THE
CHOPPER BOYS

OTHER BOOKS BY AL J. VENTER

The Terror Fighters (Purnell, Cape Town) 1969

Underwater Africa (Purnell, Cape Town) 1971

Report on Portugal's War in Guine-Bissau (California Institute of Technology, Pasadena, USA) 1973

Underwater Seychelles (Verhoef, Victoria, Seychelles) 1973

Under the Indian Ocean (Nautical, Hants, UK) 1973

Africa at War (Devin-Adair, Connecticut, USA) 1974

The Zambezi Salient (Robert Hale, UK) 1974

Coloured: A Profile of Two Million South Africans (Human & Rousseau, Cape Town) 1974

Underwater Handbook (Ed. Atlantic Underwater Club) 1974

Africa Today (Macmillan, London) 1975

Black Leaders of South Africa (Siesta, Johannesburg) 1976

Vorster's Africa (Keartlands, Johannesburg) 1977

Soldier of Fortune (W.H. Allen, London) 1980

South African Handbook for Divers (Ashanti, Cape Town) 1987

Second Underwater Handbook (Ashanti) 1988

Challenge: Southern Africa in the African Revolutionary Context (Ashanti, Gibraltar) 1989

Underwater Mauritius (Ashanti, Gibraltar) 1989

Where to Dive: In Southern Africa and off the Islands (Ashanti, Gibraltar) 1991

THE CHOPPER BOYS

Helicopter Warfare in Africa

AL J. VENTER

IN ASSOCIATION WITH
NEALL ELLIS AND RICHARD WOOD

Greenhill Books

Originally published by Ashanti Publishing Ltd, Gibraltar
A division of Ashanti International Films Ltd
Published by
Greenhill Books
Lionel Leventhal Limited, Park House,
1 Russell Gardens, London NW11 9NN
Design and Layout: Al and Madelon Venter
Typesetting and Reproduction: Photo-Prints (Pty) Ltd,
112 Long Street, Cape Town
Colour Separations: Photo-Prints (Pty) Ltd, Cape Town
Final Proofs: Madelon Venter
Printing: Singapore National Printers Ltd, Singapore
Printing Adviser: Patrick Chung
Front Cover Photo: Al J. Venter
Endpapers: Dean Simon
ISBN number: 1 85367 177 0 © 1994

THE CHOPPER BOYS
HELICOPTER WARFARE IN AFRICA

CONTENTS

A CONTINENT OF VIOLENCE

Africa has always been a source of anecdote. No less so during the modern period, following the brief period of European Imperialism. Some of the stories are tragic; others are impossible to relate without generating a smile.

Former Military Attache in Washington DC, Fred Rindell, tells of the time that he served as a very young, somewhat delinquent lieutenant at Katima Mulilo. Hostilities were still very low-key; an occasional mortar barrage here, a spot of sniping there. The 'enemy' at that stage were Zambians.

The South Africans had an advantage in that they could field choppers, usually based nearby at Rundu Air Force base. And, since the region was, literally, alive with snakes – mambas, cobras, puff-adders and so on – Lieutenant Rindell devised one of his more devious ploys.

One Saturday morning he included in Daily Orders an instruction for section leaders to bring in "half a dozen large snakes, preferably mambas". He then contacted the Air Force base. After lunch, Lt Rindell, armed with no-

PREVIOUS PAGES: AAA position at Ongiva, southern Angola, shortly after it had been captured by the South Africans and used as a forward strike base. The weapon on the roof, a ZSU-23, was captured from the Angolans; Mountain rescue in the Drakensberg, South Africa – a magnificent photo by Anthony McMillan.
THIS PAGE: Portuguese Air Force *Alouette* on bush operations in Mocambique.

ABOVE: SAAF *Pumas* at the ready during *Op Protea* at Ondangua Air Force base. BELOW: French Air Force in Chad. LEFT: South African Air Force *Super Frelons* almost caught in a brush fire in the Magaliesberg Mountains. These large choppers were not up to the task allotted them while at altitude in African conditions, a situation for which they were clearly not designed by Aerospatiele of France.

ABOVE: Rhodesian Air Force *Alouette* approaches a military base inside one of the more "active" Tribal Trust Lands in the south-east of the country. BELOW: A Russian-built and flown Mi-17 of the Angolan Air Force, similar to four of those shot down by South African *Impala* jets (see Chapter 18).

TOP: A battle casualty is evacuated to Salisbury's Andrew Fleming Hospital and, BELOW: Gunner's eye-view of the bush terrain around Mtoko where there was much ZAPU guerrilla activity.

BUSH OPERATIONS WITH RHODESIAN AIR FORCE *ALOUETTE* K-CARS AND G-CARS

thing more than several large baskets, took off from Katima's heli-pad just behind the infirmary. The *Alouette* pilot was more than a little nervous of his slithering cargo. His instructions were to climb a few thousand feet – just beyond rifle range – and head for Shesheke, a Zambian village, across the Zambezi River. There was apparently a football match on the go.

What happened next would have done justice to something more reminiscent of the *Carry On* brigade. With the chopper at about 7 000 feet – hovering over the football 'stadium' – Rindell, the future senior military diplomat in the American capital, dumped his snakes overboard and watched them twirl, head over tail, towards the ground. As Rindell watched them fall, they became smaller and smaller as they cartwheeled towards earth. To those on the ground below, the snakes were getting bigger and bigger... There were about a thousand people in the stadium watching the match, and the majority did not have to wait for these reptiles to hit the ground before making for the exits.

Years later, Rindell, by now a Colonel, met the Zambian military commander of the region. He had been in the stadium at the time. The two men could laugh about it then. But, he confided, his efforts were well rewarded. It was months before the Zambians harried South African positions again.

Clearly, combat helicopters have played a crucial role in warfare in Africa. The Algerian War would not, ultimately, have been fought the way it was without them. The Rhodesians would not have lasted a year without their *Alouettes*. Similarly, United Nations Somalian operations would long ago have been bogged down in the sand, dirt and dust if the American forces did not have adequate chopper backup.

Nor, are many people aware, that it is on the African continent that a helicopter actually shot down a fixed-wing military plane; the first and only time that it has ever happened.

The incident took place during the Rhodesian War. In the course of a cross-border raid on a Zimbabwe Peoples Revolutionary Army base near Francistown, in Botswana, a RhAF *Alouette* III, flown by Charles Goatley with Beaver Shaw manning the 20mm cannon, was 'buzzed' by an *Islander* of the Botswana Defence Force.

The *Islander* – clearly unhappy with the Rhodesian military presence – made several passes and, since it was armed, was regarded as a threat. Nor was it an easy matter for the gunner to get a bead on the plane since the *Alo* cannon had a very limited angle of traverse. And, in any event, he had to aim low to avoid shearing off his own rotors.

Shaw 'talked' Goatley, port-side on, into the appropriate position during one of the *Islander*'s passes and, aiming ahead, he let go with a full burst which crippled the plane. It made a forced landing at Francistown Airport. The event was subsequently debated at the UN Security Council. Again, a point was made: though many cross-border raids into Botswana took place, the Rhodesian Air Force was never again buzzed by the Botswana Defence Force.

In this book critical observers will notice several variances of style. It would have been easy to make all measurements metric, but then, even in nations that took that road decades ago, there are many pilots who still talk in terms of 'nautical miles' and so many 'feet' when referring to altitude. I have left it that way, using metric where appropriate.

The same with time: GMT or *Bravo* (two hours before

GMT) time. Authors such as Tom McCann, Neall Ellis and Richard Wood have it their own way. None of these little idiosyncrasies should affect the nature or the accuracy of the book.

My special thanks – as far as production is concerned – to Peter Stuckey, Richard Harrison and Richard Younghusband, all of Photo-Prints, for putting so much effort into making this a fine volume. Patrick Chung of Singapore saw me about printing and the consequence of his advice, you see before you.

My wife, Madelon, handled the proof-reading. In this task, again, she was invaluable. Thank you *Baba*.

ACKNOWLEDGEMENTS

*T*he Chopper Boys is not the work of one man. It could never have been; its scope is too vast and the book ranges over a period of almost half a century across an entire continent.

The idea first came to me about five years ago when I tasked Neall Ellis, then a Commandant in the South African Air Force, to take time off and put pen to paper. Neall has contributed several of the most important chapters of this book, made all the more interesting because *he was there*. I don't know of another chopper pilot in the world who has had as many SAM-7s fired at him as this man. That he survived, without even being wounded once, is remarkable. The same with Terry Chap-

Russian-built Mi-24s played a major role in prolonging the war in embattled Ethiopia where largely conventional forces were pitted, usually unsuccessfully, against insurgent forces. The rebels eventually ousted the Addis Ababa regime. These *Hinds* were maintained and serviced by East European personnel, including a large contingent of East Germans.

lin and Gary Fonternel who took some of the photos included here.

Richard Wood is no stranger to those who know Africa and its conflicts. I originally published his *War Diaries of André Dennison* (Ashanti, Gibraltar 1989) so I am familiar with his breadth of vision and technical knowledge. His two chapters on the Rhodesian War are instructive. All the maps in this book are the work of Richard; in this he has enhanced the value and scope of this volume.

One of the most interesting sections was contributed by US Marine chopper pilot. Captain Robert Doss, who was one of the first to take his CH-46E *Sea Knight* into Somalia, at night, to pull out diplomats and civilians threatened by Somali's rampaging warlords. Thanks, Robert, for a job well done.

Permission to publish the chapter on *Operation Sharp Edge,* the US Marine rescue that took place in Liberia, by Lt-Colonel T.W. Parker was obtained from the publication *Proceedings* by authority of the US Naval Academy at Annapolis, Maryland.

Friends Willem Steenkamp and Peter Younghusband, both old hands on the Africa beat, contributed work of their own; Willem on the Angolan War and Peter on Chad where he was eventually made Honorary Colonel of the

RIGHT: This Portuguese soldier with G-3 rifle was lost in the Angolan jungle for three days with only his knife for protection. Here he climbs into a rescue helicopter, still not aware that he is safe.

BOTTOM LEFT: A Special Forces team prepares demolition charges on a Russian PT-76 Soviet-supplied amphibious tank lying half submerged in the Kunene River within sight of Xangongo in southern Angola. A SADF *Alouette* hovers nearby, giving air cover.

BOTTOM RIGHT: A Chad rebel soldier cleans his sidearm; alongside rests his SAM-7 missile launcher. Libya flooded northern Chad with sophisticated Soviet hardware and, for a while, SAMs became a serious problem for French Air Force helicopters.

NEXT PAGE: French Air Force technicians service *Pumas* during anti-Libyan COIN operations in the desert north of N'Djamena in Chad. This country still experiences insurgency problems.

local French Foreign Legion detachment. My very good buddy Ron Reid-Daly gave much help with background to his period of service with the Portuguese Army in Mocambique. Some of the pictures are his.

Time spent by me in Somalia in 1993 would never have happened if it had not been for the likes of Colonel Mike Ferguson, at present serving as US Defence and Army Attache in Addis Ababa. Mike seems to spend more time doing 'strange things' in Somalia and Eritrea than he does at his 'home' posting. He provided the shots of the Mi-24s in Ethiopian Air Force livery.

Colonel Kim Henningsen who replaced Mike as Defence Attache in Pretoria pulled a lot of strings with another of his colleagues, Jim Callahan, to get me into Somalia. I had been in Somalia many times before, but this time it was very different! I am grateful to both of you.

Retired US Navy SEAL Captain Larry Bailey pulled just about everything out of the hat in getting me access to photos of ships, aircraft and men who took part in *Operation Sharp Edge* off Liberia.

Photos came from many sources. Tessa Paterson went into Somalia after I did and returned with some beautiful shots; Herman Potgieter came up trumps on the *Impala* jet-fighter in chapter 18. Thanks *Schultz!* A few of

Charles Norman's photos are used in the Rhodesian chapters – the one of the 'troopie' on the mountain I originally used as the cover for my novel *Soldier of Fortune* (W.H. Allen, London 1982); John Rubython will recognise several of his really outstanding pix in the southern African chapters. Special thanks to my *Rafiki* Mohamed Amin of Nairobi for letting me use the elephant poaching pictures in Chapter 7, and to a rather special friend and colleague, Gerald L'Ange, for *The Argus Africa News Service* photos which have clearly made such a difference to the Mocambique chapter. Rupert Pengelley, my editor at *International Defense Review* assisted historically with pictures. To all of them grateful thanks. This is your book too.

Also to Anthony McMillan of Durban for his series on the sinking of the *Oceanos*. He was one of the few professionals who was there to record the event and what a good job he did. Johan Liebenberg at very short notice provided the sequence on Untag in Namibia. Here I was helped by Gordon McGregor, also of Namibia.

Other pictures came from scores of sources and reflect much of my 30-odd years of work in Africa.

In particular, I am indebted to SAAF Colonel 'Monster' Wilkens for approaching the US Department of Defense and obtaining a selection of photographs for incorpora-

**The face of the Rhodesian fighting man at the height
of the war. The chopper is an *Alouette* III, of which
many came from South Africa and, surprisingly, from
Spain!**

tion in the American chapters. Also to South African
Navy Captain Peter Keene at the Embassy in Paris. I need
to acknowledge *Photo Cinema, Video des Armees* at
Fort d'Ivry for their permission to use these photos of
Algeria, Chad and the French contingent in Somalia.

Among those that helped were Mohamed Amin's
Camerapix, Nairobi; *The Argus Africa News Service*;
my old buddy Floris de Bonneville of *Gamma Presse
Images*; *Sipa Press*, also of Paris; *Camera Press*,
London; as well as the following American military
sources; US Marine Corps, US Army and the US Navy. I
also obtained photos from the SAAF Museum in Pretoria.

Individuals not already mentioned include Cloete
Breytenbach, Dervy of *Sipa*; Alain Mingam who I first met
in the early days of Angolan *Uhuru*; Juhan Kuus, Marion
Kaplan whom I remember well from Nairobi; Michel
Artault who covered the Shaba Rebellion; Pierre Perrin;
Jean-Claude Francolon; Pieter Seidlitz and, of course, Jim
Hooper, for his excellent Angolan coverage.

Finally, Robert K. Brown, publisher of *Soldier of Fortune* magazine. We've worked together for 20 years,
Bob, old buddy.

Last, but not least, let me not forget my very good
friend, Johan van Zyl, who is always around when I need
advice. Thanks to you all.

A trio of Russian-built Angolan Air Force (FAPA) helicopters destroyed in the war in Angola. BOTTOM: Picture by courtesy of Jim Hooper, shows a Mi-17 knocked out by Unita mortar fire at Muilungo, south Angola. RIGHT: An American *Stinger* knocked this Angolan Air Force helicopter out of the sky in eastern Angola. TOP: One of the FAPA Mi-17s 'taken out' by SAAF *Impala* jets operating from Rundu Air Force base in Caprivi. Unita later claimed this as a victory of their own. Because of the political implications of the 'coup', they were not contradicted by the South Africans (see Chapter 18).

ABOVE: A US Marine Corps AH-1W *Cobra Maverick*
fire-and-forget, air-to-surface missile. It was developed by G.M. Hughes Electronics. BELOW: The kind
of photos that were appearing on the desks of news
editors all over the world during 1993. This one, sent
out in August, is by courtesy of Agence France Presse.

MOG01C-08AUG93-MOGADISHU: An American helicopter hovers over the site where
four U.S. soldiers were killed by Somali mine while in a convoy going from UNISOM II
headquarters to the Mogadishu airport 08 Aug. U.S. soldiers serving with the U.N.
operation have come under attack twice in recent weeks in the same area. Color Key:
Green trees. AFP PHOTO   Alexander JOE/aj-wai
#1513A * Decod:3156 - 08/08/93 13:17:01

CHAPTER 1

THE SOMALIAN IMBROGLIO

Looking Back on How the Americans Lead the Way in the Horn of Africa

Somalia is one of those modern conflicts that is likely to be with us for a long time. In the words of one participant, "It is a mess. What else?"

It is also an imbroglio in which the helicopter has been found in great numbers; American, French, Italian, Belgian and others. But it is not the last trouble spot in Africa in which the chopper will excel.

The United Nations Operation in Somalia (Unosom), early 1993 under Special Envoy, Robert Oakley and Commander of US Forces, Robert Johnston, involved the armed forces of twenty-two nations – including several from Africa. It was not, strictly speaking, a war, though by the end of that year there were numerous confrontations, raids and punitive measures in which American and UN troops found themselves in action against Somali warlords and their brigands. These were fairly hefty fire-fights in which many people died.

From the beginning it was clear that these unconventional Somali forces had acquired a remarkable array of modern weapons, bought over a period of years from just about every arms-producing country in the world. These included British and Soviet landmines (from Libya?), Russian small arms and rocket-propelled grenades, Italian, Spanish, Portuguese, Chinese and Brazilian carbines, Belgian and German sidearms, as well as a miscellany of weapons from Israel, South Africa, Germany, Iran, Syria, North and South Korea as well as France.

In a sense, the more than 30 000 Allied troops in the country in 1993, constituted more of a rescue mission than a fighting force; there was also the effort to feed a million hapless children and refugees, which was why these soldiers were there in the first place.

For those involved on the periphery of conflict, it could be even more dangerous than some of the minor wars, largely because of the brutal nature of the Somali social system. Conflict within this society had, in recent years – at a conservative count – cost more than a hundred thousand lives, including those of countless women and children. Famine, too, had taken a frightful toll.

The problem lay, essentially, in the brutal excesses of more than a dozen Somali warlords. These tribal or factional leaders were not circumscribed by any Geneva Convention. It was fundamentally clan warfare, often affecting anyone who was in any particular area at the time; aid workers, foreign media personnel, innocent civilians; the old, the young, men and women. Always it was conducted by stealth and subterfuge. It was, and still is today, a truly brutal society.

During the first year of UN operations, there was no 'front line' as students of modern conflict understand the term. The 'war' was fought wherever armed men were gathered. But for the presence of a UN force, it would have been much more intense and certainly far bloodier. Also, while these warlords maintained a strangle-hold on food distribution centres – and access to Foreign Aid compounds – many more people would have died of starvation had the United Nations not intervened. It is a curious paradox that there are so many people critical of this presence in Somalia who, rather conveniently, forget why it was that the United Nations went into Somalia in the first place.

Those who arrived there for the first time found an extraordinarily violent society which knows few parallels in modern times. No fewer Somalis died with their throats cut while they slept or were stabbed in the back in the marketplace than in outright battle, which often took place outside a village, in any one of the dozens of towns, on the roads linking them, or on the 'green line' running through Mogadishu; the war borrowed some of its jargon from the Beirut of the eighties.

After a while in the country, it soon became apparent to people like myself that the Somali fighting man was little more than a thug. He was never regarded by members of international aid contingents, by the media or by the Unosom troops as a particularly brave, imaginative, resolute or resourceful soldier. "Devious" would have been a more appropriate description. Many of the epithets used by the Allied forces were unflattering. But even today, they are appropriate.

It was in this half-war or pseudo-war that the combined forces of the United Nations and the United States attempted to restore some degree of peace and order in a desolate region on the Horn of Africa. Because of the very nature of the troubles there, said Farouk Mawlawi, a UN spokesman in Mogadishu in mid-February 1993; "It is not and will not be a passive peace observer group. Force would be opposed with force." As we have seen, it has been...

As Third World, or more pertinently, African conflicts go, there have been a number of firsts for the peacekeeping force in Somalia.

Women were found serving in many military capacities; among others, as pilots of helicopters, gunships and medevac aircraft; Australian military police and convoy escorts; members of British air crews; Scandinavian and Canadian flight engineers; medical personnel, drivers, general duty soldiers, guards and so on.

This was also the first conflict in which both aid personnel and the media had taken steps either to arm themselves or to acquire weapons for guards hired for their protection. Journalists in Vietnam, Rhodesia, Lebanon and elsewhere would very occasionally arm themselves, but that was a matter of personal choice, and certainly not commonplace. In Somalia, if you do not have a gun with which to protect yourself – or, at very least, someone else with a gun to do the protecting, you are regarded as taking an unnecessary risk. This applies as much today as it did a year ago.

Examining individual logbooks, I discovered that every UN roadblock between Mogadishu and the former Soviet air force base at Baledogle (which was quickly revamped by the Americans) showed evidence of weapons in international aid vehicles. In each case the personnel were identified, serial numbers of the weapons listed and these then handed back for the rest of the journey. Significantly, this had never happened with aid personnel in places like Ethiopia or Cambodia.

In contrast, weapons found among Somali citizens were confiscated. But there seemed to be an endless amount of it! By early 1994 it became clear that, in spite of efforts to counter the trend, more arms were reaching the warlords each month. Some of it is believed to have come from Iran.

OVERLEAF: Flight deck of a US Air Force C-130 entering Somali air space at dawn: (Photo Tessa Paterson). RIGHT: (Clockwise from top left) American soldiers onboard an Army *Blackhawk* at Baledogle; helicopter gunship over the Central Somali plains; Gull's eye-view of Mogadishu Airport; Insignia of 10th Mountain Division at Baledogle; Baledogle Control Tower and one of the many airwomen assigned to US Forces in Somalia.

Mohamed Amin, who at that stage was managing the Reuter's Television and News Service in Somalia from Nairobi, admitted that he had acquired four AK-47 carbines at $100-00 each for the protection of his crews. He declared firmly that his journalists were not armed; only their guards. These weapons did not prevent three members of a Visnews team, including Dan Eldon, from being hacked to death by Somali militiamen in mid-1993. Three months later, five CNN drivers were slaughtered by a militia band; they had been armed!

Other journalists, though reluctant to be drawn on the matter, were known to have been carrying weapons; they usually skirted the issue when asked. Not to carry a weapon for self-defence in the streets of Mogadishu, or Kismaiyu in the early days of the UN presence, could lead to serious consequences, such as getting murdered, one of them explained.

While this writer was in Mogadishu, a French journalist approaching the US Military Headquarters compound next door to the American Embassy was accosted by a Somali with a pistol. Without warning the latter shot the Frenchman in the arm, within sight of the US Marine guards on duty.

The journalist fell to the ground; a few seconds later the Marine on duty killed the Somali with a burst of automatic fire.

Somalia must have been the first country in which UN forces were unable to have 'R & R' within the borders of the country. Most of those who wished to get away from the stresses and strains boarded a C-130 transport aircraft of the US Air Force, the RAF, the Canadian Air Force or one of the aid flights plying between Mogadishu and Mombasa in Kenya. Either way, there were also flights to Nairobi. It is a two-hour journey.

The fact is that anyone who steps outside one of the dozen or so military compounds in Somalia without an escort would, in all likelihood, be plundered. Quite a few have been killed.

There was also a strong possibility of being stoned by bands on the rampage if you were not prepared to hand over whatever you happened to have in your pockets or in your hands at that moment. Wrist-watches and dark glasses are usually the first items of personal apparel to be snatched.

The dry, dusty country with its Biblical air and the narrow rutted streets is almost tailor-made for a riot. All the roads are in disrepair and we found, to our dismay, lined with stones and the crowds tended to use them.

As a relief operation the Somali campaign has, so far, achieved only partial success. Once the main body of the American force had left by May 1993, conditions deteriorated ever further. But even then the objectives have been limited; the main one being to get food to the starving masses. The UN force has also been trying to disarm the

fourteen principal warlords, but without any success.

Observers who are familiar with the country pointed to several serious problems which have not been dealt with.

The first and most important of these is the inability of the UN (or anyone else) to limit the political and military power of the Somali faction leaders. One very well known foreign correspondent who was in the country while I was there, said that the only way to bring peace to Somalia would be to put all the warlords against a wall and shoot them. Either that, or pull all United Nations personnel out of the country immediately.

It has also been admitted by every single spokesman or officer who had been in the country for any length of time that there is simply no effective alternative but to remove the warlords from power unless it were accepted that Somalia would be in a permanent state of anarchistic turmoil in one or ten years time!

Most civilian and military personnel in Mogadishu who I spoke to regarded these tribal leaders as crass and brutal, heedless of the suffering and deaths of children. Most of them, I was told, were bent on acquiring more weapons, plenty of the *khat* drug to which they are addicted and more 'real estate' belonging to other tribes.

A look at the record of some of these belligerents is instructive.

The best-known and most obstreperous of the warlords has been Muhamed Farrah Aideed, a seasoned military tactician, but at the same time, as the UN quickly discovered, devious, unreliable and not averse to confrontation. Aideed drove the former dictator Said Barre out of Somalia and has ruled over much of southern Somalia as well as the southern half of Mogadishu.

The northern sector of town for much of the past year was in the hands of Ali Mahdi Muhamed, a former hotelier who was also, like Aideed, addicted to *khat*. That is not unusual; almost every adult Somali chews the leaf which is mildly narcotic. It is, nevertheless, a drug.

Colonel Mohamed Said Hersi Morgan (he called himself General Morgan) has been closely linked to the former President Barre (Morgan is his son-in-law) and has controlled Bardera and parts of the region round the port of Kismaiyu, several hundred kilometres south of Mogadishu.

Morgan's principal adversary was, for a while, the man who dominated most of Kismaiyu, Colonel Omar Jess; he waged war against almost every one of the fourteen warlords, but was then allied to General Aideed; at least until he was killed and replaced by another tyrant. Aideed and Jess, we were aware at the time, proposed to split the country between them: Aideed in the north and Jess in the south. His successor, apparently, now has similar plans.

And so the list continues. Few of these self-appointed leaders have any real military or political experience. But they have plenty of hardware, and they use their clout ruthlessly. Until the Americans and some of the other Coalition Forces began to use force to separate the unruly hordes (or at least to deprive them of their arsenals) they tended to regard all Allied forces with total and utter contempt and they displayed the animosty. If they believed they could get away with it, they would fire at every UN patrol that came within range, often using women and children as 'human shields'. And when the UN retaliated, they called "Foul".

But, in the early days, things changed for the better in a comparatively short time. Within the first two months of the arrival of the Americans, there were more than a dozen air and ground attacks, mostly led by US, Belgian and French forces on known strongpoints all over the country. Some of these were successful and huge numbers of weapons were seized.

Elsewhere they failed dismally, mainly because the Americans had a self-defeating habit of dropping leaflets on the towns that they intended to attack in an attempt to warn innocent people to keep clear. That, of course, gave the clan leaders time to stow their hardware. The French, with their great experience of African conflicts over the past three decades have not, in contrast, been prone to such acts of protocol.

While the stoning of Coalition Forces and the occasional sniping attack has continued unabated in some parts (mostly where the US forces have been active, because initially they were not allowed to use live ammunition to retaliate) it has stopped completely where the French (and the French Foreign Legion), as well as Turks, the Australians and some other nations are in control.

The French, Turks and Australians tended to react smartly at the first hint of a mob approaching with stones; and although they maintained that they fired over the heads of rioters, the numbers of dead and wounded in some 'incidents' indicated otherwise. The gist, evidently, is that the mobs in those places had read the message; and there was no more stoning of French or Turks, or Australians for that matter.

The Somali campaign must be the first operation of its kind where helicopters have been the principal means of transport in every sphere of internal communications: troop movements, coordination of attack and general-purpose air transport. Apart from the C-130, C-141s and Italian G222 transports (which are mostly used to bring in food, water and other supplies) there were no small, fixed-wing aircraft for general transport in Somalia in the initial stages.

By March 1993, the US forces (the US Army and the US Marines) must have had nearly a hundred helicopters deployed in Somalia, more than half of them based at Baledogle, north of Mogadishu where the US 10th Mountain Division and the US Marines shared the base. The US Army alone listed 65 of these; thirty UH-60s (Black-hawks) (Alpha and Lima), fifteen UH-60s Blackhawks (Victor) for medical evacuation (medevac); ten Kiowas OH-58s; eight AH-1 Cobras and two Blackhawk UH-60s (Command and Control).

Chinook CH-47s of the US Army were shipped to Somalia from Germany but were not unloaded. Most of the helicopter transport in Somalia was performed by the CH-53 Sea Stallions of the US Marines.

Other nations using helicopters in Somalia have been the Belgians, the Canadians (whose first shipment arrived in February 1993), the French (mostly Pumas) and the Italians (who used a variety of craft including Chinook CH-46s and the Agusta version of the American Cobra gunship as well as Agusta-Bell 206s.

While the exclusive use of helicopters in Somalia has been convenient and efficient, it has also been expensive, especially in terms of fuel and maintenance. A squadron of small, fixed-wing aircraft would certainly have served everyone's purposes better: aerial observation, the movement of small amounts of gear, weapons, personnel and senior officers between their bases and units in the interior and headquarters in Mogadishu.

Somalia, with its population of only four million, is a big country, nearly three times the size of Yugoslavia or roughly as large as Spain and Portugal together. It has presented the UN with some serious logistic problems. Radio communications between Mogadishu Airport and low-flying helicopters was initially limited to about 50 kilometres. The result was that machines flying the 350 kilometres between Mogadishu and Kismaiyu were in 'dead' areas without communications for a good part of the flight. Moreover, the distances made an additional fuel supply system necessary.

Part of the problem was solved by fitting the UH-60 Blackhawks with twin fuel wing-pods; the E-Triple S system. The tanks have increased the flying time of a Blackhawk from two hours to four-and-a-half hours.

Again, the US Army and US Marine helicopters never fly solo into the interior; they always work in pairs and all – except the OH-58 Kiowa scouts – are armed.

The United States authorities admitted to me that if their helicopters were fired upon from the ground their pilots had authority to reply "with maximum effect" without asking permission from headquarters.

Coalition Forces in Somalia faced huge deployment, consolidation, logistical and support problems from the very first day.

The Americans and the United Nations entered a country in a state of anarchy; there was no potable water, no electricity, no police and no effective military or civil administration. The roads everywhere were hardly usable. The capital, Mogadishu – and every other town along the coast and in the interior – showed the results of two years of barbarous fighting. It seemed like an only slightly less

CLOCKWISE FROM TOP: American Army Engineers leaving a *Blackhawk* at Bardera in the Central region; Mogadishu Harbour at the start of the UN Operation, December 1992; French Reaction Force at their base in north-east Somalia; French Air Force *Puma* caught in a 'brown-out' while landing; Turkish forces as part of the UN Force in Somalia, a no-nonsense contingent that tolerated little disruption from 'dissident' Somalis; Patrolling the Somali coastline in a US Army OH-58 *Scout* and, the largest used-aircraft 'dump' in Africa at Mogadishu Airport; many of these planes are still serviceable. LEFT: Italian technicians service one of their gunships at Mogadishu Airport; US Marine chopper in Somalia airspace and above, scene of much bitter fighting in the past.

intense version of Beirut at its worst.

Because the removal of the dead was far down the list of priorities of the warring leaders, the danger of epidemic disease has been serious from the beginning. We noted that in some areas where bodies had been buried, the dead were hardly covered by the soft sand; once or twice after a strong wind we saw skeletal hands and feet sticking out.

Although there are no dogs in Mogadishu (they have all been eaten), jackals, vultures and hyenas had dug up many corpses.

As a result, there were reports of cholera and other infectious diseases from every aid centre, and a huge increase in the incidence of tuberculosis, measles and meningitis in the ill-fed children and adults, who were already trying to cope with kwashiokor and rickets.

Malaria has, of course, always been endemic. In the first months there were numerous reports of the disease among the Allied forces, some of them critical because almost all the anopheline malarial strains along the Indian Ocean coast have shown strong resistance to available anti-malarial drugs.

As a prophylactic, the MO at Baledogle gave me anti-biotic *doxycycline hyclate* tablets, which is more generally used to cure light venereal and amoebic infections!

The result of all this dislocation was that American and Unosom forces have been obliged to bring with them every item of food, equipment, fuel, power, spares, machinery and water necessary for the maintenance of men and women in Somalia.

Drinking water alone had very early on become a factor and needed to be dealt with immediately. Most of it was shipped or, at first, flown in from the Gulf or from Kenya, and sometimes from Europe. The European contingents, for instance, were prepared to provide their forces only with bottles of water from their home countries. The Italians and the French were immovable; they would drink nothing else. They were right, of course. Bottled water that came through from Saudi Arabia was, at one stage, found by chemists attached to US forces, to be contaminated by faecal matter.

The Americans quickly took appropriate steps. Accompanying their force was a ship specially equipped for the desalination of seawater. This was connected to a shore station by a flexible hose.

Within a month they had also established two desalination plants on shore, each capable of producing 200 000 gallons of fresh drinking water a day. Even so, water was strictly rationed everywhere. Troops are allowed to shower during only one or two hours a day.

RIGHT: US Army Navigator's hand-written map of Baledogle Airport, north of Mogadishu. It was circulated among all Army and Marine contingents.

Up-country, in places like Baledogle, Bardera or Kismaiyu on the coast to the south, the problems were not so easily solved. Some local water sources were 'purified' for washing and bathing, but all drinking water was, for a long while, still brought in by road or air. During my time at Baledogle in the interior I counted several C-130s landing or taking off each day, many of them bringing in full loads of palleted drinking water.

While the problem of sand and dust whipped up by coastal winds had been partly solved at Mogadishu Airport by the laying of huge areas of AM2 aluminium sheeting, that was not possible in the interior in a country covered with powdery red 'talcum' dust that wreaked havoc on aircraft engines, precision equipment, generators, cameras, computers and other electronic equipment. When the wind blew at Baledogle you woke up in the morning with a layer of red sand on your sleeping-bag. For some time it was the same at Mogadishu Airport; only there the sand is white.

Travelling on the dusty roads obliged every man to

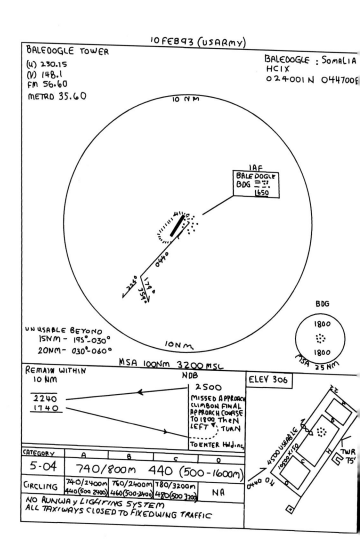

CLOCKWISE FROM ABOVE: Camouflage netting also forms a protection against the powerful East African sun. Captain Tom McCann PAO with the 10th Mountain Division detachment in Somalia is seated, centre foreground; Mogadishu from the sea – in its day it was a delightful though remote Italian colonial posting on the Horn of Africa; *Chinook* transporters attached to the Italian Air Force with UN Forces in Somalia in Mogadishu Airport.

wear a set of *Afrika Korps* goggles.

At Baledogle, all difficulties were compounded by the heat; dust falling on fuel-oil emissions crystallised after a day or two, which meant that aircraft engines had to be subjected to daily cold water engine flushes and solvent flushes once every ten flying hours. Flying and stationary helicopters were equally affected by the corrosive dust effect, according to *Cobra* gunship pilot CW4 David Coates, who was one of the few Vietnam Vets in the unit.

In a bid to lessen the effect of the red Somali dust, a soil stabiliser GDD-152 was sprayed on all the aprons alongside the runways. This created a temporary crust but tended to break up after a short while.

Maintenance has probably been the single most difficult task allotted to Allied forces in Somalia. Some technical teams preferred to work after dark because of the heat, but that was often impossible because of the demand made on airworthy helicopters by individual commanders.

The Italian Air Force seemed to be the most responsive; their technicians appeared to me to be busy round the clock, but with more than three thousand men in various Somalia postings in the interior by mid-February it was no doubt necessary. The Italians, clearly, did not have the logistical capability of the Americans.

In the first five weeks in which the 65 US Army helicopters were working from Baledogle, I was told that the unit recorded nearly fifteen hundred flying hours. There was also a US Marine helicopter detachment of about twenty aircraft there, with their own technical and maintenance units.

Night-flying at Baledogle took place regularly until about an hour or two after midnight. The commander of the unit, Colonel Mike Dallas, of the 2nd Brigade, 10th Mountain Division, said that since many of the air crews were based either in Germany or at Fort Drum in New York State, they had little opportunity for routine exercises at night on home ground, largely because of civilian constraints. There were then very few civilian settlements in the region round Baledogle, and the pilots appeared to take advantage to fly at night while they could.

Comparing conditions in Somalia with Saudi Arabia in *Desert Storm* most of the pilots at Baledogle to whom I spoke were of the opinion that though Somalian conditions were bad on aircraft, the situation – on a broader scale – was better than in the Persian Gulf. Firstly, they were operating from generally improved areas and there was less dust because the air traffic intensity was lower. Also, the Saudi desert sand was more abrasive, resulting in main blade erosion.

Bardera was regarded as possibly the worst location out of which to operate helicopters; the Marines had put bulldozers in to "clean the place up". This had increased the dust problem ten-fold. One result was that in landing at Bardera, you were 'blind' in the final 15 or 20 feet before touchdown.

TOP: Business-end of one of the US Army single-engined AH-1 *Cobra* gunships deployed in Somalia; MIDDLE: Army Lieutenant John MacPherson used to box for the US Army. In Somalia he had to 'make do' with an improvised bath while on duty in Baledogle. BELOW: The US Marines deployed a major Aviation Combat Element at Baledogle. Most transport requirements were handled by US Marine CH-53 *Sea Stallions*.

CHAPTER 2

FALCONS VERSUS FAMINE

Baledogle, Somalia.
Captain Tom McCann reports:

It seemed like another 10th Aviation Brigade field exercise. A 3-17 Cavalry Scout weapons team lifted into the blue African sky. Crew chiefs of the 3-25 Assault Helicopter Battalion serviced their UH-60 Skyhawks. Staff planning continued without a break in the tactical operations centre. Mechanics and cooks carried out their tasks.

But this was not a typical operation, and its setting was not typical of Fort Drum.

There were no piney woods and snowy fields with high Adirondack peaks in the distance. Instead, the thorn trees and blowing clouds of dry red dust that coated soldier, vehicle and aircraft alike were the norm. The sign read: "Welcome to Baledogle, Somalia".

Over 900 soldiers of the 10th Aviation Falcon Brigade and attached units from the 10th Mountain Division and from other army posts traded 1992 winter's cold and snow for the heat and dust of East Africa. Instead of facing ice, they were pestered by bugs, boredom and the occasional Somali bandit.

The Brigade's presence at the crumbling, Soviet-built airfield at Baledogle, about 90 kilometres north-west of the capital Mogadishu, was the result of over 30 days of intense planning, preparation and movement. On 2 December 1992, when the US Government identified the 10th Mountain Division as the major US Army unit to deploy to Somalia, the Brigade's schedule became a blur of activity.

Its staff officers wrote and rewrote operations plans. Motor sergeants inspected vehicles to certify deployability. The men that made up the bulk of the force – the soldiers – endured immunisation against a legion of diseases found in this corner of the world. Its family members sat through support briefings designed to help them cope with their absence.

Preparations for deployment ranged from the simple – each man packing his field bags with the right mix of equipment needed to survive in a hostile environment, to

the complex – modifying deploying aircraft with enhanced electronics and navigational aids and then wrapping them in plastic to ward off salt water contamination on the sea voyage to the Horn of Africa.

The first group of 10th Aviation Brigade soldiers, led by commander Colonel Michael Dallas, departed Fort Drum on 20 December 1992. The next three weeks saw a continuing flow of Brigade soldiers through Griffiss Air Force Base and across the 12 000 kilometres between New York State and East Africa. The main body of Brigade soldiers arrived the week of 4 January and moved as quickly as possible from Mogadishu to Baledogle, the designated base in the interior.

Here, the terrain was found to be more like the Army's National Training Centre in the Mojave Desert. Somalia's major dry season was just beginning; the days are long, hot and humid. The soldiers, clad in khaki flight suits and desert pattern battledress, moved about amid thorn bushes, low trees and the rubble of neglect scattered around the air base's old buildings with a level of apprehension. Most of them had never seen anything like it before.

The Brigade's encampments were models of expediency and ingenuity. Revetments that once sheltered Soviet-built MiG jet-fighters now sprouted tents and camouflage nets. Old buildings became storerooms and motor pools, their nooks and crannies holding make-shift showers and laundries.

Unusual things were found to be routine. At the entrance to the 3-17 Cavalry encampment, a battered, French-built *Panhard* armoured car sat, its 90 millimetre gun spiked by a force or forces unknown. The vehicle had been recovered from the nearby town of Uanle Uen, and within a week was sporting the Squadron's red-and-white 'Bandit' symbol.

While Baledogle was occupied, American, Moroccan and Somali flags flew atop the administration building and control tower. Task Force Falcon coordinated all Army aviation activities from there, including a combined Air Cavalry/assault team in the southern port of Kismaiyu, 350 kilometres towards the south as well as detachments of the 159th Medical Company (Air Ambulance) in Belet Uen, Bardera and Kismaiyu.

Many different elements made Task Force Falcon work. Elements of the Brigade HHC; 3-17 Cavalry; 2-25 Attack Helicopter Battalion; 3-25 Assault Helicopter Battalion; and attachments from 3-62 Air Defense Artillery (serving as UH-60 door gunners), 110th Military Intelligence (operating ground surveillance radars and sensors) and Company E, 25th Aviation (aviation intermediate maintenance) represented Fort Drum.

From Europe elements of the 5th Battalion, 158th Aviation; the 7th Battalion, 158th Aviation; the 159th Medical Company (Air Ambulance); Company B, 7-159 Aviation (intermediate maintenance); Company B, 3rd

CLOCKWISE FROM TOP LEFT: Colonel Mike Dallas, CO of the 2nd Bde HQS of the 10th Mountain Division in Baledogle: CW4 Dave Coates in the cockpit of his AH-1 *Cobra* gunship; Medical personnel formed a large proportion of US Force deployment; US Army soldiers prepare to board a *Blackhawk*: US Army *Blackhawk* lifting off from a Somali airstrip in the interior; Former President George Bush addressed US forces in Somalia during his visit in December 1992. OPPOSITE (TOP): SSG Keith L. Morton in the bomb blasted control tower at Baledogle; (BELOW): Chopper pilot's eye-view of downtown Mogadishu.

Battalion, 58th Aviation (Air Traffic Control) and augmenting units comprised TF 5-158 Aviation. From the Aviation and Troop Command in St Louis, Missouri, an Army Logistics Assistance Team added both military and civilian maintenance, logistics and acquisition experts to the force.

Task Force missions in the early phase included infantry air assaults into the towns of Belet Uen, Jilib, Marka and Afghoi. These high-profile events – in the glare of news media interest – contrasted sharply with the routine of logistics resupply for forces scattered throughout Somalia; continuing reconnaissance of isolated villages and road nets to identify potential trouble spots and areas where food relief was still essential.

The mission cycle took place against a backdrop of dust kicked up by every passing vehicle or launching aircraft. It turned black boots reddish-brown and coated tents, uniforms and skin. An army of ants, flies, mosquitoes, scorpions, millipedes and other creatures of the African bush, made life each day much more demanding.

CLOCKWISE FROM TOP: Technical area at US air base set up in central Somalia at Baledogle. The Americans even brought their own portable aircraft hangars (centre right); US Marine CH-53 *Sea Stallion* partly disassembled at the main Marine Air Force base in central Somalia; Italian Air force technicians at work in an improvised bombed-out workshop at Mogadishu Airport; 'Franky's Body Shop' at Baledogle all but stripped most of the US Army choppers that needed repair.

OPPOSITE (TOP CLOCKWISE): CW2 Jeffrey Ylitalo inspecting the Tow Missile System on his *Cobra* gunship; US Army technicians at work at the Baledogle air base; In Somalia everything was improvised. In the East African heat working outside was hell!

CHAPTER 3
MAINTENANCE AND LOGISTICS EQUALS SUCCESS

In most army units, 'M' means manoeuvre. But for any military mission to succeed, maintenance is essential. If equipment cannot be used because of mechanical or electronic failure, all the effort and goodwill in the world can't achieve results. This is true in the United States, in Asia or in Germany. It was especially so at hot, dirty, dusty Baledogle in Somalia. And herein lies the strength of most of the national forces deployed in that sad country.

For a while Fort Drum's 10th Aviation Brigade spearheaded the army aviation effort in *Operation Restore Hope*, a unique organisation providing a strong maintenance and logistics base that kept Task Force Falcon's 65-odd aircraft flying, its ground equipment running and its soldiers as productive as possible in an environment as harsh as it is desolate.

Task Force Falcon's Aviation Support Battalion (Provisional) assembled operational, administrative, maintenance, acquisition and logistic expertise from the United States and Germany. From Upper New York State came elements of Company E, 25th Aviation and the Logistics Assistance Office; from US Army, Europe, Company B, 7th Battalion, 159th Aviation; and from St Louis, Missouri, an Army Material Command (AMC) Logistics Assistance Team from ATCOM; the US Army Aviation and Troop Command.

While Lt-Colonel Donald Burke was normally the AMC AH-1 *Cobra* Attack Helicopter 'Product Manager' at ATCOM, he was suddenly thrust in command of the ASB(P) in Somalia. He maintained that it was a challeng-

ing, rewarding difference for an Acquisition Corps officer like himself – with experience mainly on the Army's 'business' side – to command a tactical organisation.

The road to the ASB began early December when the Brigade received its initial notification. The ATCOM Commander, Major-General Donald Williamson sent the ALAT to Fort Drum to assist the Brigade's pre-deployment activities.

Major-General Williamson created the ALAT concept and reinforced it with lessons learned from *Operation Desert Storm* and from *Hurricane Andrew* relief operations in Florida. It certainly supported aviation-related logistics; ATCOMs subsequent creation from the merger of the Aviation Systems Command (AVSCOM) and the Troop Support Command (TROSCOM) expanded it to address troop-related items such as water, POL and army watercraft.

It identified and adjusted issues such as equipment shortages and required modifications, such as rotor blade taping and global positioning system installation, to ensure that the Brigade could operate in East Africa's austere desert terrain.

After assisting the Brigade States-side, it deployed to Somalia and set up to both support it in theatre and provide liaison back to ATCOM.

While at Baledogle, Burke worked directly for both Colonel Michael Dallas, the 10th Aviation Brigade Commander, and Colonel Patrick Kirby, the commander of the AMC Logistics Support Centre in Mogadishu, to whom he reported daily.

Another unique feature of the ASB in Somalia was the presence of civilians – both government and contractor – in its ranks. Some of these people were ALAT members; others were civilian contractors from Agusta Helicopter in Europe. Quite a few were identified as Logistics Assistance Representatives (LAR).

The senior LAR at Baledogle, Mr James Climer, normally the chief of the Fort Drum Logistics Assistance Office, lead an eight-man team of expert logisticians in multiple fields.

Two Communications and Electronics Command (CECOM) LARs specialised in ground communications and aviation electronics (avionics). A Tank and Automotive Command (TACOM) LAR covered ground vehicles. An AMCOM (armament) LAR was responsible for general armament, while a MICOM LAR put all their effort into AH-1 attack helicopter armaments.

Two additional ATCOM LARs covered multiple aviation-related specialties and aircraft types; a supply and maintenance specialist rounded out the team.

"Ours is an assistance programme to enhance readiness," Climer said. "Our goal is to work ourselves out of a job", he added, referring to an ideal situation free of problems requiring his team's help.

Together, the LARs combined the multi-disciplines associated with generations of experience; they used it to support all American units stationed at Baledogle. They visit units, gather information, provide on-the-spot advice, conduct training where necessary, monitor round-the-clock readiness, track the status of maintenance and reports, and generally assist units in equipment acquisition. They also coordinate directly with agencies such as the Defense Logistics Agency and the General Services Administration.

Two aviation intermediate maintenance (AVIM) units provided ASBs muscle. Company B, 7-159 Aviation originally from Giebelstadt, Germany, near Wurzburg, where it normally formed part of the 3rd Corps Support Command. Company E, 25th Aviation was the AVIM unit for 10th Mountain Division. Together they provided direct support and back-up intermediate maintenance to Task Force Falcon's aircraft.

Major Patrick Sherman, commanding B/7-159 Aviation, explained that both companies operated from a consolidated production control office. From there, his soldiers had primary responsibility for aircraft from Ger-

many, while E-25 elements took charge of Upstate New York aircraft. Together, they supported each other when the workload increased, sharing assets to cover all requirements and contingencies.

E-25 Aviation elements, led by Captain David Riley, had specific responsibility for the AH-1F model *Cobra*, OH-58A model *Kiowa* and UH-60L model *Blackhawk*. One of B/7-159 Aviation's great strengths while in Somalia was its 100 per cent mobility; this allowed it to initiate operations at Baledogle while other units searched for in-theatre transport to move out of Mogadishu. This versatile capability also enabled the company to pitch in and line-haul much of the Brigade's equipment, allowing it to start with operations that much sooner.

The AVIM units also performed all periodic phase inspections and installed Modification Work Orders (MWO) such as the External Stores Support System (ESSS) on the UH-60 helicopter and the Global Position System (GPS) on the AH-1. They did so successfully while working in a hot, dusty, austere environment while linked in with a support tail extending all the way back to the US.

Some of the obstacles they overcame, Burke said, were lack of water for aircraft and engine washing; constantly blowing red clay dust that coated every surface imaginable and invaded electronic systems; and a sometimes sluggish, often unresponsive transportation system that required coordination with both Air Force and Marine Corps. Both services often had different delivery priorities. A real challenge was that parts for the Task Force received at Mogadishu Airport – unsegregated by the service addressee, unsorted and redirected – sometimes appeared at other service shops or perhaps not at all. Clearly, the infallible system did not always work.

One of the ASBs major accomplishments, besides its positive efforts to keep the aircraft flying, was the erection of a temporary 'clamshell' hangar on one of the hard-surfaced taxiways in the battalion area at Baledogle. This was some achievement.

The hangar, designed to augment or replace permanent hangar structures, allowed the boffins to work 24-hour shifts, performing necessary maintenance and periodic phase inspections, well away from the damaging environment.

Natural conditions and environmental hardships notwithstanding, Task Force Falcon continued to operate throughout the period of hostilities and consolidation. This was due in many ways to the efforts of almost a thousand soldiers and civilians, but most of all to the 240 individuals who manned the Aviation Support Battalion with a fairly unique mix of tools, experience and professional commitment.

Obviously, this is not the last time that committed professionals like these will be deployed in Africa. Somalia provided an excellent 'learning curve'.

CHAPTER 4

ALGERIA'S SAVAGE WAR

The First Deployment of Helicopters in Combat

The Algerian War of the fifties proved to be something of a watershed in the cycle of European colonial politics. It was the first conflict of the modern period involving a major European power in Africa. It was also the first war that was militarily and politically 'lost by an imperial force': consequently it set the pattern for a frenzy of political activity in dozens of other African states eager to reject European rule.

But to understand the cause and effect of such an evolutionary process, it is necessary to examine the historical backdrop.

To appreciate properly what happened in Algeria a generation ago it is necessary to look at the development of the country early last century. Dr L. Hahn is an Executive Director, Association of Third World Affairs, Washington D.C. His views are instructive.

Dr Hahn points out that the French entered Algeria in 1830 with a punitive military expedition against the Dey of Algiers, the recognised ruler of a state which for years had maintained diplomatic and commercial relations with several European countries.

After the surrender of the Dey, they continued to wage a relentless pacification campaign lasting seventeen years against the indigenous Arabs and Berbers who were fighting to retain the land that they had inhabited for centuries and their Islamic way of life. The conquered territories were subsequently divided into three French *departements*, which juridically constituted an integral part of France.

French settlers in Algeria, who began to arrive during the pacification, were soon joined by others from Spain and Italy, all of whom subsequently received French citizenship.

The fact was that ninety per cent of the Algerian economy was in the hands of French interests and one hundred thousand French settlers cultivated nearly two and a half million hectares, most of it good arable land that they had cleared themselves. On the other hand six million Algerian Arabs tilled little more than four million hectares.

After nearly a century of imperial rule, no event had the signal effect on the mind of the average educated Algerian Arab as the second world war, especially the humiliating defeat of France by Nazi Germany in 1940.

Even the French were aware that the Islamic psyche had always been particularly sensitive to prestige; *Baraka* is the special blessing of Allah on people who have acquired grace. France, it was felt in North Africa, had suddenly run out of *baraka*. The almighty French, it was realised, were fallible, after all.

Much the same thing happened at the other end of the continent not long afterwards, after the fall of the Portuguese African colonies in the mid-seventies. Suddenly a European power had been overthrown by black nationalists. If it could happen in Angola and Mocambique, then surely the same could take place in Rhodesia and South Africa. It has …

It is significant that throughout the period of French occupation of North Africa, Arab opposition to rule from Paris was never far from the surface. Many of P.C. Wren's stories about the French Foreign Legion – which kept generations of schoolboys in the English-speaking world enthralled – were based on actual exploits by the Legion in the Algerian Sahara. Uprisings were brief and bloody; and they were equally brutally suppressed.

By the end of the last war, the position of France in North Africa had been weakened, and the serious insurrection now known as the Setif Bloodbath broke out in 1945. Nationalist forces alleged that twenty thousand Arabs were killed by the French. Official reports give the number of about one thousand five hundred rebels shot by security forces; Walter Laqueur believes that the real figure is probably between five thousand and eight thousand. Without doubt, Setif experienced a dangerous conflagration; it would undoubtedly have drawn the attention of the United Nations if it had been in existence at that time.

Simone de Beauvoir recalls that the French public heard very little about what happened at Setif. The communist publication *L'Humanite* acknowledged only a hundred or so casualties, while de Gaulle in his memoirs dismisses the whole bloody episode in one terse sentence: "Beginning of insurrection, occurring in the Constaninois and synchronised with the Syrian riots in the month of May, was snuffed out by Governor-General Chataigneau."

Any form of military action must clearly have been sanctioned by de Gaulle's government. It must have been equally aware of the bloodbath; after all, many thousands of people were killed.

As one observer said: "On both scores it is to be noted that the communist ministers shared responsibility without a murmur." But then the French have always taken a solipsistic view of events beyond their borders; they prohibited the sale of arms to Israel, but made a great profit by selling weapons to both sides during the war between

BELOW: An Arab guerrilla suspect boarding a French Air Force helicopter for transport back to base. Most of these civilians were often brutally tortured.
LEFT: Mountain operations in Algeria involving the use of US-built French Navy HSS-1 *Sikorsky* helicopters.

Burning French Air Force *Sikorsky* helicopter after a crash near one of the bases; this aircraft had obviously been delivered fairly recently; it still had its manufacturer's markings in English.

Iran and Iraq. They stopped selling arms to South Africa, but still sold them to Angola, dominated as it then was by the Russians and Cubans.

It is also important that the Algerian war only got properly under way after the ignominious defeat of a French force by the Viet Minh at Dien Bien Phu, an apparently invulnerable South-East Asian strongpoint in the heart of North Vietnam, fortified, almost, like Verdun. It fell on the *eve* of the ninth anniversay of VE day, 7 May 1954, at a cost of 13 000 dead among the French.

A colonial resistance army had inflicted a terrible psychological defeat on a regular Western army. In the *souks* of Algiers and Oran nationalists took careful note of the event and swore that if the Vietnamese could do that in Asia, they could follow suit in North Africa.

Naturally, the average French *colon* rejected the idea. Many Frenchmen consoled themselves with the thought that *even* after the defeat in South-East Asia, at least Algeria had remained calm. After all, there had been nine years of tranquillity there after the Setif *evenements*.

The Algerian revolt began in 1954, and by 1957 the Arab controlling body, the *Front de Liberation Nationale* (FLN), thought that victory was at hand. The war went on for five more years.

THE WAR

There was a certain logic in the choice by the FLN of November 1, 1954 for the launching of their "jihad" against the French in Algeria.

It was the *eve* of the Christian festival of All Saints' Day, and most of the devout French colonial *pieds noirs*, it was assumed by the FLN leaders, would be off their guard. At least the vigilance of the police would be relaxed. The settlers themselves assumed (just as the Israelis did just before the Yom Kippur War in 1973) that the Muslims surely would respect the sanctity of a religious holiday.

They did not. The country had already been divided up by the FLN into six *Wilayas* or autonomous military zones, and there were attacks in each of them. Some were the work of a small group of armed men; in other areas, such as Biskra, a group of rebels attacked the police station half an hour before the predetermined hour of 3 am.

The attack on the barracks at Batna went off roughly as planned, but not before its occupants were aroused by alarm bells and flashing lights. Two of the guards, 21-year old *Chasseurs*, were mowed down because peace-time regimental orders required that their rifles should be unloaded and their ammunition *sewn up in their pouches*. They were the first military personnel to be killed in the war.

The first officer was killed by machine-gun fire as he emerged from his quarters in the small garrison at Khenchela. He was a Spahi, Lieutenant Gerard Darneau. Other attacks took place at the Ichmoul lead mine where the guerrillas intended to seize a quantity of explosives but failed; it was the same at the tiny *gendarmerie* post of T'kout and in the Tighanimine Gorge a few hours later. The local bus travelling between Kiskra and Arris was ambushed and a loyal *caid* or government functionary was shot. Two young French teachers were wounded in the attack.

There were five targets in Algiers: the radio station, a fuel depot, the telephone exchange, the gasworks and a warehouse belonging to a prominent French politician. All five attacks were frustrated, largely because the attackers were ill-trained and badly equipped. Similarly in Oran, none of the groups fulfilled their objectives. One of the attacks being launched prematurely, the authorities were on their guard, and by morning eight insurgents had been killed, six of them with weapons in their possession.

Elsewhere in Algeria, the attacks took on a similar pattern, some of them successful many others not, largely because of a lack of modern weapons. A few of the attackers were armed with knives. Ben Bella later said that the FLN began the rebellion with between three hundred and fifty and four hundred firearms, "and virtually nothing heavier than a machine-gun".

Most of the bombs exploded on All Saint's Day were primitive devices made locally by inexpert artisans. Only months later did military supplies begin to arrive in Algeria from Morocco and Tunisia.

Alistair Horne, the British historian, says that not a weapon at that time or for several years to come was provided by the communist bloc; nor was more than a modest quantity of guns acquired elsewhere abroad with the slender funds of the FLN. Thus, from the very beginning the theft of French arms from depots or their recovery on the battlefield became a prime military objective.

A French doctor reported later that most of the wounds he treated in the early days had been inflicted by hunting rifles and shotguns.

The French had been warned as early as six months before the attacks on All Saints' Day that an offensive was being prepared. The office of the Governor-General even received a warning from an informer that this was about to take place, but it was apparently filed away in some pigeon-hole and retrieved only after the attacks had taken place.

The French reacted, of course. The Commander-in-Chief in Algeria, General C. de Cherriere, had about 55 000 soldiers at his disposal, though few were ready for action, since most of the best French counter-insurgency forces were either still in French Indo-China or on the high seas on their way home. According to Jacques Chevallier who wrote *Nous les Algeriens* (1958), Cherriere reckoned that he had fewer than 4 000 *usable* combat troops in the entire country when the revolt began. There was only one helicopter in Algeria at the time and

eight second world war *Junkers* bombers. There were sixty thousand Algerian troops in the French Army, many of them serving 'at home'. These were branded collaborators and became a prime target of the insurgents throughout the war; their families sometimes suffering a worse fate than the men themselves.

Reinforcements soon arrived, however. By the end of that year the French Prime Minister, Mendes-France, had sent 20 000 more troops and twenty companies of riot police.

It took little more than three weeks for an extensive counter-insurgency operation with artillery and air support to get underway. Terrorist attacks on Europeans stopped as suddenly as they had begun.

Many suspects were rounded up, various Arab organisations were proscribed, offices were raided and documents confiscated. Large numbers of innocent people fell into the bag. Curiously, the Algerian revolt raised little public interest in Europe, comparable, say, to Israel's *Intifada* of late 1987 and 1988 or the black rebellion in South Africa which started in 1984/5.

Alistair Horne observes: "On the ground, the physical reaction or over-reaction – was predictable. It was predictable, not specifically because of the *pied noir* mentality, but because this is the way an administration caught with its pants down habitually reacts under such circumstances; whether it were the British in Palestine, Cyprus or Northern Ireland, the Portuguese in Mocambique or the French in Indo-China."

"First comes the mass indiscriminate round-up of suspects, most of them innocent but converted into ardent militants by the fact of their imprisonment; then the setting of faces against liberal reforms designed to tackle the root of the trouble; followed finally, when too late, by a new progressive policy of liberalisation."

In spite of the accumulation of forces, the war began slowly. At first, the rebels were astonished at the fury of the French response, although much of this stemmed from the indignation of the *pied noirs* over the fact that the Arabs should reject a colonial system that was so obviously of benefit to all.

Few French settlers were aware of the hardships suffered by the *fellah* indigenous population; widespread unemployment, and often less than rudimentary education and medical facilities for most Arabs, or of the irreconcilable political differences between the French and the Arabs. To most French people in Algeria, it was fine to have Algerian Arabs working as menials on the farms or in the factories at wages none of them would consider on the mainland, or as domestic servants, but any notion of integration on any other basis was not to be considered.

Some settlers demanded the immediate execution of all captured members of the FLN. In the *Depeche Quotidienne*, a local senator demanded that "the evil be pur-

sued where it be found and the ringleaders rooted out… "
He also insisted that security measures should be increased and called on his metropolitan associates to create the political atmosphere to launch "the proper solution" to the rebellion.

Obviously, the response of Paris paid dividends. Between November 2, 1954, the day after the revolt began, and early February the following year, not a single *pied noir* was killed by insurgents. Terrorist attacks against the Algerian population continued unabated, however. It was the typical Third World pattern of coercion by violence to make it very clear to the Algerian people that to be associated in any way with French colonial authority meant brutal consequences which often included women and children among the victims.

The guerrilla war began hesitantly in 1955. Apart from sporadic acts of violence most of the country was peaceful.

As John Talbot says in *The War without a Name – France in Algeria 1954-1962*: "For at least a year after All Saints' Day, three of the district chiefs (of the six *Wilayas* or command structures) had almost no followers or weapons at their command. Violence was confined almost entirely to the three *Wilayas* of eastern Algeria, from the outskirts of Algiers to the Tunisian frontier. The western *Wilayas* from Algiers to Morocco were for months nearly as peaceful as Paris on a Sunday morning. For most of the war the Sahara saw more oil prospectors than guerrillas."

By the end of 1955, as a result of concerted undercover work and the deployment of mainland forces as well as a strengthening of security throughout the country, most of the original members of the FLN had either been killed or gaoled.

But the war was beginning to gather momentum. Repression was first replaced by some measure of Soustelle's reform, but it was generally agreed that it made little impression on either the settlers or the Algerians. Although the FLN had few successes, its mere existence was enough to force Paris to deploy huge numbers of men. The French Air Force was expanded and prepared to start

This twin-rotor *Boeing* H-21 in French Air Force livery was operated in Algeria by the Navy and Aviation *Legere de l'Armee de Terre* (ALAT). They could transport 20 fully armed soldiers in combat conditions.

its programme of bombing and strafing selected targets. But that was to come later. And when it did, leaflets were usually dropped in advance to give the local people warning of the attack in time for them to seek shelter.

The air force dropped thousands of warnings on *fellah* settlements in the interior. One read as follows:

APPEAL TO THE MUSLIM POPULATION
Agitators, among them foreigners, have provoked bloody trouble in our country and have installed themselves notably in your region. They are living off your own resources. .
Soon a terrifying calamity, fire from the sky, will crash down on the heads of the rebels. After which *la paix Francaise* will reign once more.

With the arrival of the vaunted 25th Airborne Division, the first French paras led by the legendary Colonel Ducournau – who had recently returned from Indo-China – set up headquarters in Arris in the Nementcha mountains near the Tunisian border.

Following the same principles that he had applied in South East Asia, Ducournau decided immediately to apply Mao's maxim of "merging with the people like fish in the water" and pursuing the rebels in their own strongholds. It was not easy. The *paras* had some successes but many failures.

In retrospect, what disconcerted the FLN command was that after the first attacks, most *pied noirs* resumed their way of life as if nothing had happened. There was no mass exodus back to France and, in France itself, the war was relegated to the inside pages of the press.

Precautions had to be taken, of course. After the first acts of terrorism in Philippeville and Bone in the east and the increase in military aid from Tunisia and, indirectly, Egypt to the FLN, no one travelled anywhere without an

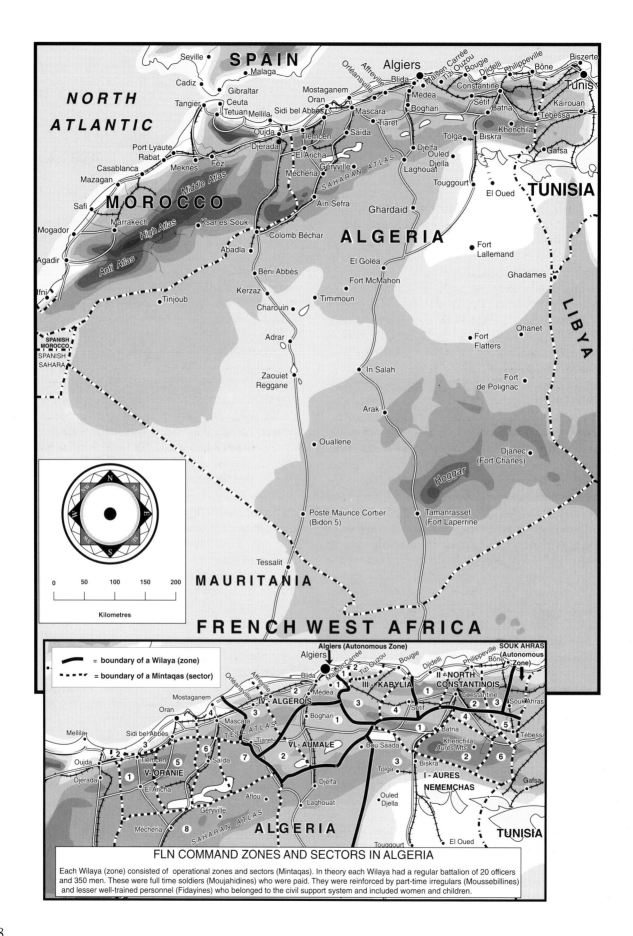

FLN COMMAND ZONES AND SECTORS IN ALGERIA

Each Wilaya (zone) consisted of operational zones and sectors (Mintaqas). In theory each Wilaya had a regular battalion of 20 officers and 350 men. These were full time soldiers (Moujahidines) who were paid. They were reinforced by part-time irregulars (Moussebillines) and lesser well-trained personnel (Fidayines) who belonged to the civil support system and included women and children.

escort. Six months after the All Saints' Day attacks, actions averaged about two hundred a month.

That included road ambushes, isolated attacks on farmers and their property, the cutting down of telephone poles, shooting members of the local militia on leave and occasional skirmishes with the army.

By a year later these figures had greatly increased. According to official reports they rose to 900 in October 1955, to 1 000 in December and to more than 2 500 in March 1956.

Much of this activity was due to the opening of the second front. By the beginning of 1957, almost thirty months after the outbreak of hostilities, FLN guerrilla fighters were active in five of the six *Wilayas,* the forces in the west having linked up with their compatriots in the east on the high plateau between Saida and Tiaret.

At that stage Soustelle estimated that there were between fifteen thousand and twenty thousand members of the FLN, although these figures included sympathisers and 'night-time guerrillas' who would carry on with their normal jobs during the day. The FLN command claimed double that number of loyalists; war always results in hyperbole. But even fifteen thousand guerrillas raised from a community of almost ten million could hardly be regarded as a nation in arms.

Gun-running increased enormously. As the FLN hierachy made headway in Algeria, so its influence spread beyond the borders. More money was contributed by friendly Arab states and more weapons made available for the fighters. At the same time the revolutionaries, even during the most favourable times, never had enough modern weapons for every man. Settlers and soldiers were being beaten or knifed to death right to the end of the struggle.

Gradually the war turned from 'hard' targets such as police barracks and patrols to 'soft' civilian objectives and the so called 'Muslim friends of France'. These might include *caids* or village constables or even lower functionaries such as postmasters and tax collectors.

A fundamentalist influence also acted strongly on the rebel forces. Muslims were forbidden to smoke or drink. Penalties were severe; first offenders had their noses or ears cut off; for a second offence FLN cadres would inflict what the army called "the Kabyle smile" – slitting of the throat.

The FLN also turned to economic sabotage; maiming and killing of cattle (which was soon to be emulated by the Mau Mau in British-controlled Kenya), rooting up of vines and poisoning of wine vats. Dogs were often found with their throats cut. In May, four French civilians caught unarmed on their farms were murdered in this barbarous manner.

In August 1955, there were the massacres at Philippeville. A group of rebels convinced several hundred peasants that the hour of their deliverance was at hand. Armed with axes, knives, sickles and other implements, the mob set upon settlers and Algerians alike.

At the small pyritis extracting town of El Halia, Algerian miners slaughtered European overseers and their families. Some were hacked to death; others were disembowelled; still more had their throats cut while their arms were pinned behind their backs. It was a gruesome report that arrived on the desk of the French Governor-General in Algiers. Altogether about 150 people were killed, about half of them settlers.

The French army and the Foreign Legion arrived on the scene at El Halia while the massacre was still going on. In reprisal they killed over a thousand Algerians, including women and children, and took many more prisoners, some of whom later died in custody, although this was strenuously denied by the authorities. The worst fears of the French settlers were being realised.

In Paris, meanwhile, arguments developed between the two factions; the one opposed to greater violence and those who were all for using maximum force to put down the rebellion. The French government, in turn, maintained that France was facing a revolt of French citizens, since technically, everyone in Algeria was French; Arabs and *pieds noirs.* They were rebelling against their own government. It was stated that in Algeria the army was not fighting a war but conducting what was called "operations for the maintenance of order".

There were a few parallels with what was then happening in Malaya. The British, like the French, never referred to "communist terrorism" in South-East Asia as a war, but rather as an "emergency". This fiction was adopted because to place the country on a war footing would have enormously increased Lloyds' insurance premiums and, no doubt, would have had many other undesirable results. It was the same in Kenya as that insurrection developed.

The same motives operated in Algeria also. After all, it was argued, for Algerians to rebel against their own government was to put them *hors la loi.*

In April 1955, accordingly, the government – with parliamentary assent – declared a state of emergency in Algeria, which although curtailing civil liberties, stopped short of actual war.

The extent to which the war had grown is shown by statistics issued at the time by the French Ministry of Defence. During 1955 the number of French troops in Algeria increased from about 80 000 to nearly 200 000. A year later, in the autumn of 1956, a third of the entire French armed forces were on active service in Algeria.

This was no longer a limited holding operation to suppress a few disaffected "rebel groups running wild on the fringe of the Sahara". The FLN had grown to its full strength.

Meanwhile, conflict intensified. The government of the

time, under Guy Mollet, acknowledged that by the end of 1956 France had committed more than 400 000 men to North Africa. As George Armstrong Kelly stated in *Lost Soldiers: The French Army and Empire in Crisis, 1947-1962* (Cambridge, Mass. 1965), there were "perhaps as many as twenty soldiers for every FLN guerrilla in the bush".

Less than ten per cent of this force did actual fighting. The main task of the majority was to protect the persons and property of settlers and Algerians, to keep the main roads and rail links secure and open and to protect strategic installations from FLN sabotage. The task of the rest – perhaps between 30 000 and 40 000 men – was to hunt down the cadres of the FLN. The term "search and destroy", long familiar to those who have followed the wars in El Salvador, Vietnam, Namibia and Angola originated with the French in Indo-China. It became typical of the classic guerrilla struggle in Algeria.

By early 1957, one out of every three Europeans in Algeria wore a French uniform. The next time that Africa was so heavily under arms was in the Rhodesian war, which lasted for seven years and ended in 1979. As in Algeria, Rhodesian insurgents in 1965 would certainly have been willing to settle for a good deal less than Robert Mugabe got at the end of the conflict. So, also the FLN, no doubt, would have been willing to settle in 1956 for less than they were finally granted in 1962.

Keeping several hundred thousand French soldiers on active duty in North Africa was also costing France a billion dollars a year. It is no wonder, therefore, that the conflict gradually lost support at home. When de Gaulle made his first conciliatory remark that perhaps force was not the ultimate answer to the problem of Algeria, the vast sigh of relief throughout France was almost audible.

It was close. While the French army had at first underestimated the extent of the rebellion, they very quickly brought in the men and systematic measures to deal with the menace. The FLN rebels lost the initiative. They were further hampered by the fairly secure Morice Line along the Tunisian border, which made infiltration from outside difficult; and by the *regroupement* of villages (along the lines of the Portuguese *Aldeamentos* system, in Angola and Mocambique which came later) and which effectively "denied water to the guerrilla *fish.*"

Walter Laqueur says that by 1961 the number of *fellaghas* inside Algeria was down to about 5 000 men, scattered in small groups.

The situation was not much better for the French, although they always put on a brave front, especially when the press was about. According to Laqueur: "If FLN morale was low, among the French it was at breaking point." They could not keep huge garrisons indefinitely in all the main towns and huge mobile reserves besides. There were twenty thousand insurgents concentrated in

Tunis, beyond the reach of the French, and the European population of Algeria was up in arms against the *defaitistes* in Paris.

The end came seven years after the first shot was fired, and half a million Frenchmen in uniform were sent home. Tens of thousands of people had been killed. More than a million people were uprooted, and Algeria became a dictatorship where the rule of law was at least as severe as it had been at the height of the war.

Socialism was adopted and, now towards the end of the century, it is interesting to look at the results of nationhood in Algeria compared with what might have been if the country had accepted the French offer to make Algeria a real, not merely theoretical, part of France.

If the rebels had accepted, Algeria would now certainly be in the European Common Market; and what a different situation that would have created for the present generation of bankrupt, almost leaderless and politically oppressed Algerians of the nineties.

HELICOPTER WARFARE IN THE MOUNTAINS

What is astonishing about the Algerian war of the fifties is that it took so long to establish that the helicopter was an unusually versatile fighting machine; remarkably adaptable to combat. It was in the Algerian war that for the first time an army commander in the field strapped a man to a hovering machine in order to rout the enemy.

Edward Bavara, writing in the US *Army Aviation Digest* in November 1984 (Volume 30, November 11), described the event as follows:

"In the mid-1950s, during a battle with Algerian rebel forces, an enterprising French unit commander undertook to arm a helicopter. This occurred in the heart of the Aures, a group of peaks in the Atala Mountains south of Algiers.

"The commander's troops were pinned down by rebel fire from a hillside above their position and he could not get his ground troops into position before dark where they could provide a base of fire. Improvising liberally, he had an observation helicopter with two litters attached to its sides near his command post and strapped a man with an automatic rifle in each litter and sent the rotor wing up against the rebels. The enemy was routed from their position by the helicopter's fire and the French unit occupied its objective.

"Another, more conventional use of an armed helicopter was devised by the French during the same period. The FLN rebels knew that after French fighter aircraft had cleared helicopter landing zones (LZs) and departed, the assaulting helicopters were extremely vulnerable during their run-ins.

"When the enemy became proficient at shooting at helicopter pilots during their approaches to the LZ, the

CLOCKWISE FROM TOP LEFT: French Army conscripts take a breather in the interior of Algeria. Helicopters quickly became a valuable adjunct to the kind of colonial military operations initiated by Paris; General Charles de Gaulle, the French President, takes the salute on his arrival in Algiers. It was he who eventually 'pulled the plug' on French military operations in North Africa when he became aware that a political solution to the war was the only option; French 'Special Forces' go into battle in Algeria from a modified *Sikorsky* and, *Agusta Bell*-47s were widely deployed in Algeria as the war progressed. They operated mainly out of Boufarik and Oran bases near the coast.

French began arming helicopters to cover the assault force in these crucial phases.

With the arrival of H-21s in 1956, the French tried to develop heavier armaments. They experimented with .30 calibre machine guns and rocket launchers. The rockets were 37mm, carried in canisters holding 18, 36 or 54 missiles to each launcher.

"At the same time French Army headquarters were experimenting with anti-tank missile systems. Anti-tank missiles do not depend on kinetic energy; they use chemical energy in their shaped-charge warhead, and that also had its application to helicopters.

"The tank-dominated battlefield envisaged during this time in Europe put a premium on long-range weapons against heavy armour.

"The French SS-10 ground-to-ground anti-tank missile of the early 1950s was followed by a larger version with a longer range called the SS-11 in 1956. An air-launched version, the AS-11, was tested on the *Alouette* in 1958.

"An important advantage of aerial delivery of anti-tank missiles was the fact that the target presented a larger silhouette from the air than it did from ground level. Still more important, however, the French discovered that their helicopters could engage tanks from a variety of aspects and angles. It was an ideal evolution of tactics."

This capability, combined with the inherent speed of response that helicopters could provide, created a new dimension for the application of fire-power, and Algeria became a testing ground, the results of which were eagerly awaited far beyond the borders of France.

And so we had the evolution of the combat chopper as we now know it. But it was a long road that had to be travelled. The wars in Korea and Malaya came and went without this new weapon being explored or even seriously considered. It had been mentioned in the past, but never acted upon until the French were forced to adopt novel tactics to suit the counter-insurgency action in North Africa.

Yet there had been a beginning of sorts some time before.

Curiously, the idea of arming helicopters in the US Army had a hesitant history going all the way back to World War 2. In 1942 the US Army studied the possibilities of mounting a 20mm cannon in the nose of a *Sikorsky* R-5 helicopter.

Later they mounted a bazooka on a H-13 helicopter in 1950, and a makeshift grenade launcher, also on an H-13, in 1953.

When the H-19s were used in Korea, the need for a ground suppression system became apparent because of their vulnerability during assault landings by troops. Any real interest in pursuing this need, however, faded away after the Korean War ended.

None of these experiments matured, largely because no sincere support was provided by the various arms of the US Defence Department, and they suffered from the lack of a formal research and development programme. Again, one of the main obstacles that had to be overcome in arming helicopters was the inaccuracy resulting from the instability and vibration of the platform, and for a while the problem was regarded as insurmountable.

The real development of helicopter armament in the US Army began in 1956 at Fort Rucker, Alabama, when Brigadier-General Carl I. Hutton established a group to undertake a special project: the fabrication and testing of weapon systems for Army helicopters. One of the main considerations was, again, the need to provide covering fire for assault troops.

By now the idea of air-mobile operations was becoming a more attractive tactical idea to the American defence establishment. But more than that, General Hutton envisaged helicopters specially designed as weapon platforms.

In July 1956 General Wyman commanding general, USCONARC, approved Hutton's request to experiment with air-mobile weapons and to the industry in the development of an aerial fighting vehicle. With that, the forging of the "saber in the sky", as it was termed, was under way.

The French success in Algeria, of course, further encouraged American efforts to put firepower on Army helicopters.

Experiments were carried out at various installations in the United States, but those done at Fort Rucker were the most extensive. By March 1957 the Aviation Center directed the organisation of a Sky Cavalry Platoon. This test unit was later reorganised by Third Army General Order in March 1958 and redesignated the 7292d Aerial Combat Reconnaissance (ACR) Company (Experimental).

These 'Sky Cav' men worked intensively to develop weapon systems for US Army helicopters. They later extended their scope to include the development of armed helicopters and experimented with machine-guns (.30 to .50 calibre), rockets (up to 5-inch) and various cannons.

The US Marine Corps did its own research, but did not receive authorisation to arm its helicopters until 1964.

Naturally, the Russians were not far behind. They watched events in Algeria with great interest. In the use of armed helicopters in full-scale military operations they saw a gap and they plugged it, naturally to their own advantage. Even so there was a school of thought in Moscow at the time that did not believe that the armed helicopter could survive on a modern battlefield.

Nevertheless they did put machine-guns on their helicopters: single-barrelled guns in Mi-4 *Hounds* and Mi-6 *Hooks*. However, as the concept of air-mobility came to be seen as tactically sound, the Soviets mounted 'strap-on' armament packs on the lifting helicopters, notably the Mi-8 *Hip-Cs* and *Hip-Es*. These packs consisted of rockets to provide covering fire during assault, capitalising on the experience of both the French in Algeria and the United States in their experiments.

The Soviets, like most countries employing armed rotary craft, adapted an existing machine as they evolved these new tactics. Russian helicopter armament slowly progressed from single machine-guns and strap-on systems on general-purpose utility helicopters to modern attack craft with integrated armament.

At first the guns were 12.7mm (Mi-4 *Hound*) manually aimed machine guns intended for defensive purposes. By the 1970s (and by then Vietnam had entered the picture) rotary-action remote-controlled Gatling guns mounted in ball turrets in the chin of helicopters (such as those on the *Hind*) had become typical.

The *Hind* was soon (with some alarm) observed in one variation with twin 23mm cannons. While those *Hinds* were considered experimental and intended solely for testing purposes, the Russians were by then already giving serious thought to increasing the armament of their attack helicopters, no doubt spurred on by the Americans, who were putting a 30mm cannon on the AH-64 *Apache*.

So much for development of a concept. The French in Algeria had moved from one phase of helicopter armament to the next, so that when hostilities ended they had more than 600 helicopters working in transport, reconnaissance, medevac and fire support functions.

By using helicopters in that war the French had achieved the kind of versatility it had never possessed during the disastrous Indo-Chinese campaign. In Algeria they were able to move their forces forward at will, and at very short notice to give the infantry support that quickly frustrated attacks or ambushes. North Africa is mountainous; and before the advent of the helicopter it favoured the insurgents, who knew the land, its deserts and its mountains, and as Arabic-speaking Muslims were at one with many, but not all of the inhabitants and, at need, could slip across the border to be still among friends and supporters.

Several different helicopters were used in Algeria:

Bell H47: used primarily for liaison and the evacuation of wounded.

Alouette 11: turbine-powered, about the same size as *Bell* but with greater lift and power; also used for liaison and wounded.

Vertol H21: primary troop assault helicopter; also logistics.

Sikorsky S-55 (H-19), also known in the US as the *Chickasaw*, but built by Westland in Britain as the *Whirlwind* and supplied to France. General-purpose and troop transports.

Sikorsky S-58: built in France under licence and used as an all-purpose helicopter.

To understand the use of aircraft in Algeria by the French, it is necessary to appreciate how this country was administered for purposes of war.

All French military units, ground and air, were assigned to one of three corps areas into which northern Algeria (where most of the fighting took place) had been divided. Each corps area was further subdivided into four zones which, in turn, had the support of an Air Force Tactical Air Group.

French Army Aviation, as distinct from the Air Force, consisted of light aircraft platoons (VMO), one to a zone, and one helicopter group.

The light helicopter squadron of the French Air Force and Army were assigned in ones and twos to the variously dispersed Army garrisons and placed under their operational control. It was significant that relations between the various French arms, including the Navy, were excellent.

The expression 'air-mobility' quickly found its way into French terminology and it was defined in the earliest period as "the ability of a unit in combat to free itself from the constraints imposed by physical obstacles such as rivers, mountains, desert and so on". It gradually became a generic term, in the words of one writer, "used with reference to all airborne missions and operations".

According to Commander Howard Wheeler USN (Rtd), the French Army distinguished between two forms of air-mobile operations. The first allowed a unit to move easily by helicopter. An artillery battery moved by helicopter was an "air-mobile battery". The second provided more of the simpler elements of military operations such as reconnaissance air support, fire and transport.

Helicopter-borne command and control were also part of the new conception.

In Algeria the main command using fixed-wing aircraft and helicopters was known as *Groupement* ALAT 101, located at Setif in eastern Algeria. The second unit, similar to ALAT 101 and identified as EA/ALAT, was located at Sidi-bel-Abbes in the western region. Its purpose was to train operational pilots, and it did not engage in combat. It had about ten *Vertol 21s*, ten H-19s and thirty assorted fixed-wing aircraft.

Major David Riley of the US Marines spent some time with the French in Algeria. In an article that he wrote for the *Marine Corps Gazette* in February he said that, in spite of problems, the helicopter pilots in that war had achieved enviable records of safety. He attributed that to the "excellent basic training received in France".

Air Force helicopter trainees, he said, put in 160 hours of flight time during their six-month training course. "All but the most advanced students progress from light to heavier types of aircraft by a balanced recognition of proficiency and time-in-type."

The missions and areas of operation in Algeria, according to Commander Wheeler, were shared between the

Army and the Air Force. The Army operated its helicopters in eastern Algeria and the Air Force in the west.

'Combat cells' were another feature of the French campaign. *Groupement* ALAT 101 was divided into two heli detachments of seven H-21s and one *Alouette* each. "When a cell went into action," typically, six H-21s and two *Alouettes* were used. The spare H-21 from the *Alouette* Squadron stood by in case one got lost.

Officially, French Air Force policy was to arm one helicopter out of six deployed, and they did not carry troops. Their sole job, according to Wheeler, was to provide "very close-in air support immediately prior to and during an assault landing".

A flexible, mounted rapid-fire weapon at least one calibre heavier than that of the enemy was used.

At first the French armed their helicopters with 68mm SNEB rockets and .30 calibre machine-guns mounted on either side of a helicopter. The rockets were later replaced by a twin combination of thirty-six 37mm SNEB rockets to port and starboard. The wider dispersal of fire was more effective against insurgent targets.

Quoting an official publication *French Army Helicopter Operations in Algeria*, June 1956-September 1959, Commander Wheeler tells us that the French Army considered one of the best weapons combinations for the H-21 helicopter to be two .30 calibre machinge-guns each with 250 rounds (one tracer in five) and the side-mounted twin-pod rockets with 72 SNEB 37mm projectiles. The *Alouette* IIs, by contrast, used only the rocket combination because of its weight limitations.

The naval H-21 helicopters were each equipped with a swivel mount in the doorway for a 20mm cannon. Quoting Major Riley, Commander Wheeler gives details of an attack that took place in the Constantine area, where a regiment was ordered to sweep an area suspected of harbouring a band of nearly a hundred rebels. The use of helicopters, which was planned two days beforehand, was considered necessary because of the mountainous terrain.

A regiment in the Constantine region was ordered to sweep an area suspected of containing a band of eighty rebels. Because of the rough terrain it would be necessary to use helicopters. The operation was planned to include all forces. The helicopter annex to the operations order was based on the technical advice of the helicopter unit.

On the afternoon of the day before, the pilots of the four helicopters gathered for their orders with a representative of the fixed-wing SNJ squadron that was to give the first air support. Maps were issued, studied and marked, together with aerial photographs of the landing site. The briefing, although informal, was thorough and precise.

The troops arrived by truck at the air base before dawn the next morning. They were formed into four helicopter teams of eight men each. Coloured strips of cloth looped through their shoulder-straps contrasted with their khaki-green uniforms. This type of identification, modified on succeeding operations, was used to distinguish between friendly forces and rebel bands wearing captured uniforms. Embarkation in the warmed-up H-21s went smoothly. The troops did not fasten their safety belts, which would have been difficult if not impossible because of the hundreds of rounds of ammunition and hand grenades festooned about the cabin. Automatic weapons were distributed among them. Except for the portable communications equipment carried in the leading helicopter, neither the composition, equipment nor task of any heli-team differed from that of any other.

They were airborne thirty-five minutes before the drop. The troop-carrying helicopters were preceded by fifteen minutes by a light reconnaissance aircraft; its task was to observe and report conditions in the landing zone that might affect the helicopter assault. In particular, it was to report on the presence of the enemy in the zone, and whether it received fire or not. Then two SNJ fixed-wing *Scouts*, circling out of sight, were called in for strafing runs by the observation pilot. At one minute before the planned helicopter landing the observation pilot marked the landing zone with smoke.

Control of the strafing aircraft was the duty of the pilot of the leading helicopter. With the wind direction and velocity clearly indicated, he turned in to his approach. The SNJs drew up and circled, ready to resume strafing.

Thirty-two men disembarked on a hilltop in a few minutes. In the valley below there were lines of troops, some stationary, others cautiously advancing. Behind them were the trucks that had brought them up the winding roads in the early morning hours. Overhead the H-21s flew to a secondary pick-up zone where a truck-borne platoon of forty-eight men stood waiting. This second lift required all four helicopters for the first run and a second trip by two of them. Upon completion of this lift, the helicopters formed a shuttle racetrack pattern to begin a third lift of a rifle company to the landing zone.

All possible avenues of escape in the area were now either occupied or covered by fire from the helicopter-borne troops commanding the ridge lines. Twelve minutes' flying time from the area there was a clearing to which the helicopters withdrew to await further orders.

A variation of this type of helicopter assault was known as 'contact engagement'. It was less formal than the planned scenario, it was used when flexibility was essential.

When a rebel flare-up was reported, the helicopters were alerted and sent at maximum speed to the garrison nearest the action to pick up men. If large rebel bands were present, support aircraft and additional truck and helicopter-borne troops would immediately be dispatched to the area. The operation would then take the same form as a planned operation.

CHAPTER 5

THE CONGO DEBACLE

Mercenaries and Helicopters

One of the saddest chapters of post-independent African history is the one dealing with the Congo, since renamed Zaire. Formerly a Belgian possession, this huge Central African country which Joseph Conrad referred to, rather critically, as The Heart of Darkness, is bigger than Texas and Alaska together.

Its problems are of equal size, for in almost 35 years of Uhuru, it has been in a state of constant turmoil. Since independence in June 1960 there have been a succession of wars in Angola/Zaire, quite a few of them involving the United Nations who brought the first helicopters into the country.

Katanga – the southern province, today known as Shaba – for all its problems, has always been regarded as one of the best endowed mineral regions of the world. The first uranium to be used in the atom bombs that obliterated Hiroshima and Nagasaki in Japan during World War 2 came from Katanga. Much

of the copper wire that today lies under the streets of the cities of Europe, Britain and quite a few in America came from this part of Central Africa. But in 1960 in Katanga civil war developed apace and the age of the mercenary in Africa came into being.

Hugo Mercks, writing in Colonel Robert K. Brown's Soldier of Fortune magazine in the 10th Anniversary Edition (August 1985) sketches the earlier backdrop.

Indian United Nations forces set up a roadblock on the main road north out of Elizabethville in Katanga, the southern province of Congo (Kinshasa); today Zaire. The Congo UN operation, which involved action against South African, French and Belgian mercenaries was a sad debacle in the history of early UN military operations.

Wishing to maintain close ties to the West, which poured huge amounts of capital into the area, Katanga seceded from the emerging Congolese nation and declared itself an independent state eleven days after Congolese independence. Provincial Governor Moise Tshombe appointed himself president of an independent Katangese state.

Tshombe's immediate problem was raising an army to defend Katanga against threats from the *Armee Nationale Congolaise* (ANC), warriors of the Baluba and other tribes in northern Katanga, as well as forces of the United Nations which vigorously opposed the secession movement. He began by hiring foreign mercenaries to serve in the Katanga, many of them South African and Rhodesian volunteers. That single move is credited by military historians with reviving the mercenary profession in modern times.

One of the men who answered Tshombe's "call to arms" was a Belgian national, born in the Congo, who knew its people, customs, languages and who had been farming in the east of the newly independent territory. He was Colonel 'Black Jack' Schramme.

Schramme joined up at Kamina base in Katanga. His prior Belgian military service immediately landed him a leadership position. After proving himself in battle around Elizabethville, today Lubumbashi, he was ordered to Kansimba in northern Katanga where he recruited teenage soldiers from local tribes to form his Leopard Group. They were the nucleus of what later became the infamous Ten Commando of the bloody Congo war.

Schramme was not the only man seeking soldiers to support Tshombe. Altogether three mercenary battalions were formed including Five Commando under Mike Hoare, Six Commando under the Frenchman Bob Denard and Schramme's Ten Commando. These battalions formed mobile groups, operating throughout Katanga. They were under the supreme command of Belgian staff officers who, officially, were attached as 'technical' assistants' to Tshombe and his staff.

Initially, Schramme, Hoare and Denard were commissioned majors in Tshombe's growing army, but it was not long before they were appointed Colonel.

At the beginning, Schramme's unit – about ten whites and 60 blacks – was active in the north of the province. It was the large number of Africans under his command that earned him the nickname 'Black Jack'.

By 1961 full-scale recruiting of mercenaries started in Europe, South Africa and Rhodesia.

The United Nations estimated there were 512 contracted mercenaries as well as twelve regular Belgian officers in Katanga alone. It was not long before the blue-helmeted troops, which had been under orders to shoot only in self-defence, were active participants in the civil war. With the benefit of hindsight, it is clear that this decision probably caused a great deal more bloodshed than it prevented, and it was due in large part to the machinations of a group of European liberals who knew little about Africa and understood its traditions even less; they were led by one man with a great penchant for personal publicity, Conor Cruise O'Brien.

In a bid to ensure that Katangese mercenaries and Belgian regulars left the Congo, UN Secretary General Dag Hammarskjold appointed Conor Cruise O'Brien, a British left-winger, as his special representative in the Congo, to organise *Operation Rumpunch*. He had always regarded white Africans as an inferior lot. Consequently, in line with his instructions, except for about 100 of the total force on combat patrols, all the Belgian regulars and mercenaries in Katanga – including Schramme – were rounded up in a single day without a shot being fired.

Schramme was picked up at Kamina and sent with four other mercs to Leopoldville (Kinshasa) as prisoners of the Congolese Army. After three months' incarceration, it was a chaplain who reportedly helped him escape by catching a plane to Brussels. Schramme promptly returned to Katanga by way of Rhodesia.

Schramme and the rest of the soldiers of fortune intensified the rebellion. Increasing tactical successes in Katanga led to even more military pressure being exerted by the Congolese Army and UN forces. Schramme, Hoare and the hundred or so other mercenaries who were now in the region formed the hard core of all future rebel military activity in the Congo.

Not to be outdone, and clearly emboldened by the success of *Operation Rumpunch*, Conor Cruise O'Brien decided to foment a *coup d'etat* in Katanga aimed at ending secession and bringing the province back under Congolese rule. But, for a while yet, it was not to be.

Following premature victory announcements, a Katangan mercenary force captured the entire UN garrison in Katanga and Dag Hammarskjold, the UN Secretary-General was, in rather suspicious circumstances, killed in an air crash in neighbouring Northern Rhodesia three days before a ceasefire was ordered. His successor, U Thant, a Burmese national, summarily sent O'Brien packing and the Katangese cheered. Effectively, the First Battle of Katanga was over.

In the Second and Third Battles of Katanga, mercenary forces did not fare as well. But they never surrendered to more numerous and powerful forces.

Tshombe's power was eventually broken in 1962 when the United Nations established a kind of tenuous control of Katanga or, at least its major centres; no one controlled the jungle interior. Schramme's Ten Commando made a dangerous march through hostile territory to link up with Denard's Six Commando. Under a unified command, the force of perhaps 100 mercenaries and several thousand

CLOCKWISE FROM TOP: Some of the FNLA troops which – in the seventies – took part in the abortive raid into Zaire's Shaba Province; Civilians murdered by rampaging Katangese troops; Marion Kaplan took this historic photo of a dissident Congolese soldier during *Les Evenements* around Bukavu: Katanga, January 1963; UN troops, rebuilding a bridge destroyed during mercenary-led rebellions in Mobutu's Congo, today the Republic of Zaire.

Katangan soldiers retreated across the border into Portuguese Angola, then still a colony, but by now engrossed in its own nationalist conflict, spurred in part by help received from the northern Congo. One of the Angolan revolutionary movements, the FNLA under Holden Roberto, was headquartered in the Congolese capital Leopoldville and received much CIA aid.

The departure of the main supportive combat force effectively marked the end of the independent state of Katanga. Tshombe went into exile in Spain. Schramme meanwhile, still in Angola, continued to train his troops for more than a year.

The United Nations left the Congo on 30 June 1964, four years to the day after independence was declared from Belgium. Tshombe, his past forgiven, returned from exile in 1963 and became the Congo's fourth prime minister under President Joseph Kasavubu.

His main rival, a professional soldier formerly attached to the *Force Publique*, Joseph Desire Mobutu, still commanded the national army with advice from Belgian military officers who remained in this vast land to lend expertise and help secure a measure of stability. (He was later to change his name to Sese Seko Kuku Ngbendu Waza Banga Mobutu and which started his period of self-glorification which persists to this day.) For years on national television Mobutu was referred to as 'The Redeemer'.

Shortly afterwards two rebellions, both with some East European help, erupted among the local population in the interior. It would be simplistic to conclude that they were aimed, solely, at toppling the Tshombe regime; instead their roots and their origins had much darker motives, dominated in some areas by youths barely into their teens who reflected a blood-lust since seen only in the townships of South Africa. The rebellions became known jointly as the 'Simba Revolt'.

In some of the tortured Congo's bloodiest brutality, acts of terrorism and barbarism were carried out by young Simba tribesmen known as *Jeunesse* against settlers, traders, missionaries, nuns and travellers. Anyone associated with the government, with the church or education, or in fact, any form of order or control were slaughtered in the most horrific rituals imaginable.

Mobutu's ANC – the only organised military unit in the country – was unable to stop what had quickly developed into a reign of terror. The Congolese army was powerless to stop these people who were described in the Belgian press as being "without any any conscience whatever". Nuns were raped and their abdomens slit open, babies thrust onto bayonets and innocent women thrown into cauldrons of boiling water. This was Africa at its worst!

Tshombe recalled his old mercenary force late 1964. Denard, who had left Angola for Yemen, did not return to the Congo for another year, but Schramme promptly

Flashback to May 1978; Shaba Province (formerly Katanga), Zaire. Burnt-out aircraft wreckage on the tarmac at Kolwezi Airport; in the background, a French Air Force *Alouette III*.

marched 8 000 men from Angola back into Katanga. Hoare headed back into the action from South Africa.

Schramme's designated task was to control the Maniema district in Kivu province, with his headquarters at Yumbi. Composed of about 12 white mercenary officers and 600 black troops, he was placed in absolute command of the region and brought it to heel in a very short time. Hoare at the head of Six Commando launched an onslaught in the east and took Stanleyville in record time. They wasted little time with the rabble or the recalcitrant youth. Batches were executed but order was quickly restored. The mercenaries answered in the only language that primitive Africa comprehends very well indeed; matching violence with more violence.

It took a great deal of effort and several battles and much bloodshed, but once the Simba Revolt had been defused, a power struggle developed between Prime Minister Tshombe and President Joseph Kasavubu. Mobutu, by then a general, promptly stepped into the gap and staged a coup on 25 November 1965.

Kasavubu retired to his farm and Tshombe returned to exile in Spain. Two years later he had been kidnapped by, it is said, operatives in the pay of the CIA to Algeria where he died not long afterwards.

Mobutu Sese Seko, as he was to call himself, has been in power ever since and the country slowly, inexorably, slipped backwards into a state of regression from which it is likely to take a century to recover. Today, Zaire has all but reverted to its roots.

CHAPTER 6

THE EAST AFRICAN ARMY MUTINIES

Army coups d'etat have almost become a feature of life in Africa. By early 1973 half of the forty-odd independent African states had been affected by military coups in one way or another. There had been six army take-overs or attempted revolutions in Dahomey alone. In Sierra Leone there were four changes of government in as many years, and still conditions remain unsettled with the military remaining in power.

It was really East Africa that set the ball rolling. For although the army mutinies in Kenya, Uganda and Tanganyika (Tanzania) were unsuccessful, more revolutions followed

in short shrift to other parts of the continent.

One of the most important political developments in East Africa in the post-uhuru period was a succession of army mutinies which plagued Kenya, Tanganyika (now Tanzania) and Uganda shortly after independence in 1964. The Dar es Salaam mutiny is particularly interesting, principally because it presaged the Chinese entry into East Africa. It is also true that but for the intervention of British troops at the behest of President Nyerere, Tanzania would almost certainly be ruled by a military government today.

ABOVE: Mutinous Tanganyika Army troops held under armed guard by a British force on the outskirts of Dar es Salaam.
RIGHT: Tanzanian children undergoing military training shortly after President Nyerere had embraced Socialism as an answer to his nation's economic woes. This eventually led to the total bankruptcy of Tanzania.

"Relax, you know what their delivery dates are like!"

Cartoon that appeared in the London *Daily Express* during Africa's 'Stormy Sixties'. The event refers to the South African purchase, from Britain, of Westland *Wasp* helicopters for maritime use.

Because of stringent security measures implemented directly after the event, much of what happened remains obscure. Questions such as where President Nyerere (above, right) hid while his troops were on the rampage remain unanswered, although the author's usually reliable sources of information indicate that the British were to a large extent responsible for his safety.

But first let us look at a brief chronology of events covering the period which was immediately preceded by the bloody Zanzibar revolution which brought the tyrant Abeid Karume to power. All dates below refer to 1964.

January 20th

The 1st Battalion of the Tanganyika Rifles mutinied before dawn and occupied key points in Dar es Salaam. Messages during the day said that the mutinous troops in Tanganyika moved into Dar es Salaam from their barracks, saw members of the Government and demanded more pay and the replacement of British officers by Africans. An aircraft took British officers and NCOs to Nairobi, where they were joined by their families.

Reports received in Nairobi spoke of shooting and loot-ing by crowds who smashed windows and damaged cars in some parts of Dar es Salaam, shouting: "Colonialists go home".

Figures of casualties made available by the hospitals in Dar es Salaam showed that, as well as fourteen dead, there were twenty who had been treated for serious injuries and one hundred for minor injuries. There were no white casualties.

The Nairobi reports said that soldiers at Colito Barracks told reporters that they were "very upset" at the casualties. They had intended that their demands for better pay and for African officers "should be met peacefully". A British High Commission source said that the situation seemed "definitely eased". There was no word, however, on the whereabouts of President Nyerere or Vice-President Rashidi Kawawa. Mr Nyerere was said only to be in "a place of personal safety".

An unconfirmed report said that 'Field Marshal' John Okello the "strong man" behind the Zanzibar coup, who arrived in Dar es Salaam the previous afternoon, was at the barracks during his stay. During the day an official at the Tanganyikan High Commissioner's offices in London had said: "There has been a misunderstanding between Tanganyikans and the British officers of the 1st Battalion of the Tanganyika Rifles. The situation in other battalions remained normal".

January 21st

The 2nd Battalion of the Tanganyika Rifles mutinied at Tabora in central Tanganyika. It was announced that Mr Oscar Kambona, the Minister of Foreign Affairs, had appointed an African, Captain M.F.H. Sarakikya, to command the 2nd Battalion. All European officers were dismissed and were put on board an aircraft bound for Nairobi. A long-awaited broadcast by President Nyerere was transmitted to the nation.

CLOCKWISE FROM BELOW: British naval officers visit Zanzibar 48 hours after the start of the revolution – their role was to evacuate British families; Nigerian troops repair barbed wire fence at Dar es Salaam barracks; British troops airlifted into Dar es Salaam from the Royal Navy carrier HMS *Centaur*: President Nyerere, with British troops, was saved from an army mutiny and, Tanzanian troops on the march after normality had been restored.

January 23rd

British troops from Kenya were flown into Uganda after unrest was reported among white-officered troops at Jinja Barracks, on the shores of Lake Victoria. In a broadcast statement Mr Milton Obote, Ugandan Prime Minister, said the British troops – stated in London to number about four hundred and fifty – had been flown in at his request to help maintain law and order in a confused situation. But he denied reports of a mutiny on the lines of that which had shaken Tanganyika three days before. Earlier a British officer of the Uganda Rifles had said: "There is no doubt it is a mutiny. We are being held by non-European members of the Uganda Rifles."

President Nyerere held a press conference in Dar es Salaam. In a statement of remarkable candour he admitted that it would take "months and even years to erase from the mind of the world what they had heard about events this week". The lesson was that the end did not justify the means. He said that there was absolutely no link between the Tanganyika Rifles revolt and the Zanzibar revolution. The Army action was "a protest or a revolt". The Government was still discussing with the Army new pay scales and the promotion system, he said.

January 24th

A battalion of the Kenya Rifles at Nakuru tried to mutiny late at night. There was a certain amount of firing, but troops of the Royal Horse Artillery moved in very quickly and secured the armoury and officers' mess. They had apparently been in an ambush position all day, waiting for this situation. Britain had agreed earlier to a request by Mr Jomo Kenyatta, the Kenyan Prime Minister, for military assistance in maintaining order if the situation deteriorated in the wake of the Zanzibar revolution and the army mutinies in Tanganyika and Uganda.

It was reported quiet in Uganda. The London *Daily Telegraph* reported that the swift arrival of British troops had probably saved Uganda from an outbreak of rioting and looting which could have destroyed her stability. Mr Milton Obote said there had been every likelihood of the security position getting out of control following the "sit-down" strike of two hundred men of the Uganda Rifles. He said: "This would inevitably have followed, and lives and property would have been in great danger. The presence of British troops in Uganda is for the sole purpose of preventing this eventuality taking place."

January 25th

In Tanganyika the sound of diversionary gunfire from the destroyer HMS *Cabrian* heralded the landing of five hundred Royal Marine Commandos from the aircraft carrier

Centaur. They stormed into Colito Barracks, near Dar es Salaam, and when mutinous members of the Tanganyika Rifles refused to surrender, fired a rocket at the guard-room and seized control. Three Africans were killed. Service families were evacuated. President Nyerere in a broadcast denounced the mutinous soldiers of the Tanganyika Rifles. He said he was neither proud nor happy to have had to appeal for external help, but he had no alternative. An army which did not obey the laws and orders of the peoples' government was not an army of that country and was a danger to the whole nation. He had therefore decided that the only thing which could be done was to disarm all troops and punish the ringleaders severely. This was not easy, as part of the field force police were absent in Zanzibar to help maintain law and order there. He had, therefore, sought help from Britain.

The President called on members of the youth league of the Tanganyika African National Union to enrol in the republic's army. "From this group we shall try to build the nucleus of a new army for Tanganyika." He said that already there was foolish talk of the British returning to Tanganyika to rule. They were in the country to help and no one should be frightened.

In Uganda men of the Staffordshire Regiment moved into Jinja barracks during the night. The Staffordshires disarmed the troops affected, and leaving a single company behind, set off again for Kenya with the captured weapons.

January 26th

Mr Obote announced that men of the Headquarters Company and the 'A' Company of the Uganda Rifles had been dismissed from the Army.

January 27th

President Nyerere called for an emergency meeting early the following month of the Foreign and Defence Ministers of the Organisation for African Unity. He said that the situation in East Africa was critical and that the army revolts constituted a grave danger to the whole continent. He also announced in a broadcast that Mirisho Sarakikya was to be commander of Tanganyika's military forces in place of Brigadier Sholto Douglas, with Major Elisha Kavana as his second-in-command.

January 30th

The six hundred men of the 45th Royal Marine Commando who had put down the mutiny of the Tanganyika Army left Dar es Salaam. In the months which followed President Nyerere invited Peking to take over the training of his defence force. China has been in East Africa ever since.

This sickening 'Dance of Death' took place after the slaughter of another elephant in Kenya's once-magnificent Tsavo National Park. Even the use of helicopters to patrol this huge area did not prevent Kenyan and Shifta rebels from almost wiping out the region's elephants, all within less than two decades after independence from Britain.

CHAPTER 7

WAR AGAINST THE IVORY POACHERS

In spite of para-military forces on the ground and helicopters in the air, the war against elephant poachers in Kenya has been a failure; a dismal battle against a better-armed and, on the face of it, a more efficient adversary who knows what he wants and how to go about getting it.

At the time of independence, Kenya had more than 100 000 elephants. In all of Africa, it was estimated in 1979 by one of the world's foremost authorities on the subject, Iain Douglas-Hamilton, that Africa's total elephant population was 1,3 million. Little more than

ten years later this figure has fallen by more than half.

Kenya today has a fraction of these creatures for which the country was once world renowned and immortalised by the likes of Teddy Roosevelt, Ernest Hemingway and Robert Ruark; perhaps five per cent of the original tally.

In more than 30 countries, according to Jeremy Gavron, in his book *The Last Elephant* (Harper Collins, London 1993) elephants have been under fire. In Burundi they were wiped out altogether. Similarly in The Gambia. I quote Gavron:

THESE PICTUR
SO ARE MOST
ELE

ARE HISTORY,
EAST AFRICA'S
NTS

ield Force return to base with poachers captured in pos-
restrictions on the export of ivory, such scenes were
how for export to the Middle East; Chopper patrol over
lands near a stash of poached ivory in the Tsavo Park;
ching patrol with some of the poisoned arrows used by
for the elephants.

"In Uganda, Idi Amin's rule had reduced the country's 20 000 elephants to around 2 000. In Central Africa, Bokassa had presided over an even greater slaughter. In southern Sudan, northern Arab horsemen and southern Dinka rebels – all armed with automatic weapons – had killed as many as 100 000 elephants in a decade.

The same in the Tsavo National Park in Kenya where these pictures were taken. Twenty years ago there were about 42 000 elephants (in Tsavo); today there are only a fraction of that number left. Soon, if present trends continue, with Shifta rebels from Somalia hunting elephants with automatic weapons, there will be none."

According to Gavron, the reason is simple. The price of ivory has risen dramatically in recent years with particularly heavy demand from the Far East. He points out that between 1950 and 1970, the ivory price remained at a level of about $5 a kilo. By 1978 it had soared to $75. "An ordinary bull elephant with a pair of 15-kilo tusks was now suddenly worth $2 000."

BELOW: A Kenyan policeman uses a knife to remove a barbed poisoned arrow from the carcass of an elephant killed by poachers.
ABOVE LEFT: Kenyan Field Force base camp with the day's 'haul' of poached elephant tusks.
ABOVE RIGHT: One of the officers with the Kenya Field Force interrogates a captured ivory poacher; Some of these criminals had come from Somalia. Many were Kenyan.

CHAPTER 8

PORTUGAL'S AFRICAN WARS

Portugal's former African colony, Angola, has been wracked by conflict of one kind or another for more than thirty years. In that time about half a million people have died. Millions have been displaced from their homes and many hundreds of thousands have been left destitute or are refugees.

There have also been several hundred thousand people of Portuguese extraction – the Portuguese ruled Angola for five hundred years – who have been forced to leave the country and return to Europe in the past twenty years. Altogether, the past three decades have in military, political and socio-economic terms been a disaster. And what could be one of the wealthiest and most prosperous countries in Africa lies in ruins, one of the poorest countries in the world.

A Portuguese Air Force *Alouette III* hovers high over the Ruvuma Valley in northern Mocambique. Beyond the river lies Tanzania, the nation responsible for fomenting many of southern Africa's revolutions during the past 30 years.

The recent history of Angola has developed essentially from its colonial origins. For centuries Angola and other African colonies such as Mocambique, Portuguese Guinea and the offshore islands of Sao Tome and Principe were administered directly, and often brutally, from Lisbon. Those countries were considered an extension of Portugal, where the people were regarded more as instruments of production than as human beings with their own legitimate aspirations.

Lisbon invested only the bare minimum of capital in her colonies and gave little in return for the ample flow of natural resources from the Dark Continent. Portugal flourished while its African possessions remained stagnant and neglected. Nothing was ploughed back into Angola itself.

The population suffered as a result. Throughout the colonial period the Angolan people were paid the lowest starvation wages. Any protest or dissent was harshly crushed. The Portuguese did not hesitate to use force against peaceful protest. African lives were held cheap.

Then came the sixties, when Britain and France – partly as a result of libertarian pressure at home but also from simple recognition of the fact that any serious attempt to suppress the growing political movements in

CLOCKWISE FROM TOP LEFT: Portuguese *Commandos Africanos* deploy after being dropped off by a squadron of *Alouettes* in central Moçambique; An insurgent – injured in a contact – is brought into base by helicopter. Most of these youngsters had never seen the face of the enemy before; For centuries African border posts reflected a European influence; Wounded Portuguese soldier prepared for helicopter evacuation; Chopper lands nearby after an emergency call; Most counter-insurgency operations in Angola and Moçambique were helicopter-orientated; Ground forces indicate a bush LZ after one of their number had been injured in a landmine incident.

MBIQUE AGAINST FRELIMO

the African colonies themselves was no longer practicable – granted independence to numerous of their African possessions.

Many of these countries were unprepared for even limited self-government, let alone full independence.

During the ten years after the granting of independence to Ghana in 1957, more than thirty countries achieved self-government and joined the United Nations: notably Nigeria, Kenya, Tanzania, Senegal, Zambia, Madagascar, the Congo and others.

But Portugal tenaciously held on to its four African colonies. The very idea of Angola or Mocambique becoming independent states in their own right was firmly rejected by the semi-fascist dictator Salazar. When protests in Angola were followed by violent rebellion, Salazar sent in the armed forces to crush the dissidents. But by now it was not so easy. African liberation forces were being armed and prepared for war against the Imperialists.

Similar rebellions ensued in Portuguese Guinea farther north and in Mocambique to the east.

Soon Lisbon was fighting three wars on a dozen fronts thousands of kilometres from home. The insurgent movements, with grandiose styles and titles such as the Popular Movement for the Liberation of Angola (MPLA), The Front for the Liberation of Mocambique (Frelimo) and the Union for the Total Liberation of Angola (Unita), were solidly backed by their independent neighbours, among others, Zaire and the Congo in West Africa and Zambia, Kenya and Tanzania in East Africa, and by Libya, Mali, Benin, Ghana and the then-Marxist Ethiopia.

The USSR, Cuba, China, Bulgaria, Vietnam, Poland, East Germany and other states in the Eastern Bloc gave the arms, funds and instruction necessary for these insurrections.

For fifteen years Portugal fought a succession of rearguard guerrilla actions, and while the wars remained static for a while because of poor African organisation, the Portuguese never achieved any real successes either.

In Angola they did better than in Mocambique, mainly because there were many permanent settlers living there. The Angolan settlers (who were in a sense more Angolan than Portuguese) were prepared to fight for the land that they had cleared and cultivated for centuries. In Portuguese Guinea, where there were few Portuguese farmers or traders, the defending colonial forces were almost entirely European conscripts with little zeal for a war that they were not prepared to die in and for a cause that most ridiculed.

The extent of conflict rapidly widened. Portugal, one of the poorest nations in Europe, could never keep up hostilities on such a scale indefinitely. By now the rebel insurgents in all three colonies were receiving the most modern weapons and training from their friends in the Eastern Bloc.

The end of all three wars came suddenly. In April 1974 a group of young officers carried out a *coup d'etat* in Lisbon and demanded an immediate end to conflict. A year later, almost without formality, Portugal's five-hundred-year-old Portuguese empire in Africa was brought to an ignominious end. In about fifteen years of fighting Portugal had lost six thousand men in action and another six thousand dead from other causes, most of them to the tropical conditions in which they fought.

Under various obscure agreements it was declared in Luanda, Bissau and Lourenco Marques – soon to be renamed Maputo – that free elections would be held and democratic governments would be established in all three countries. It never happened.

Radical forces, with Portuguese Communist Party, Russian and Cuban collusion, seized power even before the last Portuguese soldier had left Africa. They established militant one-party states that tolerated no opposition. One brutal regime had merely been replaced by another all in the space of a year.

In Angola it was the MPLA under Dr Agostinho Neto that forced both the Western-orientated FNLA and the Chinese-supported Unita back into the bush and protracted guerrilla warfare. All opposition to the Marxist one-party MPLA was ruthlessly crushed. Tens of thousands of people regarded as enemies of the state were put to death. Many more were tortured.

You were either *for* or *against* the MPLA. If you attempted to profess neutrality you were regarded as an enemy and killed. It was the same in Mocambique and the newly renamed Guiné-Bissau which also became client states of Moscow.

Such draconian measures did not end the conflict. They exacerbated diverse and often hostile sentiments.

The FNLA, backed by America, suffered a disastrous defeat at the hands of the MPLA army led by Cubans, known as Fapla (The Popular Armed Forces of Angola) early in the civil war that followed independence. Unita, headed by a young revolutionary educated in Switzerland who embraced the theories of Mao Tse-tung, fled to eastern Angola to fight another day. That was in 1975.

Since then Dr Jonas Savimbi has slowly and systematically built up his guerrilla force. Unita, then as now, drew most of its strength from the Ovimbundu tribes of eastern Angola.

When Savimbi's aid from China dried up, he turned first to the South Africans, who were themselves then fighting a guerrilla war in South West Africa, south of Angola and then to Washington. The Americans, eager to oppose Soviet influence in Africa, and not particularly keen to see the South Africans expand their base of influence on the African continent, acted swiftly. They gave Savimbi solid material and financial backing to stop the military thrust by the MPLA.

ABOVE: During the Portuguese Colonial period, Luanda, the Angolan capital, was regarded as one of the beautiful cities of Africa. Its culture, traditions, heritage and architecture were distinctly Iberian. Within months of the Portuguese pulling out of Africa, after the April 1974 putsch, this delightful tropical metropolis became a filthy, festering slum, which is how the visitor will find Luanda today.

CLOCKWISE RIGHT: Members of a crack Portuguese Commando group line up on the runway to prepare for bush operations against rebel insurgents in the Angolan interior; A Portuguese Air Force *Alouette III* hovers over a road convoy on the main road northwards out of Tete in Moçambique; Heavily protected road convoy in Angola, just south of Nambuangongo, north Angola; "Lisboa 13,999 kms" says it all! – the airstrip at N'Requinha, in eastern Angola. The hearts of these young metropolitan conscripts were in Europe, not in a remote African war…

Angola : 1966

Legend

┼┼┼┼┼┼	= railways
─────	= main roads
─ ∙ ─ ∙ ─	= district boundaries
▬▬▬	= international frontiers

Miles
0   50   100   150   200

0   100   200   300   400
Kilometres

By the mid-eighties Unita had extended its sphere of military activity and influence almost to Luanda itself, far to the west of Savimbi's country. He even sent in his men to the oil-rich enclave of Cabinda, across the Congo River north of Luanda. Because of unpopular and often brutal repressive measures by the MPLA Government in Luanda, Unita, by then, found ready support among the people wherever they infiltrated.

Several times the MPLA regime, in conjunction with the Cubans and the Russians, made elaborate plans to remove the steadily increasing influence of Savimbi by attempting to invade his headquarters region in the far eastern corner of Angola. They knew that if they could take and destroy Jamba – his bush capital – Savimbi could be dealt a crippling blow by wiping out his command and control centres and blocking his supplies, and thus his ability to continue to fight. As Mao preached, he would be deprived of a secure guerrilla base inside Angola.

Huge armoured attacks were launched by Fapla, the military wing of the MPLA, always with solid Cuban, Russian and East German support. Each time these great columns of fighting vehicles and infantry were driven back by Savimbi's men in concert with South African military forces.

The South Africans in turn had good reason to support Unita. They knew that as long as Angola remained unstable, the South West African guerrilla movement, Swapo, would not be able to carry their insurgent struggle into the neighbouring territory.

Throughout of the eighties some of these MPLA attacks on Unita lasted for months. They always entailed the use of advanced jet aircraft, helicopters, tanks, armoured personnel-carriers and tens of thousands of men. By 1984 it was no longer a bush conflict; it had assumed the proportions of real war.

But each time the Luanda regime was forced – by long distances, bad roads, poor communications and aggressive retaliation on the part of Savimbi – to withdraw, Unita and its supporters were strengthened in their resolve and in the amount of Russian military material that the rebels

were able to capture from the retreating enemy. What the South Africans took on the battlefields after their own victories over Fapla was also handed over to Savimbi. The value of such captured war material (as in *Operation Protea* in 1983) was often reckoned in terms of thousands of millions of dollars.

The years 1987 to early 1989 saw some of the most intense fighting yet experienced in any African country south of the Sahara in the years after the Second World War. Great tank battles were fought round the eastern towns of Mavinga and Cuito Cuanavale and in the south round Ongiva, Xangongo, Cahama, Mupa and elsewhere.

In an attempt to stop a big armoured attack, the South Africans in 1987 poured three thousand men into the field backed by multiple rocket-launchers as well as heavy 155mm G-5 guns, all of which were superior to anything that the Russians could put into the battle. Although the Angolans had by then achieved domination of the air it eventually proved to be of little real value because of the vast distances and remote bushy terrain in which the battles were fought.

The American *Stinger* missiles provided to the Unita movement by Reagan and Bush were also a powerful deterrent. By the time the twentieth Angolan jet, transport aircraft and helicopter had been brought down, Luanda was naturally reluctant to commit more aircraft to the war effort.

It was therefore the men on the ground who suffered. The writing was on the wall.

By 1989 there were pressing grounds for peace negotiations. Unita and the MPLA met for the first time under the auspices of the Americans, the Russians and the Portuguese. Not long afterwards the South Africans were also brought to the negotiating table.

Thus it was that a peace or sorts between the MPLA government in Luanda and Unita under Dr Jonas Savimbi was at last signed in June 1991. A bloody chapter in the brutal history of Africa had hopefully ended. But it was not to be. An even bloodier era of conflict continued well into the nineties…

PREVIOUS PAGE: Portuguese Air Force base in Mocambique showing *Fiat* G-91 jet-fighter and *Alouette III* in anti-mortar revetments.

THIS PAGE – ABOVE AND CLOCKWISE: The face of the Portuguese fighting man in one of Lisbon's African empires; Portuguese troops with an *Alouette* helicopter overhead patrolling the streets of Luanda after the April 1974 army *coup d'etat*; Many of the best soldiers in the Portuguese Army in Africa were black. One of the most outstanding men in Portuguese Guinea was Captain Joao Bacar (right) who was killed shortly after he took the author on a three-day patrol in an area south of Bissau; *Harvard* T-6s were often used in counter-insurgency roles in Angola; A casualty is rushed to a PAF *Alouette* in Mocambique; Two of Portuguese Africa's most prominent leaders during the revolutionary period and afterwards – the late President Agostinho Neto of Angola (right) and Marcelinos dos Santos, who later became Vice President of Mocambique.

CHAPTER 9

ANGOLA AND MOCAMBIQUE IN THE COLONIAL PERIOD

In Angola and, later, in Mocambique the war was debilitating from the start. The first 250 guerrillas who entered Portuguese East Africa were trained in Algeria (as were also the first 300 Angolan MPLA insurgents). They opened their campaign on 25 September 1964 with their first foray into northern Mocambique. Mueda and Cabo Delgado immediately became contested regions, and remained so for the next 11 years.

Grim battles were fought by the Portuguese when they still strode tall – as they did for five centuries – over vast regions of Colonial Africa.

Forewarned by the uprisings in Angola and Guinea, Portugal had already built up its strength to about 16 000 men in Mocambique, although at first it had only about five aircraft available.

By 1973 the figure for Mocambique had grown to about 70 000, and the air force comprised twelve *Fiat* G-91s, fifteen *Harvard* T6s which I found to be ubiquitous in all the war zones, fourteen *Alouette* and two *Puma* helicopters, five *Noratlas* transports and seven DC-3 *Dakotas*. Although some of these planes were hit by ground fire and the occasional SAM-7 missile, the Portuguese Air Force in Mocambique suffered relatively few losses compared with what was then happening in Guinea. There had been several hits on G-91 jet-fighters

in the West African territory, severely limiting air superiority.

On another occasion a DC-3 carrying foreign military attaches and members of the senior Portuguese military command was hit by a SAM-7 in one of the engines. The crippled plane nevertheless managed to land safely. They were the lucky ones.

In Angola, Mocambique and Portuguese Guinea, the Portuguese took some time to learn to use their French-built *Alouettes* effectively. When these helicopters first arrived in Africa, some unit commanders would try to squeeze five or six men on board, besides the usual two-man crews, although it was designed for a maximum of four passengers. French technicians attached to the Portuguese forces warned them this kind of weight would strip the gearbox if they were not careful; so numbers were later reduced. It was difficult when there were casualties, since the use of helicopters was so limited in this war.

Most of the infiltration by Frelimo into Mocambique took place across the Ruvuma River separating Mocambique from Tanganyika (later Tanzania); the target was the heartland of the traditionally bellicose Makonde people, who lived on both sides of the river. The Makonde had never been totally pacified in five centuries of colonisation, and they proved to be natural allies of Frelimo, although they were cast aside once independence had been achieved. Later, when Zambia entered the fray, Frelimo groups would come through from Lusaka and cross into the western regions of Mocambique.

It was then that Tete Province in the central heartland of this huge country twice the size of the state of California, became the guerrilla cauldron from which the conflict was ultimately extended to Rhodesia. In 1967, the war progressed farther southwards from the Makonde country to Niassa.

Ian Beckett tells of this period: "The size of Frelimo units (in Mocambique) steadily increased as the movement approached a maximum strength of perhaps 8 000 guerrillas by 1967/68, but these numbers subsequently declined after the internal splits within Frelimo of 1968/69, as represented by the disputes of the Second Party Congress and the assassination of Eduardo Mondlane.

"Frelimo did succeed in closing many sisal plantations along the northern frontier, but had been mostly contained when General Kaulza de Arriaga, who had become Portuguese ground force commander in May 1969, undertook a large-scale offensive, *Operation Gordian Knot*, in the dry season of 1970. Involving some 10 000 troops, the campaigns countinued for seven months, in which time Arriaga claimed to have accounted for 651 guerrillas dead and a further 1 840 captured, for the loss of only 132 Portuguese. He also claimed to have destroyed 61 guerrilla bases and 165 camps, while 40 tons of ammunition had been captured in the first two months.

"The coordination of heliborne assault after initial artillery and air bombardment, followed by mine clearance and consolidation on foot, undoubtedly severely damaged Frelimo's infrastructure in the north. But, in the manner of such large-scale operations, it did not totally destroy the guerrilla capacity for infiltration, which Arriaga's critics maintained that his predecessors had achieved at much less cost and effort. Further operations were thus required in the north such as operations *Garotte* and *Apio* during 1971."

The problem with *Gordian Knot* and similar operations is that in military jargon, when a counter-revolutionary campaign becomes spectacular (and they were spectacular, since they involved nearly every man in the security forces who could carry a gun, including office staff, cooks and bearers), the writing is already on the wall.

Yet, when the Ruvuma and Tete regions were visited by the South African vice-consul in Luanda (now Brigadier Rtd) 'Kaas' van der Waals, he did not think the war was going too badly for the Portuguese. He was soon made aware of the fact that, as a result of very heavy insurgent attacks in Tete Province, Rhodesia was suffering because of the inability of the Portuguese upper ranks to cope with the situation.

They tried hard to clear Frelimo out of Tete, but they were unsuccessful. By then *Operation Hurricane* had been launched into the adjacent Mount Darwin area of Rhodesia by the Zimbabwe African National Liberation Army (Zanla), the military wing of Robert Mugabe's Zimbabwe African National Union (ZANU).

Ron Reid-Daly, then an acting captain with the Rhodesian Light Infantry, was the first Rhodesian officer to be attached to Portuguese forces. Other Rhodesian officers, including some Rhodesian SAS specialists, were also seconded from time to time. Some of their comments about the way in which the Portuguese fought their war in Mocambique (and, ultimately, why they eventually lost it) are illuminating.

From Reid-Daly's experience with the British SAS in Malaya, it was clear from the start that the top Portuguese brass in Mocambique had no ready understanding of the nature of guerrilla warfare, and they were certainly far behind anything that the British had experienced in Borneo, Malaya or even Kenya during the Mau Mau rebellion. That was surprising, since many Portuguese commanders had by then seen service in Angola and Guinea.

The counter-insurgency pattern was the same each time. Some intelligence of guerrilla activity would come in and the local garrison commander would spend days getting together a force of several hundred men who would make a huge cross-country sweep, often 500 men strong. They would never act immediately on a tip-off, with the result that when an operation was at last launched, the birds had usually flown.

CLOCKWISE FROM TOP: General Antonio de Spinola in Portuguese Guinea wrote a book which caused the military putch which brought Portugal's African campaigns to an end. He was a dynamic military leader but a poor politician; Parade at Unita Headquarters, with Dr Jonas Savimbi taking the salute; Guerrilla patrol in Portuguese Guinea – cruel terrain in which to fight a war; Marines in Mocambique, a photo by Juhan Kuus and one of the best photos of the war in Northern Angola by Cloete Breytenbach.

During bush operations everything in their path would be destroyed; livestock would be slaughtered, crops and villages burnt, the local people rounded up for questioning and anyone acting in a suspicious manner would be arrested and taken back to base. Tribesmen who attempted to escape this treatment were regarded as 'fleeing terrorists', and they would be shot and the death recorded as a 'terrorist kill'.

If they escaped into the bush, well and good; there was no question of sending a force to follow them. By nightfall the unit would be back at base, congratulating themselves on a job well done. Naturally, any one of the local people who had experienced the force of a Portuguese 'search and destroy' mission was by then firmly a supporter of Frelimo; the business of 'hearts and minds' came only much later. In that way many neutral tribesmen soon became Frelimo sympathisers.

The *Aldeamentos* programme of resettling rural communities in organised camps was by then already in full swing in all three African provinces. Large numbers were moved into areas where they would be under Portuguese control, and, in theory, out of reach of the insurgents. The justification for this policy was, ostensibly, that it denied the guerrillas the ability to wage war because there would be no popular indigenous support and no food, which was supposed to be essential for survival in the bush.

In reality, although a million people, roughly 15 per cent of the population were resettled in Mocambique, the programme failed utterly. Beckett says that a third of the food grown in the *Aldeamentos* went straight to the guerrillas.

Sometimes the *Aldeamentos* programme was welcomed by the black leaders of the Muslim Yao and the coastal people, who were opposed to Frelimo influence because it was largely tribally based. Most correspondents who visited the war areas up to the 1974 *coup* tended to disregard the fact that although guerrilla activity was extended to the Niassa region in 1967, the Makonde and the Nyanja were only two of 19 tribes from nine main ethnic groups speaking 17 different languages in Mocambique. For that reason the war was confined to the north. Lourenco Marques, with its tourists and bright lights, might have been in another country.

In the actual fighting, the South Africans and the Rhodesians found the Portuguese clumsy and inept. Their patrols were too large; thirty or forty men at a time when people like Reid-Daly used four-man 'sticks' and achieving good results with such small numbers.

Most of the failures, the Rhodesians believed, resulted from a lack of regular professional troops and the fact that most of these boys from the metropolis neither understood Africa nor wished to be in Africa in the first place.

Their radio communications were poor, which was probably one reason why they worked in such large num-

bers; the fear of being overrun by the enemy, as in Vietnam, was a real one in the minds of such unprofessional soldiers.

Again, their radio sets were unwieldy American instruments designed rather for vehicles than the backs of soldiers in the bush, and they probably dated from the Korean War; communication with base was a long and complicated business. At one main base the Portuguese were using large antiquated German sets from the Second World War.

During all the operations in which the Rhodesians took part in the Tete panhandle the Portuguese were found to be completely base-bound. They fought much as the Americans had fought in Vietnam.

The upper command was quite happy to let the insurgents control the bush while the Portuguese held onto the towns, communications links and strong-points. Reid-Daly said that in Tete, patrols lasting from four to six weeks should have been normal, supplied by air. The idea was regarded as preposterous by the upper command. At that time, the Portuguese would not consider anything beyond three days, spending every night in camp if at all possible. The Rhodesians always emphasised the need to dominate the bush by night as well as by day, and although the Portuguese officers agreed, they very rarely did anything about it.

The ability of Frelimo to move freely at night was clearly illustrated by the number of mines, both anti-tank and anti-personnel, that they were able to lay. This freedom extended all the way from Ruvuma to Tete. During one morning's clearing operation in the Mueda area, Portuguese sappers cleared 189 mines along ten kilometres of track, about a third of them TM-46s. The rest were APs. There were roughly fifty mines laid in the short three-day journey I completed from Tete to the Malawi border in 1971.

Physically, the Rhodesians regarded the average Portuguese conscript as a "poor physical specimen". They could not march any distance without frequent rests. Most of these young men had come from poor backgrounds, and although they did their first PT the day they joined the army in Portugal, they were barely fit or strong enough to meet the fairly rigorous demands of their officers. There were exceptions, of course. One of their worst faults on the march was that the column was noisy and straggling. They talked loudly instead of maintaining silence, which even Frelimo knew was absolutely necessary in counterinsurgency warfare.

At night, Reid-Daly found, when an ambush had been set up, the Portuguese soldiers would cough and fidget. "It was as if they were warning the enemy to keep clear, so that they would not be compelled to fight. It was an impossible situation."

On the other hand, some of the *Flecha*, parachute and

CLOCKWISE FROM TOP: The only way to get into some jungle bases in Angola – such as this one at Nambuangongo, in the north – was by air; Jungle convoy as seen from chopper escort in Angola; Portuguese Para nurse directed to correct LZ in Guinea; Cahorra Bassa from the air. While the dam was being built a savage war was being fought in the surrounding Mocambique bush; Some idea of the conditions under which the Portuguese Army fought in Africa can be gained from this convoy in Cabinda jungle.

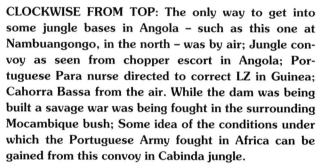

black commando regiments were excellent operators in the bush. Most of them were superior to Frelimo, and most of the kills in Mocambique were attributable to them and to the air force.

While most operational plans were carefully prepared by the brigade staff, Reid-Daly found that they seldom allowed the battalion commander any scope for flexibility or personal initiative. It all had to be done according to the book. There was a marked reluctance to change plans in spite of fresh information and developments as the operation progressed.

A sorry example of this was the failure to capitalise on the discovery, towards the end of 1967, of a huge insurgent camp, about 500 metres across, by one of the helicopters during an operation in the mountains near Cahora Bassa. It was only a day later that an infantry attack was revised, because the Portuguese were not prepared to change the original plan and the sequence of events that they had mapped out shortly before.

Reid-Daly was with them at the time. He insisted that they should scrape together another body of men and try a vertical envelopment. That would have been possible, because there were eight *Alouettes* available. The operation only got off the ground several days later, and it was unsuccessful.

The Portuguese soldiers were very badly equipped, considering the nature of the war. Apart from the standard G-3 rifle of .762 NATO calibre, they had no night illumination flares, no claymores and none of the elementary means of protection.

They had no idea how to use smoke grenades to call up helicopters, or how to use small mirrors to attract the attention of aircraft – many of the little things that most Western forces take for granted. Whereas the Rhodesians maintained excellent liaison between pilots and ground forces, that never existed in Mocambique, and no one ever took steps to improve the situation. They just were not talking to each other. Another device taught by the Rhodesians and eventually taken up in Mocambique was to set up radio relay stations on hills. Rhodesian officers began to take some of the elementary equipment that was lacking, which attracted great interest. Reid-Daly even ran a course showing them how to make a simple claymore mine from a plough-share.

He and other Rhodesian officers also explained to them the principle of a stop group in a frontal attack. They needed to work hard at it, for the Portuguese choice of positions was usually bad; they did not plan escape routes, and were simply not trained for that kind of warfare which by then had become second nature to Rhodesians and South Africans.

The very idea of taking a prisoner immediately after a skirmish was frowned upon. Although not all Frelimo captives were shot, they would argue that they *ought to have*

Dimensions of the Alouette SE 3160/316B

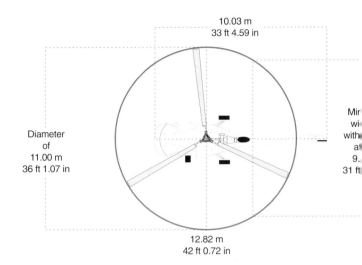

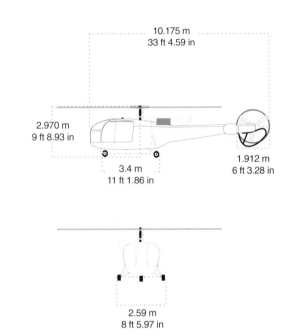

been. It depended on the attitude of the officer in charge at the time. On more than one occasion Reid-Daly stepped in; it took a long time for the army to understand the need for interrogation and the importance of proper intelligence. PIDE, the secret police, was always calling for prisoners, which sometimes resulted in friction.

The Rhodesians noted that Portuguese military vehicles, the West German *Unimog* and the French *Berliet*, and their maintenance, were excellent. Like their uniforms, of which they were issued two per tour of duty, it was all they had and they looked after them. But not their weapons.

Perhaps because the G-3 was virtually proof against

ANTI-CLOCKWISE FROM TOP: Frelimo insurgent troops on patrol near Mavue on the Rhodesian border; Portuguese Air Force *Noratlas* in eastern Angola; Angola, Mocambique and Portuguese Guinea were regarded as nothing but Portuguese, until Lisbon lost its African possessions; Portuguese *Alouette* brings flood victims to safety in Mocambique and, FNLA rebel strongpoint near the Zairean border at the height of the war.

stoppage, few Portuguese soldiers bothered to clean their guns, either before or after an operation. They would smile among themselves at Rhodesian officers who took great care of their rifles at all times. One young captain told Reid-Daly that the last place where he had seen a man actually cleaning his rifle every day when not ordered to do so was Goa, after he had been captured by Indian troops. The situation was bizarre.

Morale among Portuguese forces was seriously affected by the lack of facilities for the evacuation of casualties. That was due mainly to the shortage of operational helicopters. Also, while most of the camps had medical officers, most of them were young conscript students who did only the bare minimum. A man injured by a mine would usually have to be moved to an airstrip, where a small plane could be landed. Depending on how remote a base was, that could take a whole day. Many Portuguese died of wounds because of such delays.

The Rhodesian officers found it curious that the Portuguese in Mocambique had never developed reconnaissance patrols. They would seldom reconnoitre a position beforehand, or use aerial photographs for intelligence purposes once a Frelimo camp had been spotted. Instead they would deploy special forces in an operation which would often include the necessary primary reconnaissance at the same time as the attack; very much a hit-or-miss affair.

Reid-Daly spent time with one of the *Flecha* units; he became a close friend of Colonel Oscar Cardoza, who was brought from Angola to establish the *Flecha* concept in Mocambique. Unlike so many of his fellows, Cardoza proved to be an excellent soldier and tactician.

While the *Flechas* worked in smaller groups they also lacked scouting ability. They were composed mostly of captured terrorists, turncoats and local recruits and were paid bounties for kills, captures or recovery of weapons. Their training was hard but simple. Discipline was draconian. A petty misdemeanour would be treated as a serious offence.

But they made good soldiers. Their ability to shoot straight with a rifle was unmatched even in the Rhodesian army; they either got one- or two-inch groups at fifty yards or they were thrashed by their officers.

The *Flechas* considered a 40 kilometre patrol between sunrise and sunset as normal, in spite of the difficult mountainous and jungle terrain. Some Rhodesian SAS men who worked with them were amazed at their ability to keep going and were themselves hard-pressed to keep up the pace. They were also militarily correct in their actions; they would cross a river or other obstacle by first tactically sending two sections across, scouting the area and then bringing the rest of the group through. During the entire day they had only one break for a smoke, the respite that most soldiers regard as a natural right.

CLOCKWISE FROM TOP: Guarding a PAF *Alouette* in Guinea; Lonely vigil at a Portuguese Army base in northern Angola; Sunset over a civilian *Aldeamentos* – heavily fortified – in Mocambique. Note the trench-lines (foreground).

The Rhodesians achieved some success in Mocambique. They managed to teach some units how to run a proper operations room and to set up an efficient Joint Operations Command (JOC). Trackers gradually began to come into their own, and here members of the SAS under Brian Robinson played an important part. Unfortunately, in the long term there were simply too many Portuguese and too few Rhodesians to have any real effect on the war.

The Rhodesians never succeeded in goading the Portuguese into effectively following up tracks after a contact. Under Reid-Daly, they would often refuse outright to go into the bush unless a large force had been mustered. Helicopter support was essential. The result was that Frelimo units were able to snipe at Portuguese patrols with impunity. They knew that the Portuguese would rarely detach men from a column to go after them.

To the conscript army, capturing a Frelimo camp was the pinnacle of success, even though it had often been abandoned because the rebels had foreknowledge of the attack or could hear them coming. Holding ground was the ultimate achievement, even if they abandoned that ground an hour later.

Reid-Daly recommended on his return to Salisbury that RLI units should be allowed to work with the Portuguese, not so much for political reasons, but rather to demonstrate what ordinary young white soldiers (the RLI was an all-white unit) were capable of when properly led and trained. He knew that the presence of special forces like the SAS might have been regarded by the Portuguese command as an attempt by the Rhodesians to "show them up", with consequent bad feeling.

In the opinion of most Rhodesian and South African soldiers who came into contact with the Portuguese, the quality most needed was initiative. As it was, it was almost entirely lacking. Occasionally a brilliant officer would be encountered; a man who knew the war, the enemy, the ground on which he was fighting and capable of inspiring his men to better results; but they were rare.

Discipline was also bad; and it has been well said that an army usually reflects its national character.

Thus the Portuguese, while respectful to their officers (except during the last phase of the war after the *coup d'etat*), were sloppy in dress and bearing and slack in military operations. Often a battalion commander would be of the best type imaginable, but he would lack good professional officers to support him. Senior commanders usually had a handful of regular officers supplemented by many more *milicianos*, temporary officers from the universities.

There were other problems. A battalion colonel would often have senior visitors from Nampula, Beira or Lourenco Marques; brigadiers and generals, breathing down his neck in his own operations room, often countermanding instructions that he had just given to his men in the field. Four or five would sit about and veto the next phase; at other times they would change his entire operational plan. Certainly it would never have been tolerated in Guinea, or to the same extent in Angola, where the conflict was much more professionally handled. In Mocambique the high command had lost control. As correspondents we were all aware when visiting Mocambique, that Arriaga (the 'Pink Panther') as his men called him was frequently accused of employing too many subordinates who had failed elsewhere. He was recalled in July 1973; but by then the damage had been done.

Mocambique, from the beginning of the campaign in 1963, was never imbued with the kind of determination displayed in Angola or during the early stages in Guinea; the belief was that this was a war that could not be won. Even to the end, it was never lost; but there was no will to win.

Because it began late and most intelligent Portuguese knew that Mocambique was their third African war and that Portugal was becoming over-extended, the Mocambique campaign lacked the necessary impetus for any effective or lasting counter-insurgency measures.

As Beckett says, the Portuguese had growing problems in Mocambique by 1974, but not serious enough to ensure military defeat. We must therefore look elsewhere for the failure to consolidate the Portuguese position along the Ruvuma and to take advantage of the serious splits that were developing within the Frelimo hierarchy.

Porch speaks of deteriorating morale among regular cadres. This was manifested in the steady desertion rate in Portugal itself.

Nor were matters helped by the dictator Salazar, who, like Hitler before him, ignored the advice of his generals. He was warned repeatedly against fighting on more than one front at a time; he had three fronts in three different regions of Africa. To give him his due, there was not much he could do about it.

Again, the antiquated Portuguese war machine in all three African possessions had been souped-up by trebling its strength form 60 000 in 1960 to 210 000 twenty years later. Caetano admitted in 1974, when he was in exile in Brazil, that "we had no organisation capable of directing the army in operations". Most of the Portuguese defence was haphazard and piecemeal which, as Porch says, meant that the army was "ill-equipped to cope with a long war".

Matters were further compounded by the fact that relations between the Portuguese army and the settlers in Africa were bad. In Mocambique particularly, the colonists doubted the ability of the Portuguese army to fight. They questioned their courage, their morale and their integrity. They also hated the increasing reliance of the army on black troops. There were economic factors also. The Portuguese civilians were among the most heavily taxed in Europe. In Lourenco Marques they used to say that when the army arrived, prices went up. There was no love lost between settlers and soldiers.

The crunch came in January 1974, when a group of whites attacked an officers' mess in Beira after the murder of a white civilian. This event accentuated the isolation of the army still further. It resulted in the closing of the army rest centre in Beira.

The official military publication *Revista Militar* gives some indication of the ratio of black and white soldiers towards the end of the war. These figures themselves are illuminating, giving a clear indication of the increasing need for indigenous troops to do their fighting for them. It is significant that in January 1989 the ratio between black-white troops on the Angolan border was even higher. Most of the units deployed in northern Namibia were black.

Guinea		Angola		Mocambique	
Black	White	Black	White	Black	White
24 800	6 200	37 800	25 000	19 800	24 200

No one can predict what might have happened if the war in Mocambique had continued. Although Frelimo was not successful in taking strongpoints, it had extended the war to such a degree that so much attention was devoted to protecting the Cahora Bassa dam that the rest of Tete had become guerrilla country, which the Rhodesian insurgents used to good advantage.

By 1972 Frelimo was beginning to move south and east from Tete. The Vila Pery area was infiltrated that year and the Beira region in 1973. So constant were attacks on the Umtali-Beira rail link (one of the lifelines of Rhodesia) that they eventually stopped running trains at night. Armoured mine detectors known as *zorras* were placed ahead of the engine on this line.

Frelimo was equally active against the local population. In the Tete region alone more than fifty traditional chiefs were murdered in 1971, most of them because they refused to pay cash or tribute to marauding bands. Hundreds more were murdered in other areas. The level of hostilities had also escalated meanwhile. Mocambique, says one report, accounted for twice as many Portuguese casualties in the three months, November 1973-January 1974, than either Guinea or Angola.

Speaking in Lourenco Marques two weeks after the *coup d'etat* in Lisbon, General Costa Gomes, one of the architects of the revolution, said: "Our armed forces have reached the limits of neuro-psychological exhaustion." These were strong words, and they have often been quoted since. Rightly or wrongly, General Costa Gomes echoed the sentiments of the nation. It was time for Portugal to vacate its African possessions.

CHAPTER 10

THE CHAD WAR

An Ideological Struggle for a Desolate Corner of Africa

Although France relinquished power in Africa more than thirty years ago, the French military presence remains. Nowhere is this more evident than in the Chad Republic, where fanatical religious and ethnic passions have smouldered for years. Matters came to a head in the mid-sixties, when a band of dissident Moslem north-Chadians launched a major guerrilla operation against the black quasi-Christian Fort Lamy government from bases in the Sudan and Libya.

The President of Chad reacted by calling in the French. The Elysee government, then still under General de Gaulle, sent in the Foreign Legion together with thousands of young French conscripts.

The uproar which followed this action was similar to the young American reaction against US Vietnam involvement, and although considerable pressures were successfully brought to bear and the majority of the French troops were repatriated, France in the nineties continues to be involved in an African war which will not be reconciled as long as revolutionary Arab states maintain a vested interest in its outcome.

Peter Younghusband, correspondent for various British and American publications entered the fighting zone with the French forces and drew his own conclusions. He saw the Legionnaires in anti-guerrilla operations and this was his report.

They killed a cow in the market place. They held it down and tied its legs.

Then they cut its throat so that the crimson blood spurted forth onto the yellow dust.

As the beast bellowed and gurgled in its death throes, several of them climbed onto it, and stamped on it and pressed their feet into it to hasten its end and speed the flow of the blood. While they did so, they laughed and joked and spoke of other things.

Overhead, vultures wheeled and hovered, waiting for offal.

You don't often see vultures flying over the nations's capital in an African country. Farther out, in the bush, yes, but not over the main city. To see this seemed rather like an ill omen.

But this is Chad, primitive and poverty-stricken – the wild, savage heart of Africa where civilisation is still struggling for a foothold.

In Fort Lamy – since renamed N'Djamena – camels led by turbaned nomads plod past the plate-glass doors of the American Embassy. From the verandas of the air-conditioned hotel La Tchadienne you can watch women drawing water from the muddy river in stone jars, as they have done for a thousand years. Beyond the precincts of the city lies a medieval wilderness still locked in a dark age.

Yet Chad is an independent nation, and at the United Nations General Assembly, its vote equals that of the United States of America.

In 1966 a simmering discontent among the predominantly Moslem Arab tribes in the northern region burst into open rebellion and began to win some support from

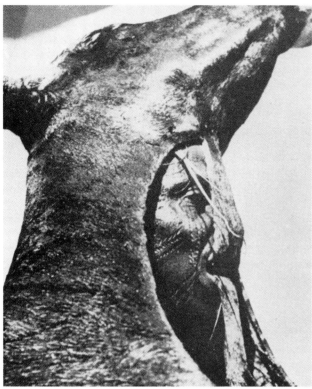

the African tribes in the south. The rebellion spread until it began to assume civil war proportions. Traffic on the few miserable roads spanning the nation's gaunt deserts and bushlands came to a standstill. By late 1967 the Government had lost control of two-thirds of the country and rebels were striking at villages close to the capital itself.

The Chad army, a sorry lot, were beaten back, losing their automatic weapons to attackers armed in the main with primitive spears and muzzle loaders. The government was spending nearly forty per cent of the national revenue on defence, and the rebels were receiving aid and base facilities from the neighbouring Arab states of Libya, Algeria and Sudan. The revolutionaries, calling themselves 'Frolinat', set up headquarters in Algeria.

The position had been reached where the Christian-animist black government of Chad was in imminent danger of being overthrown and replaced by a Moslem Arab-dominated regime.

In January 1969, President Tombalbaye invoked the defence treaty with Paris under which France had agreed to assist Chad if threatened by attack from abroad or by internal revolt.

France has not always answered appeals for assistance from its former African colonies, but the Gaullist regime had always had a special relationship with Chad. This deeply emotional tie had its origin in 1940, when Chad was the first French colony to rally to General Charles de Gaulle's resistance appeal.

It was from Chad that General Jacques Philippe Leclerc set off on his long march across the Sahara to join the Free French forces of de Gaulle that ultimately led to the liberation of Paris.

The war in Chad has been a particularly brutal conflict. At one time or another it involved just about every French Army and Air Force unit, including the French Foreign Legion, seen here in the early days in a village 'sweep' (top). The Chadians were equally brutal to their own people. A favourite 'ritual torture' (centre) was to sew a man into the hide of a freshly slaughtered ox. As the leather dried in the sun, it shrank, crushing the victim slowly to death.
BOTTOM: A Legionnaire consoles the wife of one of the men who had just been killed by his men.
OPPOSITE (CLOCKWISE FROM TOP RIGHT): Parts of Chad are incredibly beautiful; French Air Force *Super Puma* caught in an approaching desert dust storm; Technicians load a HOT anti-tank missile (developed by Aerospatiale and Messerschmitt-Bolkow) on to a UTM 800 electric turret in readiness for a Libyan counter-strike; French Paras move at the double to board; A wrecked Russian-built Mi-24 Libyan gunship after a combined French-Chadian strike at Faya-Largeau.

But this was not the only reason. Chad had also always had a special strategic significance for de Gaulle which became almost an obsession with him. He regarded Chad as the bastion of French influence in Africa, blocking the tide of communism and the particular brand of Arab socialism preached by Egypt's late President Gamal Abdul Nasser. At the same time he feared that French-speaking Africa was being menaced from the West by Anglo-Saxon and Russian influences in Nigeria and Congo (Brazzaville) respectively. This was why he gave support to Biafra. He was also wary of American influence spreading northwards from Zaire.

But the major impact of the moment was an Arab threat. It was the domino theory all over again. If Arab communism was allowed to succeed in Chad – and Frolinat had made it perfectly clear that it favoured the extreme left-wing brand of Arab socialism – then the other former French colonies lay wide open to subversion and to the ultimate collapse of French influence on the African continent.

So President de Gaulle decided to send military aid to President Tombalbaye's tottering, poverty-stricken regime deep in the desolate heart of Africa.

An immediate airlift of two hundred and sixty French troops – one hundred Foreign Legionnaires and a hundred and sixty Marines – was carried out from Nice. A cadre of three hundred French officers, most of them with colonial experience, were sent out to put some leadership and fibre into the thoroughly demoralised Chad Army.

They were followed by one thousand men of the French Air Force with half a dozen *Noratlas* transports, a dozen *Sikorsky* H-64 assault helicopters, half a dozen *Alouettes*, a few single-engined *Broussards* for observation and communication and five elderly piston-engined Douglas *Skyraiders*, which began noisily to pound rebel positions with bombs, rockets and machine-guns. Strategic transport was provided by *Transalls*.

This was only a holding operation. But it was soon clear to the French that the terrain, the climate and the elusiveness of the enemy were adding up to a long campaign. More troops were airlifted to Chad, including the 1st Battalion of the Foreign Legion's Second Regiment based on Corsica.

By early 1970 there were 3 600 French troops in Chad – including 900 Legionnaires, 1 000 Marines and 1 000 Air Force personnel – and public opinion in France began to express unease over the situation. The French press – backed by opposition politicians – pointed vociferously to the danger of "another Vietnam".

It was clear that black Africa, as a whole, was not in favour of the French intervention. The *Ghanaian Times* in Accra summed up African criticism in a leading article deploring Tombalbaye's use of French troops. It said that African leaders who had lost contact with their people

"should retire honourably instead of using foreign troops to support their wavering regimes". And it added that defence agreements with foreign powers should be abrogated by African countries, and requests for aid channelled through the Organisation for African Unity.

Certainly the build-up of French forces had become a bigger affair than expected. The bitter experiences of Indo-China – suffered by France and later by the United States – was a powerful influence on the French public.

Algeria, too, was a still painful memory. The military return to the scene of a former colonial power to prop up a regime so manifestly corrupt and unpalatable as Tombalbaye's was proving a hard diplomatic burden to bear – even for the cynical French. Furthermore, the spotlight of world publicity was focusing more and more on what had begun as a furtive little civil war in remotest Africa.

In short, de Gaulle's strategic ambitions were being hard paid for in political protest at home and sheer embarrassment abroad.

De Gaulle, meanwhile, was no longer President of France. Pompidou had taken over. He ordered Brigadier Edouard Cortadellas, the military commander in Chad, to end the war at all costs by not later than July 1970.

I spent two weeks in action with the Foreign Legion in Chad in January, 1970. The Legion was delighted to be back. Having spent the period since France gave up her last African colonial possession kicking their heels in Corsica and glumly aware that political pressures were building up in Paris to bring about their total disbandment, they saw this as a chance to prove themselves again as the world's roughest, toughest and most ruthless body of troops.

They were in their element once more, back in the desert, fighting Arabs and African rebels. It was, as an American magazine put it, the last *Beau Geste*.

I went with them to attack a village where, according to intelligence reports, rebels were hiding. As we approached, a troop of baboons gave us away. They capered on the cliffs above us, grunting and barking at our approach.

The Legionnaires cursed them with a vivid flow of obscenities, and the lieutenant ordered us into a charge, although the village was still five hundred metres distant.

We swept into it at a dead run, lungs labouring and tongues leathery in the fierce noonday heat. The rebels were shrieking and leaping onto horses and getting away, like a scene from a bad Western movie. Some just ran into the bushes, clasping loin cloths about themselves.

Someone pitched a hand-grenade. It fell short, but the fright of it sent a horse and rider careening sideways through the flimsy structure of a grass hut. The rider, riding bareback and grasping the horse's mane, kept his seat with amazing agility and galloped away.

Shouting in fury and frustration, the Legionnaires

chased the riders on foot, firing from the hip, through camelthorn that tore at their battle dress and sand that brought them, finally, to a heavy-booted, panting, swearing halt.

On the fringe of the village a prayer rug lay rumpled in the dust and the pages of a Koran riffled in the breeze. Someone had been praying when we arrived.

Only women and children remained in the village, the women clutching the infants and mutely enduring the kicks and blows of the soldiers, who pushed them from the huts and tossed kitchen utensils and calabashes about in their search for weapons and documents.

The Legionnaires who had pursued the rebels returned with two prisoners, driving them before them with thrusts of their rifle butts. The prisoners had been among those who had fled on foot. They clung to each other, the older man with his arm about the neck of the younger, apparently consoling him and calming him. We were to discover later that they were father and son.

The Legionnaires dragged them apart, wanting to interrogate them separately. The older man protested, pointing appealingly at the younger.

The officer slapped his face and shoved him so that he fell. He was kicked and pulled to his feet and dragged into a hut.

Suddenly there was a shout of warning. The younger prisoner had broken away and run to where the soldiers were piling the arms dropped by the fleeing rebels or gathered from the huts. He snatched up a spear and rushed at the officer who had struck the older man. The officer lifted his submachine-gun and fired a burst at point blank range.

The attacker jolted to a halt as though he had run into an invisible wall. He whirled half round, dropping the spear, and flopped onto his face.

There was a moment of utter silence. Then a startling, eerie wail burst forth, on an ever-ascending note, as if a spirit of retribution had descended among us. The sound came from one of the women, the mother of the youth, who fell on her knees and beat her head in the dust and rocked back and forth in a traditional African lament.

They had killed the son of the chief.

The officer walked over to the dying youth and kicked him. "*Imbecile – c'etait votre faux pas!*" he said bitterly.

The youth gasped and choked as death closed in on him. Thick swarms of flies settled on his body wounds and the froth of blood about his lips.

"Finish him," the officer ordered curtly. Two Legionnaires seized the dying youth by the ankles and dragged him behind a hut, out of sight of the women. There was the sound of a single shot.

We marched the five kilometres back to our vehicles and returned to field headquarters, where Commandant Roland Meudec – a tall beetle-browed Breton command-

ing the 1st Battalion of the Foreign Legion's Second Regiment – was lunching on Strasbourg sausages and a bottle of red wine.

He was not pleased with our results. "It is always so," he grumbled. "They will not fight us. They are hard to find. And most of the time they escape. And when you do corner them it is pathetic to kill them. They have one gun for every ten of them – the rest have spears. It is not what I call war. It makes you feel bad."

The Legion was finding – not for the first time in its colourful history – that Africa was on the side of the enemy, defending her own with every element, pestilence and hazard at her command. Blazing sun, malaria, dysentery, sand, bush, lack of water, the freezing cold of the desert at night – they were all there, harassing to the white man, but a way of life for the black man, and therefore his shield.

And the drums. The eerie drums. We heard their throbbing beat in the dark dawn of each morning as we broke camp, signalling our movements to all the population – primitive drums that were as efficient as our own modern field radio communications.

One morning we reached a wadi called Bahr Zrouk. A porcupine roasting over a still-glowing campfire and signs of a hasty departure told us we were hot on a trail.

Suddenly our machine-gunner, perched high on our six-wheeled, nine-geared troop carrier, yelled; "*Les types – a droit!*" (To the Legion all enemy and suspects are *types*.)

We hastily shoved our section mascot – a little grey monkey with bright blue genitals – into a C-ration box for safety, and tore off on a wild careening, bumping, ploughing pursuit, engines whining and labouring, springs and axles groaning and twanging, smashing down bushes and young saplings in our path and cleaving through the neck-high elephant grass like a flotilla of surfboats.

A score or so of turbaned men galloped ahead of us on nimble bush ponies, just out of gun range.

The rebels suddenly veered left and crossed a ravine where we could not follow.

"*Merde!*" yelled the Legionnaires, throwing their bush hats down and stamping on them. There was a furious lighting up of Gauloises and more cursing. Glumly we drove away.

That night, as we dined delicately on tinned *pate de foie* and drank a bottle of Chateau Neuf du Pape beside a campfire, Commandant Meudec sighed and said: "With a hundred helicopters I could clean up this situation in a month…"

But the Department of Defence in Paris had made it clear there would be no more helicopters. Acutely mindful of the criticisms that they were creating a Vietnam-type situation, the French Government wanted the war cleaned up without any further reinforcements of troops.

CLOCKWISE FROM TOP: French Air Force *Gazelle* with Astazou engine in temporary base in the Chad Desert; Pilots operational in Chad tend to fly low for fear of SAM-7s; French troops board during operations against Libyan forces; Technicians in maintenance hangar at N'Djamena Airport, the Chad capital.
OPPOSITE: The war in Chad was more extensive than was officially acknowledged; six French Air Force *Jaguar* fighters and four *Mirage* bombers were sent to N'Djamena to provide cover in the event of a Libyan attack. When it came, hostilities were restricted to the north of the country.

Commandant Meudec made no apologies for the methods used by his men. The Legion did not win its reputation for toughness by adhering to nursery rules. I saw rebels tortured to force them to reveal information during interrogation. They were cuffed, slapped, beaten and given water torture or electrical shocks. When their interrogators were satisfied they had told all they knew, they were left alone.

All prisoners were given the chance of rehabilitation. One of the first prisoners taken by the Legion became the barman in the officers' mess at the Legion's headquarters at Mongo.

The desert rebels are notoriously ruthless and cruel when they have the advantage. They show a special flair for techniques when it comes to torture. One favourite method is to sew a victim into the skin of a freshly killed cow and leave him in the blazing desert sun to die slowly of hunger, thirst and the asphyxiating squeeze of the cowskin as it dries and shrinks in the sun, attended by dense swarms of flies.

A Legionnaire who had seen two friends struck down in rebel ambushes – one by a hail of machine-gun fire and another by a lion-hunting spear that went clean through his chest and the pack on his back – told me: "We are not playing games here. We do to them exactly what they do to us when they get the chance."

But I also witnessed acts of compassion by the Legion. In one village a non-combatant was accidentally shot by Chad troops in a combined operation. Commandant Meudec radioed for a helicopter and an army doctor, and the wounded man was flown to hospital. The Commandant then went to great lengths personally to console the grief-stricken wife, assuring her repeatedly that her husband would return healed.

When France gave Chad its independence in 1960, it was inevitable that unrest and rebellion would follow. All the ingredients for civil war were there – poverty, tribal divisions, long traditions of feuding, and religious differ-ences. And, to cap it all, the independent government which took over from the French colonial administration proved to be despotic.

The new independent government under Francois Tombalbaye, a Christian African from the south of Chad, was composed mainly of blacks from the south – animists and Christians.

Tombalbaye – now long gone – whose face was mar-red by tribal scars, had no substantial education and, apart from his tribal dialect, spoke indifferent French. He was one of the founder members of the PPT (*Partie Progressiste Tchadien* – Chad Progress Party) which is still the only recognised political party in Chad.

The country which Tombalbaye took over on its birth as a new nation would have taxed the abilities of the most sagacious of leaders. In addition to being one of the poorest countries in Africa, it is one of the largest, with an area of one and a quarter million square kilometres – larger then France, Italy and Spain combined. It lies in the middle of Africa's great land mass and stretches from the sandy wastes of the Sahara to the edge of the great tropical rain forests in the south.

Most of the country is a vast depression that drains into Lake Chad, a shallow, marsh-fringed body of water of fluctuating area. Surrounding Lake Chad on all sides except the west are a series of mountains and plateaux.

The land is entirely tropical, with no cold season. The south is mostly under savannah grassland or woodland vegetation, since it receives an annual rainfall of up to 1 250 centimetres. The north, which receives a meagre 150 centimetres rainfall a year – and some years none at all – is part of the great Sahara Desert, where life is concentrated in a few isolated oases and around some watering-points of nomadic herders.

At the height of the rainy season (July to September), the south is transformed into extensive, malarial swamps as the Chari and Logone Rivers overflow their banks.

Since prehistoric times Chad has been the meeting-

place of the races of Africa. Across it runs the watershed of Arab Islam's great tide. The vanguard of this Moslem force in Africa – the veiled, blue-painted Touareg tribesmen – range fast and far on their camels and horses through Chad's northern provinces of Ennedi, Tibesti and Borkou. In the days of French colonial rule they were difficult to control, and these three provinces were permanently under military rule from the great Foreign Legion base at Fort Lamy.

Over the course of centuries, Arab invaders from the north left their stamp on the south – mainly in the form of their Moslem religion and through intermarriage, but also in the hatreds they evoked with their massacres of the African tribes and the slaves they took.

Christianity and animism predominate in the south. The Chari people, the largest single group in Chad – living in the Chari and Logone River valleys – are still pure black African, and so are the Massa, the Baguirmi as well as the Kotoko, who live near them in the south-western part of the country. Ethnically black, but more Arabise, are the Peuls and the Toubou and a far-flung division of the Kotoko. Most of these are nomadic herders, Moslem, and strongly hierarchic.

Although Chad's three- or four million population – no one knows for certain what it is – is predominantly Moslem, the French colonial administration, in its withdrawal, took steps to ensure that the reins of government were left in Christian-animist hands.

That is where the trouble began. The Arab elements of the north were incensed that the peoples they once enslaved and whom they considered inferior were now their rulers. Unrest began to foment almost from the day independence began.

Tombalbaye governed uneasily for the first two years. In 1962 he banned two opposition parties and in 1963 he gaoled their Moslem leaders, Ahmed Koulamallah and Jean-Baptiste. In the same year he arrested several Moslem ministers in his own cabinet whom he suspected of plotting a coup; in the fracas that followed more than one hundred Moslems were shot dead in the streets of Fort Lamy. In 1964 Tombalbaye announced that Chad was a one-party state and would remain so in the future. It has been so ever since…

But the repressive measures merely served to fan the flames of a growing discontent in a country where oppressive tax collection and corruption had been added to the basic burden of poverty. In the north the fierce, nomadic Arab tribes refused outright to pay the government taxes, and Tombalbaye's raggle-taggle security forces proved unable to force them. This led to more taxes on the less aggressive African tribes in the south to make up the balance – with the result that they, too, became roused to rebellion.

The situation was ripe for exploitation. It came with the

formation in 1966 of a rebel organisation called 'Frolinat'. The popular name was derived from the initials of the movement's name in French, which means 'the Chad Liberation Front'. Dr Abba Siddick, a former education minister and co-founder of Tombalbaye's Progress Party, who had escaped the purge of 1963 and was living in exile, became the leader of Frolinat.

The rebel organisation worked busily at drawing together into one cohesive resistance movement the various rebellious elements – the nomadic tribes in the Saharan desert lands of the north, the strongly religious Moslem emirs and sheikhs along the Sudan border in the east and the oppressed African peasants of the riverine central provinces, suffering a miserable existence and continually being harassed by corrupt tax collectors. The movement was joined by disgruntled students and government officials who had been sacked.

Frolinat guerrillas began to murder tax collectors and to attack government administrative outposts and river traffic. This was the situation that gave birth to open civil war.

Colonel Gadaffi's recognition of his African arch-rival Chad Head of State – then President Hissene Habre – and the Chad government on 25 May 1988 could, at the time, be regarded as roughly equivalent to Mrs Thatcher embracing the Irish Republican Army. The comparison – absurd as it is – reflects the often inconsistent nature of politics and war in Africa; especially between two nations that have been opposed to each other for so long.

The war in Chad has involved France and the CIA in more than two decades of heavy intrigue and subterfuge and a succession of border wars.

After years of conflict, Gadaffi in 1988 abruptly called for a unilateral truce and offered his friendship. If another analogy may be allowed, this was like the Vietcong embracing everything American at the height of the Vietnam war.

But Gadaffi at the time was apparently sincere in his gesture. There was good cause. Libyan forces had earlier taken a hard thrashing at the hands of what disdainfully he had always referred to as "primitive Sahara natives". There was reason for this:

By the end of 1986, purportedly with strong French backing on the ground and in the air, the Chad Army pushed northwards to retake large tracts of northern Chad that had been occupied by Libyan forces. The attack was made on two flanks: one in the north-west part of the Tibesti Plateau; the second onslaught came in the east; towards the oasis of Fada.

To the foreign observer the operation was problematical. Throughout the campaign Chad forces were obliged to keep to isolated roads – the only roads – in a region half the size of France. They had no air power of their own and their weapons were simple, though practical; at that stage forces lacked the kind of sophistication enjoyed by Libya with its Soviet weapons. Chad had no heavy artillery, few mortars, claymores or mines. Almost no anti-tank missiles. They did have a variety of vehicles that were nothing more than a logistics officer's nightmare. Spare parts were almost non-existent and most of the vehicles were consequently badly maintained.

There has been some speculation in Africa and elsewhere that as this conflict developed there was a good deal more French support for Habre than the Elysee Palace was prepared to admit. The French Air Force had maintained a presence – jets and helicopters – in Chad, but largely, according to the French, as a precautionary measure to limit Libyan air attacks on Chad towns south of what is still called the *Red Zone*. This follows the 15-degree line of latitude north of the capital, N'Djamena (formerly Fort Lamy).

That there was real European support emerged only afterwards. Once severe fighting had taken place round

the two oases still in enemy hands – in which the Chad Army routed both the Libyans and their dissident allies in Chad headed by Goukouni Oueddeye – the government was able to push farther north to the heavily defended and strategic oasis town of Faya Largeau, a nodal point of northern Chad where Colonel Gadaffi had established a strongpoint for his forces. Here he also controlled the adjacent airstrip of Ouadi-Doum with a large force of Libyan MiG-21s and *Sukhoi* jet bombers, some of which had on occasion penetrated as far south as N'Djamena.

The attack on both these northern points came in March 1988. Habre's men poured out of the desert in a surprise attack and put Libyan forces to flight in disarray. Millions of dollars' worth of Libyan war material was abandoned, and Gadaffi was obliged to withdraw behind his own frontiers. His supply lines had been cut.

There was no apparent explanation for this debacle. The Libyans were well entrenched behind prepared lines of defence and were far better equipped that the "rabble Chadians", as it was phrased in a Tripoli newspaper. Subsequent investigation and interrogation of Libyan prisoners of war indicated a serious lack of zeal and sloppy command. Many of the officers who managed to return to Libya were later shot.

Gadaffi accused the French of interfering in the war, but this was strenuously denied by the French Minister of Defence, Andre Giraud. His reply that "not one French soldier took part" appeared to most of us in N'Djamena at the time as though he were, perhaps, protesting too much.

French Air Force *Gazelle* hovers over a Chadian village in the interior of the country.

American participation was obvious from the beginning when, during an earlier campaign, Gadaffi said he had captured some troops with *Stinger* missiles. These were put on show to foreign reporters in Tripoli. What in fact he had found were US *Red Eye* missiles and Franco-British *Milans*. So much for Libyan intelligence.

After that the Libyans regrouped and once again captured various strongpoints in Chad. This time they took large quantities of American equipment. Gadaffi made various guerrilla feints from the Sudanese border town of Darfur, but nothing really developed in that direction.

Clearly, American intervention in the fifteen-year-old Chad-Libyan dispute has been obvious for some years.

From roughly the time that President Reagan came to power, Chad was seen as a convenient means of creating problems for Gadaffi, a leader the average American was quick to equate with everything that is evil.

Bob Woodward, in his book *Veil: The Secret Wars of the CIA 1981-87*, Simon and Schuster, New York and London, 1987), revealed that the US had channelled millions of dollars to Chad both before Reagan took over as president and afterwards. US military aid to Chad loyalists by June 1987 had been estimated at about $35 million. More was promised when Habre visited the White House in November 1987 and he got it.

It has also become clear that France had been subjected to a considerable amount of arm-twisting by the US over Chad. The part played by the Americans, according to the European intelligence services, was covert; while supplying much of the weapons, they let the French appear to take the responsibility threatening that if Mitterrand were to withhold support for his former colony, they themselves would step in. The French would never allow that to be seen to be happening; next thing the Americans might want to do is interfere in Corsica!

The question that puzzled strategists for nearly thirty years is why two African nations should commit so much effort and material to fighting for a useless piece of real estate in the middle of the Sahara Desert. Apart from the fact that things have progressed vastly since the days of Tombalbaye, one reason propounded is that the often-contested Aouzou Strip is considered by some to be rich in minerals. There may be oil or uranium. No one is certain, although these theories must be based partly on fact, considering the number of lives that have been lost over what most regard as little more than a totally isolated desert backwater.

What is known is that from the beginning Gadaffi has seen the conquest of Chad – or the very least, the presence of a government favourable to Libya established in N'Djamena – as essential to his long-term objective of bringing much of West Africa within his grasp. There are uranium mines at Arlit in the northern part of neighbouring Niger, which export almost 6 000 tons of uranium oxide annually. The Niger Republic is one of the world's ten largest producers of the ore.

With Chad under Libyan control, it could be argued it would be less difficult for Gadaffi to bring similar pressure to bear on the government of Niamey, the Niger capital.

At least one consignment of uranium oxide has already disappeared from Niger "without trace". A truck loaded with uranium from the mines in Arlit appears to have been hijacked by Libyan agents during the early eighties and is believed to have been smuggled overland across the Libyan border. This consignment is said to have eventually reached Pakistan for use in its nuclear programme, but that has never been confirmed. It makes sense.

Pakistan and Libya maintain excellent relations; Gadaffi has given financial support to the Pakistani nuclear programme over the years to develop what has been called an Islamic nuclear bomb. There also appears to be an Iraqi interest in acquiring uranium. Iraq is also on good terms with the Libyan leader. And so, incidentally, is North Korea.

These developments have drawn the attention and the appropriate response from Washington. Obviously, Israel also takes a keen interest in the matter, and no doubt the Mossad is watching the situation closely.

The Americans, Israel and several African nations are also aware of a new Libyan plan to destabilise a number of pro-Western states in West Africa, including Togo, Niger, the Ivory Coast, Mali, Senegal, Nigeria and The Gambia. For a while Colonel Gadaffi wanted Burkina Faso to join Benin in acting as a springboard for activities that included sabotage of public services, subversion, and attempts at military *coups d'etat*. It is clear that – at this stage – the new Burkinabe leader is not willing to cooperate, although it is known that his precedessor, Blaise Compaore, discussed the matter with Colonel Gadaffi during a visit to Tripoli early in 1988.

Libya first occupied the Aouzou Strip in 1973, justifying it by a treaty signed in 1935 between France and Italy (which then controlled Libya).

Chad, in turn, based its claim on the 1955 treaty, which shifted the border northwards in line with contemporary maps of the region. The matter has been constantly disputed, with each side claiming ownership of the territory, but it has never been settled in favour of either party. Even if it were, it would still need the signing of a new agreement, but others have been signed in the past and come to naught.

Both Libya and Chad appear to rely on the international law principle of *uti possidetis juris*, which confirms the permanence of border disputes in at least two dozen other African countries which have shown themselves dissatisfied with the colonial demarcations, some which date back to the Treaty of Berlin of 1878. These include Zaire, Nigeria, Ghana, Togo, Somalia, Kenya,

Tanzania, The Gambia, Malawi, Botswana (with regard to Namibia's Caprivi Strip), Lesotho, Angola, Mocambique and Swaziland.

Clearly, the question is a potential hornet's nest on the African continent. It could lead to more war.

The Chamber of the International Court of Justice recently held – in the frontier dispute between Burkina Faso and Mali – which also led to conflict, that pre-eminence should be accorded to legal title over and above effective possession as the basis of sovereignty. Therefore, it is argued, in the case of Chad and Libya, it would not be necessary for either party to show that it had exercised control before independence; which, in theory, would have greatly strengthened the Libyan case.

Chad maintains that the frontiers it inherited from France at independence are inviolable, and that, in any event, the treaty of 1935 is invalid, as the French National Assembly never ratified it.

As the century draws towards a close the matter remains in a state of stalemate. Habre was deposed by Idriss Deby in December 1990 and who can tell how long he will last.

Libyan troops construe to occupy several positions in northern Chad, at Aouzou, Elwigh (south-western Libya) and Toumo, near the border between Libya and Niger. For a while, Chad forces were drawn up in a long defensive line to the south. Gadaffi's earlier offer to recognise Chad remained the only hopeful development for several years. But some sceptics pointed out that this may have been a gesture in an attempt to obtain the release of large numbers of Libyan soldiers captured during the first Aouzou attack, most of whom have since been released.

TOP: French Air Force *Super Pumas* over Chadian air space, and (right) The French Army made much use of smaller observation helicopters for intelligence gathering purposes.
PREVIOUS PAGE: French Legionnaire with unit mascot; In background a French Air Force C-160 *Transall*; Improvised fuel pump in Chadian desert – war in Africa is never easy...

The question is still further complicated by the fact that some captured Libyan soldiers publically declared that they were forming an opposition movement against Gadaffi. Among those who condemned the "terrorist, barbaric and arbitrary regime of Tripoli" were Colonel Khalifa Belcassim Haftar, the commander of Ouadi-Doum during the spring offensive of 1987 and Gadaffi wants him returned home; obviously he would like to make Colonel Haftar shorter by the head.

At the same time whichever Chadian president is in power is aware that he cannot survive without strong French support. Chad is one of the poorest nations in the world. It depends heavily on cotton for foreign earnings; but it has been severely affected by drought and the locust plagues of the past few years.

Some aid has been coming, but nothing really substantial. The International Development Association, the concesssionary lending affiliate of the World Bank, has been providing some credits. The African Development Bank contributed cash and Saudi Arabia has donated about $10 million.

More money has been promised, but with a conflict still threatening the one country in the world least able to afford a full-blown war, Chad continues to spend valuable foreign exchange in preparation for more conflict.

It is reckoned that it would cost several hundred million dollars just to put N'Djamena "on the map again". Like Mogadishu, the city is a blistered and scarred shell of what it was before the French departed.

It hardly possesses a real economic infrastructure; many of the buildings are in ruins, public services exist in name only and the military remain dominant. The only facility that works is the market, but markets tend to spring up everywhere, whether there is conflict or not.

It is only recently that traders in the town stopped taking the evening ferry across the Bahr Ergig river to safety in Cameroon, returning each morning to open their stalls.

Perhaps, after Gadaffi goes, matters might ease a little and allow for a more permanent social, economic and political structure.

CHAPTER 11

THE WAR IN RHODESIA 1962-1980

The Beginning of the End of an Era for Southern Africa

Guerrilla conflict in Rhodesia lasted eight years; from the first incursions north of Salisbury, the capital, in the Mount Darwin area during Operation Hurricane *to late 1979 when a British-brokered settlement was reached in London as a consequence of the Lancaster House Agreement. Before that, there had been a decade of sporadic infiltration by groups of insurgents, but nothing that the Rhodesian security forces, in the early days, could not contain.*

Rhodesian Air Force *Alouette* IIIs prepare for a fire-force operation from a Forward Tactical Headquarters near the Mocambique border. Many South African pilots were involved in this eight-year guerrilla war.

CLOCKWISE FROM ABOVE: At the height of the war – and under cover of much subterfuge – the Rhodesian government acquired a dozen Bell 205/UH1D *Iroquois* from the Israeli Air Force. They were in a poor state, but local technicians soon had them operational; 'Hot extraction' was often used when clandestine, cross-border raids were compromised; Salisbury, Rhodesia's capital city during the mid-seventies; Tactical headquarters in mountainous terrain near the Mocambique border; RAR patrol in bush country; Rhodesian troops set ablaze abandoned village believed to have been used by insurgents; Wounded civilian 'casevaced' to hospital at Mount Darwin in the north.

t was a low-key struggle. Throughout, it was not nearly as intense or as widespread as similar wars that were then taking place in South-East Asia. Altogether about 1 500 members of the security forces died during the course of hostilities. Of the 25 000 people of African origin who were killed, roughly two-thirds were insurgents. The rest were civilians, caught in a crossfire of a conflict that many of them did not comprehend.

It is significant that by the time the first disaffected tribesmen – armed and trained by a variety of countries in Africa, Europe and Asia – crossed the border into Rhodesia, several other 'liberation' struggles in nearby territories were already well-established. The Belgian Congo had burst into a dreadful protracted insurrection and state of anarchy on independence in 1960; that was preceded by Kenya's Mau Mau emergency which involved a full-scale reaction by the British Army and the Royal Air Force.

The Portuguese colonial territories of Angola and Mocambique had their own wars; full-scale guerrilla struggles which gathered in intensity and eventually drained Lisbon and its people of the will, the resources, and the ability to fight. The Zimbabwe African National Union (ZANU), a Shona tribal-orientated movement, led by the Reverend Ndabaningi Sithole and, ultimately, by Robert Mugabe.

The War of Liberation, or as it was phrased locally, 'Chimurenga', began in 1962, after ZANU sent numerous young men for guerrilla training in China. The first of the insurgent killings began with the murder in the Eastern Districts of Mr P.J.A. Oberholzer, who was ambushed in July 1964.

Rhodesian whites in rural areas were particularly vulnerable. But at the end of it all, in 1980, most of the farmers – some 6 000 of them – were still ensconced on the land. Many, though, had left. Quite a large proportion had emigrated.

But first there was Rhodesia's Unilateral Declaration of Independence (UDI). On 11 November 1965, Britain recoiled in anger at this rebellion by a British territory, the first since the American revolution.

Yet Wilson dared not use force because he had only a tiny majority in Parliament. He believed that his security forces might not fight against a 'white' Rhodesia. Instead, Wilson applied economic sanctions and deployed two Royal Navy carrier task forces to cut off Rhodesia's supply of oil. In 1966 Wilson invoked the United Nations to secure world cooperation through selective mandatory sanctions in 1966. He made sanctions total in 1968. The world seemed to cooperate but trade continued clandestinely.

Cooperation by Rhodesia's neighbours, Portuguese-ruled Mocambique and South Africa cushioned the broader effects of sanctions. Neither of these governments recognised Rhodesia but they helped to keep her routes open to the sea.

South Africa supplied much of Rhodesia's wants. Rhodesia also later provided military aid to keep her forces in the field. Rhodesia's economy grew steadily until in the 1970s, drought, world depression, high oil prices, the steadily escalating costs of war and, finally, the loss of Mocambique as an ally in 1975, imposed severe strains. But all these factors together were never severe enough to force a Rhodesian surrender.

The unravelling of conflict in this African state was a slow process and, to the outsider, the end was predictable, even though the first attempts by the African nationalists to foment an insurgency by sending in groups of guerrillas into Rhodesia from neighbouring territories were easily defeated. The widening rebellion against the Portuguese in Mocambique during the sixties, however, allowed the rebels – Frelimo in Mocambique – to offer ZANU's armed wing, the Zimbabwe African National Liberation Army (Zanla), sanctuary close to the populated area in north-east Rhodesia. The Portuguese proved powerless to stop them, to the alarm of the strategists in Salisbury.

Zanla soon established a foothold among the tribesmen. Consequently, while the insurgents would not be able to control the towns, and although the Rhodesian forces could and sometimes would achieve kill rates of eighty to one, the security forces were never able to regain the rural areas permanently. Towards the end of the war, something of a stalemate had been reached, exacerbated by the increase in Rhodesians leaving the country. By early 1979 Ian Smith was losing the equivalent of a Company of his fighting men a month.

Throughout the period of hostilities, clear victory for either side was never in sight. In the end both forces were largely going through the mechanical motions of fighting a war, although casualties remained high. Clearly, a political solution was the only way to peace.

It is interesting to observe how the Rhodesians fought their war.

In the early days, any government counter-insurgency effort was led by the police, the British South Africa Police (BSAP). Bungling of their first operation in 1966 led to inter-service cooperation through JOCs, or joint operational command centres, comprising the army, police, air force and the district administration representatives.

Nationally there was the Operational Coordination Committee on which the commanders of all services sat. Later coordination was further tightened, in 1977, by the creation of the Combined Operations Headquarters under the command of Lieutenant-General Peter Walls, also referred to as 'Supremo'.

The involvement of both the armed wing of ZAPU, the Zimbabwe People's Revolutionary Army (ZPRA), and the South African National Congress in the first serious incur-

sion in 1967 provoked South Africa to reinforce Rhodesia with a battalion-sized force of policemen deployed largely as infantry. The South African Police provided welcome assistance to the small Rhodesian security forces fighting an insurgency in a country three times the size of England.

But they would be withdrawn in 1975-1976 as part of the pressure from South African Prime Minister Vorster on Smith to settle in order to relieve pressure on South Africa over the issue of South West Africa (later Namibia) and South Africa's support for Rhodesia.

The security forces comprised both police, army and the men of the district administration.

The British South Africa Police (BSAP) contributed its regular policemen, small anti-terrorist units (PATU); a para-military Support Unit of battalion strength; a large police reserve; and the Special Branch which gathered intelligence.

The Army, in turn, fielded a regular white battalion, the Rhodesian Light Infantry (RLI); an enlarged black battalion (later enlarged to a second battalion), the Rhodesian African Rifles (RAR); white national service independent infantry companies; a small but crack regular specialist reconnaissance unit, the Special Air Service (SAS) and

eight battalions of territorials and reservists of several Rhodesia Regiments with varying commitments due to age. Asians and coloureds were drafted into a defence regiment with whites and Africans.

There were also units of engineers, signals, armour, artillery and the like. Later the army formed a mounted infantry regiment, the Grey Scouts; an intelligence corps, a psychological warfare unit and the formidable special warfare unit, the Selous Scouts under a highly experienced SAS veteran of the Malayan Campaign, Lt-Colonel Ron Reid-Daly.

When the example of Malaya was followed and the tribesmen were moved into protected villages, a separate defence unit, the Guard Force (Internal Affairs) was created using African regulars and white part-timers.

The need to call up men from the workplace put the already embattled Rhodesian economy at risk. Thus the forces deployed on any one day in the war amounted to a few thousand. Total mobilization would only be employed to protect national elections and Rhodesia could certainly not afford to keep all her forces in the field for longer than three weeks.

Constant call-ups badly affected businesses, morale,

Body of a Rhodesian soldier killed in cross-border raid at Chimoio in Mocambique is choppered out.

family life and led to a steady stream of young emigrants seeking a normal life elsewhere. Emigration hurt the army more than any loss of casualties. There were always more than enough willing black regular recruits to replace the white losses but these forces, combined, could not compensate for the economic damage of emigration.

Air support, so crucial and often decisive, was supplied by the eight squadrons of the Rhodesian Air Force.

There were sufficient *Hunter* ground-attack fighters, *Canberra* light bombers, *Vampire* fighter bombers armed with cannon, rockets and deadly locally-manufactured blast, shrapnel and napalm bombs to devastate external camps and other targets. To this the RhAF, defying sanctions, added light aircraft for liaison, reconnaissance and light attack. Most important was a small squadron of French *Alouette* helicopters. More *Alouettes* would be acquired, including some from Spain, and others loaned by South Africa.

The acquisition clandestinely, in 1978, of elderly *Agusta-Bell* 205s from Israel gave the helicopter forces greater range and load-carrying capability. The helicopter was to play a vital role by enabling the forces to cut off and surround guerrilla units on bush operations.

The security forces suffered only moderate casualties throughout the war, largely because their enemies did not press home attacks against even light resistance. But that was part of the insurgent philosophy. Basically, the attitude went along the lines of: "hit the target, withdraw quickly and live to fight another day…"

Zanla and ZPRA instead concentrated on indoctrinating the population and on recruiting or abducting tribesmen. They were preparing for the ultimate 'political indoctrination' which would bring Mugabe to power.

Courage among the Rhodesians was never found to be wanting. One and two-man missions deep into neighbouring countries were not rare. When external camps were attacked, the shortage of aircraft, pilots and trained personnel could mean that the attacking force was often little more than a reinforced platoon, often ranged against thousands.

An example of the remarkable combat ability of the Rhodesian security forces can be gained from the results of an external attack on an insurgent stronghold at Chimoio in central Mocambique on 21 November 1977. Named *Operation Dingo* the target was a series of about a dozen Zanla camps spread out over an area of five square kilometres. The force attacking was comprised of 97 SAS and 47 RLI troops; 144 men altogether, backed by air support.

At the end of it there were 2 000 enemy dead for the loss of one Rhodesian killed and eight wounded.

It was a 'first of a kind' attack devised by the then OC of the Rhodesian SAS, Lt-Colonel Brian Robinson. The ground forces were air dropped and their task was to seal off three of the four sides of the enemy bases in a 'box' operation. Helicopter K-Cars (*Alouette* gun-ships) were responsible for the remaining 'side of the box'. Air strikes followed by *Hunter* bombers and *Canberras*, after which the ground forces moved inwards to mop up.

A day later a similar force hit at another Zanla camp at Tembue, which lay a short of distance to the north of Chimoio; here about 400 insurgents were killed using similar tactics, but the element of surprise was not quite as complete as at Chimoio.

Many such operations were embarked on by the Rhodesians during the course of the war and, apart from an abortive raid on the headquarters of Joshua Nkomo in Lusaka, the Zambian capital, most were remarkably successful. All underscored the quite astonishing ability of the Rhodesians in unconventional or semi-conventional warfare.

CHAPTER 12

FIRE FORCE

The Evolvement of Helicopter-Orientated Bush Operations

Richard Wood, formerly of Rhodes and Edinburgh Universities as well as the University of Zimbabwe is an authority on conflict in Rhodesia. He wrote the definitive work, with Sir Roy Welensky, on the original Central African Federation. More recently, his War Diaries of Andre Dennison *was published. He has made a study of Fire Force operations in the Rhodesian War.*

This is his report:

Outward bound in an *Alouette* III helicopter on a casualty evacuation mission from Rutenga in south-eastern Rhodesia on a hot afternoon in late 1976, Flight-Lieutenant Victor Bernard Cook began his descent from 800 feet to collect

an African civilian, who had been wounded that morning. He did not see the 27 members of the Zimbabwe African National Liberation Army (Zanla) (supporting Robert Mugabe) based up in a clearing in the trees beneath him but their rude welcome of a burst of fire severed the *Alouette*'s tail rotor shaft and ripped through the floor, damaging Cook's Uzi submachine-gun under his seat, and wounding Cook in the right foot and arm. Two rounds penetrated the flak-jacket of the technician, Finch Bellringer, leaving him semi-conscious. Only the medic was unhurt but shocked.

To regain some control of the crippled *Alouette*, Cook pushed the nose down to acquire forward speed and with great skill, presence of mind and courage, brought the stricken aircraft in a wide spiral to earth, crashing among his scattering attackers. The impact jerked Cook forward onto the control stick, stunning him and cutting his chin deeply. Yet, despite his wounds, the small stocky Cook's thoughts were only to get his crew away from the threat of fire and the enemy around them. He tore off his harness, shook the medic into action and together they dragged Bellringer into cover close by.

Sensing the presence of the enemy in bush around him, Cook ran back to the aircraft for his Uzi, not knowing that it was damaged. As he struggled to cock the Uzi, Cook suddenly saw a prone Zanla some yards away aiming his AK-47 Russian assault rifle at Bellringer and the medic. Dropping the Uzi, Cook rushed the insurgent, tore the AK from his hands and shot him dead with it.

Cook then fired at the movement in the trees, hoping to gain time to get Bellringer to greater safety. When all was quiet, Cook and the medic carried Bellringer to higher ground nearby. Then, moving tactically, firing double taps, limping from cover to cover, Cook returned to strip the dead Zanla of AK magazines before beginning a protective patrol of the area.

Cook was fortunate because the Rhodesian Army unit which had summoned him from Rutenga, had heard his crash and the subsequent firing, and had called the nearest helicopter-borne reaction 'Fire Force'. Fifty minutes later a Reims Cessna FTB 337G *Lynx*, twin-engined light aircraft, led in the Fire Force. Cook and his crew were evacuated by helicopter and a follow-up on the tracks of his attackers began. As so often happened, however, the tracks were soon lost.

For his gallantry, Victor Cook was awarded the Silver Cross of Rhodesia.

counter-insurgency war in 1962-1980. Indeed, the Rhodesians were to produce a unique and deadly variant of the tactic of 'vertical envelopment' of a target by helicopter-borne infantry called 'Fire Force'.

Rhodesia, with terrain over 2 000 feet above sea level and a hot climate, was unsuitable for helicopter operations until the French development of light turboshaft engines encouraged Sud-Aviation (later Aérospatiale) to produce a range of jet helicopters in the late 1950s. By then, African nationalist opposition to the short-lived Federation of Rhodesia and Nyasaland, 1953-1963, and to white rule in general led to a demand for the rapid deployment of troops. With no suitable helicopter available, the use of paratroops was considered in March 1960 and the Royal Rhodesian Air Force adapted *Dakota* aircraft for tests.

Unrest in the Federation and mutinies of African soldiers in the Congo in 1960 prompted a general expansion of Federal security forces, including the establishment of white professional army units such as C Squadron of the SAS and the Rhodesian Light Infantry (RLI). The RRAF ordered the newly available *Alouette* III helicopter which was also the choice of the South African Air Force, which meant training facilities and expertise could be shared. The Portuguese Air Force likewise purchased *Alouette* IIIs and would be the first to arm them with French 20mm cannons.

The *Alouette* III was the product of an experiment in 1953 when Sud-Aviation replaced the piston-engine of the SE3120 *Alouette* [Lark] with the new Artouste Mark II gas-turbine. The resulting performance made the Société Turboméca the leading supplier of small turbine helicopter engines in the west. The *Alouette* II achieved a new world height record for helicopters in June 1955 at 26 932 feet. The next engine, the Astazou, gave the *Alouette* II constant power at height and in hot climates, doubled its load-carrying capacity, and in June 1958 set a new record at 36 037 feet. In 1959 the more powerful Artouste engine resulted in the larger *Alouette* III SA316B which also set new records. The next engine, the Astazou XIV, made the SA319B *Alouette* III of 1969 even more effective and economical in 'hot and high' conditions.

Although both versions of the *Alouette* III had maximum speeds of 124 mph at sea level and could cruise at 115 mph, service ceilings of 13 100 feet and ranges (at optimum altitude) of 335 miles, in practice their perform-

When the helicopter was adopted by the small, if potent, Rhodesian Air Force (RhAF), its agility – its ability to hover, decelerate rapidly, land and take-off vertically in almost impossible terrain – was exploited to the full in the

Rhodesian Light Infantry 'Troopies' – in shorts and no socks – prepare to board for an ongoing Fire Force operation. In its day, this was one of the finest fighting units on the sub-continent.

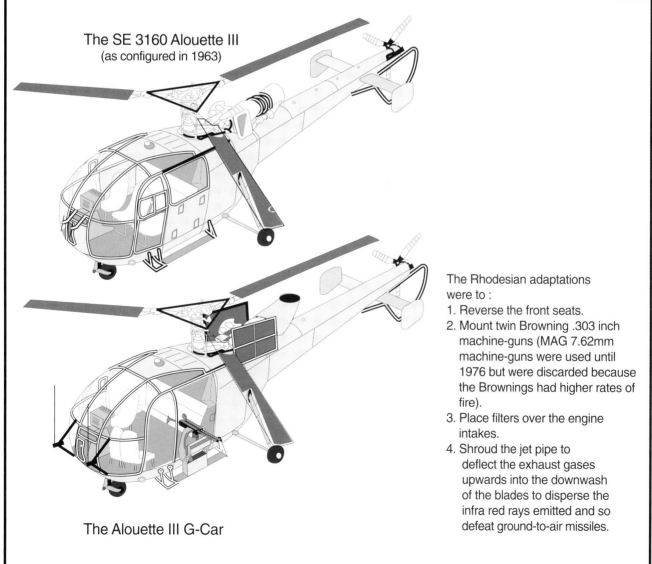

The SE 3160 Alouette III
(as configured in 1963)

The Alouette III G-Car

The Rhodesian adaptations
were to :
1. Reverse the front seats.
2. Mount twin Browning .303 inch
   machine-guns (MAG 7.62mm
   machine-guns were used until
   1976 but were discarded because
   the Brownings had higher rates of
   fire).
3. Place filters over the engine
   intakes.
4. Shroud the jet pipe to
   deflect the exhaust gases
   upwards into the downwash
   of the blades to disperse the
   infra red rays emitted and so
   defeat ground-to-air missiles.

ance was more modest. Rhodesian *Alouettes* flew at 65-84 knots (75-97 mph) with a range of 242 miles (210 nautical miles). The *Alouette* III 'K-Car' gunship, armed with a 20mm cannon and ammunition, a crew of three, and 600 lbs of fuel had an endurance of 75-90 minutes. The troop-carrying 'G-Car' with 400 lbs of fuel, a crew of two, a 7.62mm MAG machine-gun, and four fully equipped troops would fly for 45 minutes. Experience in combat led the Rhodesians to remove the doors and to reverse the front passenger seats to widen the available floorspace for casualties and cargo and to permit rapid evacuation. Two stretcher cases and two seated wounded could be carried and there was an external sling for cargoes up to 1 650 lbs (750 kgs) and a 380 lbs (175 kgs) capacity hoist to winch up casualties and the like.

Stiffening African resistance led Harold Macmillan, the British Prime Minister, to scupper the Federal experiment by granting independence to Northern Rhodesia (Zambia) and Nyasaland (Malawi) on the basis of majority rule. Southern Rhodesia was self-governing and the British Government could not do likewise. The Southern Rhodesian Government countered African unrest with a mixture of reform and tough security legislation and action. Over a thousand African nationalist supporters were arrested and the Zimbabwe African People's Union (ZAPU), led by Joshua Nkomo, was banned.

Frustration led the African nationalists to send young men for training in Ghana, Tanganyika and at Soviet and Eastern Bloc insurgency warfare schools. The Rhodesian police began to uncover arms caches and arson became the order of the day. Thus the war of liberation, known as the 'Chimurenga', began in late 1962. The pattern of urban violence continued for a year or more and then fizzled out because of good police work and the effectiveness of the law. The African nationalists split into two factions, ZAPU and the Zimbabwe African National Union (ZANU) of the Reverend Ndabaningi Sithole (later ousted by Robert Mugabe), and established themselves in sympathetic Zambia across the Zambezi. From there, after Ian Smith had unilaterally declared Rhodesia independent (UDI) on 11 November 1965, they sent men into Rhodesia to foster rebellion. The towns remained uncooperative but the rural areas began to harbour the insurgents in 1972 when the success of Frelimo rebels in Mocambique provided the Rhodesian African nationalists with supplies and safe havens close to the border.

The Rhodesian *Alouettes* were generally unarmed until the insurgency intensified in the late 1960s. However, until 1973, the hazardous 'gunship' role was excluded because international sanctions, the consequence of UDI, made it very difficult to replace helicopters. Indeed, they were treated so reverently that Rhodesian soldiers liked to believe that the pilots would not allow them on board without clean boots. Correctly all weapons had to be cleared and magazines removed. The pressure of war relaxed such rules to the extent that at Marymount Mission in the north-east an African soldier accidentally discharged a rifle grenade through a helicopter roof.

When the war gathered pace from December 1972, and white farmhouses were attacked in north-eastern Rhodesia, quick reaction forces were needed and troop-carrying G-Car *Alouettes* (armed with 7.62mm MAG machine-guns) were pressed into service. Later, in 1976, they were re-armed with twin faster firing Mk2 .303 Brownings (the RAF's turret and wing guns of the Second World War) with 500 rounds per gun. South African G-Cars (flying in Rhodesia after 1967) mounted single .303 Brownings and when South African *Puma* helicopters were brought in, they had twin .5 or .303 inch Brownings.

As dedicated helicopter gunships could drastically enhance the effectiveness of the reaction forces, 'K-Cars' were created by installing Matra MG151 20mm cannons on floor fittings, aiming out of the rear port doorways. Like the German MGFF and MG151 20mm cannons of Messerschmitt 109 and Focke-Wulf 190 fighters, the Matra MG151 used a short cartridge with less than normal propellant, reducing recoil and muzzle velocity. This. and a slow rate of fire, made the MG151 suitable for helicopters. For deflection shooting it had a Collimateur reflector gun sight, calibrated for a cannon firing at 90 degrees to the fore and aft axis from an altitude of 800 feet at a speed of 65 knots. A good gunner could fire accurately at lower heights. Some preferred 600 feet. The MG151s were initially obtained from the Portuguese and for a long time so were the high explosive incendiary (HEI) rounds. The rounds were expensive – Rhodesian $35 each – and difficult to procure and because the weight of the ammunition (in trays of 200 or 400 rounds) limited the helicopter's range, the cyclic rate of the gun was adjusted downwards to 350 rounds per minute. Gunners restricted themselves to bursts of three rounds or less and regarded themselves as off form if more than five rounds were expended per enemy killed.

The HEI rounds were highly effective except when fired on soft ground which absorbed their explosive effect or caused the shells to fail to explode because the inertial fuses had to decelerate sharply to ignite. Gunners would look for rocks or hard ground to fire at to maximise the effect of the shrapnel. A high proportion of the enemy were killed or wounded by 20mm fire. The HEI shells were also prone to explode harmlessly on contact with trees, so the gunners loaded ball rounds on a ratio of one ball to five HEI shells. The problems of soft ground and trees resulted in other weapons being tried. Twin Browning .5 inch heavy machine-guns were discarded because they were heavy and, instead of shells, they fired bullets which required direct hits to score. In 1979, some K-Cars

Bush operations could take place in 10 foot-high elephant grass, or in the *gomos* around Mount Darwin.

were re-equipped with four Mk2 .303 Brownings slaved to a remote hand operated sighting and hydraulic driver system developed in South Africa as the Dalmatian Project which involved Group Captain Peter Petter-Bowyer, then Staff Officer (Planning) of the RhAF. He field-tested it in Rhodesia in 1978 with Squadron Leader Ted Lunt flying a Dalmatian-fit *Alouette* while Petter-Bowyer found targets, using skills learned as a recce pilot. They would attack the target and then call Fire Force to get troops on the ground to complete the operation and were so successful that in the first week of trials 31 Zanla were killed. The Dalmatian four gun fit was mostly used in the role of a second K-Car. The Dalmatian K-Cars flew at tree top height and, with .303 ammunition freely available and with each gun firing at a cyclic rate of 1 150 rounds a minute, achieved devastating results. The Dalmatian K-Cars were used to drive the enemy into the open where they became targets for the 20mm.

The *Alouette* III is a magnificent military machine. It burns jet fuel (paraffin) but can operate on diesel and petrol [in a dire emergency and only for a short flight]. It can absorb astonishing quantities of small arms fire and even hits from anti-tank rockets. Ted Lunt's K-Car, carrying Major Pieter Farndell of Support Commando, RLI, was hit in the tail section by an RPG-7 rocket but came home safely. On 14 October 1978, Dick Paxton's K-Car, with Major Nigel Henson (also of Support Commando)

aboard, was riddled by small arms fire when Paxton flew slowly and low over a hidden insurgent camp. With all instruments shattered and a blade punctured, Paxton was still able to climb to his operational height (800 feet), orbit, and put down suppressive fire, before flying out. The celebrated pilot and, later, Selous Scout, Michael Borlace, brought an *Alouette* III into Fort Victoria airfield with tail rotor control failure, landing it without harm to its crew. Vic Cook brought his *Alouette* down with its tail rotor drive shaft severed. Yet the *Alouette* was not invulnerable – a hit in the engine or the main rotor gear box could be fatal. The *Alouette* III lacked the aerobatic capabilities of more modern helicopters. Nevertheless a K-Car, flown by Charles Goatley, with Beaver Shaw manning the 20mm cannon, had the distinction of shooting down a Botswana Defence Force *Islander* on 9 August 1979 during the recovery of troops from an external operation against a Zimbabwe People's Revolutionary Army base at Francistown.

The *Alouette* IIs and IIIs had limitations in range, carrying capacity and, in particular, they were designed only for clear daylight flight. Poor weather conditions – hail, heavy rain *et al* – and winds in excess of 30 knots make the aircraft difficult to fly. Crosswind velocities of 10-15 knots and downwind velocities above five knots will affect the direction of landing or take-off. The helicopter is inherently unstable and a loss of control for more than a few seconds spells disaster. Yet, because of their agility, the *Alouettes* were flown under marginal weather conditions. They were not equipped for night flying. Indeed, the French had fitted, as the principal compass, an E2A, which in other aircraft was a standby device. The Rhodesian pilots, nonetheless, flew in the dark until Air Lieutenant G. Munton-Jackson and his technician, Flight Sergeant P.J. Garden, fatally crashed during an attempted blind radar approach in a heavy thunder storm on 17 January 1972. Thereafter flying was only officially allowed when a horizon could be discerned but urgent calls to evacuate casualties and personnel resulted in that ruling being ignored. Then the constant danger of their daily lives had the reverse effect and pilots began to refuse to take greater risks and transgressed the rule less and less. The *Alouettes* were fitted with Becker radio direction finders after Petter-Bowyer strayed into south-western Zambia in 1969 when flying ammunition and weapons in the pre-dawn darkness from Thornhill, Gwelo [now Gweru], to Binga, on the Zambezi River. Low on fuel and lost, Petter-Bowyer landed next to a farm, near Livingstone, to ask where he was. An African obliged but did not tell him that he had landed next to ZAPU's 'Freedom Farm'. Petter-Bowyer learnt that from Air Vice-Marshal Harold Hawkins, the Commander of the Air Force, when he flew on to the Victoria Falls in Rhodesia.

Rhodesia (and 68 other countries) bought both versions of the *Alouette* III. Some 50 *Alouettes* flew in Rhodesia but, given the international sanctions, how many were actually owned by South Africa is not clear. Within the RhAF's No. 7 (helicopter) Squadron, the South African *Alouettes* formed Alpha Flight, with a strength at one stage of 27 helicopters. It is known that, after an initial procurement in 1962-1963 of eight helicopters, 32 helicopters were purchased from 1968-1980, in defiance of sanctions. At least five of them were damaged beyond repair or shot down. As all *Alouettes* are rebuilt totally in the course of their preventive maintenance cycle (the engine would be changed after 1 200 flying hours and the airframe after 3 600), it is clear that not only were some repaired but that many helicopters were built entirely from spares. In 1980, when Rhodesia became Zimbabwe, the Air Force of Zimbabwe was left with eight *Alouettes* which gives some indication of the true strength. Eleven Italian Agusta-Bell 205As (the Rhodesians called them, *Cheetahs*) were also acquired in August 1978 by devious means. They arrived from the Comoro Islands after being delivered to Beirut and bartered for arms from Israel for Major Haddad's Christian militia in southern Lebanon. The AB205A was the celebrated American *Huey* of Vietnam fame built under licence in Italy with a range of 400

kilometres and a maximum speed of 126 miles per hour. Although designed to carry 11 passengers, these AB205As were elderly, and the addition of armour and twin .303 inch machine-guns reduced the load to eight troops. Nonetheless they outranged and doubled the carrying capacity of the *Alouettes* and their allocation to cross-border operations in 1979 meant that the Fire Forces engaged in internal operations were not constantly robbed of their *Alouette* IIIs. In addition, large 'Jumbo' Fire Forces could be created, inflicting increased casualties on the insurgent forces.

The RhAF was always small. Its maximum strength in the 1970s was 2 300 personnel (150 of them pilots), including the General Service Unit which guarded its installations. The importance of helicopters, however, was such that, at the height of the counter-insurgency war, No. 7 Squadron was the largest helicopter squadron in the world with 40 Rhodesian pilots and 20 seconded South African Air Force pilots, flying 45 aircraft.

The South African helicopters and crews initially supported the South African Police units which served in Rhodesia between 1967-1975. Later, crews were seconded to the RhAF's Alpha Flight or 'joined' the RhAF for tours of duty – some for as long as three years. When major cross-border operations were mounted, such was the cooperation with the South African Air Force that the Rhodesians could field 50 helicopters.

This assistance was, however, a double-edged sword. The South African Prime Minister, B.J. Vorster, used it to apply political pressure on the Rhodesian Government. In 1976, for example, when he was seeking to coerce Ian Smith into accepting majority rule, Vorster withdrew 27 pilots on the pretext of protesting at the escalation of the Rhodesian war by the Rhodesian Selous Scouts' raid on the ZANU camp at Nyadzonya in Mocambique on 8 August. The loss of pilots was made up by senior qualified personnel from headquarters (after a five-hour refamiliarisation course) and by calling up former pilots who had returned to civilian life. Vorster also cut off Rhodesia's supplies of ammunition and fuel, forcing Smith to accept the settlement proposals offered to him in September by the US Secretary of State, Henry Kissinger. Once Smith's

CLOCKWISE FROM TOP: During the earlier phases of the war, captured insurgents were often brought into base by helicopter; *Dakota* DC-3s drop a large contingent of RLI troopies during a major onslaught on known ZPRA positions; Cross-border operations in Mocambique with 'Scouts' leading the way and, the war spawned its own hybrids – anti-landmine vehicles in the Honde Valley.

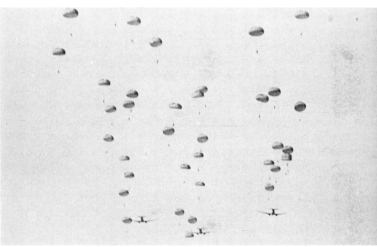

acceptance of majority rule had produced the first African-dominated government of Bishop Muzorewa, the South African support was liberally renewed, including two South African-manned Fire Forces in the south of Matabeleland, with four *Pumas* each, South African Parabats (paratroopers) and assisted by Rhodesian pilots and soldiers.

The initial role of the *Alouettes* was to assist the police in the turbulent urban unrest of 1962-1963. The first two pilots, trained in France and South Africa, were immediately employed dropping leaflets on rioting crowds (and tear-gas grenades on occasions), 'sky shouting', and acting as airborne command posts. As pilots only have time to listen to snappy, brief transmissions, the police and army were forced to revise their ponderous radio procedures.

In the immediate aftermath of UDI, Rhodesia experienced incursions by insurgents based in Zambia. This led, on 28 April 1966, to the first use of armed helicopters supporting ground forces, which reached a level approaching farce but had important consequences. The incident is now graced with the title of the 'Battle of Chinhoyi' and is celebrated in Zimbabwe as a public holiday to mark the beginning of the 'Chimurenga or War of Liberation'.

On 3 April 1966 20 armed members of ZANU crossed the Zambezi near Chirundu from Zambia and marched southwards through the bush to the power-line to Salisbury (now Harare) from the Kariba hydro-electric dam. Following the line the group reached the small town of Sinoia (Chinhoyi) where it split up. Five men left for Umtali (now Mutare) to blow up the oil pipeline and to attack white farmers, two for Fort Victoria (Masvingo), six for the Zwimba Tribal Trust Land and seven were destined for the Midlands but first based themselves near Red Mine on Hunyani Farm just north-east of Sinoia and attempted to sabotage pylons on the power-line. The main aim was to recruit local support. Various members were killed or captured over the coming weeks, but not before they had murdered a white farmer, Johannes Viljoen, and his wife Johanna at Hartley (Chegutu) on 16 May 1966. The seven at Red Mine were inept. Their training was deficient and they often inserted the detonator into the Russian TNT slabs in the wrong place, missing the primer, and simply blowing the slab to pieces.

Peter Petter-Bowyer, as the standby pilot and fresh from a conversion course to helicopters, was sent to Sinoia in an *Alouette* III to support the police efforts to arrest the saboteurs co-ordinated by the district commander, Chief Superintendent John Cannon, DFC, a former Second World War RAF bomber pilot. The saboteurs had sent one man to Salisbury to make contact with African nationalist politicians, not knowing that he was a police informer. On 27 April he told the police in Salisbury the location of his comrades, their intention to attack white farmers near Sinoia and that he was returning to them early the next morning in a blue Peugeot.

Cannon and Petter-Bowyer suggested that the elimination of this gang was a task for the Army and the Operations Co-ordinating Committee but the Police Commissioner, F.E. Barfoot, insisted it was a purely police affair.

In the early dawn of 28 April, an *Alouette* pilot, Murray Hofmeyr, whose aircraft had been hastily armed with a MAG machine-gun (with basic infantry sights) mounted on an A frame at the left rear doorway, followed the Peugeot at 11 000 feet. The informer had said that he would rendezvous with his comrades in the bush left of the main road just beyond the intersection with the old strip road to Sinoia, a kilometre before the Hunyani River bridge. Accordingly, Cannon planned a sweep and search operation in the triangle formed by the roads and the river, using his mixed force of 40 blue-denim clad police and farmers in the Police Reserve, armed with venerable Lee Enfield .303 bolt-action rifles – hardly adequate against the ZANU's five AK-47s, the rocket-launcher, light machine-gun and grenades.

Hofmeyr, however, reported that the Peugeot had turned on to the strip road, had stopped after a hundred metres. The informer had got out and had disappeared into the bush on the left. This meant that the ZANU were outside the triangle. Cannon hastily placed half his men in a sweep line from the main road to the parallel Kariba power line to the south of the main road. The other half moved along the powerline to cut off anyone escaping.

With four helicopters (three of them unarmed) circling above, the sweepline advanced through the bush towards the last sighting. Realising that Peter Petter-Bowyer could control the operation from the air, better than he could on the ground, Cannon gave him immediate command. Petter-Bowyer took off with four policemen on board. He could not, however, communicate with the sweepline for lack of compatible radios. Thus the helicopter pilots had to land to confer with the advancing line. In the south-western corner, where the two police lines started to converge, Pilot Officer David Becks had to land hastily to prevent them shooting each other.

Flying in the vicinity of the last sighting, Petter-Bowyer pointed out to his passengers (by shouting as he had no spare headset) what seemed to be a policeman standing under a tree. Petter-Bowyer was so outraged when one of his passengers responded by firing his Sterling sub-machine-gun through the spinning tilted blades that he deposited his passengers on the road. He resumed his patrol alone and near the river a white shirted man opened fire at him. Having never been shot at before, Petter-Bowyer was further outraged. He banked into a right hand orbit, and called Hofmeyr in to use his MAG. Due to inexperience, Petter-Bowyer did not realise that Hofmeyr was circling left to bring his gun to bear and was on a colli-

sion course with him. Petter-Bowyer, while watching the man on the ground running with dust spurting around him, suddenly saw Hofmeyr's incoming shadow and broke away.

It took Hofmeyr's technician, George Carmichael, 147 rounds, fired in four bursts, to bring down the runner just south of the powerline. Such expenditure, Air Force Headquarters found intolerable. In fact, it was modest and there was an obvious need for deflection sights.

Traversing the ground, Petter-Bowyer next spotted two figures in the bush off the old road but before he could summon help, they looked up and he saw their white faces. He waved them back to the road. They were Detective Inspectors Bill Freeman and 'Dusty' Binns who had driven up the road and plunged into the bush ahead of the sweepline, anxious not to miss the fun.

Another pair to join the party was Major Billy Conn of the RLI and his sergeant who, en route from Kariba, had come upon the helicopters and the armed police. Conn volunteered his services to his friend John Cannon. Cannon readily agreed and Conn drove along the strip road to join the sweepline, arriving just as it killed an insurgent. As the inexperienced police clustered around the body, Conn shouted at them to disperse and as he did, two ZANU rose out of the nearby grass and bush, one aiming his rifle and the other brandishing a grenade. Conn opened fire killing both. The grenade exploded harmlessly. The chastened sweepline continued and eventually killed the remaining four insurgents.

In the aftermath, Petter-Bowyer was awarded the Military Forces Commendation for his coolness under fire and for his control of the operation. This incident forced the security forces to review their procedures. All future operations became combined efforts, controlled by Joint Operations Centres (JOCs) on which all services were represented. The gathering and use of intelligence was centralised with the Special Branch reporting to the Central Intelligence Organisation. In March 1977 all opera-

tions came under a single commander, Lieutenant-General Peter Walls, as Commander, Combined Operations. There was a glaring need for compatible radios. The Air Force prepared its pilots better for action. They were taught to fly with maximum loads since flight control is affected drastically by weight and balance. The Air Force also insisted that their map reading be accurate to 50 metres, a task which was not assisted by the necessity of keeping the right hand on the cyclic-pitch control column. Generally, the standards set the pilots stiffened as the demands of war asked more of them.

At UDI in 1965 the Air Force was concentrated at two bases – New Sarum near Salisbury and Thornhill near Gwelo (now Gweru). New Sarum housed the administration, the photographic and the air movements sections, the aircrew selection centre, the apprentice training school and the parachute training section. Its air units were No. 3 Squadron (transport), No. 5 (bomber) with *Canberras* and No. 7 Squadron (helicopter) with *Alouettes*. Thornhill had No. 1 Squadron (fighter) with *Hunters*, No. 2 Squadron (fighter) with *Vampire* FB9s and No. 4 Squadron (flying training) with *Provosts*. As the conflict widened the RhAF used its Volunteer Reserve to staff forward airfields (FAFs) in the operational areas to provide immediate air support for the ground forces. Eventually there were nine such bases: FAF1 (Wankie); FAF2 (Kariba); FAF3 (Centenary); FAF4 (Mount Darwin); FAF5 (Mtoko); FAF6 (Chipinga); FAF7 (Buffalo Range); FAF8 (Grand Reef); and FAF9 (Rutenga). Impromptu FAFs were also created anywhere there was a 1 000 yard runway.

The Fire Forces were based at the FAFs to be within an hour or so's flying time of any incidents such as ambushes, farm attacks and sightings, and to be able to reinforce trackers or cross-graining patrols (usually sticks of four) when they made contact with the enemy. Thornhill and New Sarum provided facilities for major maintenance and repair but the helicopters were mostly self-sufficient because each had a qualified technician to maintain it as well as manning its weapons. The jet squadrons based at Thornhill and New Sarum, being in the centre of Rhodesia, were able to provide quick response anywhere when a target tough enough to need their attention presented itself.

Although based in the operational areas, the helicopter's high consumption of fuel still limited its range and loads – the load carrying capacity decreases with increases in altitude, humidity and temperature. The *Alouette* carried a two-stroke pump for refuelling and therefore dumps of aviation fuel were placed across the country at district commissioners' camps, rural police stations and other points. Fuel tankers were also sent forward with the 'land-tail' of Fire Force reinforcements to get within ten minutes' flying time from the target. If vehicles could not supply the fuel in time, *Dakota* aircraft flew fuel to the nearest airstrip or parachuted it close to the scene of the action. On external operations fuel was para-dropped into temporary administrative bases set up in remote areas of Zambia and Mocambique along the flight path of helicopters flying troops to attack external camps. The second phase of *Operation Dingo* in October 1977 required two bases to allow the helicopters to reach Tembue camp in central Mocambique near the Malawi border. On *Operation Mascot* in 1978 the drums landed amongst a cluster of 'Buffalo Beans'. A stinging encounter with Buffalo beans is never forgotten.

The Rhodesians compensated for the helicopters' limited troop carrying capacity by using their venerable Douglas C47 Paradaks (*Dakotas* configured for paratrooping) which could deploy some 20 paratroops in a single drop against the four or eight men delivered by the *Alouette* and the AB205A *Cheetah* respectively. The Paradaks, however, were less able to make a concealed approach and could not land anywhere. They had a greater range but once their paratroops were dropped, their swift recovery was difficult without helicopters. The Rhodesian compromise was to use paratroops to reinforce heli-borne troops both on Fire Force operations and external raids and ferrying them back by helicopter.

Given their unique agility, the helicopters had a variety of tasks including Fire Force. A daily task was placing radio relay teams on high features and resupplying them. There were casualty evacuations. The wounded could be reached within an hour which drastically reduced fatalities and boosted the morale of the ordinary soldier. Helicopters recovered damaged or discarded equipment and captured weapons. The *Alouettes* lowered the police

Special Urban Emergency Units 'SWAT teams' onto the roofs of buildings. Troops needed rescuing at times and Rhodesian Army units on external operations wore 'Pegasus' harnesses which, when clipped to a trapeze bar on the *Alouette*'s cargo sling, permitted their 'hot extraction' literally from the grasp of a pursuing enemy. 'Hot extraction' could be uncomfortable if the pilot, under fire, dragged his human cargo through the trees. Usually, however, G-Car pilots landed quickly rather than hazard men on the end of a rope. On occasions, escorting aircraft would attack, driving the enemy pursuers to ground, while the G-Car landed. 'Hot extractions' were dreaded by aircrews because they involved flying deep into hostile territory, sometimes refuelling twice to reach their objective.

The helicopter's unique ability to fly close to the ground allowed trained trackers to follow spoor from the air, overhauling the enemy quickly. Dogs with radios strapped to their backs, enabled the helicopter to follow at a discreet distance until contact was made. Scents are based on moisture and in the dry, hot conditions of the Rhodesian veld, they were gone by mid-morning, reducing the value of the tracker dog.

As helicopters permitted great flexibility in the placement of troops and weapons, *Alouette* pilots were trained to carry mortar teams and to observe the fall of shot. The mortar was rarely thus used because the 20mm cannon of the K-Car gave potent, instant fire power. Helicopter crews also corrected the fall of shot for artillery. Vic Cook did this at night, flying above Leopard Rock Hotel in the Vumba, on the eastern border of Rhodesia, spotting for 5.5 inch medium guns harassing Machipanda in Mocambique. The second shell hit the target.

The three Fire Forces usually deployed did not employ every helicopter. Individual or pairs of *Alouette* III G-Cars were positioned at non-Fire Force bases, for example at Inyanga Barracks, to support local efforts. They would place stop groups in cut off positions during follow-up operations. Working on their own, these pilots had to be remarkably ingenious. The success rate was never high but the disruptive effect was enormous as the pilots and their (often reservist) troops harried the enemy. Vic Cook

OPPOSITE (CLOCKWISE FROM TOP): Hastily erected barricades on the main road into Umtali form a helicopter Temporary Base; Tough Rhodesian African Rifles contingent waiting for lift-off in an *Alouette* lll; Chopper pilots wore little – or nothing at all – because of the tropical heat. The flak-jacket was mandatory because of ground fire; News photograph showing helicopter antics in the presence of local tribespeople – Psy-ops; Scouring the bush for the enemy.

recalled the constant use of simulated 'dummy' drops of stop groups as he tried to convince insurgents that they were surrounded when in reality he was moving only four men at a time. And the groups that a single helicopter might confront need not be small. Cook found himself alone in the air on one occasion when tackling 85 heavily armed Zanla who crossed the eastern border from Mocambique to attack Inyanga Village and Grand Reef Airport, Umtali [Mutare]. Led by John Barnes, flying a K-Car, Cook and Bill McQuaid, an American, had flown from Mtoko [now Mutoko] in the north-east to join a company of the Rhodesia Regiment in the Inyanga North Tribal Trust Land where it had discovered that African tribeswomen were feeding a large group. A couple of the women were carried aloft to point out the group but nothing was seen. Contact was made through the K-Car firing searching rounds into a wooded area and provoking a murderous reply from a heavy 12.7mm machine-gun and other weapons. The K-Car was hit but stayed in action until its 20mm cannon jammed. McQuaid just managed to fly his severely damaged chopper over a nearby hill before going down. The K-Car returned to Mtoko, leaving Cook alone in a running fight of seven to eight hours. Cook used the terrain to advantage, popping up from behind ridges to fire on the Zanla, drawing hot responses. He moved the troops, in sticks of four, to cut off the enemy and late in the fight put all the MAG gunners into an ambush position. The Rhodesian effort was rewarded by the harried Zanla retreating.

By then Cook had made so many hard landings that his left undercarriage axle broke. As the upper oleo strut, from which the wheel still hung, was banging against the helicopter's side, Cook, unable to land, hovered over a tree to allow his tech to break off a branch and wedge it into the broken undercarriage to hold it in place. On arrival back at Mtoko, Cook faced the problem of landing without damaging the aircraft further. This was resolved by the ground crew building a mound of sandbags on which Cook could rest the broken strut. Cook eased down onto it, ending a long day.

Given a controlled airspace, helicopters permit the placement of firepower and troops virtually anywhere, in tactical formations, ready for action, giving the battlefield commander great flexibility in exploiting a tactical situation. This was the *raison d'être* of Fire Force.

Deployed in January 1974, the Fire Force enjoyed its first action a month later, on 24 February, after being called in by Lieutenant Dale Collett of the Selous Scouts. Stunningly successful from the outset, Fire Force went through three phases of development: Phase One – 1974-1976; Phase Two – 1977-1979; and Phase Three – 1979-1980 after the election of the first black majority government led by Bishop Abel Muzorewa.

Before any Fire Force was ready for action, there was much to be done. Much depended on the Fire Force commander and the senior pilot, who flew him in the K-Car and commanded the other aircraft, and the rapport between them as well as the efforts of their troops, pilots, the FAF commander, the Special Branch, the technicians and base personnel.

As the senior Army officer, the Fire Force commander had a plethora of duties which included the strategic and tactical siting of the Fire Force base and its defences. He needed effective communications, intelligence and call-out systems. Among the detail, he had to know what other forces were available in his area as reinforcements for Fire Force actions. He could never have enough men.

The basic Rhodesian Fire Force unit was a 'stick' of four men – a junior NCO, with a VHF A63 radio and a FN rifle; two riflemen; and an MAG-gunner. The MAG and its ammunition was heavy but its high rate of fire was greatly prized. For rapid movement, the troops wore camouflage tee-shirts, shorts and light running shoes. They carried only ammunition, grenades, water, medical kits and basic rations. Short sharp actions meant that they were usually back in base by nightfall for re-deployment the next morning. If they expected to set a night ambush after a contact, regulation camouflage denims would be worn and light sleeping bags and claymore mines carried.

The life of Fire Force facing two or three daily call-outs was tough. Many missions were 'lemons' for many reasons – faulty intelligence, the disappearance of insurgents in the meantime etc. With deployments of six-ten weeks, the strain told. Three operational jumps a day was something no other paratrooper ever faced. In 1950-1952, the French Colonial Paras in Indo-China boasted of their fifty odd combat jumps, which more than doubled the 24 operational jumps of the two vaunted French Foreign Legion Para battalions between March 1949 and March 1954. Against the hundred major French combat jumps in Vietnam, the Americans had only one.

The combinations of aircraft used by the Fire Forces depended on what was available. Before the arrival of the AB205As, the Fire Forces were constantly stripped of their helicopters to support external operations by the SAS and other units. Occasionally Fire Forces were reduced to a K-Car and a G-Car, making them almost ineffective. The Rhodesian Intelligence Corps concluded in 1979 that the most successful combination was a K-Car and 32 soldiers carried in four G-Cars (each with four) and a *Dakota* (16 paratroops) reinforced by a *Lynx* for light air strike with 63mm SNEB rockets, mini-Golf bombs [blast and shrapnel], napalm, and twin .303 Brownings mounted above the wing. As contacts typically involved 6 to 12 Zanla, this gave the Fire Force a three to one ratio of superiority, producing an 80 to 1 kill rate.

This is not to say that the enemy did not fight back. Comparatively few helicopters were shot down (consider-

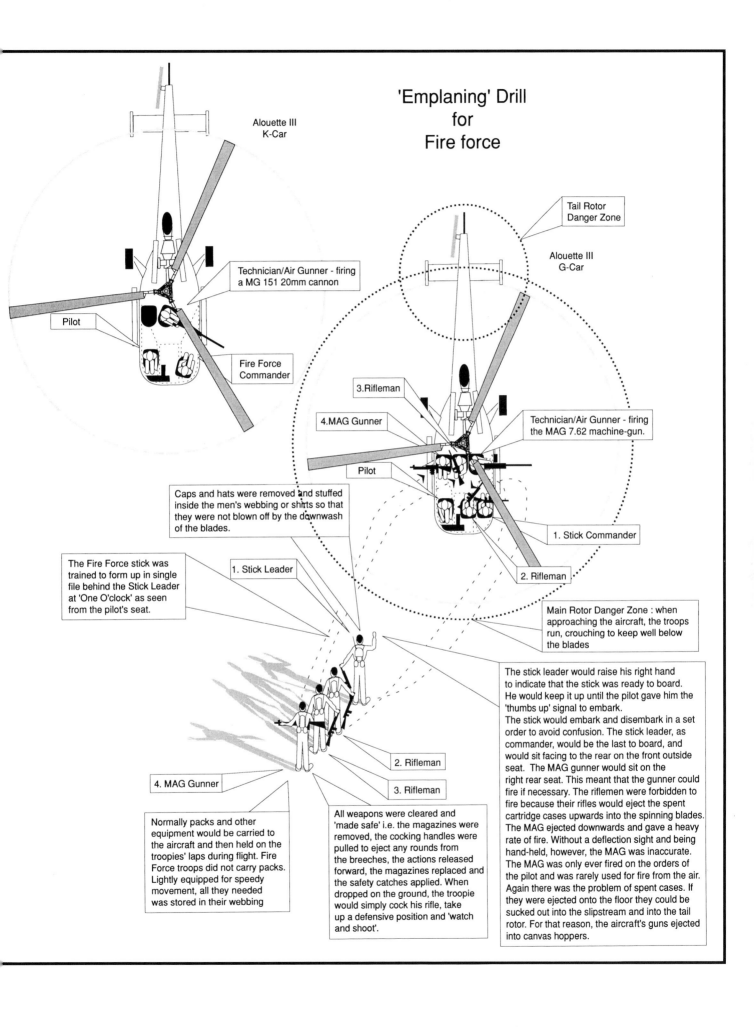

'Emplaning' Drill for Fire force

Alouette III K-Car

Technician/Air Gunner - firing a MG 151 20mm cannon

Pilot

Fire Force Commander

Tail Rotor Danger Zone

Alouette III G-Car

3.Rifleman

4.MAG Gunner

Technician/Air Gunner - firing the MAG 7.62 machine-gun.

Pilot

1. Stick Commander

2. Rifleman

Caps and hats were removed and stuffed inside the men's webbing or shirts so that they were not blown off by the downwash of the blades.

The Fire Force stick was trained to form up in single file behind the Stick Leader at 'One O'clock' as seen from the pilot's seat.

1. Stick Leader

Main Rotor Danger Zone : when approaching the aircraft, the troops run, crouching to keep well below the blades

The stick leader would raise his right hand to indicate that the stick was ready to board. He would keep it up until the pilot gave him the 'thumbs up' signal to embark.
The stick would embark and disembark in a set order to avoid confusion. The stick leader, as commander, would be the last to board, and would sit facing to the rear on the front outside seat. The MAG gunner would sit on the right rear seat. This meant that the gunner could fire if necessary. The riflemen were forbidden to fire because their rifles would eject the spent cartridge cases upwards into the spinning blades. The MAG ejected downwards and gave a heavy rate of fire. Without a deflection sight and being hand-held, however, the MAG was inaccurate. The MAG was only ever fired on the orders of the pilot and was rarely used for fire from the air. Again there was the problem of spent cases. If they were ejected onto the floor they could be sucked out into the slipstream and into the tail rotor. For that reason, the aircraft's guns ejected into canvas hoppers.

4. MAG Gunner

2. Rifleman

3. Rifleman

Normally packs and other equipment would be carried to the aircraft and then held on the troopies' laps during flight. Fire Force troops did not carry packs. Lightly equipped for speedy movement, all they needed was stored in their webbing

All weapons were cleared and 'made safe' i.e. the magazines were removed, the cocking handles were pulled to eject any rounds from the breeches, the actions released forward, the magazines replaced and the safety catches applied. When dropped on the ground, the troopie would simply cock his rifle, take up a defensive position and 'watch and shoot'.

ing the numerous daily call-outs) but many were damaged by ground-fire and a number of Fire Force commanders and aircrew killed and wounded. The enemy displayed some ingenuity. For example, in failing light at 5.20 pm on 17 August 1976, Support Commando, 1RLI, commanded by Major [later Lieutenant-Colonel] Patrick Armstrong, tackled 20-30 Zanla after an 'aircraft ambush' near Mount Darwin in north-east Rhodesia. The Zanla planned to draw a Fire Force into the trap which comprised a 75mm recoilless rifle, a 7.62mm machine-gun with an anti-aircraft sight, 60mm and 82mm mortars, six electrically-fired anti-aircraft 'mines' of TNT buried in a foot of earth with 8-10 stick grenades on top. The Zanla contrived to lead a stick of men, who were tracking them, into the area. The supporting *Lynx* took the bait, put in an airstrike and was badly damaged by fire from the ground and by the explosion of three of the 'mines'. The Zanla split into small groups and awaited the arrival of the Fire Force. The Fire Force was deployed without the K-Car which had to be recalled from a trip to Salisbury. Stops were put down but nothing transpired until, in the fast fading light, the K-Car arrived and drew heavy fire. The stops advanced and drew long range mortar, rifle and machine-gun fire. Corporal Crittal was slightly wounded by a mortar bomb and Corporal Titlestad was mortally wounded aboard a helicopter. There were no immediate Zanla casualties but a night ambush by 2 Independent Company, Rhodesia Regiment, killed one and captured two who were wounded.

Fire Force deployments were underpinned by much careful planning, preparation and equipment checks. The Fire Force commander, his second in command, his officers, the senior and other pilots, the FAF commander and the operations and intelligence staff would review the current intelligence, call-out drills, and general *modus operandi*. Aircraft and men had to be properly equipped. Items such as spare headsets in the helicopters, to keep troop commanders informed, and recognition devices such as strobe lights carried by the stop groups, improved efficiency markedly. Standard drills were equally important. In the K-Car the division of responsibilities between the pilot and the commander was crucial for the elimination of confusion. On the ground, the troops had to defeat the enemy with swift efficiency, which included accurate shooting. To this end extensive briefings would be held to familiarise everyone with all operational aspects – radio channels, callsigns, heights of para-drops, aircraft formations, target marking, casualty evacuation, the composition and command of the supporting 'landtail' and much more. The Fire Force commander had much to remember about his own role. In action he had to orientate himself, using a prominent feature, as it was easy to become confused in an orbiting helicopter. He had to ensure he knew where his stop groups where, to avoid 'friendly fire,

casualties and to block the enemy's escape. He was not to set his men impossible tasks. He had to encourage them, keep them informed using clear, confident tones and unambiguous language. There were fundamental rules with regard to tactics which could not be broken. The first was: never to sweep uphill – always downhill; the second: never to sweep into the sun; and the third was always to sweep from cover into open ground – never from open ground into cover. Major Henson recalls that, whenever he broke these rules, he lost men (five in all). And he would only break the rules because time was pressing, the sun was setting and there was no time to get his men round to the top of a hill to start a downward sweep.

Thus prepared the Fire Force would wait for the klaxon to announce a call-out. Calls for Fire Forces were generated in a number of ways. There could have been an incident – a farm attack, an ambush. Or cross-graining patrols or trackers on spoor might have contacted the enemy. Intelligence gathered by the Special Branch and other agencies like the fearsome Selous Scouts, might indicate a target. Selous Scout 'pseudo-gangs', disguised as insurgents and 'operating' with them, provided the times and locations of meetings. Good results were obtained from intelligence but often it was dated or inaccurate and produced 'lemons' for the Fire Forces. Enemy could be found electronically by the 'road runner' – an adapted portable commercial transistor radio receiver. The 'road runners' were placed in rural stores and were given to double agents, such as the Reverend Kandoreka (who, although a close colleague of Bishop Muzorewa, supplied Zanla). The 'road runner' was activated, when the radio was switched off. The insurgents might be alarmed by the sound of an aircraft and switch off their radio to listen to discover if it was threatening. The 'off' switch, however, switched on a homing device which could be picked up by a searching aircraft's Becker radio direction finder. Two aircraft, flying on parallel or opposing courses, would secure co-ordinates to identify the square kilometre from which the 'road runner' was transmitting and numerous insurgents were surprised by the unheralded arrival of a Fire Force. But the lack of precision in target identification and the absence of personnel on an observation post (OP) to direct the Fire Force allowed many to escape.

Aerial reconnaissance was an important method of detecting the insurgents. By the early seventies, the pilots of No. 4 Squadron, then commanded by Peter Petter-Bowyer, and flying *Provosts, Trojans, Cessna* 185s and later *Lynxes*, became highly skilled at spotting 'crapping' patterns – radiating paths made by insurgents going about their daily functions. The most skilled reconnaissance pilot was Kevin 'Cocky' Benecke whose phenomenal success was attributed by the Air Force's Medical Officer, Doctor Brian Knight, to a minor visual defect in the green-brown range which enabled Benecke to distinguish dark objects

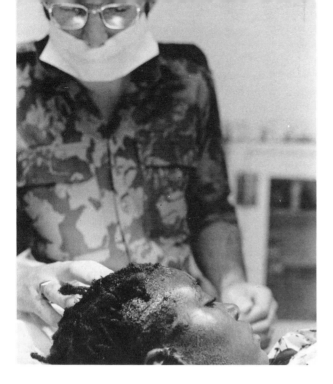

LEFT: Landmine victim being tended by a South African doctor in the *Operation Hurricane* area. ABOVE: BSAP detachment takes away civilian bodies killed by insurgent group and BELOW: Landmine victim is 'casevaced' by helicopter.

in shade which people with normal eyesight could not see.

Success was more likely if OPs were involved. These were established on hills overlooking infiltration routes, villages of sympathisers and other likely areas. By observing the pattern of life, an OP would detect anything out of the ordinary – unusual amounts of cooking or lines of women carrying cooked food into groves of trees and other hiding places. The major problem was to conceal the OP from the local population and considerable skill was needed. Success also depended on accurate map reading so that the Fire Force could be directed with precision to the target. Although all units served on OPs, the most skilled OP operators were Selous Scouts. Major Nigel Henson, who commanded Support Commando 1RLI for two and a half years (1977-1979), flew on 111 Fire Force missions. 73 were in 1979 and 68 of them resulted in contacts. In 1979 only one in six call-outs were unproductive 'lemons'

which Henson attributes to the full deployment of the Selous Scouts on OPs as much as to the competence of the aircrews, himself and his men. There was always a high rate of unsuccessful call-outs but many of them were the result of the Fire Force not spending enough time combing the area if nothing was immediately apparent.

In Phase One (1974-1976), the commander and the K-Car pilot would make a quick appreciation of the problem presented them and, if Fire Force was not needed immediately (if necessary, the Fire Force could be airborne in four minutes), they would give the aircrew and stick commanders a preliminary briefing before take-off. All aspects would be covered – radio channels, aircraft formations, air support, route to the target, target-marking, enemy numbers, likely escape routes, stop group positions and callsigns, action on contact, casualty evacuation, second-wave reinforcements, the 'landtail' (which would approach on tarred roads, where possible, to avoid land-

mines), the provision of trackers for following-up on any who escaped, the need for captures for intelligence (these would be flown out immediately for interrogation and possible use by the Selous Scouts' pseudo-operations). Stick commanders would be reminded of pro-words such as 'Ters visual' which was most imperative. Another was 'Stop; Show Map' – the waving of the white back of a map in lieu of smoke signals to indicate a stop group's position on the ground. When a veteran Support Commando stick leader, 'Messus' Moore, was ordered to show his map, he replied that, as he had forgotten his map, he would hold up his cigarette packet. His Fire Force commander, Major Henson, surprised to be able to see the upheld packet, responded '*Stop One*, are they Kingsgate or Madison?' [two Rhodesian brands].

A problem to be considered was how to take the enemy by surprise and here aircraft noise was of prime importance. Some idea of when approaching helicopters could be heard was given during *Operation Dabchick* (a raid on Mucheneze Camp in Mocambique on 5 February 1979) when the SAS OP heard approaching AB205A *Cheetahs* eight minutes before they arrived. Usually the OPs reported hearing aircraft four minutes from target which allowed the insurgents time to run a kilometre and a half. Every minute wasted, allowed them gains of 400 metres. Terrain and wind direction were crucial in achieving surprise and 'contour-flying', hugging hills and trees for cover, was used when possible. On occasion, Fire Forces would fly in a wide half-circle, refuelling on the way. Where the terrain could not assist, a noisy aircraft, like the *Trojan*, could arrive first to mask the sound of the approaching helicopters. On *Operation Dingo* in November 1977 a DC8 jet airliner overflew early morning muster parades in Zanla camps near Chimoio in Mocambique, prompting a stampede into cover. When nothing happened, the ranks reformed and, believing the DC8 was off course, did not disperse at the next sound of jet engines – those of *Hunter* fighters diving out of the sun.

If noise could not be completely masked, the reflection of the sound could disguise direction. To drive the enemy to ground before they could flee, an initial air strike could be put in by light aircraft (using rockets, Frantan or mini-Golf bombs) or, if the target warranted it, by *Canberras* or *Hunters*. An alternative was for the entire Fire Force to arrive from all directions simultaneously, but usually the K-Car pilot would fly ahead of his G-Cars to allow the Fire Force commander time to orientate himself, confirm the OP's information and reassess his plan.

The briefing over, the aircraft would take-off. In the G-Cars, the stick commanders sat on the left front seat to use the spare headset to follow progress, their riflemen took the middle rear and front seats, leaving the MAG gunners the rear right seats to give the aircraft additional firepower if the pilot requested it, (for example, to keep enemy heads down when landing). The riflemen would not fire from the aircraft because they might hit the blades in a tilting helicopter. Furthermore, unlike the MAG, the FN ejected its spent cases upwards towards the spinning blades and, in any case, loose cases could be sucked out of the open doors and rearwards into the tail-rotor – for this reason, the G-Cars' own guns ejected into shoots.

The K-Car would fly ahead to be talked onto the target by the OP. The K-Car pilot and commander would use the time in flight to review their plan and inform the pilots and stick leaders of any changes. Second-wave reinforcements would also be ordered to standby for uplift by the G-Cars once the stop-groups had been deployed. The commander would also keep the JOC informed so that it could frame its plans accordingly.

Difficulties of parallax, of judging the position of an aircraft in the sky to a point on the ground, often caused delays in precisely identifying the target, allowing the enemy to escape. The OPs sometimes indicated targets with tracer bullets, flares, shoulder-launched smoke rockets or other means. Sergeant Ron Flint of the Rhodesia Regiment aimed his pencil flare projector and informed the incoming K-Car just behind him: 'Marking Target NOW!' The pencil flare refused to ignite. Coolly observing Flint's agitated efforts, the K-Car pilot laconically commented from above: "Don't worry. I can see where your finger is pointing." On another occasion, great difficulty was experienced because the African Selous Scout sergeant of the OP had marked the target so well that his rocket was buried in the chest of one of the enemy, dampening the smoke. The Selous Scouts did not, however, usually mark targets themselves because, acting as pseudo gangs, they wanted to appear to the local tribesmen as survivors of the contact. Instead, when over the approximate area of the target, the K-Car gunner would throw out a smoke grenade to create a reference point for the OP to use to direct the K-Car onto the target.

Once the target was identified, the K-Car would pull up to its optimum orbiting height of 800 feet and open fire, seeking to kill the enemy or drive him to ground. Meanwhile the G-Cars would fly in a wider pre-arranged orbit, waiting for the Fire Force Commander's orders to put their stop groups down on the escape routes in a pre-defined counter-clockwise order. This was a somewhat rigid, slow and cumbersome procedure and was often fruitless because the enemy had time to flee. It was soon realised that the aircrew had to look constantly outside the circle as the insurgents covered the ground at their astonishing rate of 400 metres a minute.

The Fire Force commander would bring in his reinforcements as soon as possible as he could never have enough troops on the ground and might need a reserve on hand for decisive action or for unforeseen eventualities. When the reinforcements arrived the K-Car would lead their helicopters through the pattern of landing zones, ordering each G-Car to deploy its troops when the particular landing zone was flown over, to maintain the order of the deployment.

The Fire Force commander would make maximum use of fire from the aircraft into known insurgent positions. He would use the G-Cars for flushing fire so that the K-Car remained on station above the target. Flushing fire or 'Drake' shooting, was also used by the sweeplines. The troops would fire several rifle shots into bushy thickets to drive out the insurgents from hiding places.

Once the enemy was trapped, the troops had to disarm and to frisk all insurgents alive or dead immediately. This was to be done because many feigned death only to abscond. Captives would be flown out for interrogation and the area thoroughly searched and all abandoned equipment, ammunition and spent cartridge cases were picked up for ballistic and intelligence purposes and to deny the survivors ammunition. Even if no enemy were encountered, care was taken that nothing of intelligence value was missed. The troops would be recovered or, if appropriate, left to ambush the contact area or to follow up on the tracks of the fleeing survivors. The last task was a full debriefing back at base.

The changes made in Phase Two in 1977 drastically improved the success of Fire Force. The initial briefing (which would now include details for the paratroops – dropping zones, parachute recovery etc) would normally be held at the refuelling stop on the way to the target, to save time and because by then the OP would have crucial information on any enemy movement. It also was realised that the K-Car had to fly in from behind and over the OP in order to see what he was seeing and therefore waste no time in finding and marking the target with white smoke.

As before, once sure of the target, the K-Car would pull up to 800 feet and fire on the enemy. When the G-Cars arrived, they would fly directly to prescribed stop positions on the escape routes and orbit them individually. Instead of having to wait for the Fire Force commander, the G-Cars were given some autonomy. If the G-Car crew spotted the enemy, they could land their stop group without reference to the K-Car. Likewise they would fire on any escaping enemy. If there was no sighting, the stop groups would remain airborne for quick deployment elsewhere. For flexibility, there would be an alternative plan – Plan *Alpha*. The Fire Force commander would simply state 'Plan *Alpha*' and the G-Cars would deposit their stop groups on the predetermined stop positions. This meant minimum delay in bottling up the enemy.

In the meantime, the Paradak would be flying around an 'IP' (intermediate point) four minutes away, out of earshot. Once the escape routes were sealed, the Fire Force commander would have his paratroopers dropped to sweep the area, driving the quarry into the open, where the K-Car's 20mm could deal with them, or into the waiting stop groups. Before the para-drop the K-Car, or a delegated G-Car, would have verified the suitability of the landing zone (LZ) – a few trees were no impediment but dense woodlands, rocky ground, steep slopes and winds in excess of 15 knots were. If time permitted, the G-Car which might land to transmit the precise altitude of the LZ for the QNH setting of the *Dakota*'s altimeter. The K-Car or G-Car would mark the centre of the dropping zone with smoke and talk the *Dakota* in. Where possible, the troops would be dropped facing the contact area, in the direction of their sweep. It took considerable skill by the pilots to position the *Dakota* precisely, when flying at 90 knots (to create sufficient slipstream to open the canopies), so that the paratroopers landed on the often small dropping zones. For mutual defence and for efficiency it was essential that the paratroops came down close to each other. To expose the paratroops to ground fire for the shortest time, the prescription for the drop was from 500 feet and never lower than 450 feet. In fact, drops were often made from 300 feet so that none of the paratroops drifted off the dropping zone. The Fire Force paratrooper, carrying little more than his weapon, ammunition, grenades and water, was not as heavily burdened as other paratroopers.

The advice was 'Rather too high than too low'. On

Conditions in the Operational Area were often primitive. Drums of fuel and supplies had to be dropped by DC-3s or hauled in by road, usually with resultant landmine casualties.

17 February 1978, however, paratroops from A Company, Second Battalion, the Rhodesian African Rifles, were dropped at 300 feet due to an error of 150 feet in the setting of their *Dakota*'s altimeters. Their commander, Major André Dennison, estimated that the canopies were open for only nine seconds before the men struck the ground – unharmed. A Support Commando drop in 1979 near Rushinga left 14 of 22 men injured when their *Dakota* maintained a constant height over rising ground. The last man jumped under 200 feet.

Once on the ground the paratroops would abandon their parachutes and marry up with their sticks and then with the senior stick using a separate radio channel. They would lay out an identification panel and face the contact, before the senior stick commander reported 'ready' to the Fire Force commander. The parachutes would be collected later by the closest troops after the contact or a 'wanker' stick would be dropped to recover them.

The achievement of Phase Two was that the quick positioning of stops often trapped the enemy.

Phase Three was the product of the constant availability of G-Cars in 1979 because the forces deployed on external operations at last had available the longer-range and greater troop carrying-capacity of the AB205A *Cheetahs*. The Jumbo Fire Force was created by bringing two Fire Forces together, giving it two K-Cars, eight G-Cars, a *Dakota* and a *Lynx*, often with the support of *Hawker Hunters*. When the Fire Force was seven minutes out from the target, the two K-Cars would accelerate and pull ahead. Once directed onto the target, the K-Cars (being used like tanks on the battlefield) would immediately attack without pulling up, seeking to traumatise, if not kill, the enemy. The Fire Force commander might bring in the jet aircraft immediately with their devastating Golf bombs to lower the enemy's morale further. The effect would be to 'stabilise' the situation. Those insurgents who survived would go to ground. The stops would be in position quickly and the paratroops would follow to sweep the area. Actions that used to take an entire morning or a day thenceforth were often over in an hour. The commander of Support Commando, 1RLI, Major Nigel Henson recalls tackling and killing 22 insurgents at 6 am. By 7 am his Fire Force was in action against ten more and, having dealt with them, was by mid-morning in a third contact.

Rhodesian national servicemen in the independent companies of the Rhodesia Regiment at times served as Fire Forces, as did the First and Second Battalions of that regiment, and many impromptu Fire Forces were created by available troops. The permanent Fire Forces, however, were drawn from the Rhodesian Light Infantry, whose white regular soldiers achieved the highest kill-rate with relatively small loss to themselves, and the Rhodesian African Rifles whose black professional soldiers also attained enviable results. An RLI commando or an RAR company

would serve as a Fire Force at a forward airfield. By 1977 all regular infantry were trained paratroops and took turns to be deployed by helicopter or parachute or brought in as reinforcements by the vehicles of the 'landtail'. In 1979, in the last phase, the RLI took over the exclusive task of Fire Force, scoring formidable tallies of kills. After the election of Muzorewa's Government in April 1979 until the cease-fire in December 1979,

One Commando, RLI, killed	450 insurgents
Two Commando	350
Three Commando	410
Support Commando	470
	1 680

André Dennison's fine 'A' Company, 2RAR, by contrast killed 403 insurgents in the period September 1977 to July 1979. Perhaps there is no comparison but in nine years of campaigning in Malaya, the British SAS killed 108 of their enemy.

The records of Support Commando, 1RLI (then commanded by Major Nigel Henson) in the crucial months of February to May 1979 give a taste of Fire Force action at the height of the war, at the moment when the new constitution of Zimbabwe-Rhodesia was brought in, conceding majority rule for the first time.

In late April 1979, Bishop Muzorewa and his United African National Council gained the majority of the seats in the new Legislative Assembly with the overwhelming support of the electorate who defied the orders of Zanla, and the Zimbabwe People's Revolutionary Army (the military wing of Nkomo's ZAPU), not to vote. Muzorewa's popularity quickly faded because Western governments, and, in particular, the new British Conservative Government of Margaret Thatcher, refused to recognise the legality of his election.

The forces ranged against Muzorewa – Zanla and ZPRA – took a terrible pounding from the onslaught of the Rhodesian security forces in Rhodesia and externally in their host countries of Mocambique, Zambia and, on one occasion, deep inside central Angola. Support Commando was in the thick of the fighting. In February 1979 Support Commando supplied troops for two Fire Forces, *Delta* and *Echo*.

On 22 February, at 1.45 pm on a bright, very hot afternoon, Support Commando's Fire Force *Delta*, commanded by Lieutenant V.A. Prinsloo, contacted twelve green-clad Zanla cadres in the mopani forest and thorn bush of Sengwe Tribal Trust Land in the extreme south of Rhodesia, close to the South African and Mocambican borders. A callsign of the mounted infantry regiment, the Grey Scouts, had been tracking a group of Zanla and had killed one before calling *Delta* to seal off the escape routes with stop groups and sweep the area. *Delta* (comprising a K-Car, three G-Cars and a *Lynx*) had been pre-positioned nearby but in the five minutes it took to reach the Greys, the Zanla unit was fleeing south-east. As *Delta* flew in, a keen-eyed trooper in a G-Car spotted the insurgents some three kilometres from the contact area. The K-Car attacked them while *Stop One* was put into a river line a kilometre to the west. *Stop Two* was dropped a kilometre south on a track and both stops advanced eastward parallel to each other. *Stop Three* was placed in a small kraal 800 metres to the west of the sighting. By this time the insurgents had 'bombshelled' (fleeing in all directions). One insurgent surrendered to the K-Car and, with a wounded man, was taken into custody by *Stop Three* who immediately killed a third. The K-Car's 20mm cannon knocked down three more in a gully a hundred metres away and *Stop Two* was sent to investigate. The K-Car scored its fourth kill another hundred metres on and dispatched *Stop One* to clear the area. The *Lynx* pilot then spotted two Zanla running west behind *Stop One*. The *Lynx* put in two unsuccessful Frantan attacks while *Stop One* turned about to search the other side of the river line, immediately killing a Zanla and two more on a re-sweep.

Nine Zanla in all were killed, two captured and one escaped. Four SKS self-loading rifles, six AK assault rifles, an AKM, six stick grenades, twelve thirty-round AK magazines, one forty-round AK magazine, three percussion grenades, 2 000 rounds of 7.62 intermediate rounds, five RPG-7 rockets and four RPG-7 boosters and an 82mm mortar secondary were recovered. The twelve RLI troops had expended 250 rounds of 7.62mm ball and a white phosphorous grenade. The K-Car had fired a hundred rounds of 20mm and the *Lynx* had dropped two Frantan bombs and fired 120 rounds of .303 inch ball from its front guns. A mini flare projector had been lost as well as three FN magazines. What was notable, Prinsloo wrote in his report, was firstly the poor state of the Zanla weaponry, with its woodwork old and rotting, and secondly that interrogation revealed that the Fire Force had achieved surprise even though it had been waiting close by for the call-out.

Two days later, at 10.30 am on the rainy morning of 24 February, Support Commando's other Fire Force, *Echo*, commanded by Major N.D. Henson, contacted an unknown number of Zanla in the Chiweshe Tribal Trust Land, north of Salisbury. Henson was faced with many problems: he had only a K-Car, a G-Car and a *Lynx*; the target area was large (five kilometres by three) and covered in thick bush; visibility from the air was poor; and heavy rain swept in at ten minute intervals throughout the day. Henson had responded to a confirmation received at 10.15 am from Special Branch that 95 insurgents were in the area but he was not given a precise location. He had been forewarned and, having only one troop-carrying helicopter, had positioned his second wave reinforce-

ments, comprising six RLI and ten Police Anti-Terrorist Unit sticks [64 men in all] with fuel about five minutes away.

No movement was seen from the aircraft on arrival over the suspected area. Henson deployed *Stops One, Two, Six* and *Seven* in a curving line from south to north along the banks of the Ruya River. *Stops Three to Five* started sweeping northwards and, once across a small tributary of the Ruya, contacted an insurgent who wounded Trooper Cummings. Requesting airstrikes by the *Lynx* with Frantan and a mini-Golf bomb, Henson reinforced *Stops Three to Five* with *Stops Six* and *Seven*. Zanla replied with mortar fire. Henson moved *Stops Eight* to *Eleven* to the west and had them sweep north-eastwards. *Stops Three to Seven* killed a Zanla 60mm mortar-man on the hill in front of them and then resumed their advance. On the second central hill, *Stop Eight* reported Zanla ahead. The *Lynx* and the K-Car attacked but an immediate sweep found nothing. Henson ordered a further sweep of the area, and this time *Stops Three to Seven* came under intense fire from the summit. Further airstrikes were put in and the sweepline found three Zanla bodies on the northern flank of the hill. Fifteen Zanla had escaped and four had been killed in return for the wounding of Trooper Cummings. The size of the area of operations and the heavy rain had militated against a bigger kill. An AKM assault rifle, a PPSH submachine-gun, the 60mm mortar, grenades, ammunition and documents were recovered and handed to the Special Branch at Mount Darwin. Henson confessed that the idea of tackling 95 Zanla with only a K-Car and a G-Car was daunting because his ability to move his troops had been drastically limited. Those killed, Henson wrote, had been more inept in attempting to escape than he had yet seen.

At 6.30 am in the difficult light of the early morning of 6 March, Lieutenant Prinsloo's Fire Force *Delta* contacted seven Zanla in grassland with scattered trees and thorny undergrowth in the Mtetengwe Tribal Trust Land, north of Beit Bridge on the South African border. Intelligence gathered by One Independent Company, Rhodesia Regiment, (1 Indep) had led the JOC to devise an all-arms programme to attack five Zanla camps. The first and second camps were to be bombed by a *Canberra* at first light. Simultaneously, supported by a K-Car, three G-Cars, a *Lynx* and a Police Reserve Air Wing aircraft (PRAW), *Delta* was to attack the third while the fourth and fifth were engaged by artillery. The plan went somewhat awry. The artillery bogged down on the mud road and could not get into position. The *Canberra* had communications problems and had to abort.

Undaunted *Delta*, pre-positioned nearby, decided to attack the third camp. *Stops One* and *Two* were dropped on a 'cut-line' [a bush-cleared fire break] to the east of the camp. *Stop Three* was placed in the south on a ridge

CLOCKWISE FROM ABOVE: Cross-border raid into Mocambique involved two South African Air Force *Super Frelons* with a 'Trooper' G-Car. The weapon is a captured 12,7mm DSh K-38 heavy machine-gun; Fire Force in heavy bush country in the north; RAR troops on the move near the Mocambique border; Nearing Salisbury in an *Alo*.

OPPOSITE (CLOCKWISE FROM TOP LEFT): The Rhodesian Government launched a massive programme in rural areas to entice tribespeople to hand in weapons' caches; Tactical Base in *Operation Hurricane,* near Mtoko; Rhodesian African Rifles on the move near Fort Victoria; Rhodesia also had its share of American and European 'Bounty Hunters' who were offered rewards by the Government for insurgents killed and; Defensive position in the south of the country, near the Limpopo River.

MAKE MONEY
LOOK FOR THESE

THESE ARE SOME OF THE THINGS CARRIED BY TERRORISTS
AND YOU WILL BE PAID UP TO $1000 FOR SHOWING OR
SAYING WHERE THEY CAN BE FOUND.
YOU WILL BE PAID UP TO $5000 FOR INFORMATION
LEADING TO THE DEATH OR CAPTURE OF A TERRORIST.

beside the river which flowed directly north through the camp. When the K-Car flew over the camp, Prinsloo could see sleeping places and blankets but no movement. *Stops One* and *Two* moved directly west along the cutline to the river and then along its banks southwards towards the camp. Close to the camp they killed three Zanla in thorny undergrowth so thick that the troops spent much of their time on their hands and knees. A fourth Zanla killed himself by blowing his head off with a grenade. Seeing movement in the bushes, the troops fired and killed two African women. Prinsloo had *Stops Four* and *Five* dropped in the east on a tributary of the main river to work down it towards the camp. *Stops One, Two, Four* and *Five* then swept the swamp just to the north, working up the main river towards *Stop Three*. In the thick thorn bush six more African women were killed. The sweep returned towards the camp and captured two females. The bodies of a female and an insurgent were recovered. The thorns were so impenetrable that the bodies of the three insurgents and the African women could not be recovered and were left behind. The captured females informed the security forces that the camp had held seven insurgents and eleven women. In the aftermath, the troops were sent on foot to check the other four camps, finding them unoccupied. Four Zanla and eight women had been killed. An AK, a SKS, two stick grenades, an offensive grenade, seven AK magazines and 500 rounds of 7.62mm ammunition were picked up. The twelve RLI and eight 1 Indep riflemen had fired 500 rounds and had thrown four white phosphorous grenades and a high explosive grenade. The K-Car had fired fifteen rounds of 20mm. The troops had lost a MAG belt.

At 11 am on the next day, Prinsloo and *Delta* were back in action, responding to a sighting by the Selous Scout OP, callsign *Three Three Bravo*. *Delta* contacted eight insurgents in the Godlwayo Tribal Trust Land, south of Bulawayo. Despite time being wasted by a bungled talk-on, the K-Car killed an insurgent in the camp. Prinsloo had *Stops One* and *Two* dropped to sweep the area. During the sweep, an orbiting G-Car noticed two insurgents about two kilometres north-west. The K-Car flew over, shot both of them and diverted *Stops One* and *Two* to search this area while *Stops Three* and *Four* were dropped to the east to sweep the original camp. *Stops One* and *Two* found only one of the two victims of the K-Car and it was concluded that the other had escaped wounded. After searching the area, all stops were recovered. The Fire Force returned to base.

An hour later, the same OP, *Three Three Bravo*, called *Delta* to a sighting of three insurgents on a hill five kilometres north-east of the contact area. One insurgent broke cover as *Stop One* was landed. The K-Car killed him. *Stop Two* joined *Stop One* and swept the northern flank of the hill while *Stop Three* searched the kraal to the

south of the hill. *Stops One* and *Two* flushed two insurgents off the hill who fled north-east only to be killed by *Stops One* and *Two*. An SKS, three AKs, five stick grenades, an armour piercing rifle grenade and 400 rounds of AK ammunition were recovered and handed to Special Branch at Gwanda. Recording the score of five Zanla killed and three escaped, with one of the escapees being wounded, Prinsloo felt that, if the first talk-on had been accurate, all eight insurgents could have been killed.

On 9 March 1979, the Fire Force manned by Three Commando 1RLI and commanded by Major Frederick Watts, contacted 23 Zanla and killed 21 of them. At 4 pm that day, Major Henson's Fire Force *Echo* (a K-Car, three G-Cars and a *Lynx*) contacted an unknown number of Zanla in the Masoso Tribal Trust Land in the Zambezi Valley near the northern border with Mocambique. The country was flat, covered with thick jesse thorn bush interspersed with patches of mealie lands and a northward flowing riverbed. *Echo* had been diverted from another call-out only to endure an inaccurate and confused talk-on by the OP, callsign *One Two Charlie*, which wasted twenty minutes while the aircraft milled about over the Muvadonha Valley. Henson was particularly annoyed by the OP's refusal to fire his target marker. A target was only acquired when the K-Car's aircrew caught a fleeting glimpse of two insurgents where an east-west track crossed the riverbed. The K-Car fired its 20mm and the *Lynx* followed with Frantan. Henson had *Stop One* put down on the track where it skirted a mealie land to the west of the river. *Stop Two* was dropped on a mealie land close to the riverbed and just north of the sighting. *Stop Three* was put down on a third mealie land in the south. The first in action was *Stop Two* who killed an insurgent shortly after landing. They advanced to the site of the airstrike where blood spoor and an AK were found. *Stop One* killed an insurgent on the eastern edge of their mealie land. *Stop Three* working up the riverbed, soon encountered an insurgent and killed him. The light had faded so ambushes were set up on the riverbed. A sweep at first light yielded no signs of further insurgents. Henson blamed the talk-on, the thick bush and the poor light for what he considered a poor score of three Zanla and one wounded escaped. An RPD light machine-gun, a PPSH submachine-gun, two AKs, grenades, ammunition and documents were recovered and handed to Special Branch at Mount Darwin.

On 12 March, Second-Lieutenant Simon John Carpenter distinguished himself in a contact with insurgents while commanding a sweepline of ten men from Support Commando's Fire Force *Delta*. When the sweepline was held up by five hidden insurgents, Carpenter coolly outflanked them, enabling his section to kill all five. A month later, in April 1979, Carpenter accounted for two insurgents who were concealed in a well-sited defensive position which completely dominated his own.

At 4 pm on 12 March, Henson's Fire Force *Echo*, contacted an unknown number of Zanla in the Makoni Tribal Trust Land, east of Rusape. The action took place in open fields divided by thickly bushed river lines, a central river and a range of heavily wooded rocky hills The OP was on the summit of a north-western hill. The target seemed important enough for Fire Force *Echo* (comprising a K-Car, three G-Cars, a *Dakota* and a *Lynx*) to be summoned at 1 pm from Mount Darwin, 210 kilometres away. The briefing was held in the Selous Scouts' Fort at Rusape. *Echo* was told that there were three targets – huts – within a square kilometre. The first hut was at the bottom of the OP's hill, the second across the river line directly east between two hills and the third also across the river at the foot of a south-eastern hill.

Once over the target, Henson had *Stop One* put down to the west of the first hut, *Stop Two* was landed on the riverbank to the north and *Stop Three* just south of the third hut. Then the orbiting K-Car spotted an insurgent sitting in a zinc bath in a maize field close to the second hut and opened fire. Two African women abandoned their roles as bath attendants and fled but the bather reached for an AK-47 and fired back. The naked African stood his ground until he was out of ammunition. Then he ran and was killed by a 20mm shell. The K-Car crew spotted two insurgents in the riverbed just beyond at the confluence of a small tributary and fired at a further insurgent who was captured by *Stop One*. Henson ordered the dropping of *Eagle Three* and *Four* [para-sticks] the west of the first hut. *Eagle One* and *Two* were dropped either side of the confluence of the river and a tributary in the north and began a sweep down the river, promptly killing two insurgents. At that moment, a G-Car, departing to refuel, saw 12 insurgents running in a ravine two kilometres to the south-west. *Eagle Four* was moved to the ravine but could not overhaul the enemy and Henson could do nothing more to cut them off because his aircraft were running out of fuel. The K-Car left to refuel from drums which the Special Branch had said had been placed nearby. Finding nothing, which enraged Henson, the K-Car had to return to Rusape to refuel. A Police Anti-Terrorist Unit stick supplied the G-Cars with some diesel, refuelling them with watering cans, but jet fuel for them did not arrive until 20 minutes before last light. Thus no fire from the air could be brought to bear on the fleeing men and the stops could not be re-positioned. All that Henson could do, shortly before last light, was to have *Stop Two* and *Eagle Four* uplifted and placed in ambush. Sweeps the next day yielded nothing. Henson recorded the score as three Zanla killed and one captured. Two SKS and two AKs and miscellaneous documents were recovered.

Twenty-four hours later, at 4.15 pm on 13 March,

Henson's Fire Force *Echo* – comprising a K-Car, two G-Cars, a *Dakota* and a *Lynx* – was back in the Masoso Tribal Trust Land in the north-east. Fifteen Zanla were contacted in an area of low, sparsely vegetated hills intersected by thickly bushed river lines running north. Called out to a sighting of ten-fifteen insurgents in a base camp the Fire Force *Echo* had taken off from Mtoko at 3.40 pm. The talk-on was inaccurate and, after some searching, the K-Car finally spotted some insurgents one kilometre to the east and opened fire. *Stop One* was positioned in the north at the confluence of the two river lines. *Stop Two* was placed east of the southern hills. The para sticks were dropped in the south. *Eagles One* and *Two* swept north along the westerly river, contacting and killing two Zanla. *Eagles Three* and *Four* joined *Stop Two* and swept the southern hill from the east. *Eagles Five* and *Six* searched the northern flank of the next range before joining *Eagles One* and *Two* on their advance northwards along the western river. The K-Car killed an insurgent on the southern side of the second range and another in the riverbed ahead of *Eagle One*. *Stop One* then killed an insurgent at the confluence.

The early success of *Eagles One* and *Two*, led by Temporary Corporal Neil Kevin Maclaughlin, was attributed to his clever use of minor tactics. Exposing himself to enemy fire, Maclaughlin placed himself in the open riverbed to control the sweep effectively. After *Eagles Five* and *Six* joined him, Maclaughlin's sweepline was fired on by a third group of four insurgents, hidden in thick cover near a hut on the eastern riverbank. The sweepline returned fire, killing two of the enemy. Undeterred, the remaining Zanla kept firing and knocked down Trooper M.J. Jefferies. They fired at Maclaughlin as he ran forward to Jefferies. Maclaughlin administered first aid before carrying Jefferies to safety, while the aircraft and the sweepline fired to distract the enemy. The K-Car ordered a G-Car to casevac Jefferies, delaying the advance. When Maclaughlin led his men forward again, they killed an insurgent within the first few metres. *Stops Two*, *Eagle Three* and *Four* killed three insurgents on reaching the easterly river line and another on the western flank of the southern hill. They then swept the second range.

Action continued during the night. Ambushing the area between the two ranges of hills, *Stop One* opened fire on locals coming in to remove three undiscovered but wounded insurgents. One local was killed adding to the tally of twelve Zanla dead. The three wounded Zanla escaped into the night. Three SKSs, one DP machine-gun, two FN and six AK rifles, and documents were recovered and handed to the Special Branch at Mount Darwin. Henson concluded that, if he had not had to delay to casevac Jefferies, a complete kill could have been achieved. The discovery of FNs worried him because of the danger which their powerful rounds posed to his troops and aircraft. He recommended the decorating of Corporal Maclaughlin, who was awarded the Bronze Cross of Rhodesia on 8 June.

At 9.30 am on 19 March, Support Commando's Fire Force, commanded by Lieutenant Prinsloo, contacted ten more insurgents in the Masoso Tribal Trust Land, after a sighting by a Selous Scouts OP in a hilly, bushy area with a river flowing eastwards across its northern sector. Prinsloo had *Stops One* and *Two* placed in the west at the foot of the first hill. The paratroops were dropped with *Eagle Two* across the river, *Eagle Three* to the west on the southern flank of the hill and *Eagle One* just south of the river in the west. *Stops One* and *Two* swept up the eastern stream of a tributary and then worked back down it towards the river where *Eagle Two* joined them. They moved back towards the main hill at the foot of which was the insurgent base camp behind a rocky outcrop. Half-way to the hill they killed three Zanla. They moved on to the base camp where they met *Eagle Three* who had come in from the west along the hill. *Eagle Three* continued along the hill and killed an insurgent in front of a small village before moving north. *Stops One* and *Two* and *Eagle Two* moved north. *Eagle One*, in the west, moved south and immediately killed an insurgent. Shortly afterwards they killed another and then another further on, before sweeping back to the north. In all seven insurgents were killed and three escaped. Seven SKSs and a nearly new AK were recovered along with webbing, grenades, magazines, ammunition and documents which were handed to the Special Branch at Rushinga. The OP continued to observe the area. Prinsloo was complimented for a well controlled action.

Support Commando seems to have been stood down for a rest but was back in action on 1 April, when Corporal Christopher William Rogers and his section were pinned down by accurate fire from four men at close range. Rogers and another RLI soldier were wounded but Rogers continued to exchange heavy fire with the insurgents and managed to kill two of them. Roger's sustained fire enabled other troops to close with and eliminate the entire group. He was awarded a Military Forces Commendation (Operational) for his deeds.

The first majority rule election was approaching and it was known that Zanla and ZPRA would attempt to deter the Africans from voting by sending into Rhodesia a substantial number of their more experienced men to ensure that the tribesmen did not vote. Measures were taken to counter them. Later in April 1979 there was a mass mobilization of all territorials and army and police reservists. Before then the Fire Forces went to work. Support Commando was deployed on Monday 2 April. A small sub-unit was detached to provide protection for some of the more vulnerable polling stations and the remainder of the Commando was divided into two Fire Forces, one

stationed at Grand Reef airfield, near Umtali, and the other at Inyanga, further to the north on the Mocambican border.

By 1 pm, that day, 2 April, Henson and 36 Support Commando men (flying in a K-Car, three G-Cars, a *Lynx* and a *Dakota*) were in action in what would be a four and a half hour long contact with an unknown number of Zanla. The Zanla had been spotted by an OP, manned by Peter Curley of the Selous Scouts, just north east of the Inyanga Downs and close to the Gairezi River on the hilly eastern border.

Curley thought he could see a weapon in the doorway of a hut but was not sure. Henson knew that Fire Force would not have been summoned without the Selous Scout being confident that there were Zanla present. Thus Henson put his stops down, placing *Stop One* in the south on the western flank of a long range running northwards. *Stop Three* was placed in the middle and *Stop Two* in the north. The para sticks were dropped to form a sweepline to search three thickly bushed river lines which flowed eastwards to a river at the foot of the eastern range. The southern end of the sweep encountered thirteen insurgents and killed them before discovering their camp on the side of a spur. Most were killed in the main river valley. Henson noted that the Zanla had adopted the tactic of running, hiding and then throwing grenades. In support of the troops, the K-Car fired eighteen 20mm rounds and the *Lynx* dropped three Frantans. Henson praised his troops for their good soldiering, saying "the troopies were complete stars". The troops managed to lose two MAG belts, two sleeping bags and two pangas and sheaths.

After being called to a sighting by an OP, Henson's Fire Force (36 men, a K-Car, 3 G-Cars, a *Lynx* and a *Dakota*) at 9.30 am on the next day, 3 April, contacted an unknown number of insurgents on the Wensleydale Estate, a white-owned farm, north of Headlands. The contact lasted one hour on a thickly bushed rocky ridge. Henson strung out his troops in a sweepline in heavy bush from a river in the north to south of the ridge. The capture of two Zanla was immediately followed by a K-Car kill and one by the sweepline. One AKM and two SKS rifles were recovered.

Success came again that day for Henson. At 3 pm his Fire Force (still 36 men and a K-Car, 3 G-Cars, a *Lynx* and a *Dakota*), contacted ten Zanla on the Rathcline Estate, north west of Inyanga Village. Again they had been summoned by an OP. This contact lasted one and a half hours in thick bush in front of a hill round which the Inyangombe River flowing north, curved round to the east. The K-Car killed three insurgents while the troops killed four, two in the bush, one on the hill and one over the hill by the river. Four AK and three SKS rifles were recovered and handed to the Special Branch at Inyati.

Success continued the next morning, on 4 April, but

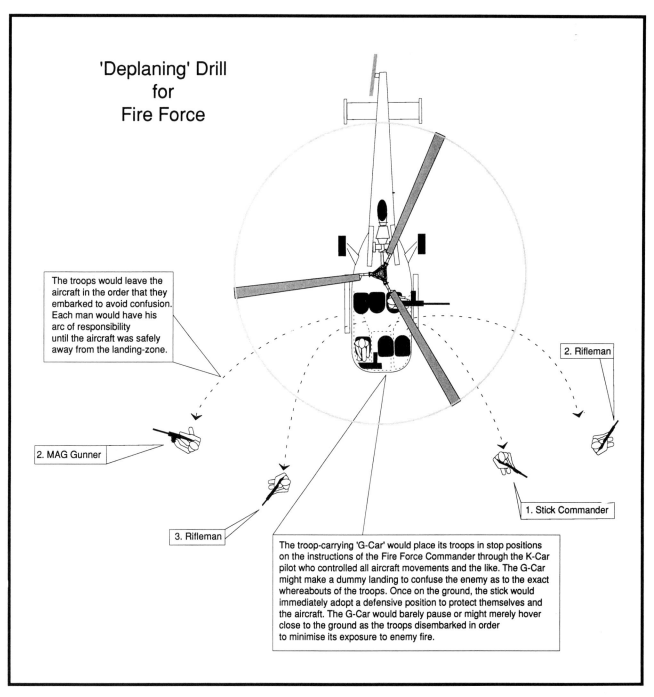

'Deplaning' Drill
for
Fire Force

The troops would leave the aircraft in the order that they embarked to avoid confusion. Each man would have his arc of responsibility until the aircraft was safely away from the landing-zone.

2. Rifleman

2. MAG Gunner

1. Stick Commander

3. Rifleman

The troop-carrying 'G-Car' would place its troops in stop positions on the instructions of the Fire Force Commander through the K-Car pilot who controlled all aircraft movements and the like. The G-Car might make a dummy landing to confuse the enemy as to the exact whereabouts of the troops. Once on the ground, the stick would immediately adopt a defensive position to protect themselves and the aircraft. The G-Car would barely pause or might merely hover close to the ground as the troops disembarked in order to minimise its exposure to enemy fire.

cost the life of Lance Corporal M. Overbeek. Fifty-six Support Commando men led by Major Henson were called to a sighting by Sergeant 'Jenks' Jenkinson of a Selous Scouts' OP of some 50 Zanla in a base camp on the Rathcline Estate. At 10.30 am contact was made and action continued for eight hours on a square mountain, crowned by a series of summits and stretching four kilometres in one direction and two in the other. Facing 50 Zanla, Henson called in an initial strike by a *Canberra* bomber which hit the target with precision as the Fire Force's K-Car, three G-Cars, *Lynx* and *Dakota*, arrived.

On the summit of the northern hill, the stick of Temporary Corporal Peter Malcolm Binion was surprised by point blank rifle fire from two Zanla hidden in a clump of rocks which killed Overbeek. Binion returned the fire. Then, while his stick put down covering fire, Binion dashed forward into the open to kill the two insurgents. Shortly afterwards, Binion received a minor shrapnel wound from an exploding RPG rocket, fired at short range by a third Zanla. Ignoring his wound, Binion closed in and killed this man. A further insurgent was killed close by.

Later the sweep killed two Zanla on the western end of

that hill, two on the eastern flank of the second northern hill, one on the west of its southern flank. Two more insurgents were killed near a stream that ran to the southeast across the feature. The K-Car killed an insurgent at the southern base of the easternmost summit. In all twelve insurgents, dressed in the green uniforms of Mocambique's FPLM, were killed and one wounded escaped. Ten AKMs, two SKSs and an RPG-7 were recovered. Corporal Binion was awarded the Bronze Cross of Rhodesia for this and numerous other successful actions.

On the way back to base, the K-Car began to vibrate, forcing the pilot, Luigi Mantovani, to land it. It was found that the blades were so badly damaged by ground fire that flying was impossible. Mantovani radioed for new blades. The request was relayed to No. 7 Squadron at New Sarum, outside Salisbury, which sent new blades immediately by *Dakota* to Grand Reef and by G-Car to the stranded K-Car. Mantovani, the technician and Henson fitted the blades and the afternoon light was going when the K-Car lifted off. The technician, however, had been unable to calibrate the blades in the bush and Mantovani had to make frequent landings as the continuing vibrations affected the engine.

All Fire Forces were scoring similar successes. For example, on 5 April, a Fire Force from One Commando, 1RLI, commanded by Major Frederick Watts, contacted two groups of insurgents totaling 27 men and killed 21 of them. In the next eleven days, until 16 April, Watts, his men and the aircraft of his Fire Force eliminated 106 Zanla.

Corporal Binion again scored at 3 pm on 7 April, when Henson's Support Commando men contacted seven insurgents, dressed in green FPLM uniforms and kit in the extreme south of the Weya Tribal Trust Land, just north of the white farming area of Headlands. One insurgent escaped and six were killed with Binion accounting for four of them on a low ridge just north east of a high rounded hill. The K-Car killed the fifth insurgent on the ridge and the sixth at its western end. Rifles, grenades and ammunition were picked up and handed to the Special Branch at Inyanga.

On 11 April, Support and Three Commandos and a detachment from the Rhodesian African Rifles were sent into Mocambique to attack a complex of five staging camps which were believed to hold up to 250 Zanla. The operation was aborted when the helicopters and *Dakotas* were circling the camps because Zanla had already left. Support Commando returned to Grand Reef where it was reinforced by its Inyanga detachment. That day, Rhodesia mobilised its territorials and reservists to protect the election. They would be stood down on 24 April.

At 10.15 am on the next morning, 12 April, Henson and 28 of his men, supported by a K-Car, three G-Cars, a *Lynx* and a *Dakota*, made contact with an unknown number of Zanla in the Sabi Tribal Trust Land east of Buhera, after a sighting by an OP. The contact lasted four hours. For once the terrain was favourable and was divided by converging river lines, flowing eastwards towards the Sabi River. The K-Car killed one insurgent at the confluence of the rivers. A G-Car killed insurgents in a village in the south-west. *Stop Two* was landed astride the river in the west and killed an insurgent immediately as did *Eagle One* after dropping on the most southerly tributary. An insurgent was captured near the northern tributary and the remainder were killed just north of the confluence by the sweepline. The final score was fifteen insurgents, all dressed in FPLM kit, killed and one captured. Rifles, machine-guns, grenades, magazines and ammunition were picked up and handed to the Special Branch at Dorowa.

Four days later, on 16 April, Henson, a K-Car, two G-Cars, a *Dakota*, a *Lynx* and 29 of his men were summoned to a sighting by an OP of an unknown number of Zanla on the northern flank of a twin peaked mountain in the Zimbiti Tribal Trust Land, north-east of Inyanga. Henson dropped his para sticks to the north and formed a sweepline from his helicopter-borne troops on the eastern end of the northern flank. When the sweep reached a stream near a saddle at 2 pm, it encountered fifteen Zanla in FPLM uniforms, killing ten of them. Five escaped. Rifles, grenades and ammunition were handed to the Special Branch at Inyanga. Henson was particularly pleased by the performance of his troops during the six hours of the operation.

At 12 noon on 17 April (the day that the four days of voting by all inhabitants over the age of 18 began), Henson and 27 of his men, supported by a K-Car, two G-Cars, a *Lynx* and a *Dakota* again made contact with the enemy, this time seven Zanla, in the south of the Chiduku Tribal Trust Land, west of Umtali. The contact lasted four and a half hours among three and a half kilometres of kraal lines with brick buildings, rubber hedges and thousands of mango trees stretching along an east-west road, parallel to a river which also flowed east-west. The K-Car killed insurgents on the road just short of a stream which flowed south to the river. The sweepline killed insurgents at a house by the stream and in the houses either side of the road. Trooper M.C. Moore was killed at a pair of houses across the river in the south-east. In all nine green and blue clad insurgents were killed and two escaped. Ten rifles, grenades and ammunition were picked up and were handed to the Special Branch at Inyazura.

On 19 April, Support Commando's Fire Force *Bravo*, commanded by Lieutenant Prinsloo, responded to a sighting by a Selous Scouts OP of ten Zanla in a village, close to the last contact in the Chiduku. The result was a contact with thirteen insurgents, starting at 10 am and lasting four hours in a series of kraal complexes along a river.

CLOCKWISE FROM TOP: Operational 'Stick' deplanes in thick bush country; Missed and mourned by his men when he was killed in an *Alouette* crash, former RLI Colonel 'The King' Dave Parker shortly after the author left him at Mount Darwin; Temporary Base in the south-east of the country and, a pair of RLI 'Troopies' prepare for a 300ft para-jump into a 'Terr' contact area.

When the Fire Force was overhead the K-Car threw out a smoke marker. The Selous Scouts OP callsign *One Three Golf* indicated the target with smoke and a number of people were seen to run from the kraal. The K-Car fired on them and stops were put in with *Stop Two* to the south on the river. The paras were dropped in the west and advanced east through the kraals. After killing the majority of the insurgents, *Eagle Four* was approaching yet another kraal cautiously when Trooper R.F. Poole was shot through the chest. Corporal Binion, the MAG gunner, ran to help but Trooper Poole was mortally wounded and died. The K-Car killed the man responsible as he fled from a hut. A feature of the contact was that the insurgents were wearing civilian clothes over their denims and tried to conceal their weapons under their clothes. Some left their weapons in the kraals and ran. Four AKs were handed to the Special Branch who removed four more from burning buildings. The final tally was ten Zanla killed, two captured and one escaped. The death of three members of the Mortar Troop of Support Commando had reduced it to 13 men and to restore their morale, they were sent on four days' leave in Salisbury.

A military spokesman said on 21 April that during the elections 230 guerrillas had been killed for the loss of 12 regular soldiers and security force auxiliaries. There had been a total of 13 attacks on polling stations, most of them at night and all, according to officials, 'ineffectual'. The final result of the elections was announced on 24 April, with Muzorewa's UANC winning 67.27% of the votes and securing 51 of the 80 seats in the new Legislative Assembly of Zimbabwe-Rhodesia. The poll had been over 60 per cent and Zanla and ZPRA were stunned by the tribesmen's defiance of their orders not to vote. As Zanla and ZPRA went to ground and their leaders left the country for orders, the Rhodesian security forces kept up the pressure.

To harass Zanla further, Combined Operations Headquarters proposed *Operation Oppress*, an attack by Support Commando, on Sunday, 29 April, on freshly trained reinforcements expected at Petulia base, near Chicualacuala, fifty kilometres inside the southern Mocambican Gaza Province. The aim was to destroy the base and kill or capture any Zanla present. This logistics and transit base comprised three camps, with a resident section of 22 Zanla. The plan envisaged a combined air and ground attack with the RhAF supplying two *Hunters*, two *Canberras*, seven G-Cars, three K-Cars, two AB205A *Cheetahs*, two *Lynxes*, and 3 *Dakotas* (including a Command *Dakota* equipped with radios and teleprinters to control the operation from the air).

At Grand Reef on 28 April, Support Commando, reinforced by the Mortar Troop, was issued extra light machine-guns and RPG-7 rocket launchers and drew as much ammunition and grenades as the men could carry.

Each rifleman took ten 20-round magazines and 100 loose rounds in addition to numerous grenades, extra machine-gun belts and RPG-7 rockets. In the evening, the Commando flew to Buffalo Range to be briefed by intelligence officers. It was explained that the base was a staging post simply monitored but not attacked by Rhodesian forces. As an influx of Zanla into Rhodesia was expected, it was now to be attacked and at least two members of the Zanla hierarchy (dressed in camouflage uniforms with hammer and sickle insignia on the collars) and Eastern Bloc military advisers would be encountered. Such men had to be captured if possible. Combined Operations wanted at very least one Zanla guerrilla to interrogate. Another aspect was that the approach road was to be mined with experimental landmines to delay any reaction by Mocambique's FPLM. In the event, the survival of Support Commando depended on the mines.

On 29 April the *Hunters* attacked the target with Golf bombs, followed by the *Canberras* with 300 Mk II *Alpha* bombs each. The 50 men of Support Commando, flying in the eight G-Cars and two AB205A *Cheetahs* with an escort of two K-Cars and two *Lynxes*, landed on the fringes of the camps in the brown fog of dust and smoke of the airstrikes. Sergeant Frank Terrell, a former British marine commando serving in Support Commando, recalls the sound of continuous explosions of burning ammunition, the methodical reply of an anti-aircraft gun to the *Hunters'* repeated attacks. Eventually a *Hunter* silenced it. The RLI troops began their advance and first encountered a Zanla kitchen littered with dead. They shot dazed Zanla amid unexploded red-painted round *Alpha* bombs. The fires were burning so fiercely that the troops could not at first penetrate the lines of bunkers, weapon pits and tents. The camp was littered with equipment, Soviet Army helmets, abandoned and destroyed anti-aircraft guns. The RLI troopers cleared the trenches and bunkers and dismantled the heavy weapons. A huge haul of rifles and equipment was collected but there was no further sign of Zanla who had clearly fled, probably before the attack. The weapons, AK and SKS rifles, grenades and three 14.5mm and a 12.7mm machine-guns, were loaded on the *Cheetahs* once the area was secure. Uniforms, packs, web-equipment, propaganda leaflets and enormous quantities of tinned food were burned.

Major Henson then ordered the troops to search the surrounding bush which yielded six empty pistol holsters and a leather briefcase, containing documents bearing names and weapon numbers, messages, letters and photographs of uniformed Zanla in the company of East German or Soviet military instructors. A follow up was instituted and Terrell believes that the troops were closing on their quarry – six high-ranking Zanla officers – but ran out of time. The Command *Dakota*, carrying Lieutenant-Colonel Brian Robinson and Group Captain [later Air

THE SELOUS SCOUTS

Apart from the RLI Fire Force, the Selous Scouts was the unit most closely involved in bringing in a helicopter-led strike force. Most of their activities were clandestine, except when they combined with the Rhodesian SAS and the RLI to hit hard at cross-border targets in Mocambique. These pictures show such a raid, towards the end of the war, involving various Special Force units, *Eland* armoured cars and artillery with jet fighter and bomber back-up as well as chopper support. The bridge blown was deep inside Mocambique on the rail-link with Maputo. Founding commander of the Selous Scouts, one of the more effective southern African counter-insurgency units, Colonel Ron Reid-Daly, top right.

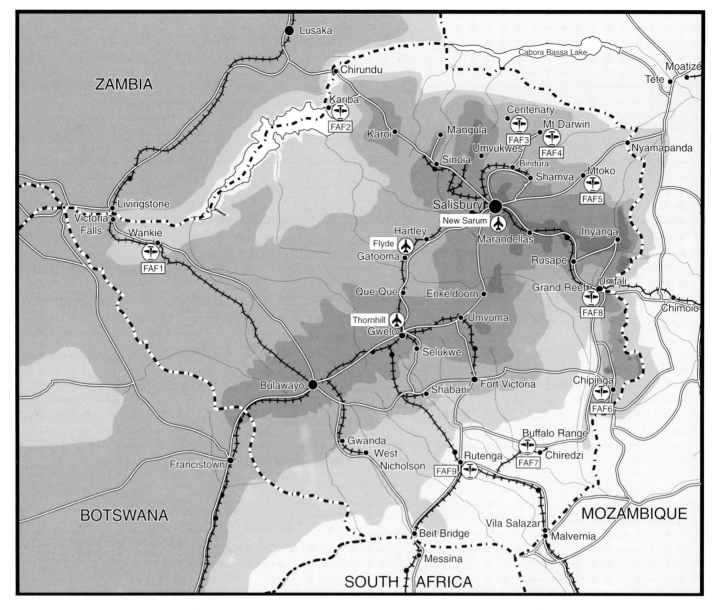

Rhodesian Air Force Forward Air Fields (FAFs) throughout the country. The main RhAF bases were at New Sarum and at Thornhill.

Vice Marshal] Hugh Slatter called off the pursuit because the remaining light was needed to airlift the attacking force out. The airlift was threatened by the approach of an FPLM reaction convoy until its trucks detonated the landmines in the road.

Although Support Commando had not secured a prisoner, *Operation Oppress* was pronounced a success because 28 Zanla had been killed without loss. As had happened so often before in the Rhodesian war, a large number of Zanla had vacated the camp on the previous night, 28 April, but Support Commando was to kill many of the escapees within days. On 14 May, it killed or captured 21 Zanla, including several high ranking officials, from a large group which had recently crossed from Mozambique. A follow-up on the border on 16 May resulted in a running, day-long fight with the survivors. Two of the dead were wearing Ethiopian camouflage uniforms with hammer-and-sickle insignia on the collar.

In a seven-week period in April/May 1979, Support Commando, 1RLI, under the command of Major Nigel Henson, together with its supporting aircraft, accounted for 165 insurgents in Fire Force operations and on *Operation Oppress*, and had seized large amounts of heavy weapons. Henson's skill, aggression and other qualities as a leader earned him a recommendation for the award of the Officer of the Order of the Legion of Merit (Military Division, Combatant). By 20 May *The Sunday Mail* reported that worn-out, dispirited insurgents were surrendering. "Their morale is shattered," remarked a senior police officer who claimed that hundreds more were longing to give up but that they feared execution by the fanatical cadres "trained in communist Ethiopia by Cubans".

CHAPTER 13

THE EARLY DAYS OF HELICOPTERS IN SOUTH AFRICA

In 1953 the decision was made by the South African Air Force to acquire long range Shackleton aircraft from Britain for reconnaissance and air-sea rescue purposes.

The South African Navy at that stage relied on ageing high-speed, deep-sea motor launches for search and rescue purposes. With the arrival of the *Shackletons*, the maritime requirement for motor launches fell away, but there was still be a need for inshore air-sea rescue craft. Helicopters were ideally suited for that purpose and in use elsewhere in the world with excellent results.

Helicopters could also be used in other roles such as assistance to the Forestry Department to combat fires in the reserves or to help the police or for flood and snow relief.

The price of a *Sikorsky* S-55, with spares, at that time was 114 000 Pounds. Feasibility studies on the suitability of the *Bristol Sycamore 171*, the *Hiller H21A* and the *Bell 47* were also carried out.

The South African Air Force (SAAF) made a decision to purchase the S-55 which finally arrived in 1955. Their prime role was to be for rescue services along South Africa's coast; they were transferred to No. 1 Marinecraft Unit and based at Air Force Station Langebaan Road, north of Cape Town.

The mainstay of the South African Air Force rotor-winged contingent for many years, was the *Sikorsky* S-55, seen here in SAAF livery. The first chopper to actually fly in South Africa, though, was the *Sikorsky* S-51 shown on page 125. It was used mainly in anti-tsetse fly spraying programmes in the Lowveld.

First, more pilots had to be converted to rotor craft and the first to be trained was Lt Membe de Jager. At the end of 1954, Lt Jeff Tatham – formerly of 28 Squadron and who had originally flown S-51s – and de Jager were the only current helicopter pilots in the Air Force. The second man to be converted was Lt Vernon Kruger. He was signed out competent to carry passengers in August, 1955.

There were no formal selection procedures for helicopter pilots. They were simply asked by Headquarters whether they would like to fly the machines and if the answer was in the affirmative, that person was posted to Langebaan Road for the course. During that period, because Tatham was the only rotor-wing instructor in the Air Force, the task of training these pilots fell on his shoulders.

In 1955 the *Sikorsky* was regarded by Air Force pilots as something of a curiosity. The SAAF could not define a role for the aircraft and most of the sorties were training flights with very few operational assignments.

Kruger recalls that during training, the instructor sat in the middle seat, with the student in the front. Behind the instructor was a bench; the S-51 was able to carry a maximum of three persons. It was during this phase that most emphasis was placed on achieving the correct centre of gravity and, for that reason, a 'weight and balance sheet' was always carried onboard.

Towards June 1956 Lt Tatham was sent by the Air Force to the Sikorsky factory in the United States to convert to the more advanced S-55s. He returned to South Africa with the first aircraft, registration A-4, in July that year.

The new *Sikorsky* was shipped out by sea, in crates, and assembled at Ysterplaat in Cape Town. The initial paint finish was all-silver, with a yellow band on the tail-boom close to the tail rotor; superimposed was a red arrow with the letters *DANGER/GEVAAR*. The serial number was also painted onto the tailboom as well as on the nose. The roundels of the SAAF were fixed on the fuselage, just behind the main gear box.

The first S-55 flight in South Africa occurred on 1 August that year and the aircraft was accepted by the SAAF three weeks later. Not long afterwards, Lt Tatham took his aircraft on a maiden extended flight to Waterkloof Air Force base in Pretoria. The route was via Beaufort West, Tempe airfield, Bloemfontein and finally Waterkloof. It was a distance of about 1 600 kilometres and took two days.

The aerodynamics of helicopters was something of an unknown factor in the SAAF in those early days; often pilots would find themselves in situations where the aircraft "decided to take over" and control was, as one pilot phrased it, "between God and machine".

On this occasion, Tatham and Kruger were flying between Beaufort West and Tempe at about 10 000 feet; Kruger was at the controls. Tatham relaxed in his seat, monitoring his charts because Kruger had no dual-training experience.

For much of the distance the flight went well. Harmse, the flight engineer sat behind the others, looking out of the slightly opened rear hatch at the terrain below.

Suddenly, the chopper flipped over onto its side at an angle of almost 90 degrees. Tatham immediately became a ball of energy; hands and feet simultaneously reaching for the controls and shouting, "I've got her, I've got her. …What the hell did you do?".

Kruger, of course, had no idea what had happened. The chopper had just flipped over; and that was bad because he was also concerned about his chances of qualifying on the S-55. He replied with the standard response, "I did nothing, the stick just jumped out of my hand!"

Tatham, clearly not accepting Kruger's version, thought the pilot had jerked the cyclic to the side and took over the flight from there on. Harmse, in the back, had meanwhile broken into a sweat; he opened the hatch a little farther to cool down. The fact that helicopter crews in those days did not fly with parachutes when at altitude did not help either. To the flight engineer these strange craft were still very much of a mystery.

The flight continued. Tatham and his crew had settled down after the incident, when quite suddenly, the chopper was on its side again. The aircraft had once more "taken control". Whereas a split second ago there was a solid fuselage between Harmse and the ground, now there was nothing. He screamed once and clung to one of the spars behind the cockpit.

Once again Tatham brought the *Sikorsky* under control. This time the flight continued at a much lower level and without incident. On reaching the Free State capital, Tatham decided to spend the next day examining the aircraft's flight controls and rigging. Nothing unusual was uncovered and the men carried on to Pretoria, but still not at altitude.

Kruger recalls:

"One thing we did learn, if that (the unusual attitude) is going happen, it is better to be a little closer to the ground. Is is bloody awful up there in the S-55 – sitting at 10 000 feet. It is definitely not fun."

Tatham wrote to the *Sikorsky* manufacturers, describing the incident. He received from them a document explaining the dangers of blade stall. From then on the S-55s were flown at 200 feet. "If we were going to fall out of the sky, it would be better to come in from 200 feet than from a great height. We had plenty of fun trying to unravel helicopter aerodynamics in those days," he said.

Tatham's main task from then on was to train additional pilots as more *Sikorskys* had arrived in the country.

The A-6 was expected early 1957. There was no formal course for the S-55 and the conversion onto type consisted of three hours dual. A pre-requirement was the S-51 qualification.

The next pilots to be trained on the S-55 after Kruger were Lt Buks Smal and Major B. Wigget. But this course was without event.

The first real 'incident' occurred in August, 1957 when a S-55 was damaged when Tatham and De Jager were carrying out an autorotation with an A-4 fitted with floats. These were only used when maritime exercises were carried out.

The A-4 had a straight tailboom and any harsh flares or hard landings would cause the rotors to come dangerously close to the tailboom. On this occasion, over the sea, Tatham flared too high with the result that the aircraft, literally, fell out of the sky. It hit the water hard, causing the rotors to strike the tailboom.

Subsequently, the tailbooms of the A-5 and A-6 were given a ten degree droop to prevent a recurrence of this mishap.

The S-55 was extensively deployed in the role for which it was intended; air-sea rescue. It was equipped with hoists and floats which allowed the crew to perform air-sea rescue and, if necessary, land on water.

In conjunction with high-speed motor launches, the SAAF had an extremely efficient air-sea rescue service along the southern tip of Africa. In addition to a strop fitted to the hoist cable, a net was available; this could be lowered into the sea and scoop a downed pilot from the water. By flying the chopper at a slow, forward speed, anyone floating on the surface could be manoeuvred into the net and raised with the hoist.

The scoop net was big enough to take a one-man dinghy, but it was too bulky to fit inside the cabin. When used, it was attached to the hoist and strung outside the fuselage; the flight engineer had to physically hold on to the net to stabilise it in the airflow.

On longer flights, it was secured to the fuselage to prevent it breaking loose and damaging the rotors.

Other tasks performed by these helicopters were aerial observation for artillery exercises, liaison work as well as general communications.

The use of the helicopter as an assault transport aircraft had been tested by the United States Marine Corps in the early fifties and choppers were deployed in Korea with encouraging results. The British in Malaya were also active; S-55s of RAF Squadron 848 carried 200 000 pounds of freight and deployed 10 000 troops during their first year of operations.

Initially, the South African Defence Force showed some interest in the deployment of helicopters, other than for air-sea rescue duties; the concept of troop movements in military situations was an early priority. Africa was showing evidence of political disenchantment with the colonial powers and ultimately, it was accepted, South Africa could be affected by unrest.

Initial training with the South African Army consisted largely of exercises where troops – acting as stopper groups – were deployed around an objective or target. The tactical value of the helicopter was accepted when the rapid deployment and uplifting of troops in a bush warfare scenario was acted out.

But the *Sikorskys* were vulnerable. Consequently, the tactical situation dictated that S-55s should not be used over any hostile areas of operation and that friendly forces would have to be dropped by chopper some distance from any enemy position. The bottom line was that trooping choppers should not be exposed to enemy fire. That basic rule is still enforced in southern Africa today.

The first 'political' use of helicopters in southern Africa came early 1960. During that year, the Anti-Pass Law protest campaign was initiated by the ANC and PAC movements and events quickly forced the government to declare a State of Emergency.

Helicopters from 17 Squadron were called on to give

LEFT: An S-55 involved in mountain rescue in the Drakensberg mountains.
ABOVE: A *Sikorsky* S-55 fitted with flotation tanks for Air Force maritime rescue work, mainly near Langebaan in the Western Cape.

close support to the SA Police and to assist with riot control. Kruger was tasked to fly command and control for the Police who were monitoring about 30 000 black activists marching on the Houses of Parliament in Cape Town, late March 1960. There was no violence, but it was a close thing.

It was clear to all that a new era for the use of helicopters in the South African Air Force had arrived.

Another milestone in the history of rotor craft in the South African Air Force was the purchase, from France, of seven *Alouette* II helicopters during the latter half of 1960. These arrived in the country in October that year. This turbine-powered helicopter had proved its worth as a very successful light helicopter and had established an altitude record of 26 937 feet in Europe in June 1955.

As far as the South Africans were concerned, it was a readily available helicopter with high performance capability and appeared to be the machine best suited for African conditions. The *Alouette* II had certainly proved its mettle with the French armed forces during the war in Algeria.

The rationale behind buying the *Alouette* II was that training pilots on S-55s was too expensive. They were also heavy on fuel. In any event, the S-55s were being used quite extensively on other tasks and were not always available for training runs. Also, the *Alouette* was easier to handle.

The S-55 was a huge craft and somewhat ungainly for command and control purposes during crowd control; a lighter helicopter was needed. At this stage there was a tendency worldwide to move towards turbine-power and the *Alouette* II seemed the logical choice.

The *Alouettes* II taken into service by the SAAF were able to carry five personnel, including the pilot, and it could mount a 37mm rocket pod weapons system. This capability was never instituted by the South African Air Force in any of their wars, largely because of political pressure from the French.

Meanwhile, the SAAF had also considered buying the French SO.1221 *Djinn* helicopter manufactured by Sud-Oest. But it was only a two-seater and was regarded as too small and frail for local conditions where long distances were a factor. In addition, there was some doubt as to the performance capability of the *Djinn* in the kind of high density altitude found on the South African Highveld.

The *Alouette* II was soon put to operational use. In December 1960, Kruger was told to fetch the first *Alouette* II which had been assembled in Pretoria and fly it to Bizana in Pondoland, now Transkei. It was to be used in riot control during a State of Emergency declared by the government in a bid to quell unrest initiated by black political activists.

Not long afterwards South Africa opened negotiations with the French Government to acquire the more advanced *Alouette* IIIs, the natural successor to the successful *Alouette* II. Also, Washington was starting to moot the possibility of an arms embargo against South Africa because of its racial policies.

Approaches had been made by the Bell Helicopter Company to sell the 206 *Jetranger* to the SAAF, but the government vetoed the purchase because of the possibility of sanctions. If these were imposed, spares would be a major problem.

In December 1961, Kruger – by then a Captain – and a Captain Steyn flew to France to undergo the *Alouette* II*I* conversion course.

The first *Alouette* II*I*s were flown out, by airfreight, to South Africa and landed at AFB Waterkloof on 9 February 1962. They were airborne over South African soil for the first time five days later.

Kruger and Steyn were the only qualified pilots on type and therefore carried out all the initial test flights. It was not long before *Alouette* II*I*s were seen in action along the length of South Africa's operational area with Black Africa.

CHAPTER 14

SOUTH AFRICA'S BORDER CONFLICT

A Generation of War
War Correspondent Willem Steenkamp
Assesses the Background to Conflict

Southern Africa's longest war effectively ended on 1 November 1988, when South Africa and the South West African People's Organisation (Swapo) finally called it quits, twenty-three long years after the first shot had been fired. It had gone on for so long that for several generations of people of all races it was hard to believe that peace had come; that (on the South African side at least) a father and son could be wearing the same campaign medal for fighting on the same front but fifteen years apart. In the latter stages, in fact, the brunt of the war was borne on both sides by young men who had not even been conceived when it had started.

Wounded South African soldier is moved to a waiting *Puma* during *Operation Meebos*. As with most other cross-border raids, South African casualties were usually about one or two per cent of those of the enemy, in this case Swapo.

To understand the Border War it is necessary also to know something about the territory which, in the past two hundred years, has been called by various names, most recently South West Africa/Namibia and now Namibia.

Physically it is immense, particularly by the cramped standards of many nations in Europe and elsewhere: 823 000 square kilometres, bounded in the west by the Atlantic Ocean, in the east by Botswana, in the south by South Africa and in the north by Angola and Zambia. Most of it is an elevated plateau between 900 and 1 200 metres above sea-level, with mountain ranges running north to south for most of its length.

It is, to use a worn-out phrase, a land of contrasts. It has an almost infinite variety of terrain; often the landscape varies so abruptly and dramatically that the traveller can scarcely believe that he is still inside the same set of borders. It has the Namib, one of the oldest deserts in the world, that runs down its western side and forms the bleak, harshly beautiful littoral that is known as the 'Skeleton Coast' because it is a centuries-old killer of men and ships, although it is redeemed by the diamonds and other minerals found under its deadly sands.

For thirty years the Imperial flag waved over German South West. The Germans were energetic developers who provided the territory with its first roads, railways, health services and structure of civil government. At the same time they ruled it sternly and, as with all colonial powers, frequently without much concern for their subjects' property and other rights.

Then in 1915 the South Africans invaded on behalf of Britain and conquered the Germans. After World War 1 the League of Nations entrusted South West Africa to South Africa as a Class C mandate, to be governed as a virtual extra province for the betterment of its inhabitants. The mandate laid down certain requirements and required the South African government to report annually to the League of Nations.

When the moribund League of Nations officially died immediately after World War 2 South Africa undertook to continue administering South West Africa in the spirit of the old mandate, although denying that ultimate responsibility had passed from the League of Nations to the United Nations. The UN, however, maintained unsuccessfully that South West Africa should be placed under its trusteeship.

In 1949 the government of Smuts's successor, Dr D.F. Malan, granted South West Africa a greater measure of autonomy. The all-white Legislative Assembly which had been founded after World War 1 became a fully elected body and substantial numbers of governmental functions were transferred to it, so that it enjoyed greater autonomy than any of South Africa's own provinces. At the same time South Africa remained in overall control and South

CLOCKWISE FROM TOP: While the war in the air included modern jets, supersonic missiles and helicopters, the ground war in this remote African region was fought in a most basic manner, usually on foot, often in conjunction with armoured vehicles but sometimes employing the most pragmatic means of making contact with the enemy, in this instance horses. A mounted patrol checks movement at an Ovambo village not far from the Angolan border; Unita troops clamber over a downed Angolan Air Force Mi-17 helicopter; Killing fields on the Angolan border from a SAAF *Alouette*.

West Africa was represented in the South African Parliament by six MPs and four senators.

In 1953 the UN appointed a committee to report on conditions in South West Africa because South Africa had refused to do so, and in 1955 and 1956 the issue of who should control South West Africa twice more ended up in the World Court.

At this stage the seeds of the eventual South West African insurgency were sown, 1 400 kilometres away from the territory itself, when a 33-year-old former railway policeman and World War 2 veteran called Herman Toivo ja Toivo living in Cape Town founded the political movement called the Ovambo Peoples Congress (OPO).

Before embarking on the story of the border war, we should say something about the population of what is now known as Namibia. The territory lacks many things, but most of all it lacks people. In its entire vast extent – three times the size of West Germany there live just over a million people; in November 1986 the-then General Officer Comanding South West Africa, Major-General Georg Meiring, put it even more aptly when he described SWA/Namibia as being four-fifths the size of South Africa, but with the same population as the British holiday resort of Blackpool.

There has been a considerable amount of urbanisation, but most of these groups are still closely linked to their traditional stamping-grounds. The Kaokolanders, Ovambos, Kavangos and Caprivians have traditional tribal homelands in the far north, immediately below the border with Angola and Zambia. The whites, Hereros and coloureds mainly inhabit the central part of the country and the Namas the dry south. The demographic distribution largely determined the battle zone in the border war; it is no accident that most of the infiltration and fighting took place in central Ovamboland, for that is where about 25 per cent of all Namibians live, including the Kwanyama and Ondongo tribes.

It is an indication of the low intensity of the border war that during its course the population increased rather than declined, and no part of the territory was laid waste. It is remarkable, in fact, how little the struggle impinged on daily life in this vast country.

South of the black tribal areas it was always barely noticeable except for the occasional urban bomb blast and a couple of small-scale Swapo raids on white-owned farms in the midlands, and in places such as Ovamboland the regional economies actually benefited from the conflict; ironically, probably the greatest consequence of the war was the accelerated abolition of most segregation laws and the inclusion of blacks in the previously all-white administration, so that by 1988 the territory's internal government was mainly black.

Real political change only really took place in 1960, when the OPO became the South West African Peoples

Organisation.

No doubt the new name helped to broaden Swapo's popular support, but (given the absence of any impartial survey of its popular support) it does not appear to have turned it into a truly representative organisation – possibly a reflection of the territory's history of internal conflict and ethnic division. Although its political wing recruited sympathisers from members of all or most other ethno-cultural groups, it still remained strongly Ovambo-based in the years to come, particularly as regards its military wing which did most of the fighting.

This can be seen from the fact that about 95 per cent of all Swapo insurgents killed or captured in the decades-long border war which was soon to break out were Ovambos.

A provisional Swapo headquarters was set up in Dar es Salaam, Tanzania, in March of 1961.

A more exact dating, however, is to be found in the fact that in 1962, soon after Swapo had set up its headquarters in Lusaka, it founded a military wing called Plan the 'Peoples Liberation Army of Namibia'. Given the South African government's complete disinclination, then or later, to yield to Swapo or any other 'liberation organisation' this effectively set the stage for a shooting war.

All this time Swapo had been recruiting fighters for its embryonic military wing. Progress was slow at first, but eventually some 900 recruits were gathered by a variety of means, ranging from signing up genuine volunteers to offering in-country youths bogus scholarships for overseas study and then diverting them to Plan.

The recruits were given basic training in Tanzania, and those selected for advanced and/or specialised courses were then sent to countries such as Algeria, Cuba, Egypt, China, the Soviet Union, North Korea and Red China. At the same time Swapo forged links with the anti-Portuguese Unita insurgents starting to operate in southern Angola, a handy and advantageous relationship because the southern Angolans and the Ovambos are part of the same broad ethnic group and such a friendship would give Plan easy access to its main target, Ovamboland. The links were so close, in fact, that when the later-to-be-famous Dr Jonas Savimbi slipped back into Angola for the first time in eight years in late 1966 he was carrying a Tokarev pistol given him by Sam Nujoma, Swapo's leader.

By September of 1965 Plan was ready to launch its first infiltration, and that month six trained insurgents slipped over the border from southern Angola into Ovamboland – an easy process, the international border existing more in name than in fact, with no-one to guard it except a handful of South West Africa's small six hundred-man police force.

The insurgents busied themselves with basic political activation and also gave about 30 young Ovambos some elementary military training before sending them home to await a call to arms. By this time suspicious tribal elders had passed word of their activities to the police, but except for surveillance no immediate action was taken.

In February 1966 a second small group set out to infiltrate southwards, only to become the authors of a total fiasco when they murdered two Angolan shopkeepers and an itinerant Ovambo in the apparent – and mistaken – belief by its members that they had crossed the border. The group then dispersed, only to have three of its members arrested by police in the neighbouring tribal territory of Kavango, where local inhabitants had wasted no time in informing the authorities about the presence of foreign tribesmen.

In July 1966 a third group of insurgents crossed the border. They were an unimpressive group, trained in half-a-dozen different countries and armed in some cases with assegais and bows and arrows – a far cry from the uniformed, well-equipped and trained insurgents of later years. In spite of this they launched the 'armed struggle' in no uncertain terms by attacking a number of Ovambo tribal chiefs, firing at a white farmer's house in the Grootfontein district just south of Ovamboland, and shooting up the South West African border post at Oshikango.

This opening phase of the struggle was short-lived, however: the following month helicopter-borne policemen attacked their camp at Ongulumbashe, killing two insurgents and capturing nine others. Later, acting on information passed on by the local inhabitants, they arrested many more, bringing the total number of captures to forty-five. This effectively strangled the infiltration and, incidentally, knocked out the only permanent base Plan ever managed to establish anywhere in the operational area during the entire twenty-three year course of the war.

Following the crushing of this latest infiltration, Ovamboland and Caprivi were now so quiet that the police withdrew their counter-insurgency unit, but the border war was far from over. In October 1968 two large groups of insurgents slipped in from Angola and restarted the Caprivian end of the moribund insurgency. Police retaliation was swift. Within a week no fewer than fifty-six insurgents had been arrested. At year's end a total of 178 Plan members had either been killed or captured, and the infiltration ended with the remaining operatives withdrawing over the border into Zambia.

The local population still declined to rise en masse, and the insurgents concentrated on harrying the security forces. In April a Russian-made mine blew up a police vehicle near Katima Mulilo, heralding a new and terrifying dimension, and during 1971 and 1972 five policemen were killed and thirty-five wounded by landmine explosions. For the next few years the landmine was to become a prime weapon against the South Africans (as it was against the Portuguese in Angola and Moçambique),

CLOCKWISE FROM BELOW: With the South Africans in the south, Angolan troops on the march north of Luanda – note French-built chopper on parade-ground (right, background); Wounded South African is helped to safety by his mates; SA *Olifant* tank crosses back into South West Africa after the *Op Modular* cease-fire; The 'Golden Highway' in northern Ovamboland; An Angolan Air Force MiG-21 knocked out by an American *Stinger* missile in eastern Angola.

SOUTH AFRICAN PARABAT
AT CUAMAT

The attack at Cuamato in January 1981 was a blunder. So
fact, it was a well-defended Angolan Army strongpoint.
Pumas. The battle raged for several hours, through trenc
14,5mm heavy machine-guns and RPG-7s predominated. T
and several wounded, including the author. Inexplicably, th
was re-occupied by Fapla. The South Africans bombed th
before nightfall. One might well ask: What was it all about?

AN ANGOLAN ARMY CAMP
TH ANGOLA

ntelligence sources believed the base to belong to Swapo. In
ent in on the attack, across open ground and, initially, in
unkers. Retaliatory fire was extremely heavy; 12,7mm and
well laid out (see below). The South Africans lost two killed
amp was vacated before dark by the South Africans when it
ly the next day, retook it once more, and vacated it again

although in due course its threat lessened and eventually became a minor one as the South Africans learnt from their experiences and developed a series of the most effective mine-protected vehicles in the world. But, right to the end of the border war, it continued to claim the lives of civilians, almost all of them Ovambos.

By the end of 1973 it was becoming patently obvious to the government – although not to the South African general public, which was still looking towards Rhodesia, where a police contingent had been campaigning for several years in support of the Ian Smith government – that the SAP simply did not have the manpower or other resources simultaneously to keep the peace in South Africa itself, secure the South West African borders and provide a Rhodesian contingent. The SAP had never been a large force, but it had always managed to carry out its tasks with reasonable efficiency; this burden, however, was more than it could handle.

This being the case, it was decided that the South African Defence Force would take over responsibility for counter-insurgency operations in the border operational area, leaving the police to concentrate on their normal duties, although still maintaining their small anti-terrorist unit.

The date for the South African Defence Force's assumption of responsibility was set at 1 April 1974, and in the second half of 1973 increasing numbers of military personnel and quantities of equipment started to arrive in the operational area.

The Army had their first casualty of war, late June 1974. Admiral Biermann, the Chief of Staff of the SADF, announced the death of Lieutenant Freddie Zeelie, saying the young officer had died the previous week "in a skirmish with a group of terrorists which attempted to cross the South African border…a unit of the Permanent Force killed and wounded a number of terrorists".

As far as is known, 22 year-old Zeelie was the first South African soldier to be killed in action on the border. The circumstances of his death were shrouded in secrecy – not even his parents were told exactly when and where he died – and remain so to this day. At the time it was not even known what unit he belonged to, although a green infantry beret lay with his sword on his coffin when he was buried with full military honours at his home town of Alberton, near Johannesburg (it later transpired that he had been a member of the super-elite Reconnaissance Commando, the forerunner of today's Reconnaissance Regiments). About six months later his parents received his posthumous Louw Wepener Decoration for gallantry.

Although most South Africans did not realise it, a new phase of the war was about to start, one which would have a radical effect on the border and would force Admiral Biermann to eat his assurances about South African non-intervention across its borders.

Till the first quarter of 1974 the support of Prime Minister Marcelo Caetano's regime in Portugal had been of great value to Pretoria in its counter-insurgency campaign in South West Africa, principally because it had meant that Plan could not freely use southern Angola as a sanctuary, training-ground and jumping-off place for infiltrations into Ovamboland.

But by 1974 years of fighting simultaneous insurgencies in its three African provinces of Angola, Moçambique and Guiné-Bissau had brought Portugal, the poorest country in Europe, to the brink of financial and spiritual collapse.

In late 1974 alone, for example, an estimated six million US dollars' worth of heavy Russian weaponry – including 122mm BM-21 multiple rocket-launchers, obsolescent weapons but highly effective against unsophisticated African troops – was shipped to remote rural MPLA depots from Dar es Salaam and later Congo-Brazzaville, and large numbers of MPLA officers were flown to Russia for training (although in fairness this happened only after Red China had sent the FNLA some instructors and 450 tons of light arms through Zaire in June of that year, followed by another shipment from Romania in August).

In addition, more Cuban military advisers and instructors were quietly slipping into Luanda. For years Swapo and MPLA sympathisers inside and outside South Africa have claimed that Cubans started arriving in Angola only in late 1975 to combat South African aggression, but in fact there was an old relationship between Neto and President Fidel Castro, and Cuba had been providing Neto with instructors and a personal bodyguard since 1966.

With dismaying rapidity Angola began to slide into full-scale chaos as the three contenders fought – for survival in the case of Savimbi and for supremacy in the case of Neto and Roberto. In July the MPLA won the first round by throwing both the FNLA and the small Unita presence out of Luanda and establishing itself in almost every sizeable population centre between the capital and the South West African border.

To the South Africans it was obvious that an extremely serious situation was developing. Refugees, who were now streaming over the border in thousands, had started bringing word of the close Cuban involvement with the MPLA, and independent proof of this involvement – and possible future plans – was obtained when one of the numerous small hot pursuits launched by the South Africans over the ever more irrelevant border turned up Cuban-origin ammunition and weapons dumps which, as one official spokesman later said, "placed the security situation of southern Angola in a completely different light".

The Americans' grasp of the issues involved does not seem to have been very strong, if one is to believe John Stockwell, who came almost straight from the disaster in

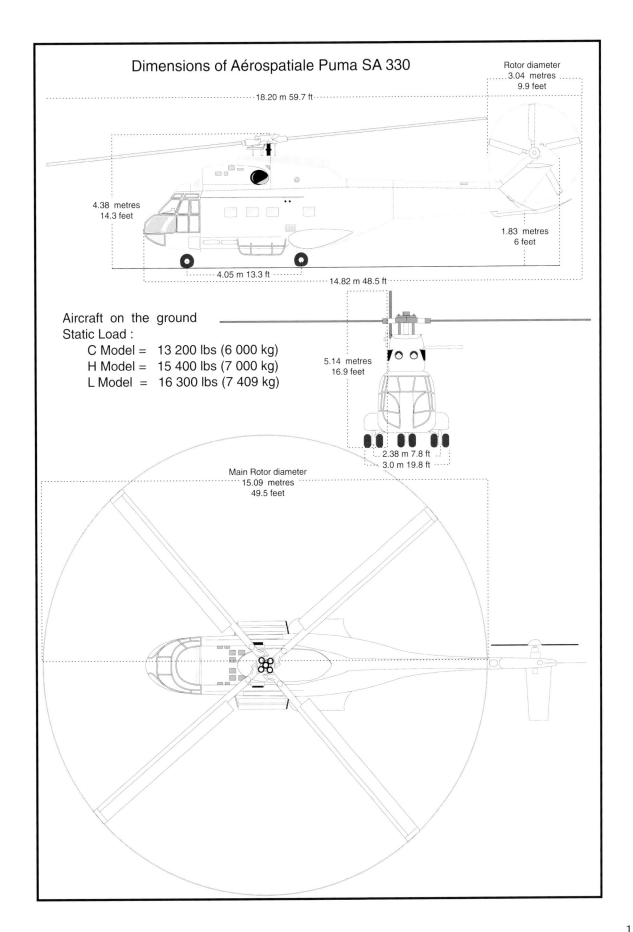

Dimensions of Aérospatiale Puma SA 330

Rotor diameter
3.04 metres
9.9 feet

18.20 m 59.7 ft

4.38 metres
14.3 feet

1.83 metres
6 feet

4.05 m 13.3 ft

14.82 m 48.5 ft

Aircraft on the ground
Static Load :
   C Model = 13 200 lbs (6 000 kg)
   H Model = 15 400 lbs (7 000 kg)
   L Model = 16 300 lbs (7 409 kg)

5.14 metres
16.9 feet

2.38 m 7.8 ft
3.0 m 19.8 ft

Main Rotor diameter
15.09 metres
49.5 feet

Saigon to be made head of the operation the CIA hastily set up in Angola in 1975. In the 1984 television documentary, Stockwell – who by then had severed his ties with the organisation and become one of its strongest critics – described the first briefing on Angola to be delivered by the CIA director to the National Security Council, US President Gerald Ford's inner cabinet:

The CIA director (said): "Gentlemen, this is a map of Africa, and here is Angola. In Angola there are three liberation movements. There is the FNLA, headed by Holden Roberto, they're the good guys. There is the MPLA, headed by Agostinho Neto, who's a drunken psychotic poet with a Marxist background. They're the bad guys" – and they used exactly that terminology, the "good guys" and the "bad guys", so that those people on the National Security Council could get straight what the game was.

The reason why Savimbi did not get a mention at this stage was undoubtedly the fact that (as Stockwell noted), "nobody knew much about Savimbi. Savimbi didn't hit the international cocktail circuit the way FNLA and MPLA activists and leaders did. Savimbi stayed in Angola, tending to his business".

The fact is that throughout the crucial first six months of 1975 the US government was virtually inert as far as Angola was concerned. No doubt the Americans' deeply ingrained parochialism was partly to blame, and in addition the US was not only still too deeply mired in its post-Vietnam nervous breakdown to take positive action but was entering its traditional pre-presidential election paralysis.

And so South Africa was sucked into the burgeoning war, a conflict that went on for another 15 years.

Pretoria's involvement in Angola has been put down to everything from blatant racism to out-and-out neo-imperialist expansion, and Stockwell's theory is that the South Africans' main reason for giving in to the American urgings was because they scented a lever which they could use to force the US to support their policies.

The border war in contrast was still of very low intensity, but an intermittent dribble of contacts, mine explosions and shoot-and-scoot rocket and mortar bombardments inexorably pushed up the casualty rate. For the Plan insurgents, operating on their home ground against relatively inexperienced enemies, the environment was still comparatively favourable; the SADF's immediate reaction was to mount intensive counter-insurgency operations.

The border war showed no signs of abating. Insurgents often operated in large groups and did not hesitate to fight if contact was made. In certain sectors of the South African public the erroneous conclusion was reached that Plan members always ran if attacked. In fact, this tactic was usually the only one that made sense. A typical contact consisted of a short, fierce fire-fight, after which the insurgent group usually gave way and headed for the Angolan border or dispersed into Ovamboland's endless stretches of bushland; to do otherwise would be to provide a sitting target for the SADFs helicopters and reaction-force units.

The border war lasted for twenty-two years (or twenty-three, if the final post-ceasefire outburst of violence is included). If the material losses of all the participants are counted, it cost billions in any reputable currency and destroyed the lives of thousands, especially in southern Angola.

Its total casualties will probably never be established; South African sources give known deaths by 1 November 1988 as 715 security-force soldiers, 1 087 SWA/Namibian civilians and 11 291 insurgents and Angolan soldiers, and it is quite possible that many more Plan fighters died, given the fact that they did not have recourse to the sophisticated medical backup enjoyed by the security forces.

These figures do not include the thousands of deaths suffered by Unita, the Cubans and the Angolan soldiers and civilians as a result of the civil war which was so intimately connected with the border fighting.

The number of dead and permanently disabled is not, perhaps, very impressive when measured against the ghastly losses suffered in greater wars. By the standards of southern Africa, however, where countries are vast but populations are small, it is a heavy toll, and particularly Angola will be a long time recovering from the loss of blood and treasure.

An interesting avenue of speculation is this: was it necessary for Swapo to embark on its 'armed struggle' in 1962? Might it not have been better advised to fight for an independent Namibia on the national and international political battlefield rather than take up arms in its own backyard?

The answer, possibly, is "no" to the first part and "yes" to the second – but the question should be seen in the context of its times. The 1960s was the era of the 'freedom fighter', not the negotiator, and in any case the South African government of the time was little disposed towards negotiations with an openly revolutionary organisation which had links with Moscow.

An intriguing idea some observers play around with in their idle moments is the theory that perhaps the war did not hasten South West Africa's progress towards independence but actually delayed it. True or false? It is difficult to say, for there is no clear answer.

An interesting question is this: Should the South Africans have fought the insurgents?

The answer is probably that, apart from personal inclinations, they had no alternative, once it had become clear that the insurgency was not a nine days' wonder. To

CLOCKWISE FROM TOP: Dead Swapo insurgents brought into Oshakati headquarters for identification; White phosphorous grenade — Willie Peter — indicates LZ to chopper back-up; Soldier with human skull at earlier Xangongo battlefield during *Op Protea*; *Alouette* engineer/20mm gunner at Cuamato; Kunene River forms the backdrop during an airlift in *Operation Protea*.

many – possibly most – of their voters they would have been seen as 'hands-uppers' or worse, and the result of *Operation Savannah* sealed the matter. After 1976, when the insurgency became really viable for the first time because Angola's new masters threw their support behind Swapo, there was no turning back. The irony of it was that the seeds of the Swapo movement were sown in the 1940s and 1950s, but did not come to flower till late in the 1960s, when attitudes had changed a good deal and gave promise of changing even more.

History teaches us a great deal. Angola's disastrous slide into chaos was largely due to the Soviet Union's undermining of the post-Caetano era in Portugal. It might well be that the Russians were not working according to a pre-determined plan but were merely seizing a handy opportunity, but that does not alter Moscow's culpability (and the 'opportunity' theory is suspect in any case, when one considers that Moscow, Cuba and the likes of Rosa Coutinho had already started working in 1974 to manoeuvre the MPLA into power).

Then there is the matter of Angola, which is generally cast as the war's (and South Africa's) greatest victim. Yet to a large extent the Angolan government could be said to have brought its troubles on itself.

There have been many statements that thousands of young white South Africans left the country to avoid service in SWA/Namibia, but this has not been backed up by any conclusive research, and it seems likely that many of those who left did so because they considered that two years of full-time conscription and 720 days of part-time service were too onerous a burden on their careers and personal lives – which is a different matter altogether.

Angola was certainly not South Africa's Vietnam in the sense that the SADF was bogged down there for any length of time. Till far into the 1980s the South Africans did pretty much as they pleased in southern Angola and scored many victories at little cost to themselves. If Angola was anybody's Vietnam, it was the Cubans'. Losses among the Cuban conscripts who were sent there by their government have never been made public, but in some circles it is thought to number thousands – almost all victims of Unita.

Another popular misconception was that it had destroyed the "myth of South African military superiority". This was a handy phrase that rolled readily off the typewriter, but the contrary was true. South African military superiority was anything but a myth, then or later.

Unlike almost every other southern African army, the SADF was a long-established body, forged by six decades of independent development and two bloody world wars into the best-organised, best-trained force in Africa. What *Savannah* proved was that the SADF was not in good shape after thirty years of peace; its equipment was outdated and there was a good deal of deadwood – both in

personnel and in doctrine – that needed to be lopped off. To the South Africans' credit they took this lesson to heart, with the border war supplying a handy training-ground. As a result they emerged with a standard of operational expertise which surpassed that of some of the most famous armed forces in the world – and the self-confidence that went with it.

Were the South African and SWA/Namibian soldiers better than the Swapo insurgents? The answer is "yes" – but one must understand why it was so. It was not about courage or cowardice but about better organisation, better planning, better utilisation and, above all, better training.

If the war proved anything, it was that although most insurgencies end in political solutions, he who has lost the penultimate military phase has no right to say anything when the armed struggle concluded not with a bang but with the whisper of papers being shuffled at a conference-table.

To those who did not know better – and to some who did, but found it more convenient to avoid facing the facts – the border war was a simple confrontation between racist whites and oppressed blacks.

The men and women who fought in it knew better, probably no other southern African war has ever featured such a motley, many-tongued array of combatants driven by such a variety of motives: patriotism, political belief, a hunger for vengeance, a desire for money, obedience to the authorities, and so on.

For some it satisfied a thirst for adventure, because in a sense the border was a fighting man's conflict, in that most of the action in it was Mark One face-to-face soldiering at whites-of-the-eyes range rather than the impersonal killing of enemies at long distance.

It has been called a 'colonial' war, but in at least one important aspect it was not. Where it differed from most such wars was that none of the fighters were foreigners, in the sense of coming to the battle-zone from distant lands, like the Americans in Vietnam and the British in Malaya. All were southern Africans of one race or another and did not experience real difficulty in coming to terms with their environment.

In some case, in fact, the difference between the protagonists was tragically small: for the insurgents on the one hand and the Ovambo soldiers and policemen of 101 Battalion and the South West Africa Police it was nothing more or less than a civil war.

RIGHT: *Ratel* Infantry Fighting Vehicles (IFVs) with approaching *Puma* during *Operation Meebos*. For several years the South African Air Force was arguably the best commercial advertisement for the astonishing efficacy and reliability of French-built helicopters — *Pumas* and *Alouettes*.

CHAPTER 15

HELICOPTER REACTION FORCE

JUST ANOTHER DAY... NEALL ELLIS RELATES:

Even before the first streaks of dawn brighten up the sky, the sounds of men preparing for conflict can be heard on the hardstand. Gradually, the familiar shapes of aircraft and men working in the half-light become apparent.

As the light improves, the activity is easier to follow. Green-clad aircrew in flight overalls and groundcrew in their distinctive 'blues' can be seen preparing the helicopters for the day's missions. There is some light-hearted bantering between the aircrew and the parachute battalion reaction troops billeted on the edge of the runway, kidding each other on the possibility of a contact with the enemy during the day. "If you croak", one of them asks, "can I have your watch?"

The troops are not inactive. They, too, are checking their weapons, ammunition pouches, ratpacks (rations), and filling water bottles. Equipment must be secured to prevent any possibility of loss in the drop. The sound of radio static can be heard in the background as stick commanders check their frequencies.

Once the aircrew and troops are satisfied that men and machines are 'ready to go', pilots and stick leaders move off towards the ops room for the morning's briefing. Much has come in during the night; consequently the immediate task is to remain on standby for an area operation just north of the base.

Ground troops had moved into the target region in the early hours of the morning, cordoned it off and started a systematic hut-by-hut search for a weapons cache that it was said, had been brought in from across the border during the dark hours.

After the briefing, the stick commanders return to the overhang where their troops are waiting. Aircrews remain in the pilots' crew-room, waiting for the radio call that will announce a contact. Time lies heavy on the minds of these men; they play cards, or read or form small groups and engage in the kind of bullshit banter than men are fond of during wartime. The siren sounds...

The scene could have been Air Force Base Ondangua in South West Africa/Namibia during the war on the Angolan border or any other forward airfield in southern Africa during the past 15 or 20 years for that matter. The procedure never differed. It was the start of a day for what could then be considered, arguably, the most effective counter-insurgent force in Africa and the world.

The Rhodesians called it 'Fire Force'. The South Africans, 'Reaction Force'. Whatever the name, this small but effective fighting element accounted for more insurgent kills than any other military contingent anywhere, during the period 1965 to 1989.

Heliborne troops supported by gunship helicopters armed with the 'Duka-Duka' (the 20mm MG151 side-firing cannon) struck heartfelt fear into the minds of those carrying their version of conflict from Angola, Mocambique, Zambia, Zimbabwe and elsewhere into the 'white South'.

INTELLIGENCE GATHERING

The aim of Swapo, ZANU, Zanla and other insurgent groups was essentially, to recruit young men and women for their revolutionary cause. Their ideology was alien to Africa; it was the product of the Dark Empire that has since been all but destroyed; East Germany, the Soviet Union, Cuba, North Vietnam and elsewhere. This was then all part of what was euphemistically termed *The Cold War*. Only this was very hot and active indeed.

These insurgents would enter selected African villages or kraals (villages), complete with their Soviet or Bulgarian arms and Polish uniforms, usually after dark, in a bid to indoctrinate locals and possibly press-gang some of the younger men to join the movement. The usual ploy was to offer the wide-eyed youngsters a university education in Europe.

If members of a local village did not react favourably or willingly, the men and sometimes the women as well, would be kidnapped and force-marched across the border before daybreak. Before leaving the target village, they would either assault or kill the headman and often his family as well.

By such tactics – in Angola, Namibia and Rhodesia earlier in the decade – the insurgents were able to establish a doctrine of fear that guaranteed food and essential provisions. It was a doctrine of fear and intimidation; unfortunately for these innocents, it worked.

Conversely, in order to protect these local people, information on the insurgents, their movements, equipment and targets became a primary objective of the security forces. Essentially, the civilian community – as in all guerrilla wars – was caught, as it is so often phrased, between the rock and the hard place!

Operational experience gained in the Rhodesian bush war and the South West African conflict proved that the most efficient method to garner intelligence on insurgent movements was either to deploy observation posts (OPs) on high points in the terrain or to use clandestine patrols, usually disguised as insurgents – as a pseudo force – to reconnoitre an area where an insurgent presence had been or was expected to be active. Because of the activity of such 'pseudo groups', areas were given boundaries and 'frozen'. No other security force operations were permitted to take place during the period that such clandestine reconnaissance was taking place.

Air traffic either had to fly at height over the area, or avoid it altogether.

These patrols spent days observing local villages. At night their members would often enter villages to gather information. It was dangerous work; only specialised Special Forces trained in this kind of subterfuge were used for the task. Once the presence of the enemy was detected, the patrol attempted – usually through a black intermediary – to make contact with their members in order to socialise, and if they were fortunate, discuss their plans and perhaps discover their objective. That was the ideal; it rarely worked quite that way.

Whatever information was uncovered was radioed back to operational headquarters in standard format or contact report. It comprised an Own Forces callsign, a grid reference of the enemy position, followed by a grid reference of Own Forces, time of the sighting or contact, or description of the enemy concerning their status – moving or static – numbers, types and quantity of armament, and also what type of clothing they were wearing for later identification or spotting work.

Control arrangements concerning the marking of Landing Zones (LZs)/Own Positions with coloured smoke grenades, VHF frequencies for communication with ground forces, as well as weather conditions describing cloud cover, wind and visibility were additionals required in the report.

If an airstrike or a heliborne assault on the insurgents' location was authorised, more information was usually asked for and radioed back to base. There could never be *too much* intelligence.

This included as much detail on the target as possible; additional information such as terrain, high spots, possible escape routes, the best route for a heliborne approach for the purpose of maintaining a good surprise ratio and, possibly, the vegetation around the target was also detailed.

COMPOSITION OF THE AIRBORNE ASSAULT FORCE

In the vast areas of thick bush in southern Africa, a small group of insurgents has always been a difficult target to detect. When spotted, they could be miles from the nearest reaction unit.

In order to maintain an element of surprise – the key factor in low-intensity counter-insurgency operations – the only practical means of deploying troops was usually by helicopter. Certainly, in its theatres of operations, the chopper as a fighting machine proved itself. The 'combat-worth' of a heliborne force with its inherent mobility, flexibility and firepower was always invaluable. However, as aircrew and field commanders will always tell you, helicopters are expensive to operate; there are certain routines that need to be followed when deploying airborne forces.

The first consideration is that all commanders should know when and how to use helicopters. During the course of both the Rhodesian and South West African wars, operations often failed because their operational planners did not appreciate the essential speed needed to muster a reaction force. Or perhaps they did not understand the often incredible ability of an insurgent force to move across the ground at speed, even on foot.

The bottom line is that any helicopter-borne reaction force should be regarded as a rotor-powered cavalry to be held in reserve and deployed only when the event warrants its use.

The composition of such a ground force, ideally, is an infantry company with a company HQ, similar to that of a rifle company, together with three platoons of three sections each containing between eight and 14 men.

Each section should have a trained tracker and an interpreter on hand for immediate liaison with civilians encountered en route. Time is of the essence – the enemy is on the move.

The Air Force element, in contrast, ideally consists of an *Alouette III* command and control helicopter armed with a .303 MG piloted by the mission leader and carrying the Army Ground Commander onboard to monitor ground positions.

For close air support, two 'gunship' Aerospatiale *Alouette III* helicopters armed with the MG151 20mm cannon was usually the preferred configuration.

The Rhodesian Air Force's Fire Force *Alouette III* helicopters were armed with this weapon and were referred to as K-cars. Fire Force elements were normally deployed in conjunction with outlying Selous Scouts spotter teams carrying out pseudo operations but they were never far from any potential contact area. For this reason, in Rhodesia, fuel was not as critical a consideration as it might have been for the reaction forces in the South West African operational area. Also, Rhodesian units seemed to prefer to have the army commander in the K-car instead of a separate command and control helicopter, but then they fought their war differently.

For airlifting reaction force troops on the Angolan border, a minimum of two, ideally, three *Puma* helicopters armed with door-mounted 7.62 LMGs were deployed. Visual reconnaissance and radio relay was taken care of by a light, fixed-wing aircraft of the *Cessna 185* or *Bosbok* range. If necessary, a larger fixed-wing aircraft such as a *Dakota* for the parachute dropping of a second wave of reserve troops could be put on standby. This combination worked successfully in the Rhodesian War except – instead of *Puma* helicopters – *Alouette III* G-cars (four troops) and *Bell 205s* (eight troops) were used; the light support aircraft was the push-pull *Cessna 337* armed with twin 7.62 MGs, 37mm SNEB rockets and the mini-Golf bomb or the Rhodesian manufactured version of napalm called Frantan.

Looking back, it is clear that the deployment of sufficient men on the ground during counter-insurgency operations has been a problem throughout the Third World since 1945. To provide for extra reserve troops, fuel and ammunition, the Rhodesians, where possible, used a convoy of vehicles called a 'landtail'. The roads used by the 'landtail' had, of necessity, to be tarred because of the imminent threat of landmines. Almost all the dirt roads in the operational area were mined and could not be negotiated at the kind of speed required for helicopter assault operations.

Likewise, the road-grid infrastructure in northern South West Africa and southern Angola was limited, often severely, and the SADF very seldom employed a 'landtail' concept. They were restricted to deploying whatever troops the *Puma's* could carry, unless, of course, there was a nearby temporary or permanent base which could provide reinforcements.

If a 'landtail' was not possible, troop reinforcements could be parachuted into the area by one or more *DC-3 Dakota* fixed-wing aircraft. The 'Dak' can drop up to two sections of ten men each.

There are two principal types of operations employing helicopters. The first is the 'Pre-Planned Attack'; the second can be regarded as a 'Reaction Attack' to reinforce and give possible close-air support to troops already involved in a contact. Undoubtedly some of these concepts will be used if the South African political and security situation deteriorates still further. Certainly, the tactics explained here will be useful in the other Third World wars involving NATO, Eastern Bloc or American troops.

PRE-PLANNED ATTACK

Almost all pre-planned attacks normally result as a consequence of confirmed intelligence. This information could be gathered by informers among the civilian population of an area of operation or perhaps by the confirmed sighting of an enemy base camp by friendly forces occupying observation posts. During the Rhodesian war, OPs proved to be extremely effective when used to pinpoint insurgent activity.

Some of the most successful pre-planned attacks on the larger insurgent camps in Rhodesia and in Angola were carried out as a result of information gathered by aerial photography or by visual reconnaissance by fixed-wing aircraft. This was particularly so in the southern Angolan war. When such photo intelligence was gathered, a small reconnaissance commando patrol was tasked to physically confirm that the camp was occupied and, if possible, by whom.

In 1982, during what can be considered the most successful heliborne assault in the history of bush warfare, *Operation Super*, a total of 45 men attached to the elite 32 Battalion supported by four *Alouette* gunships and five *Puma* medium transport helicopters attacked a 300-strong Swapo camp. A total of 250 insurgents were killed for the loss of four 32 Battalion troops.

REACTION ATTACK

The reaction attack is normally initiated when security forces require close-air support after either walking or driving into an ambush or initiating a contact with the enemy. Ideally, the reaction force should be no more than 15 minutes flying time from the contact. When a contact has taken place, the insurgents tend to 'bombshell' into small groups of between one and three men each; this can make it difficult for security forces to maintain contact with the dispersing enemy.

Experience has shown that an infiltrating force can maintain a pace of up to one kilometre per five minutes after a contact. The result is that long helicopter flight times to the area of operation, often gave the adversary the chance to disappear into thick bush. For this reason, the reaction attack is not always successful for heliborne reaction unless ground forces – who originally initiated the contact – can immediately follow up the insurgents and remain close to them until the airborne force is able to provide relief. This can be difficult if security forces have sustained casualties.

QUALIFIED TROOPS

Troops selected for reaction force need to be qualified in helicopter operations. They need to have experience in how to emplane and deplane on to and from helicopters as rotating blades and screaming turbines can create confusion for the uninitiated. During the early stages of the Rhodesian war, there were a few fatal accidents when a

couple of men accidentally ran into spinning tail rotors or the main rotor blades.

Helicopters are vulnerable when on the ground and emplaning and deplaning procedures need to be regularly practised. Every second on the ground increases the chances of an attack on the aircraft. During operations in Angola and Rhodesia, a number of helicopters were lost in those vital seconds during approach to landing, on the ground and during take-off when a helicopter is at its most vulnerable.

It is vital that the stick leader ensures that each member of his team knows *beforehand* exactly where to sit once onboard and also how to take up a circular defence position immediately after leaving the aircraft. Contingencies also need to be catered for.

Loose straps and articles of clothing must be properly secured during flight. Unsecured objects have been known to exit the open doors and foul tail rotors, sometimes with catastrophic results. Radio antennae must be taped down or removed and stored properly, close to the body.

Every soldier must know the various hand signals used by aircrew for emplaning and deplaning. This is essential as engine and gear box noise does not allow for conversation either on the ground in the immediate proximity of the aircraft or while in flight.

Each person must be aware of the dimensions of a LZ; this can mean the difference between success or disaster in the event of a medevac or a hurried extraction, more commonly known as 'hot extraction', usually in the face of heavy enemy ground fire. Troops need to show aggression and have little fear in a combat situation as very often the numbers of troops deployed by helicopters during low-intensity counter-insurgency operations are grossly outnumbered by those opposing them.

Other qualities required for reaction force operations are the ability to shoot accurately and quickly and to have the initiative to take over command of a stick at any time. Officers and NCOs also sometimes become casualties. For this reason, the Rhodesians preferred their Regular Forces for Fire Force operations, using RLI and RAR soldiers who were not part of the annual national intake.

The South Africans in Angola tended to deploy troops from the well-trained 32 Battalion or from the Parachute Battalion. They found the 32 Battalion to be among the most effective counter-insurgency troops in the entire force. The Parabats, in contrast, though comprised almost solely of one or two year servicemen, acted best with a Permanent Force leadership element. Because of the thorough training given to these youthful Parabat national servicemen – who ranged in age from about 18 to 25 years – they quickly emerged as effective heliborne troops and were justifiably feared by Swapo insurgent cadres.

Another reason for using 'select' troops was that an unspoken camaraderie between a reaction force unit and

CLOCKWISE FROM TOP: *Mirage* and *Buccaneer* bomber strikes on the Swapo headquarters camp at Cassinga during the early 'assertive' stage of this border war; 32 Battalion troops in the process of boarding; A *Puma* approaches a temporary base during *Operation Daisy*; Helicopter Administrative Group (Hag) set up in arid countryside during *Operation Super*; Wounded South African soldiers await evacuation to Oshakati after a cross-border raid into Angola.

helicopter crews was quickly established. This cut out numerous uncertain communication problems and helped develop a feeling of trust between the two participants. Curiously, it was also found that troops on the ground tended to fight more ferociously when they were personally acquainted with the gunship crews giving them close-air support. They were being 'looked after by their mates', as it were.

Commanders of heliborne operations needed – for practical purposes – to have training in the control of troops on the ground from an airborne platform. A helicopter orbiting a position over a long period can cause, for instance, directional disorientation after a few minutes of circling the target area. For this reason, army commanders must acquire skills in map reading from an aircraft and must also be able to orientate themselves direction-wise without hesitation.

They need to be able to read the aircraft's instruments to assist them with navigation when en route to the target and back again, as well as being able to communicate over the radio – air force style – and not the lengthy procedures required by normal army channels. They should recognise from the dials how much fuel is still available and not have to be reminded. It helps with contingency planning.

The aircraft commander on the other hand, must be able to understand 'army language' and have a thorough understanding of deploying troops and the interaction of moving troops over the ground in attack formation. In a sense, something resembling a culture change takes place and, for all practical purposes, is what makes heliborne assault forces different to most other units in any combat zone.

Once cooperation among the troops and aircrew has been established, the reaction force becomes a well oiled and effective counter-insurgency killing machine.

It is interesting that after independence, the Zimbabwe Army applied many of the military precepts originally deployed against them by the Rhodesian Army while combatting Matabele dissidence. They used exactly the same principles, discipline and systems against their former comrades and utterly routed them with tremendous loss of life. Clearly, some useful lessons had been learnt.

EQUIPMENT

The troops on deployment carry with them only that battle kit essentially needed for heliborne operations. This usually consists of field webbing or a special vest, containing light rations for one day and spare magazines, a light sleeping bag made from parachute material, water and additional first line ammunition, which could include grenades and claymores. Aircrew frowned on embarking troops with armed RPG-launchers; if these were accidentally discharged the results could be terminal.

Often contacts could occur at last light and troops might be required to overnight in the AO or perhaps lay an ambush. It was known that insurgents tended to return to the battle zone during the night to retrieve lost equipment and establish who among their comrades had been killed or wounded.

Sections were always heavily armed. In addition to personnel R5 rifles (in .223 calibre) troops carried items as diverse as phosphorous grenades, mini-pencil flares, day-glo panels and torches for searching underground bunkers and tribal huts. Extra armament per section could be up to two 40mm grenade M79 launchers (made in Taiwan), at least one LMG with the No. 1 and No. 2 men carrying 500 rounds each. In some cases a light 60mm assault mortar or a RPG-7 rocket-launcher was added to the pack. The average all-up weight of a reaction force soldier was approximately 250 pounds or roughly 115 kilograms.

Chopper aircrew always wore green Nomex flight overalls and survival vests. Although the contents of the vests were not prescribed, they normally consisted of a pistol and two or three magazines, water, recognition flares, as well as day-glo panels, radio-locator beacons and other odds and ends to assist a downed pilot and his engineer in escape and evasion techniques. A couple of paperbacks was a *sine qua non* of any operation to help break the tedium of waiting.

In addition, each crew member would be armed with an R5 or R1 (.762 calibre) assault rifle. Most crews had a pack of playing cards with them. The standing joke was if a crew was shot down in the bush, the first survival technique would be to haul out the cards and start playing a game of solitaire. Before long some bored SAAF rescue pilot would sidle up, peer over one's shoulder and give instructions for the next move!

LOGISTICS

Fuel was always a problem for helicopter operations, particularly in the vast, almost limitless operational areas in southern Africa. Because of the established road, rail and urban infrastructure in Rhodesia (Zimbabwe) farther to the east, Ian Smith's forces were able to locate drums of helicopter fuel (Avtur) at numerous towns or villages around the country. This ensured that a helicopter should never be more than 10 to 15 minutes away from the nearest fuel dump. Ammunition for 20mm cannon was also stockpiled with the fuel.

South African forces, in contrast, were not as fortunate; the only positions where fuel could be placed were military or police camps scattered around the operational area often hundreds of kilometres apart. Namibia's northern border with Angola and Zambia – from the Atlantic Ocean to the Zimbabwe border at Kazangulu in Caprivi – stretches more than 1 500 kilometres.

CLOCKWISE FROM TOP: Typical Ovambo countryside in the northern sector of the country; A supply column is brought to a halt by landmine clearing Sappers; Black troops waiting to embark at Eenhana; Deploying troops from a *Puma* in south Angola and, Radio operator with 32 Battalion deep inside Angola during a penetration raid.

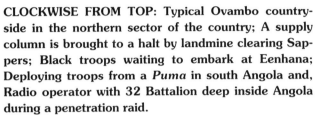

The distances between these camps were sometimes so great that a pilot occasionally had to make the decision whether to break off from a contact at a critical stage for refuelling – and therefore deprive the reaction force on the ground of close-air support – or to carry on with the action, land in friendly terrain near his ground troops with zero fuel and hope that the drums of fuel he ordered over the radio would be brought in later by a *Puma* helicopter. That action could expose the chopper to enemy fire and it was always a difficult decision.

RADIO COMMUNICATIONS

Radio communications were vital during reaction force operations; each section, ideally, needed to have up to two VHF/AM radios. In addition one HF radio was carried per platoon.

The reason for the excess in sets was that contact could be fluid; if the commander was not altogether sure of the position of his troops, accidents could and did happen.

Helicopters, by way of contrast, had a choice of two VHF/AM radios, a VHF/FM radio and a HF radio. Clearly, with so many frequencies on the net, the chatter sometimes became cacophonic, especially in the heat of battle.

To reduce traffic, each reaction force normally had a choice of three VHF channels or frequencies as well as the normal HF net. One channel was labelled the 'Battle Channel'. This was used for radio chatter between the troop commander in the air and his section commanders on the ground. All aircraft had to listen out on this channel as each pilot needed to have a mental picture of what was going on between his troops and those of the enemy to avoid putting down fire on own forces.

The second channel was allocated as an alternative battle channel. Sometimes secondary contacts would develop away from the main area of operations and a gunship might be detached to give fire support for the troops involved. If close-air support from fixed-wing ground strike aircraft was used, this channel was employed to pass on forward air controlling (FAC) information. Note that it was still the responsibility of the gunship commander to listen into the main battle channel so as to maintain his broader picture of what was going on down below.

There was always a third channel, nominated the domestic channel. This could be used by aircraft to communicate with each other, to receive instructions particular to the air effort or to guide the troop-carrying helicopters to LZs for deployment. It could also be used for the pick-up of troops without cluttering the battle frequency, and for SITREPS back to base or the handing over of command to relieving gunships.

During follow-up operations or contacts, the noise on the ground from gunfire or orbiting helicopters could be deafening. To allow ground commanders to listen to radio chatter without having to hold the radio's handset continuously in one hand, the headset was (and still is) fastened to the webbing or vest underneath the ear. If called on the radio, all he needed to do was press the transmit button with a free hand and – when required – talk into the microphone.

COMMAND

Channels of command as designated in a reaction force can be confusing, especially to the uninitiated. There are moments during a contact when the air force pilot will be in command of the operation; 'mission leader' as he is called. The army commander will be in command of the rest of the operation. As a rule of thumb, the mission leader exercises command while the troops are airborne; the army commander will assume operational command during the subsequent ground phase. For rather obvious reasons, mission leader will not lose control of the aircraft at any time during the operation.

Mission leader is responsible for the briefing of all aircrews involved. This includes navigation route/procedures to the contact area as well as the delivery of fire support, whether it be airborne or groundborne.

Mission leader must therefore be a qualified AFAC (Airborne Forward Air Controller) in order to coordinate ground attack by fixed-wing aircraft as well as a FAC (Forward Air Controller) to coordinate fire support from artillery and mortar fire. He must also be capable of controlling troops on the ground as there will be times when troop commanders are not able to become airborne. This happened fairly frequently with South African reaction forces because of the great distances that had to be covered. Fuel was at a premium and the army commander already on the ground was often not able to become airborne while the battle in which he was involved raged around him. Maximum fuel was always carried with the *Alouette III* and the additional weight of the army commander. At about 80 or 90 kilograms that meant that up to 25 minutes' flying time could be lost. When this became an issue it was just not on. He therefore continued to command on the ground together with his troops.

Each pilot is in command of his aircraft at all times. Only he is held responsible for the safety of the aircraft and the troops onboard. The pilot can decide how many men the aircraft can carry, but this is seldom a problem. When a crew and aircraft is detailed for reaction force duties, helicopters are refuelled to a specific weight so that each aircraft can carry the same number of troops. Troops will only deplane and emplane on the aircraft commander's instructions. For the same reasons, the flight engineer manning onboard armament may only fire the .303 MG or 20mm cannon on instruction from the aircraft commander.

PRELIMINARY GENERAL BRIEFING

The preliminary general briefing is attended by all aircrew, the army commander as well as responsible section leaders. The base intelligence officer will give an updated briefing on the situation on the ground in the AO followed by the ops officer on any other air/ground movements expected or planned for during the day. The mission leader will then brief the assembled officers and NCOs on general aspects for deployment.

This briefing will cover aspects such as callsigns, formation positions, frequencies, refuelling points, actions to be followed in the event of being shot down due to enemy fire, reactions if there is a radio failure and any other important point which might have a bearing on the outcome of an action. The army commander may also issue special orders to the stick commanders with respect to the order in which the troops will be deployed and which men will be held in reserve.

After the briefing, the mission leader and army commander will stay in close proximity to the ops room, monitoring the ground situation by radio while the aircrew and troops will relax in the pilots' crew room or in covered shelters alongside the ops room. In the heat of Ovamboland and southern Angola, this was always regarded as the most difficult phase.

The piercing howl of the siren rents the air. Suddenly there is confusion. Everyone is up and running. Is this a lemon, or is it the real thing? How many of the enemy are there? Questions fly around as the men get on with the business of donning their webbing and blackening their faces with 'black-is-beautiful' camouflage cream. The black troops are usually the most animated at this stage, passing smart-arse comments about their buddies doing their best to look like 'savages'.

Aircrew scramble to put on shirts, don flying overalls and gather nav equipment. Pilots race to the ops room while flight engineers and reaction force troops move quickly, weight allowing, towards their allotted aircraft to prepare for take-off.

Inside the ops room, the army commander has plotted the position of the designated contact area. He and mission leader decide on the quickest route to the target and draw up a preliminary tactical plan. Is there enough fuel? Casualties?

While the detailed information from the contact report is being analysed, a final plan is formulated. By this time, the pilots are there; maps are readied to plot flight planning information.

Strike force of 28 Swapo insurgents has been sighted at a waterhole close to an African kraal (village). According to information from 'locals', the OP has disclosed that they are resting under thick bush next to a waterhole and appear to be waiting for food to be brought to them by the villagers. All are armed with AK-47s and SKS rifles, many with anti-vehicle and personnel grenades. Unconfirmed, they also have a SAM-7 anti-aircraft missile and at least one RPG-7 rocket-launcher. The OP gives essential information such as wind direction, possible escape routes, any other civilian kraals in the area and all information necessary to ensure easy identification of the target.

Mission leader and the army commander decide that the reaction force will approach into the prevailing wind so as to allow for the noise of the approaching helicopters to be screened by thick tree cover for as long as possible. Sound travels far in the silence of the African bush and approaching helicopters can be heard up to five or six minutes away.

As a shock tactic – and to soften the target before the troops go in – the commanders decide that a formation of Impala single-engined jet strike aircraft will be sent in ahead of the force. They will rocket the area and drop 125 kilogram bombs; the troop-carrying helicopters will go into orbit 30 seconds after the last jet has completed its run while the gunships will overfly the target area for the commanders to assess the situation on the ground.

Orders are given to scramble jets as the choppers take off.

The OP team leader on the ground is informed by the army commander that the helicopters will fly over their position at such and such a time; he is instructed to fire a flare in the direction of the insurgent position as the strike force approaches. This will give mission leader an idea of the correct direction to fly and enable him to identify target acquisition.

After deciding on a battle plan aircrew and stick commanders are given the final briefing. The first two Pumas will drop their troops in stopper group positions. The third Puma will deploy the sweepline. The nearest fuel for the choppers is determined. After drawing in the route to the contact area on their maps, aircrews hurry out to their craft. The elapsed time from when the siren went off is less than five minutes.

While the pilots are strapping into their helicopters and initiating the start cycle, stick commanders give their men a quick rundown on the ground situation and which section will do what; sweepline or stopper groups.

Within a minute, the sharp clicking sounds of engine ignitors are heard over the winding up of turbines and rotor blades start, slowly at first, to beat the air. Last minute cigarettes are extinguished as pilots give the boarding signal for the troops to emplane. This is no lemon!

INBOUND TO TARGET

Moments after lift off, all the aircraft report in to the lead aircraft to check radio communications and then fly over the firing range alongside the airfield to test their guns. The *Alouettes* take off some minutes before the troopers; this allows the faster *Pumas* to rendezvous with the smaller, heavier, lumbering gunships at the contact area. On clearing the immediate airfield circuit areas, the helicopters descend to tree top level; for 21 years of this bush war this remained a statutory measure against SAM-7s. It was effective; not a single South African helicopter was ever brought down by a SAM; thick bush cover prevented the SAMs from 'locking on'.

The northern part of South West Africa adjacent to Angola is flat and virtually featureless. This always made low level aerial navigation extremely difficult.

Navigation was initially done by using maps scaled 1:250 000 and used to an easily recognisable point on the map, and then – for more accurate navigation to the contact point – by 1:50 000 scale maps. Or, on occasion, by using aerial photographs.

Because of the lack of navigation features in this vast terrain, most navigators preferred using heading and time and allowing for wind, and although this was considered a 'thumb-suck' procedure, the majority of pilots knew the area so well that they could navigate quite accurately to the point of destination.

During the Rhodesian war, in contrast, the chopper pilots were thoroughly familiar with their respective AOs. They could glance at a map before take-off, and only when the contact area had been reached did they bother to utilise the map for the final run-in to target. This was certainly because of the distinctive hilly nature of the country; there were many prominent landmarks.

There is little time for relaxation on the way in for aircrew and airborne alike. Mission leader and reaction force commander are required to obtain as much information from the OP position as possible and adjust their battle plan if they think this necessary. In addition, mission leader is required to ensure that his navigation is correct, coordinate his timing for strike aircraft as well as to make sure that all the choppers are maintaining their positions in the formation.

During the latter stages of the bush war in southern Angola, the Angolan Air Force – MiGs with Cuban or East German pilots at the controls – aggressively flew air patrols in the hope of encountering South African aircraft or helicopters within Angola airspace carrying out external missions. There was, in addition, a ground-to-air threat from SAM-7, SAM-14/16 missiles both in South West Africa and Angola. For mutual support and safety, all helicopters flew in battle formation in order to give each other all-points warning from any threat. Once a threat was visually acquired, the formation would take evasive action.

All aircrew in the formation were required to keep a constant look-out for any signs of enemy activity. Minor points which might be missed by the uninitiated were important; like the presence of cattle in kraals during the middle of the day; this would indicate that insurgents were active in the area. The local population would keep the cattle in their pens so that they could watch over them to prevent the insurgents from slaughtering an animal for food. When faced with the business-end of an AK-47 assault rifle, one tends not to argue about who the cow belongs to!

Other indications that the men looked for were behaviour patterns of the local inhabitants when the helicopters flew over them. If these people tried to hide, run away or behave in an aggressive manner by throwing stones at the aircraft or gesturing with their fists, it was more than likely that insurgents were in the area. A show of bravado, uncalled for, was a dead give-away.

Other indications were camouflaged uniforms lying drying near waterholes or kraals or women preparing food in the middle of the day. Tribespeople, these pilots knew, ate in the mornings and evenings. Never at noon.

Other features included disturbed ground away from kraals near a prominent tree or an antheap; this could indicate a possible arms cache. Such information needed to be reported back to base and acted upon later. If there was sufficient evidence of an enemy strike force present there and then, the attack would be immediately diverted. The original OP sighting could wait a few hours; unlike the Russians in Afghanistan, the watchword was always – flexibility!

Section leaders were required to wear headphones during flight so that they were kept abreast of the situation at the contact point.

CLOCKWISE FROM ABOVE: *Puma* squadron heads homewards in formation towards sunset during *Operation Protea*; Maintenance was a major aspect of mobility during the war — much of it took place at Ondangua Air Force base; Captured Russian GAZ-66 truck (left) helps with re-supply during *Operation Protea*; Zulu troops in *Puma* during an airlift to Ongiva, southern Angola.

FIVE MINUTES

"Mission A47Z – five minutes." At five minutes out from the target area, the mission leader gives a call over the radio indicating to all parties involved in the contact that the formation is five minutes away from the area and about to deploy. Mission leader pulls maximum collective allowed for the density altitude and flies the helicopter as low as possible, skimming the fuselage of the aircraft between the tree tops and with the rotor blades, often frighteningly, perhaps a metre above the branches. The rest of the formation follows suit.

The reason for flying low is to muffle the thudding sound of the approaching choppers' rotor blades. Approaching the target downwind will also help to prevent the sound from being picked up while the aircraft are far out. They were all-too-aware that these bush soldiers who had been away from normal life for a year or more often developed most acute hearing; as is the case with most people who exist in the wilds. Surprise, they knew, was possibly the most important principle in this kind of war.

As the choppers get closer to the contact area, the reaction force commander makes radio contact with the OP commander; he needs the very latest on the target insurgent group. More important, he has to know what their reaction to the approaching helicopters will be; will they 'bombshell' or stand and fight?

Aircrew and section leaders strain to hear the message over the radio. In the bush, normal speech can be heard for some distance and recce patrols tend to talk in whispers over the radio.

The broad battle plan is relayed to the OP commander. He asks that the helicopters fly over his position so that he can guide the mission leader over the insurgents by firing a thousand foot flare in the direction of the enemy position.

The callsign on the ground reports that the formation has not yet been identified by the enemy. Last minute checks of weapons are made and the pilots check their aircrafts' instruments for any deviation from the normal. By now they have calculated how much time they will have over the target before having to return to base for fuel.

TWO MINUTES!

"Mission A47Z – two minutes out and climbing." The mission leader starts a gentle climb to firing height and also to allow him to identify the target area. The OP commander calls over the radio that he has the formation visual. He also reports that the enemy have started to run, using the escape route next to the river line. He directs the lead gunship in the direction that the insurgents were last seen moving.

Over the radio a call is heard at one minute away, "Bats – rolling in, live in the dive…bombs gone and on target!" The Impala strike aircraft drop their ordinance on time and the flash of the explosion followed by a huge column of dust and smoke shoots violently skywards. A shock wave gently rocks the choppers followed by the muffled sound of bomb blasts heard through padded earphones in the helmets of the aircrew.

As the smoke and dust from the bomb strike starts to dissipate the gunship is overhead target area. Mission leader is now at firing height, 150-300 metres above ground level. He enters a left- hand orbit above the bombed area, looking for life in order to destroy it.

After a few turns, what appears to be several camouflaged bodies becomes apparent under the bushes. He quickly gives the gunner instructions to fire. Cannon fire rips into the trees while the recoil causes helicopters to yaw slightly to the right.

Immediately the popping sound of small arms fire is heard by the aircrew, accompanied by the flicker of green tracer rounds whizzing past the canopy. Stomach muscles tighten; the adrenalin begins to flow. Voices over the radio pitch an octave higher.

In order to maintain control mission leader nonchalantly transmits a slow controlled message in a monotone voice over the radio: "Contact!…it would appear as if the locals are restless today…"

Again the helicopter becomes a target. The OP commander reports that the firing is coming from a small patch of thick bush some 50 metres from where the first rounds were fired.

The gunships direct their attention to the bush while the reaction force commander

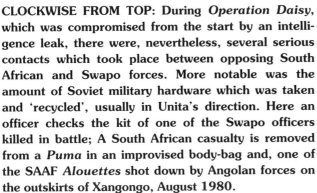

CLOCKWISE FROM TOP: During *Operation Daisy*, which was compromised from the start by an intelligence leak, there were, nevertheless, several serious contacts which took place between opposing South African and Swapo forces. More notable was the amount of Soviet military hardware which was taken and 'recycled', usually in Unita's direction. Here an officer checks the kit of one of the Swapo officers killed in battle; A South African casualty is removed from a *Puma* in an improvised body-bag and, one of the SAAF *Alouettes* shot down by Angolan forces on the outskirts of Xangongo, August 1980.

and the mission leader decide to put down their stopper groups. It seems that the surprise was complete and the insurgents have not had the chance to escape and are still confined to a relatively small area. The commanders decide to follow the original plan made before take-off.

The troop-carrying Pumas *have meanwhile remained in a wide right-hand orbit, well clear of small arms or rocket fire. They are ordered to drop their troops at designated points. The fight is on!*

Initial stages of any contact can be confusing, often disorientating, particularly if there is a misunderstanding between troops on the ground who have called in for air support and reaction force commanders. If surprise has not been attained, the insurgents use their escape routes

to maximum advantage.

Also, the area of operation can take place over a fairly large terrain. This can have a negative effect on the outcome as mutual support between stopper groups and the all-important support for the troops on the ground from the gunships can be stretched to more than the reaction force can contain. The result is a loss of kills.

DEPLOYMENT OF STOPPER GROUPS AND SWEEPLINE

The No. 2 gunship leaves the immediate contact area to give fire support, if necessary, to the *Pumas* approaching predetermined drop-off points for the stopper groups. You never know who is waiting on the ground...

As the first *Puma* approaches its LZ, the gunship pilot gives the pilot instructions; "Turn left...roll out...LZ 500 metres...slow down...LZ on your nose 200 metres...100

151

metres…call when visual." The *Puma* pilot transmits: "Visual and landing."

As this is happening the door gunners spray the surrounding bush on the approach to and around the LZ with fire from their machine-guns mounted in doorways. A thick cloud of dust spreads upwards as the *Puma* pulls into the hover. For moments the helicopter is completely obscured; as the muck clears small antlike figures can be observed leaping onto the ground to take up defensive positions around the vulnerable chopper. Within seconds the dust cloud completely obscures the *Puma* again, as it lifts off, indicating that troops have deplaned and are safely on the ground.

Out of the dust, leaves and dirt the helicopter appears once more, accelerating to obtain forward speed. Seconds later a callsign reports: "Stop 1 on the ground." These men are ready, in position for further orders.

Once all the troops have been deployed, mission leader instructs all but one of the larger helicopters to return to base and refuel. The remaining *Puma* is instructed to remain in orbit around the AO, available and ready to pick-up and re-deploy any stopper group if necessary and to be on standby for medevac should that need arise.

In the Angolan war, experience showed that following a contact, insurgent groups would follow the line of least resistance to escape from an attack on their position. If a river line was nearby they would invariably use that route to make good their getaway. Normally the reaction force commander would deploy stopper groups on a position in the direction of the flight. These deployments needed to have good fields of fire and be in positions where they could force the enemy into open areas. Not long afterwards a sweepline would be sent out at the position opposite to that of the stopper groups or to counter the largest group of insurgents trying to escape.

The task of the reaction force commander would then be to control the sweepline so that a solid front could be maintained. This was important as it was easy for troops on the ground to lose visual sight of one another in the thick bush. If the sweepline became ragged, the possibility existed that the troops may have lost direction and could end up in a fire-fight with one another. That actually happened a few times.

The danger also existed that the gunship could fire on troops that had become separated from their sweepline. In order to prevent accidents from 'friendly fire', it became custom that 'friendly' participants would have a day-glo patch stuck to the underside of their bush hats. Once on the ground the hat was reversed showing pilots above the position of Own Forces.

With more than one gunship orbiting it was occasionally difficult for section leaders of stopper groups to determine from which helicopter their instructions were coming. It was important for troops on the ground – at all times – to know exactly which helicopter was the lead gunship; troops rarely had the time to orientate their positions, perhaps with the help of a compass, to determine which direction is north, south, east or west. There were often choppers at all four points of direction.

To reduce the workload on the section leader, the reaction force commander would give directions relative to *his* position in the orbit or maybe attempt to fly over them in the direction that they were ordered to direct their fire. It was therefore preferable that the lead gunship was clearly marked so that it could easily be identified.

The most common type of identification was for mission leader to tape a square half-metre large orange day-glo panel onto the tailboom of his craft. Although this insignia tended to attract much of the insurgents ground-to-air fire, the advantages far outweighed the risk involved.

The flight engineer/gunner also had to have a consistently high standard of accuracy. All commanders were aware that the 20mm cannon is an accurate weapon and that the larger round has a lethal radius sometimes in excess of five metres.

Often contacts between the insurgents and security forces in the thick bush occurred within a few metres of each other and the gunner had to be able to put down fire support without inflicting casualties on Own Forces.

THE RECOVERY

Once the sweepline had moved through the contact area and the gunner linked up with stopper groups at the opposite end of the AO, the reaction force commander usually instructed both groups to form one consecutive line abreast formation. This would then move back through the area to the initial contact point where they were originally off-loaded to see what they could find.

By sweeping back through the contact area, the reaction force commander could ensure that all insurgent weapons and equipment was collected for transportation back to base, to locate enemy wounded and to capture or kill any insurgents that may have escaped the 'net' in the initial stages of the contact. In the confusion of combat, some insurgents would tend to return to the original cauldron of fire in an attempt to escape the sweepline moving outwards from the centre.

All prisoners, insurgent weapons and equipment was then taken to a central point where a helicopter could be called in for transportation back to base. Once that had been accomplished, the troops would gather at the nearest LZ for an uplift and to be flown back to base for the debriefing.

There was a hot meal and cold beer waiting back home, even though 'home' was usually little more than a tent in the hot, dry sand. Or another call-out…

It was just another day…

CHAPTER 16

KOEVOET OPERATIONS

The Ultimate Coin Deployment

One can usually tell how effective any particular unit or regiment is in an ongoing war or campaign by talking to their adversaries. The Japanese regarded the Ghurkas as barbarians. Of course, the sentiment was thoroughly reciprocated. In Aden there wasn't an Arab who did not invoke the wrath of Allah on the head of Colonel 'Mad Mike' Mitchell and his men of the Argyll and Sutherland Highlanders. Similarly the Germans detested kilted regiments almost as much as the Irish Republican Army does in present times.

So it is, even to this day that the name *Koevoet* – it means in Afrikaans, *Crowbar* – is regarded by South Africa's English-language press as perhaps the most pernicious unit ever formed on the sub-continent.

This Police Counter Insurgency Unit fought for more than a decade in South West Africa and Angola and were afterwards brought to South Africa to clean up township scraps. They did this so effectively that the African National Congress/Communist Party of South Africa Alliance insisted that they be disbanded. It was an ultimatum: *Koevoet* must go! And they did, early 1992.

This is a curious development, since *Koevoet* was the one unit which very quickly brought South African township disturbances to a halt. Very clearly they were an ultra-efficient, no-nonsense unit with an incredible elan that really only became evident under difficult circumstances. And South African township violence, as we have seen, can sometimes be extremely dangerous.

South African Army engineer trips a Russian TM-57 landmine laid by Swapo insurgents in main road north of Oshakati. Landmines were the single most serious threat to *Koevoet*'s mobility; This force ranged widely over Ovamboland in their *Casspir* armoured vehicles.

Koevoet in the South West African border (today Namibia) campaign was a phenomenon.

It was a tiny unit by comparison with other operational groups in the field and was composed almost entirely of policemen and former Swapo combatants who had been 'turned'. Their strength lay in their remarkable tracking skills; their staying power in the field and their ability to bring in *Alouette* gunships at the precise moment that a ground sighting was imminent. This was helicopter warfare at its most practical level and the tactics employed are likely to be studied by protagonists of this form of warfare for a very long time to come. Certainly it has an application in other 'small wars'.

Koevoet was founded in June 1979 with a strength of ten security policemen, both white and black, and 64 special constables. The aim of establishing the unit – which could react without delay to information received (unlike the army, *Koevoet* never indulged in random patrols) and also interpret insurgent spoor with all possible speed during normal operations – was to "take the war to the enemy".

In early 1980 it acquired its own small Fire Force as well. By the end of that year it had killed 511 insurgents for a loss of 12. This trend continued to the end of the war, with *Koevoet* consistently scoring the highest 'kills' of any security force unit or regiment whether army, police or marine.

In its final form *Koevoet* consisted of platoon-sized fighting teams, travelling in heavily gunned armoured vehicles, each able to operate on its own for up to a week at a time. These were named *Casspirs*. Ops K units were stationed in Kaokoveld, Ovamboland and Kavango; teams were not area-bound and went where need took them. For a while they operated in Angola.

There were a handful of men in *Koevoet's* leadership group who excelled above all others in the Swapo war. These were field commanders like Police Lieutenant Frans Conradie and his close associates, Captains Johan 'Sakkie' van Zyl, Eugene de Kock, 'Sakkie' du Plessis and others; all were physically tough, efficient and highly professional fighting men. They were prepared to risk their lives and their careers for those who fought with them, black and white, and, in turn, were adored by them, often to their embarrassment.

These men were frank in admitting to me that while they did the work on the ground, it was the choppers that came in for the kill and brought results. Other units had similar facilities at their command but it was *Koevoet* which scored the most often, largely because they worked closely with the pilots that reacted to their bidding; both on and off operations. Back at base *Koevoet* commanders were usually to be found in the Air Force mess at Ondangua. Aggressive, intelligent flying appealed to the *Koevoet* commanders and they soon had their 'favourite' gunship

pilots, although they generally got on quite well with all the fliers.

The mutual trust between the helicopter pilots and 'K' operators was especially evident in follow-up operations. The pilots would fly exactly as the 'K' commander requested – in contrast to dealing with national servicemen under the same conditions. In latter instances the pilots would usually take charge from the air and direct the movement of ground troops.

With *Koevoet* contacts, in contrast, pilots like Neall Ellis would often land in hazardous terrain, pick up the 'K' commander and his black team leader and go airborne to make an assessment, perhaps directing 'flushing fire' at thick bush areas to unsettle insurgents when necessary and drop them off with their team again when a fire-fight was imminent.

So successful was *Koevoet's* top 'scorer' Frans Conradie that he was responsible for 98 kills in 1981 and more than 80 in 1982 (the year before he died). By August 1983 – he died in September that year – his tally was already over the 60 mark.

Nor was knocking off Swapo 'cadres' an easy act to follow. The revolutionary movement was a well-trained, well-equipped force, the majority with East German, Soviet or Cuban backing. Technically, in handling Eastern Bloc equipment, they were as good as the South Africans, who had the advantage of a western background, experience, education and training.

Every kill achieved by Conradie and his men was a physical head count. An enemy was not a statistic until he lay prostrate on the ground, his weapon and pack usually arranged with other bodies in a neat little row, ready for photographing and classifying.

For his part, Conradie must have come through well over 150 contacts in a career that spanned a decade. He was never seriously wounded in action. He once took an AK bullet between the ribs, but the shock was absorbed by one of the curved AK magazines in his Soviet-style chest webbing.

He carried a Kalashnikov AK-47 of choice, maintaining that in African conditions, it was the best infantry weapon in the world. Also, ammunition was readily available; he took what he needed from those he had killed.

It is significant, perhaps, that there are entire regiments in the South African Army which have seen extended service along the Angola border and elsewhere that cannot claim such success: or even a fraction of the number of kills. It is estimated that in his fighting career that spanned all of southern Africa, Rhodesia included, he accounted for close to 1 000 guerrillas. It's a further contradiction that Conradie was not in the army. He was a policeman.

Possibly it's an irony – or a quirk of any man's ultimate destiny – that Frans Conradie's end came in a road accident. Having returned from a week-long sortie to the tiny

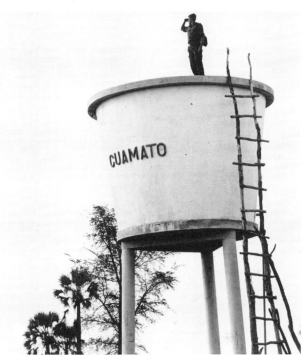

CLOCKWISE FROM TOP: Dust was always a serious problem while operating in the African bush during the dry season; Cuamato camp during the battle against Fapla forces; Soldier on the look-out on the Cuamato water tower; Troops remove the body of a Swapo soldier killed in a raid; Refuelling in remote areas required a great deal of adaptation to cope with demands.

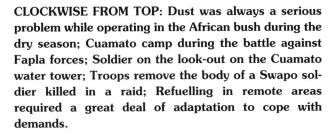

garrison town of Oshakati in Ovamboland, he was heading for home after having had a drink with the 'boys', when his vehicle overturned. Conradie was pinned in his seat; he bled to death before he reached hospital.

The man next to him – a senior NCO in the force – was hurt. He survived. Before dawn there were few people in Oshakati or the nearby Air Force base of Ondangua who did not know that Frans had gone on his last 'op'.

The following day, an entire region – whites as well as blacks who had come to know and respect this man – mourned the death of a gallant fighter.

His comrades flew back with his body to South Africa. A special flight was laid on by the South African Air Force to bury him in his home town of Rustenburg in the Transvaal. Frans Conradie was laid to rest with full military honours, and though still a lieutenant – who had worked his way to a commission through the ranks – there were generals present at his graveside that hot September afternoon.

That night, those men with whom he had shared action in a remote region of Africa for the previous three or four years used money that Frans had laid aside for just such an occasion. He had often joked about the $200 he had put away to provide the drinks "so you boys can laugh when I die. Not cry". That comment, stated in that quaint though strident voice of his and usually accompanied by his characteristic half grin, was totally in keeping with his personality. Affable, some would regard it.

At the wake they talked about little else but Frans; Frans the fighter, unflappable when under fire; the practical joker; the lover; the military historian with an awesome library of reference works; the party-giver; the provider of good things to his mates; the punctilious – for he was a stickler to detail when in the field; the collector of military trivia (which included an incredible selection of Cuban and Soviet belt buckles taken from those who would never need them again) and Frans the tactician. In this role he was superlative, in planning and in the final execution of duties.

He had a quirk of going into battle with the hi-fi speakers attached to his fighting vehicles blaring at full volume, usually something Wagnerian. The pop songs *Bad Moon Rising* and *Another One Bites the Dust* were also favourites.

But getting into the final phase of a full-blown contact with well armed and increasingly well-trained Swapo insurgents was also an experience. To some it was an exercise in skill, combined with a basic intuitive cunning that fringed on the atavistic. For Frans Conradie was essentially a survivalist.

This quality, alone, earned him the highest praise throughout his fighting career from South Africa's often hard-pressed chopper pilots who most times provided the back-up when he needed it most. They were always happy to give it, for when Frans called them in, there were results.

Using air and – when he needed it – ground support to cut off or corner a group of insurgents, Frans Conradie could manipulate his own, and often enemy forces with the kind of foresight with which few military leaders are blessed.

In the words of double gold *Honoris Crux* winner, Air Force pilot Arthur Walker, Frans was a 'natural'.

"He would never rush the contact. Nor would he let it drag on so long that the enemy had time to regroup or reorganise. He remained behind them and when he believed it the right moment, he would say 'go for it'."

Distance and fuel considerations in the vast terrain of southern Africa's largest conflict – especially where helicopters were concerned – were of paramount importance. But then Conradie used experience garnered as an accomplished forward air controller; he had become an expert, although he had done the course years before.

Captain Walker also spoke about another quality that he and his fellow pilots admired. Frans Conradie, even under the heaviest fire, always had time for a laugh. He was never known to 'lose his cool'.

"Of course this had a magic effect on the men he led into battle. They would follow him anywhere – black and white ..." said Walker.

On one occasion a *Koevoet* team scored 11 kills as a result of the remarkable powers of observation of Arthur Walker. It was about 17:00 hours and Walker was flying back to Ondangua from Eenhana base in the east of Ovamboland when he saw about seven or eight bicycles lying at the edge of a small clump of bushes in his flight path.

He was immediately suspicious. Along with his No. 2 gunship, Walker started circling the area in a bid to establish why the cycles were there and who owned them.

While circling, the two gunships were hailed from a distance by a *Koevoet* team, callsign 'Zulu Victor', who had had an uninspiring day in the area searching for fresh spoor between Oshigambo and Okankolo. 'Zulu Victor' called Walker's radio frequency and asked what he was up to. Walker told him and 'Zulu Victor' changed direction towards the hovering gunships.

At that stage the bicycle owners were nowhere to be seen but the 'K' team nevertheless spread out and moved rapidly towards the scene, with the two gunships still hovering overhead.

When they were about 75 metres from the clump of bushes, the vehicles suddenly drew heavy automatic fire; the fight was on! Walker and the other gunship had to hold their fire for most of the contact as the *Koevoet* team – according to their fashion – drove right into the source of fire. The two adversaries were having a go at one another at very close quarters.

CLOCKWISE FROM TOP: *Koevoet* officer, Captain Johan 'Sakkie' van Zyl, with his men on ops in Ovamboland; *Casspir* operational vehicles at an Ovambo village during routine patrols; Heavy machine-gun that originally graced a *Vampire* jet's wings, now mounted on a *Casspir*; *Koevoet* convoy on the move and; *Koevoet* troops douse ammunition with paraffin prior to operational duties to remove excess dust.

Meanwhile, Walker and his buddy covered the open area around the bush and in the dust and chaos killed several insurgents that had tried to escape. In the end, eleven Swapo saboteurs – all in civilian clothes – lay dead with their carbines, rifle grenades, an impressive array of TNT explosives, safety fuses and detonators. It later emerged that the group was one of the most notorious saboteur gangs that the war had produced south of Angola.

Their leader whose combat name was 'Jet Fighter'; his side-kick 'Nicky' and their team of Russian-trained engineers had successfully eluded the security forces for over a year. During that time they had destroyed telephone poles and other communications equipment, planted landmines and acquired a reputation for ruthlessness.

If it had not been for the chopper pilots' instincts that something was amiss, along with their innate bush war sixth sense, coupled with their eagerness for a scrap, the 11-man squad might have been active for a while longer.

There are dozens of anecdotes that illustrate the life of Conradie the man and the fighter, but one needs an appreciation of military logic to understand some of them.

Conradie was proud of the fact that in the three years he had been with the Police Special Task Force, he had never lost a man in combat. As the war intensified the inevitable had to happen. And so, into his fourth year, while Lieutenant Conradie was faced with other duties back at base, his squad ran into an ambush and lost one of the black trackers who had been with him since the beginning. This had been a source of great pride; it was important to him that he never lost anybody in his team, until that day.

Mortified at the news, Conradie drove 100 kilometres across dirt roads in the four-wheel-drive pick-up van that was as familiar around Oshakati as its owner, to reach the area where the dead man lay. The fact that the road could have been mined didn't matter; one of his men had been killed.

He was shown the dead man in the local clinic. Without hesitation the youthful lieutenant walked up to the body, pulled away the sheet covering the face and placed a kiss firmly on its forehead.

"*Totsiens, ou maat,*" he was heard to say in Afrikaans (Goodbye, old friend). That was Frans Conradie…

It was Conradie's physical ability which impressed everyone who knew him.

In many respects he was one of the finest trackers in the operational area, often following a spoor for days at a stretch, usually on the ground, ahead of his back-up vehicles. His staying power was regarded as remarkable.

On many occasions he would start on the spoor in the dry, desert-like sand of Ovamboland at first light and follow it at a running gait with the vehicles following behind until sunset; or until he made contact. He could easily cover 50 kilometres at a stretch like this in extremely diffi-cult terrain where the POM-Z booby-trap is king. 'Sakkie' van Zyl recalls that he had seen him a few times when he was the only person on the ground looking for a difficult spoor, his whole team having returned to the vehicles, catching a breather.

He could judge the freshness of a spoor as well as any black tracker; also how heavy the man was carrying, whether he was wounded, tired, hungry or active. In counter-tracking measures, too, he was an acknowledged fundi.

One of his last episodes involved three insurgents on the hop. For three days, Conradie – on foot and running – followed their trail heading steadily towards the Angolan border. When the enemy 'bombshelled' – split up – he followed one spoor at a time, until he killed the man at the end of it. Then he returned to the original point and started again; and so on, until all three were dead.

He would move across the sandy terrain bare-chested, in only a pair of shorts and running shoes, carbine in hand. If he needed water, he would drink it on the run. Food was for later, or before he started.

Naturally, such measures paid off. Conradie was one of the few active fighters along the Angola border to have 'taken out' fifteen Swapo in a single strike and he did it several times. He was also the only policeman to have called in a jet strike to wipe out an insurgent pocket that was showing stiff resistance. There fifteen more of the enemy died. He killed groups of ten on four or five occasions, usually going into the contact with his 20mm cannon mounted atop his *Casspir* fighting vehicle blazing.

The gun itself also had an illustrious career. It had been scrounged (with the help of a few pals in the Air Force) from an old SAAF *Vampire*; it was an original Hispano-Oerlikon. Conradie modified the weapon slightly, cutting down the barrel so it became easier to handle.

In 1979 when the new police fighting unit *Koevoet* was formed (symbolically to 'dislodge the terrorist menace') Conradie was approached by the only other man he would ever serve under: Police Brigadier *Sterk* (Strong) Hans Dreyer, who also had an incredible following among his men. The special unit, it was stated at the time, would launch a series of unconventional onslaughts against the insurgent force that would take it throughout the region adjoining Angola.

Koevoet attracted some of the best specialist combatants in the force. Designated 'Operation K' at the time, it was a development out of security intelligence gathering operations in the border area.

Koevoet methods were tough and uncompromising from the start. But they achieved results. There were many who compared the unit with Rhodesia's erstwhile 'Pseudo Squad', Selous Scouts.

CHAPTER 17

LANDING ZONE REQUIREMENTS AND PROCEDURES

STANDARD HELICOPTER LANDING ZONE

1. Surface.

The ground in the centre of the LZ must be even and sufficiently firm to support a fully laden helicopter. The surface is to be cleared of loose articles such as rubbish, tree stumps, loose gravel and loose grass. Ash and dust constitute a hazard to helicopter operations, therefore the surface is not to be cleared by burning. A natural grass covering provides the best surface for helicopter operations.

2. Slope.

The ground should be relatively level and the slope must not exceed 5 degrees (1:12).

3. Puma.

Overall Diameter - 50 metres.
Central area cleared to ground level - 35 m diameter.
Hard surface in centre of LZ - 15 m diameter.
Area between the 35 m diameter and the 50 m diameter is to be cleared to a 1 m height.
Obstructions on edge of clearing not higher than 6 m, single oustanding obstructions adjacent to the landing site to be cleared to the right height.

DIMENSIONS OF PUMA LANDING ZONE

Plan View

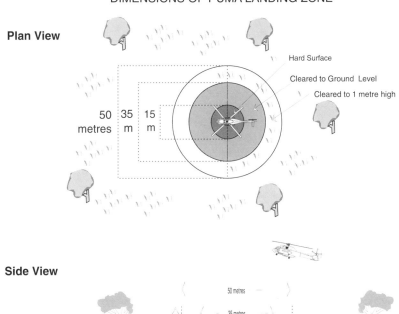

Side View

Landing a helicopter in the bush on operations far from the home base can be a problem if the troops involved have not been trained in the preparation of Landing Zones (LZs). An overloaded Puma *or* Alouette *cannot always take off or land vertically; the pilot often needs to make use of ground effect to complete the manoeuvre. When loaded to maximum, the helicopter behaves similarly to a conventional fixed-wing aircraft and needs a shallow flight path for approach and departure.*

A preferred area is usually a large open dry marsh or *vlei*, perhaps covered with grass. This is not always possible in southern African bushveld conditions. Ground forces trained in the selection and preparation of suitable areas for landing and taking off are aware that when selecting an LZ, trees and other hindrances must be taken into account. If a large enough clearing is not available, the men on the ground need to clear all obstacles in a bid to make an area large enough for the helicopter to touch down and take off again.

Although the South African Air Force (SAAF) has laid down requirements for a standard helicopter landing zone, this is not always possible in an operational scenario, especially when there is combat.

So the SAAF has a rule of thumb; the LZ dimensions must be greater than one-and-a-half times the rotor dimensions of the chopper. In the case of a *Puma* helicopter, a clearing of at least 25 metres in diameter will suffice. For the *Alouette*, the dimensions should be not less than 18 metres.

The ground must be even. It must also be sufficiently firm to support the weight of the helicopter and the slope must not exceed five degrees in any direction. Additionally, the ground surface must be cleared of loose objects such as garbage, tree stumps, large rocks, loose gravel and loose grass clumps.

Also, trees must be cut to ground level to prevent damage to the underside of the helicopter's fuselage. Ash and dust are hazardous to helicopter operations and the surface should not be cleared by burning undergrowth and grass as natural ground cover provides the most acceptable surface for this kind of exercise.

Wind direction is not an important factor when constructing an LZ, unless there are tall obstacles in the flight path. A helicopter pilot will normally land and take off into wind.

Helicopter pilots are trained to execute night landings with various forms of lights marking the LZ. The standard illumination is a trapezium shape, using four battery-powered lights mounted on stands secured into the ground. If the standard lights are not available, persons holding torches can be used. This has often been the case in the southern African military scenario.

The trapezium is designed to give a pilot an indication from which direction the wind is blowing as well as to provide visual information on the landing direction as well as the helicopter's horizontal and vertical position relative to the ideal flight path.

Most helicopter operations in south Angola were in difficult, often unchartered terrain. In dusty or hazy conditions in the bush, adequate LZs were often difficult to define and accidents did happen.

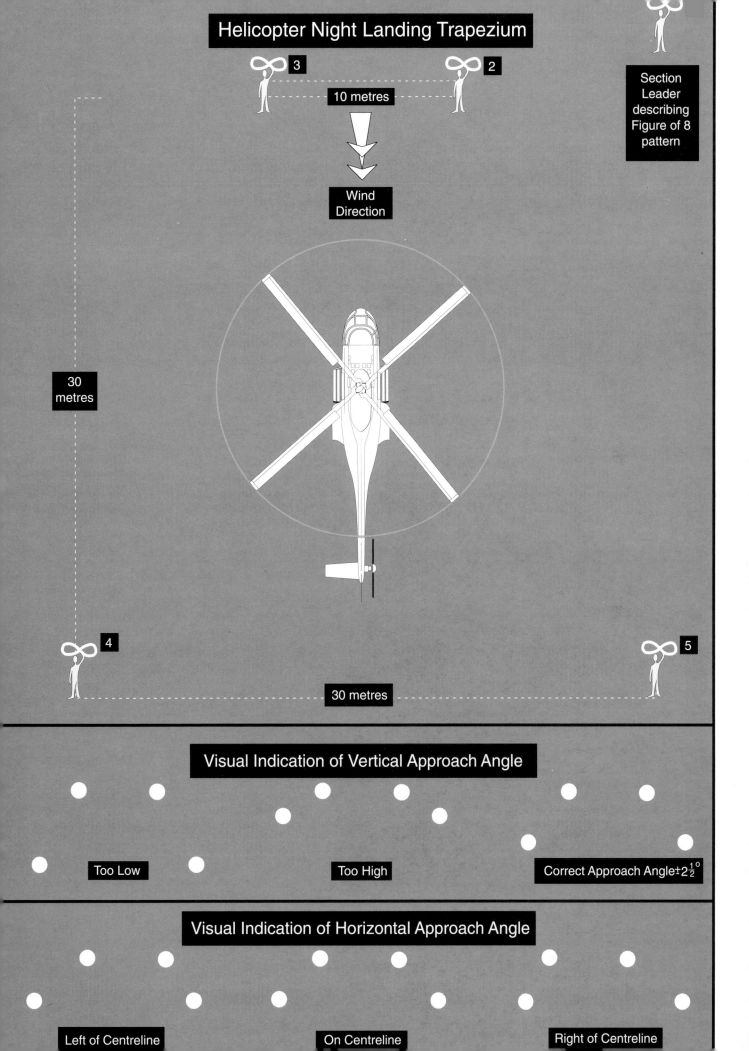

If torches are used to bring in a chopper, the ideal number of lights is five. Four individuals, each holding a torch should be positioned at the points of the trapezium where the lights would normally have been placed. They should be facing the approach direction. The torch beams should be held at an angle of approximately two to three degrees above the horizon. The fifth individual – usually the section leader with a radio for ground-to-air comms – stands at the 12 o'clock position of the trapezium and faces the approaching aircraft. He describes a figure eight pattern with his torch. This gives the pilot the visual impression of a flashing light.

The section commander continually faces the approaching aircraft, even if it circles, while the pilot – using the ground light for guidance – positions himself in the circuit for final approach.

On short finals or on instructions from the pilot, all torches are pointed downwards (at the feet) so as not to disorientate the aircrew during the final touch-down. The pilot brings the chopper to the ground in the middle of the trapezium.

Other light sources such as fires, pressure lamps, open-ended tins filled with sand and burning with an inflammable substance such as paraffin or kerosene can also be used. They often have, particularly in Angola. Many hundreds of C-130 flights were guided into Angolan airstrips using spaced cans filled with a sand and paraffin mixture along the length of often primitive runways. However, tins or lamps mush be partially buried to prevent them from being blown over by the downwash from the rotors.

Open fires should be carefully positioned and prepared beforehand as the downwash has caused the flames to set fire to the surrounding bushveld.

Vehicles can also be used to illuminate an LZ. These should be parked at the edge of the LZ, about twenty-five metres apart, but facing towards the line of approach.

Headlights must be on dim and be angled at about 45 degrees so that all the light beams centre on one central point in the middle of the LZ or where the helicopter is required to touch down.

It is essential that the chopper approach the vehicles from behind, passing between them. All radio antennae should be removed or lowered to prevent contact.

If the LZ is in an area where there are many other lights such as in an urban area or a village, a strobe position indicator light should be used. If this is not available, vehicle hazard lights should be on the flash setting.

Once the pilot has identified the LZ, these lights should be switched off.

During long-range penetration raids into Angola, planners had to allow for a good deal of improvisation, including the likelihood of ambush by the enemy with the possible loss or depletion of aviation fuel or ammunition. Order Groups were a regular event in the bush each evening.

CHAPTER 18

THE RUSSIANS LOSE SIX CHOPPERS IN ANGOLA

Neall Ellis fought as a chopper pilot in Angola for the best part of a decade. During the occasional cease-fires he would meet with some of the Angolan helicopter crews that opposed him and over a period of time got to know them quite well. Then, suddenly, several of these crews were shot down. Ellis's fighter pilot friends were responsible; four Mi-25 Hind attack helicopters and two Mi-17 Hip transporters were knocked out in two five-minute sorties.

SAAF *Impala* jet of the type that took part in cross-border raids into Angola and knocked-out six Soviet helicopters. The *Impala* is the Italian Macchi MB 326 K.

War has spawned anecdote since the beginning of time. So, too, has Angola.

A South African jet-fighter squadron equipped with SAAF *Impala* Mk2 strike aircraft knocked out six Angolan Air Force (FAPA) choppers in two sorties in the last week of October 1985, effectively bringing to an end the massive Russian-backed and supplied *Operation Second Congress* which had been launched to cripple Dr Jonas Savimbi's Unita movement.

For several years Unita had been making gains from its bush headquarters at Jamba in the extreme south-east corner of this vast country almost twice the size of Texas. It is a remote and isolated region of Angola, known since Portuguese colonial times as *Terras do Fim Mundo* (Land at the End of the Earth).

Operation Second Congress took the form of a two-pronged action, designed primarily to regain control of the Cuzombo Panhandle and to recapture Mavinga by 2 September 1985, but also to impale Savimbi on his own defences.

The combined Angolan Army (Fapla) force would then launch a final assault on Jamba (Savimbi's capital), destroying its main base of operations. That was the intent. But there were problems.

In all of south-east Angola there were only two airfields which could be used by the Angolan Air Force; Menongue, known during Portuguese times as Serpa Pinta, and

Cuito Cuanavale further towards the Zambian border.

Cuito was demarcated specifically for FAPA helicopter operations during *Operation Second Congress* while jet support fighters were based at Menongue. Obviously, though, choppers moved between both airfields in communications, support and resupply roles. Helicopter deployment at Cuito was four Mi-25 *Hinds*, two Mi-8s and four Mi-17s.

Anyone who has seen the Angolan hinterland is aware that this was a most difficult country in which to wage war. Apart from a handful of large rivers, the terrain is almost featureless with trees and huge expanses of sparse forest reaching to about 30 metres in height and mostly interspersed by savannah. The topography of eastern Angola barely changes by more than 30 metres for as much as five or six hundred kilometres northwards from the Rundu Air Force base in the Caprivi *Zipvel*.

At the time that the war was being waged, Caprivi in South West Africa (now Namibia), was the South African Army and Air Force base farthest east in the vast land under dispute; within minutes flying time farther eastwards you are over Zimbabwe. Botswana lies to the south and Zambia to the immediate north. None of these countries were particularly well-disposed towards South Africa during this period of conflict.

One of the more prominent features of eastern Angola are the vast open grasslands, often stretching for hundreds of kilometres and known locally by the Angolan Ovimbundu tribespeople as *chanas*. Catch an army or a squadron of tanks in an open *chana* and two or three helicopter gunships could cause a great deal of damage in 20 minutes.

Navigation in eastern Angola is difficult; there are no outstanding geographical features; no hills, no escarpments or any towns of consequence and the safest navigation method is still to stick to the river lines or follow the few roads that criss-cross the region like spider tracks. The word 'road' is used loosely; they are essentially sandy tracks; and if the ruts become too worn or too deep, it's easier to make new tracks alongside the old ones. Sometimes you can spot a dozen tracks in the sand alongside each other, all leading in the same direction. Bedrock lies 60 metres below the surface.

In the Cuito Cuanavale area it was principally helicopters – the *Hips* and the *Hinds* that were used to re-supply Angolan garrisons in the interior. There were times when some Fapla brigades were running desperately short of essentials because of Savimbi's tenacious policy of ambushing road convoys; few of these got through intact. Unita had mastered the art of surprise in this desolate region.

FAPA assignments were flown on a daily basis, providing such necessities as fuel, vehicle spares and medical supplies. Medevac missions were also launched when necessary, but to spend time and fuel on bringing out a wounded or ill individual meant that that person had to be a very important person indeed.

Ordinary troops were (and are, even today) expendable. No one wasted effort on them.

It was the Mi-25 *Hinds* that provided the escorts for these lumbering rotor-wing transporters, as well as giving close-air support (CAS) for ground forces. They would also sometimes provide flushing fire on to Landing Zones during troop deployments; on these missions 57mm rockets would be fired using a shallow dive attack profile and, on rare occasions, cannon fire.

Chopper formations would transit at between 3 000 and 6 000 feet above ground level (AGL) with escort helicopters a minute or two behind. The formation used would be in line astern for the transport helicopters, with the Mi-25s sometimes flying a loose echelon pattern and about 1 500 feet separation. South African intelligence had disclosed that FAPA helicopter pilots feared Unita ground fire more than any threat from a fixed-wing formation; as part of Washington's anti-Marxist Angolan policy, Dr Savimbi's forces had been given *Stinger* missiles.

Soviet advisers to FAPA had been heard to comment that the threat of RPG-7 rockets was also a big problem. Depending on the threat, helicopter formations would often be escorted by MiG-23s flying at about 15 000 feet AGL and orbiting to the rear.

In general, it soon became evident – even to the Rus-

sians, Cubans and East Germans – that the standard of flying within the Angolan Air Force was poor. Navigation by pilots was so bad that their foreign advisers prevailed on them to use physical features such as river lines, bush tracks and 'roads' to reach their destinations.

All South African intelligence briefings would mention the fact that the Angolans would very rarely fly on a direct route to any point. Also, it was clear very early on in the war that the basic lack of navigational competence was another reason for flying at height. Even then, pilots often failed to find their LZs and missions tended to be planned for the same time of day.

Radio procedures and discipline within FAPA ranks were also poor. However, this improved as losses increased or when Russian pilots flew as formation leaders.

Only two radio frequencies were used by operational aircraft; one for fighter and helicopter operations and another for transport aircraft ops. Night flights were unheard of; helicopters returned to base before last light.

By October 1985, South African forces were heavily involved in the war with Unita in a bid to stem the flow of Fapla forces southwards towards Jamba. At about this stage Pretoria decided that it was essential to deploy *Impala* ground strike aircraft to Air Force Base Rundu, in Caprivi, to give Own Forces close-air support when requested to do so. Unita and South African Army elements engaged against Fapla brigades were only a fraction the number of the enemy; the ratio was something like one to 12.

By the last week of October 1985, it became clear that the Angolan ground offensive had fallen badly behind schedule.

Intelligence sources indicated that Fapla had decided to change its basic plan and launch a drive to capture Mavinga to the north of Cuito. Jamba, the intercept indicated, would come afterwards. It was all a softening-up process. These sources also mentioned that Angolan helicopters were flying on a daily basis to resupply ground forces.

With these facts in mind, Dr Savimbi approached his South African counterparts with a proposal: Why did the South Africans not shoot down the helicopters being deployed against him in south Angola using *Impala* jets based at Rundu? It was a bombshell of an idea!

Word has it that the first reaction by the South Africans was one of stunned silence. Then someone said something about such a move possibly escalating the war and bringing MiG-23s over South African air space in search of targets of their own. Someone else talked about that not being necessarily so, *especially if the Angolans were not aware that it was jets that had been used to down their choppers.*

RIGHT: 'Sharp end' of an *Impala* on ops over Angola from Rundu Air Force base. Herman Potgieter took this outstanding photo from a *Puma*.

And so the discussion went on until everyone sitting around the table on that momentous day agreed that perhaps there was merit in such an action. The proposal was referred to Pretoria and a signal came back 24 hours later with the authority to proceed.

But Unita was not to be involved. Savimbi was not even to know that the go-ahead had been given. There was good reason for this.

No one was certain to what extent Unita's command structure had been infiltrated by MPLA intelligence agents and, in any event, the South Africans always tended to play their cards close to their chest. Certainly, they did not intend to tell their principal Angolan ally that they intended shooting down Angolan helicopters and so, perhaps, alert the Angolans who could then take the appropriate counter-measures.

Military headquarters in Pretoria immediately instituted intensive flight evaluations to determine the most efficient method to knock out enemy choppers in the air using fighter jets. It was accepted that they had to do this without giving the *Hind* pilots a moment's opportunity to fire back; or to establish what it was that had shot them down. To determine the profile to be used for this action SAAF *Puma* helicopters were drafted in to simulate enemy chopper flying techniques and formations used.

The main problem that the *Impala* crews had to contend with was that while in Angolan air space they were forced in ingress low level (50 feet AGL) to stay out of enemy radar coverage. This was essential, first to maintain surprise and second, to prevent MiG-23 escort fighters from taking any kind of retaliatory measures during

approach and on the return legs.

The most suitable profile determined was to attack from either the side or from behind and perhaps slightly above the target helicopters.

The height that the enemy helicopters flew at presented problems for the standard quarter attack. If this was attempted with an *Impala* with full underwing stores, the speed at the top of the pitch tended to be a bit low and the helicopters could accelerate away from the attacking aircraft. Naturally this presented problems with the tracking solution.

A decision was reached to reduce the rate of pitch when the attack was initiated and to flatten out the peak of that pitch so as to maintain speed. The aircraft were to fly in pairs and, when attacking, a type of 'scissor' pattern was to be flown with the lead aircraft attacking the rearmost helicopter first, and the wingman moving into the kill on the chopper next in line. This pattern was repeated depending on the number of helicopters in the formation.

For the South African fighters there was no problem with the route likely to be flown by FAPA helicopters; they knew about the preference for features such as roads or river lines.

The *Impalas* were split up into four pairs, three for reconnaissance and attack and the fourth as a back-up and for 'search and rescue' if that became necessary. Additionally a pair of *Puma* helicopters were tasked to be airborne during the mission for 'search and rescue' purposes.

The combat zone was 35 minutes' *Impala* jet flying time from Rundu; timing for the operation was critical.

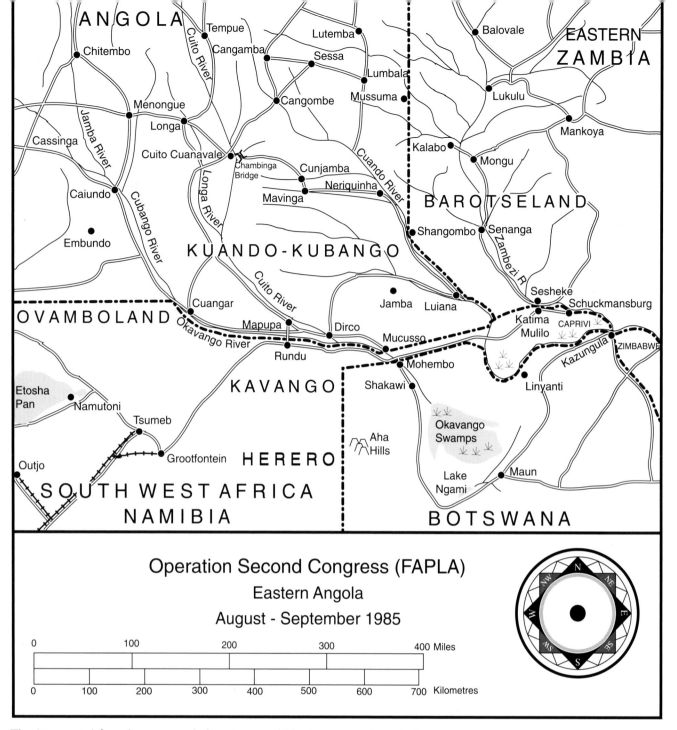

Operation Second Congress (FAPLA)

Eastern Angola

August - September 1985

0	100	200	300	400 Miles

0	100	200	300	400	500	600	700 Kilometres

The 'time gate' for when enemy helicopters would be in the most remote area between Cuito Cuanavale and the combat zone was given much attention.

Pairs of *Impalas* were to take off at four minute intervals, and to fly more or less the same route to the expected contact area and back.

Six headings were carefully calculated to give the most area coverage without placing the crews' lives or aircraft safety in jeopardy. Pilots were instructed to make one pass over the route and not to loiter if enemy helicopters had not arrived. Most important, radio silence was to be maintained at all times; the Angolans had the most sophisticated Soviet monitoring equipment and they could pin-point a position with DF equipment from a single radio emission.

To inform the pilots of the status of enemy choppers and their MiG-23 escorts, a fixed-wing single-engined aircraft was positioned nearby the area to pass on codewords; this was not unusual as these aircraft were always in the air, day and night. *Impala* crews were placed on immediate standby at Rundu; they would be scrambled as soon as word was received of enemy helicopter movement.

At approximately 16:00 hours Bravo on the afternoon of 27 September a brief radio message, in code, was received at the SAAF ops rooms, Rundu. Two enemy Mi-25

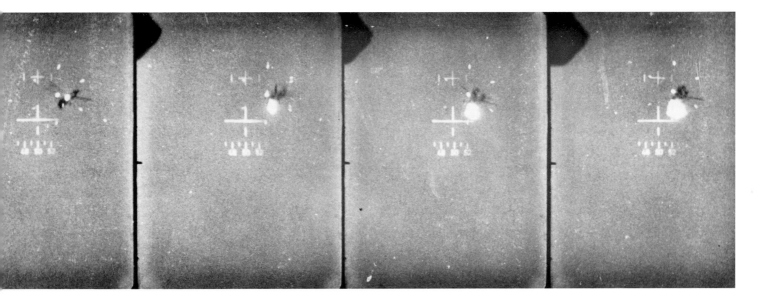

attack helicopters were airborne travelling from Cuito Cuanavale and flying in the direction of the war zone.

The *Impalas* were scrambled and headed north towards the previously designated AO.

It seemed as if only minutes had passed before the wingman of the second pair of *Impalas* made visual contact with the helicopter formation above him. The helicopters were flying at approximately 2 000 feet AGL.

As he was in the most favourable position to attack, the wingman initiated his onslaught by pitching up towards the rearmost aircraft. He attacked from the rear and above the helicopter.

The wingman's burst of fire was observed by the lead aircraft to strike towards the rear of the fuselage. Moments later, the chopper started to burn and its pilot initiated a controlled descent towards the ground. The helicopter then began to burn furiously and the pilot fired off his FFAR rockets carried in the underwing pods before jettisoning all underwing stores and carrying on with the descent.

The leader of the *Impala* formation then saw the first helicopter initiate a steep descent towards the ground. He began his quarter attack and approached the descending helicopter from below and to the side. The helicopter, at that stage, had turned a full half-circle through 180 degrees and was still in a steep, nose-down diving attitude.

Using rotor diameter and not the size of the sight reticule – relative to the helicopter – to estimate his range the jet leader pegged the firing distance on the sight to 500 metres. His aim point was the spot just below the main rotor gear box. Fixing his gunsight in air-to-air mode, he only fired when the diameter of the diamonds on the sight was less than the rotor diameter and the pipper on the exhaust port.

Though he wasn't counting, nineteen rounds followed;

Destruction of an Angolan Air Force Mi-17 caught in the gun-camera of a SAAF *Impala* at the moment of impact from the jet's 20mm cannon.

he could clearly see the strikes on the starboard fuselage of the target, exactly where the pipper indicated. The attack was carried out at approximately four to five Gs.

Recounting the event afterwards, the pilot got the impression that suddenly everything had gone into slow motion; they could observe every detail: the A side panel of the aircraft flew off; the helicopter immediately adopted a nose-high position and the rotor blades separated. The machine then went into a tail slide, hit the ground and exploded, sending a plume of smoke and flame high into the air.

By this stage the wingman had repositioned his aircraft for a second pass on the leading Mi-25 and shot it down. With the second strike, its rotor blades also separated. The Russian-built helicopter crashed into the ground nose high and exploded.

Both *Impala* pilots descended to low level in order to evade any potential MiG-23 threat and returned to base at Rundu. Mission successful.

Two days passed before another strike was possible. At approximately 09:00 Bravo on 29 September word was passed back to the ops room at Rundu that a formation of helicopters was airborne from Cuito Cuanavale again, bound for the war zone. It consisted of two Mi-8/17s and two Mi-25s. The *Impalas* were scrambled and the same tactics and procedures used on the previous occasion were observed. It was almost a carbon copy repeat of the first strike, only this one was in the full glare of the morning sun.

It was not long before the crews spotted their targets; helicopters were flying along the Lomba River – at approximately 3 000 feet AGL. The two Mi-17s were in a line astern formation, about 1 000 metres apart. The Mi-25s – also about a kilometre behind them, were in an echelon formation. Separation was approximately 500 metres. Then everything happened quickly.

The wingman of the formation was in the best position to attack. He immediately initiated a quarter attack on the rear chopper. Pitching to approximately 1 000 feet above the Angolan aircraft and waiting until he was within striking range, the wingman fired a long burst of cannon into its fuselage. The helicopter started to burn, but continued on course.

The long burst and extremely low indicated airspeed after the pitch caused the engine of this *Impala* to flame out! Suddenly there was a problem among the attackers.

By now the formation leader had positioned himself for his attack on the second last helicopter, also an Mi-25. During his run in, he crossed ahead of the burning rearmost helicopter and, for a moment, was concerned that the Angolan pilot would squeeze off a couple of rounds. Nothing happened. At approximately 500 metres from target, the leader fired a short burst; his rounds struck the tailboom and the rotor.

A second later the entire after-section separated and the *Hind* spiralled, without burning, into the ground. It exploded on impact.

There were still two helicopters ahead; the two *Hip* transporters. By now they were aware that they were under attack, having probably been warned by the first Mi-25 that he had become a target; at this stage there was much radio chatter among the Angolans.

Having re-lit his engine, the wingman attacked the rear Mi-17. As he did so the helicopter carried out what could only be described as a full rudder turn in a desperate bid to observe his attacker. The *Impala* fired and the helicopter flipped onto its back, falling towards the ground upside down and exploding.

Only one of the original four helicopters remained airborne; the last Mi-17. Having seen what the *Impalas* had done to his comrades, he immediately descended to low-level as the lead *Impala* came in on the attack. But the *Hip* was too low for the leader to track properly and the jet's rounds exploded harmlessly on the ground behind target.

The two South African pilots determined that it could not be allowed to escape. Breaking radio silence the leader called to the other formations flying nearby. By now he had lost visual contact with the Mi-17 which had disappeared into the tree-line in a desperate bid to elude its pursuers.

In the debrief later it was noted that the *Hip* pilot had turned towards the attacking *Impala* forcing him to overshoot. The South Africans were convinced that since FAPA pilots had received no aerial combat training, it was to be assumed that that chopper was being flown by a Russian. His escape tactics indicated some knowledge of anti-fighter evasive training.

It was minutes before the next pair of *Impalas* arrived in the area. By now the Mi-17 pilot – believing that the jets had withdrawn – had regained some altitude and was heading towards home. The leader of the newly arrived pair of jets following on the tail of the Russian-built craft set himself up for an attack. Aware that this could happen, the *Hip*, in a zig-zag motion spotted the predator on his tail and put the nose down once again. He hit the ground in an open space between the trees in a controlled crash, the main rotors separating from the fuselage before it came to a standstill. The helicopter then toppled over onto its side.

The third pair of *Impalas* arrived in the area moments afterwards. It was time to move out; there were too many aircraft over the target area.

They had barely started to egress for their home base when the leaders spotted two MiG-23s flying over the burning wreckage at about 200 feet AGL. The MiGs did not orbit, but carried out a single pass over the wreckage, probably in a bid to ascertain whether anyone had survived.

Surprisingly, this was a new tactic; the South Africans were aware that Angolan fighter aircraft had never previously been observed at heights lower than 15 000 feet probably because of the threat of *Stingers*. Having passed once over the burning wrecks, the MiG-29s lit their afterburners, folded their wings and zoomed up to safer altitudes.

There were two consequences as a result of the loss of the six Russian-built helicopters. The Angolans never used their helicopters again during *Operation Second Congress*. They did deploy their French-built *Alouettes* to pull all their Russian advisers out of the front-line when the South Africans threatened to overrun Fapla positions, but nothing else.

Secondly, it was also acknowledged that this was the first time in history that an *Impala* jet-fighter, originally built by the Italians as the *Macchi MB 326 K* – ostensibly a trainer – had managed to destroy enemy aircraft in aerial combat.

It remained one of the contradictions of a war that had been on the go – first against the colonial Portuguese and later between the various political factions – since 1961; more than 30 years...

CHAPTER 19

HELICOPTERS IN EGYPT WITH THE AMERICAN RAPID DEPLOYMENT FORCE

With the formation of the Rapid Deployment Force (RDF) more than a decade ago, a new dimension was added to the US Defense Establishment. This became apparent in 1982 with the Rapid Deployment Force taking part in Operation Bright Star with elements of the Egyptian Army and Air Force in north-east Africa.

Clearly, the US Armed Forces managed to project a global dimension to their activities. It was fortunate that this happened when it did, for it placed emphasis on desert training and operations in a desert environment, which became particularly valuable when the Iraqi dictator Saddam Hussein posed a threat to Free World security.

While desert and semi-desert warfare is nothing new in US Army history, Middle East conditions are a far cry from what the Americans experienced, for instance, in the war for Texas independence or, almost a century later, in North Africa during the Second World War.

Operation Bright Star showed that a new form of preparedness was essential if the United States was to play a pre-eminent role in world politics. In this, they have regarded Egyptian cooperation as vital.

A flight of US Army helicopters from America's Rapid Deployment Force in formation over Cairo's pyramids. Leading are two OH-58 *Kiowa* Scouts followed by four UH-60 *Blackhawks* and, bringing up the rear are two AH-1 *Cobras*.

CLOCKWISE FROM TOP: A group of four Soviet-built Mi-8 Egyptian helicopters deployed during *Operation Bright Star* from Cairo West Air Base; A member of the 502nd Parachute Infantry rappelling from a *Blackhawk*; A disassembled *Blackhawk* emerges from the belly of US Air Force C5A *Galaxy* with the help of men of the 101 Airborne Division; Ground forces prepare for desert exercises during *Operation Bright Star*.

CHAPTER 20

THE SCORPION'S STING

Evasion and Escape in Angola

Captain Tinus van Rensburg isn't exactly graphic about how it felt for his chopper to be hit by an RPG-7 rocket in mid-flight except that there was no real difference between the blast and his fuel tanks exploding; both happened simultaneously. And he was within sight of the enemy on the ground...

Captain (today Brigadier) Tinus van Rensburg at the controls of an *Alouette* III, of the type in which he was shot down during a cross-border raid into Angola. His adventures to avoid capture would make an epic film.

Sunset over South African Air Force base Ondangua in northern South West Africa. An *Alouette* III hovers in the distance.

The way he describes it, he did not even see the missile coming.

One moment he was hovering about ten metres above ground – and a fairly large concentration of hostile insurgents well inside Angola – the next there was a heavy sensation of blast, "somewhere next to my head". The rocket hit the helicopter engine to his rear; fortunately for him the roto-engine absorbed much of the blast. His engineer was not so fortunate.

"It all happened so fast," he recounted. Less than a second later the cockpit of the South African Air Force *Alouette* III was enveloped in smoke.

"I could feel a searing, burning sensation about my neck and back; it came all the way through my helmet and flying jacket. The blaze must have been intense," he told me.

"I looked out towards my right and saw billows of fire and smoke everywhere. Everything was alight." As he remembers, the blast had also shattered the canopy; there were slivers of metal and perspex all over the place. More immediate, at that moment, the helicopter wasn't answering to her controls.

"I braced myself. The earth came rushing up towards me; there was no time to execute emergency procedures. I just prepared for impact and took it for granted that the engineer was doing the same." He apparently, somehow, managed to get the chopper to go down tail-first which absorbed some of the impact.

Captain van Rensburg wasn't alone in the air late that 1980 afternoon.

The insurgent attack group – all of them attached to the South West African Peoples Organisation (Swapo) – was part of a force that the South Africans had followed in embattled Ovamboland during their incursion from Angola. In northern South West Africa the group had spent days terrorising locals, attacking a few minor targets and laying landmines. A South African Army patrol caught up with them shortly after they had re-crossed northwards into Angolan territory; choppers from 17 Squadron SAAF took up the chase.

As he tells it, the group the South Africans were following in a 'hot pursuit operation' numbered about a hundred men. Their column, having formed up with Angolan Government Forces, included several vehicles painted in light camouflage, a design which had become synonymous with forces operating with the Cuban Command in this corner of Africa. "There was no mistaking who they were," Captain van Rensburg said. "By the same token, they knew we were following."

"We were still beyond range of normal gunfire when they started firing; they let go with everything they had, including several salvos of RPG-7s which self-destructed 900 metres out, most of them well off target."

"Then it happened. Suddenly everything which this war had represented for me in the past became a nightmare: I was at the fiery core of it all."

Although Captain van Rensburg's aircraft fell only a short distance, other South African helicopters circling the battle area were convinced that no one could have emerged alive from what appeared to be a mass of twisted and burning debris, smoke and exploding fuel. Though they watched for any evidence of movement in the immediate area of the crash, they saw none.

But, as van Rensburg recalls, what they didn't know was that he had been thrown clear on impact and landed in the middle of a Swapo section which had originally taken up defensive positions against their airborne pursuers. Seconds later, as he came round from being stunned by the impact, he was lying to one side of the burning chopper. His back was contorted in pain and, more importantly, he had nothing with which to defend himself. He was without his flight jacket or the 9mm Parabellum pistol that he normally carried in a holster on his belt; it had been ripped off his back in the crash. There was no chance whatever to get at the FN .762 calibre R1 rifle that was normally stacked at the rear of the cockpit. It, too, had been enveloped in flames.

"I looked around me quickly; people were firing from a position close by and because there was a truck about ten metres to my left, I headed for it; on my hands and knees. By now bullets were scattering the dry white Angolan sand all around me."

At that point, perhaps because he could view the situation in a broader perspective because of its hopelessness – a sensation some people recall when faced with imminent death – van Rensburg suddenly remembered his engineer, Sergeant Koos Cilliers. He looked about him and spotted a cammo-clad figure a little distance away. He shouted at the man; there was no response. He shouted again, and then crawled to him but the figure was lifeless.

"There was a huge wound in Koos's leg and though I felt for pulse, there was none." Cilliers was already dead.

Van Rensburg again: "Fire picked up round me and several bullets ricocheted off the body of the truck. I decided that the nearby vehicle offered the best cover until I could decide what next to do. In spite of the danger, I felt remarkably light-headed and could think quite lucidly," he remembered.

"Twice I felt bullets rip through my flying suit and once

BELOW: An *Alouette* gunship over hostile country in Ovamboland; RIGHT: South African camp, typical of the one eventually reached by Captain van Rensburg after his escape from Angola.

a tracer lightly singed my forehead; I knew then that what I had always dreaded was about to happen." A green Soviet tracer ripped into one of the truck tyres alongside him and he smelt burning rubber.

Captain van Rensburg didn't know it at that moment but the small paperback novel that he had earlier zipped into one of the trouser leg pockets of his flying suit had taken a direct hit. Only later, when he reached safety, did he discover how fortunate he had been. Had the book not been there it would probably have blown his calf away making any possibility of escape impossible.

By now his nose was bleeding profusely. He was not aware of the implications but felt severe pain in his back. He later discovered that, on impact, his spine had suffered a double compression fracture of the two lowest vertebrae.

For a second or two incoming fire let up as helicopters firing heavily at targets below sped past above his head. But they did not see him. Van Rensburg had to make an immediate decision. The light wasn't as bright as it had been earlier in the day, and he knew that it was almost sunset. Also, he was in an area that was covered in thick bush which gave him a slight advantage, *but only if he was able to get out of his immediate predicament*. It would have to be along a route through the undergrowth. Clearly, van Rensburg would welcome darkness for the possibility of escape, but that was still 15 or 20 minutes away. In the tropics there is little twilight; darkness comes quickly in this part of West Africa.

Van Rensburg knew that he was a good distance from the South African border, perhaps 20 or 30 kilometres; and it would be on foot *all the way*.

The young South African pilot wasted no time. Again scrambling frantically on hands and knees at double pace he quickly edged towards a thicket of trees behind the truck. A minute later he was on his feet running in a westerly direction. The SAAF helicopters made another pass. In the confusion his attackers were not aware that he had moved away. Only later did he realise that his buddies were shooting at anything that moved and that he could easily have become one of their targets.

Van Rensburg rapidly took stock of his position. He recalled seeing a road in the immediate vicinity of the attack on the flight in; he knew that if he was to head back to base he would have to go south, towards the border, but that meant crossing the main road southwards that the enemy had raced along to avoid their pursuers. Meanwhile, he kept on running; in any direction that he felt safe and as long as the sounds of shouting and gunfire receded. Then he stopped and took off again towards the setting sun. By now it was almost dark.

For a while he kept on westward, hoping desperately that the enemy would deploy to the south and *away* from him in their search. There was obviously no doubt that the Swapo unit knew he was alive. All the while he could hear shouting and much activity even though these noises had grown fainter; trucks started their engines.

He was also acutely aware that this was one potential South African POW that they had no intention of letting go free. He would have been their first and only South African Air Force pilot captive; a big prize and worth a year's concerted propaganda in Europe and America. But already the pain from his back had become intense.

Van Rensburg pushed himself on. He willed one foot in front of the other.

He had covered a couple of kilometres when he spotted a huge anthill; in much of southern Africa these termite mounds are sometimes in excess of six or seven metres. This one was at least that high.

"I went around it, regarding it as something of a landmark and then suddenly spotted a small rag and branch lean-to that had been built nearby. It was typical of the small bush structures erected by local natives. I also spotted movement. I went cold; I knew that if I had been able to detect the presence of someone else, *they too must have seen me*! They would also have heard the commotion not far away and have been alerted by the shouting."

Van Rensburg turned and saw a man in Swapo's distinctive tiger stripe camouflage sitting on the ground, an AK carbine slung across his knees. He was trying to get up, simultaneously shouting to someone nearby.

"It could have been a basic instinct for survival or a spur of the moment decision – I don't know which – but I rushed him. That was all I could do. I knew that I had to kill him."

The young Air Force captain remembers nothing more of the event except that when he got to his feet again he had managed to wrest the gun from the insurgent and shoot him. Only later he recalled tales of men facing death being possessed of immense strength. He had subdued the man with his bare hands. But not without cost.

More shouting coupled with shots attracted the attention that van Rensburg was so desperately trying to avoid; with his new-found weapon he ducked out towards the rear of the structure into thick bush. By now several of the dead man's cadres were firing wildly in his direction but

they didn't follow him; undoubtedly they feared an ambush.

The way van Rensburg remembers the next few hours and his eventual escape to safety were punctuated by several incidents interspersed by occasional spasms of severe pain in his back that left him breathless. Fortunately, the African terrain was enveloped in the black of night with only a hint of a glow in the west – where the sun went down to give him direction.

Several times he tried to rest by sitting or lying down. Once he attempted to sleep for a couple of hours in a desperate bid to build up strength but his back would take no pressure whatever.

His condition obliged him to remain erect and on the move. He was also thirsty. But the only water he had brought with him when he left base earlier in the day had been vapourised in the crash. Nor were his assailants inactive.

Several times earlier in the evening, van Rensburg was forced to give Swapo patrols a hurried berth. Once he accidently walked through the middle of a tiny village. He was quickly spotted by a local African and both men made hasty tracks in opposite directions. He knew then that the alarm would be given afresh.

By now the pilot was in excruciating pain. He knew that if the pain got worse he would be forced to stop. Eventually, towards midnight, he could no longer carry the Kalashnikov, although it weighed only a few kilograms.

Under the circumstances, van Rensburg made a desperate decision. He would relinquish his single hope of retaliation if he were again sighted and decided to stash the gun in a clump of tall grass. There was no other way; his broken back just would not take the additional weight. This gesture, alone, was indicative of the incredible suffering Captain van Rensburg was being subjected to by his pain. It was a wise decision.

An hour before dawn, the young chopper pilot had crossed the South West African border from Angola. In that part of the world it was called the 'Cut-line'; an area cleared of bush, perhaps ten metres across and stretching from west to east.

Most of the time he had walked close to the road leading southwards and which he had used as a marker on the way into Angola. He knew that it was dangerous to walk on the road itself; it could have been mined or the enemy had placed stop groups in ambush positions, in all probability waiting for him to head their way.

John Rubython captured this dramatic shot of a *Puma* flying over south Angolan bush country at the height of the war. Much of this thick bush provided adequate cover for Swapo insurgents infiltrating southwards to Namibia. Similarly, an emergency landing in this terrain would be a serious matter.

Now, back on home soil, he had the additional task of avoiding his own army's defensive positions. The South African security forces had no knowledge of his presence or even that he had survived the crash. In the bad light he could easily have been mistaken for the enemy by an over-enthusiastic sentry.

Then, quite unexpectedly, as the African sky started to clear, he heard voices; they spoke his language – Afrikaans. He shouted to alert them of his presence; the group was on a routine patrol around the base.

An hour later Captain Tinus van Rensburg was back at the same base from which he had lifted off almost 18 hours before. He was casevaced to hospital at Oshakati in central Ovamboland under heavy sedation the same morning. He was obliged to undergo three months' treatment for his back. More significantly, he had flown his last operational tour.

South Africa's 17 Squadron, in 1980, was composed entirely of French-built *Alouette III* support choppers. The unit has a history that extends beyond the lives of all of its present members.

The squadron was founded during the early days of World War 2 as a general reconnaissance unit. At the time – in December 1940, its South African component aircraft were largely British-built *Blenheims* and were part of the Allied war effort.

Two years later the unit went on to see active service in Aden, North Africa and Italy – flying with British, American, Free French and other Allied squadrons and distinguished itself in various major operations in and around the Mediterranean. Like other South African squadrons active during the Second World War, its flyers achieved their share of honours and decorations.

After the war, in 1947, the successor to 17 Squadron was reformed in South Africa as a maritime Air-Sea Rescue unit operating from Cape Town with American-supplied *Venturas*. Much of this work was of a practical nature – the Cape sea route which handles much of the oil from the Middle East was almost as active then as it is today.

In 1954 the wing was allocated its first helicopter; a *Sikorsky S51*; two years later they were given *S55s*. The first *Alouette IIs* were taken into service in 1960, with the more advanced *Alouette III* being introduced two years later.

Most of the earlier post-war activities were uneventful; the squadron's major role was in providing civic authorities with assistance when needed during floods or natural catastrophes. At least, that's the way it remained until the first Swapo incursions into South West Africa from Angola took place in 1966.

After a break of more than two decades in military activities; 17 Squadron went to the task with the *elan* for which it has become known. Today the squadron is one of the most highly rated in South Africa. Its Honours Roll lists more than two dozen names; men who had distinguished themselves in the face of the enemy. The vast proportion achieved merit during the Angolan Civil War period when South Africa, alone, attempted to stem Soviet and Cuban aggression in this vast ungovernable territory to its north. The name Tinus van Rensburg is among them.

CHAPTER 21

DEATH OF A GOOD MAN

Operation Meebos – July-August 1983

Operation Meebos *was launched following a period of intense peace negotiations during 1983. Initially, intelligence sources had indicated that the Swapo Central Area Headquarters (CAHQ) was located in the Evale area of southern Angola. However, it was soon established that it was farther to the north, in the hills just outside Mupa.*

Ongiva, about 100 kilometres south of Mupa, was the initial Own Forces Tactical Headquarters (TAC HQ) for the operation. As a staging centre, it was an ideal choice; it stood on the main road between the South West African border and Cubango, the biggest city in the south. Much of Ongiva town had been destroyed but the airport was still intact; an ideal base of operations.

For the South Africans, a new trend seemed to be developing, and it was not a good one. Pretoria was transferring to the 'sharp-end' on three month tours, senior officers with limited operational experience. These commanders were literally "thrown in at the deep end", and tended to be most conventional in their planning.

The overall commander of the TAC HQ for *Operation Meebos* was Colonel Jan Pieterse, a professional soldier experienced in anti-aircraft operations. The troops allocated to his sector were two 32 Battalion Companies, under command of Captains Eric Rabie and Tinus van

BELOW: Into action – A *Puma* airlifting a force of Parabats into the Operational Area following a contact near the Angolan border. The men sit, weapons pointing outwards, to give fire support on landing.
OPPOSITE: Captain Tinus van Rensburg.

Rensburg. In addition, there was a company of 1 Parachute Battalion commanded by Major Jab Swart. For insurance against Fapla intervention, a Combat Group of 61 Mechanised Brigade – under the command of a well-salted fighting man, Commandant Roland de Vries, was made available.

Air support was in the form of seven *Alouettes*, six of them gunships armed with 20mm cannon and one command and control trooper. For airborne troop transport, there were nine *Pumas*, as well as *C-160/130* transport aircraft on standby for airborne operations if necessary.

Dakotas (DC-3s) were available for resupply. To give the exercise muscle, 1 and 3 Squadrons flying *Mirage* F1 fighters had been made ready at Ondangua.

22 JULY

An attack was launched on the identified Swapo camp on the morning of 22 July; ground forces backed by choppers. A massive area clean-up followed involving the insertion of troops and backup; all were in search of isolated groups of Swapo insurgents and whatever arms caches could be uncovered.

Various minor contacts with Swapo insurgents did take place, but the elusive headquarters was never found. 32 Recce teams operating on foot located evidence that the main base had been operative in the area, but when approaching these locations, they would either find a hastily deserted camp, or hear the last of the insurgents pulling out in vehicles.

On July 26th, Captain Harry Anderson and Major Pete Harvey, flying gunships, made contact with a small element of the Eastern Area Headquarters (EAHQ). Own troops on the ground were Rabie's 32 Battalion.

The final tally was 15 insurgents killed and two captured. Most of the kills came from the gunships. It turned out that among this group were the last stragglers in the camp with orders to clean up and destroy any information which could be of assistance to the South Africans.

But Swapo was unlucky; two captures provided vital information on the new location of its EAHQ and its 'A' Battalion; all were camped on the Jamba River.

There were many frustrations experienced – not only by the helicopter pilots – but also by the troops on the ground. The intelligence picture was not clear; there was a lack of experience among senior Army Staff Officers and members of the Air Force MAOT making up the Tactical Headquarters.

SAAF headquarters in Windhoek, the South West African capital city, had placed severe limitations on the deployment of helicopters; each target had to be ground 'recced' for anti-aircraft capability. Considering that all reconnaissance work was carried out at night, this was a difficult task.

It was known that once Swapo troops had detected evidence of 'recce' teams having entered the area during their early morning security patrols, the camp would be abandoned within an hour. The result was that many opportunities were squandered because senior commanders 'back home' would not allow the man on the ground to make the decision as to whether to bring in a strike force or not. Consequently, after much to-ing and fro-ing, most attacks were carried out too late in the day to have any effect. But then again, is that not the problem with most modern wars…?

Issues were compounded by the fact that the TAC HQ in south Angola was too far distant from the Area of Operations (AO). Flying time from Ongiva to the nearest troops on the ground was 55 minutes, necessitating a refuelling stop at a mini-Helicopter Administrative Group (mini-HAG) before contact could be made. If one allowed 15 minutes for refuelling, the earliest that any callsign on the ground could expect fire-support would be over an hour.

As a rule of thumb, an insurgent, high on adrenalin, could maintain a pace of ten kilometres an hour while on the run. There was absolutely no way that operational elements could convince the higher level commanders that the TAC HQ should be deployed at the mini-HAG for it to be of any use. Consequently, many kills were lost; the intransigence of senior officers would have a profound effect on the rest of the operation.

30 JULY

There was much excitement; intelligence had determined the area where Swapo's new Military Command Post was situated. Captain Willem Rutter, 32 Reconnaissance Commander – formerly Rhodesian SAS – was deployed in the target area to ascertain if it was 'alive' or not. Preliminary reports had estimated that the camp was approximately 150 strong and that they had ZSU-23mm anti-aircraft guns. According to the 'duff gen merchants' (intelligence), the insurgents were well dug-in, with an elaborate system of trenches and underground bunkers.

The basic plan was to para-drop a Company of 1 Para Battalion led by Major Jab Swart to the north of the camp by a twin-engined *Transall* C-160 and also by *Hercules* C-130s. P-hour was 05h00. While the 'Bats' were moving into position, troops from 32 Battalion would be choppered in by *Puma* and dropped at first light to the west, east and south of the enemy camp.

The *Alouettes* would be used for close-air support (CAS), but only after all AAA had been neutralised by ground forces. Until the 23mm guns had been knocked out, HQ had placed a four kilometre restriction on all helicopter flights; they had to remain beyond that distance from the Swapo strongpoint.

The *Alouettes* were to take-off at 07h00 to deploy with 61 Mech Bde; this unit was based to the east of Cuvalai just north of Mupa. The order was that 61 Mech Bde HQ would form the mini-HAG.

31 JULY

Neall Ellis, Alouette gunship commander recalls:

"I was awakened at about 04h45 by the sound of C-130s flying low overhead on their way to the DZ. The moon was full and I immediately remembered a similar situation with *Ops Daisy* when the C-160/130 aircraft had also used our base as a bearing for the run-in.

I had a sense of foreboding and I hoped that their night navigation would be better than the time before.

Unable to sleep, I got up and went to the ops room to monitor the paradrop. Willem Rutter, on the outskirts of the enemy base, was on the radio urgently requesting that the para transport hold off a short while as they were experiencing problems in marking the DZ. Apparently, while crossing a river – which was deeper than anticipated – the homing beacon for marking the DZ had been lost. As fate would have it, by the time TAC HQ were aware of his request, the transports were circling the Swapo camp, looking for the DZ. It was too late to order the planes out of the area; the pilots were instructed to return to Ondangua.

This was a critical setback. The attack had obviously been compromised; Rutter reported a sudden, frenzied activity within the enemy base which indicated a withdrawal.

The inability of putting down the 'Bat' stopper group to the north of the camp meant that the insurgents were able to move on as soon as they were ready to do so. The *Pumas*, by this time, had arrived at Ongiva and they, in turn, were tasked to return to Ondangua to uplift and ferry these men to the target area; the entire operation was delayed by hours instead of having been a first-light attack. Swapo would have plenty of time to disappear into the bush to the north of us."

The *Alouettes*, led by Neall Ellis in a command and control trooper, took off from Ongiva for the mini-HAG. He landed just before eight that morning and proceeded to the command *Ratel* (Infantry Fighting Vehicle) for a briefing by Commandant de Vries. Ellis continues:

"The atmosphere was relaxed; no one seemed to have a clue what was going on and we decided to brew up a cup of coffee. Pre-attack butterflies in the stomach had not yet settled and breakfast was not asked for, or offered.

We were sitting there, swapping the usual kind of war stories with the 'browns' when we heard a strange whistling noise followed by a loud explosion about 800 metres to the west of us. All of a sudden the relaxed atmosphere became one of intense activity. The 'browns' had made their TAC HQ *and our mini-HAG* within range of the Angolan Army 122mm D-74 artillery guns at Cuvelai!

We were not impressed with Army efficiency that morning. The whole camp was packed-up and deserted within 10 minutes.

It was astonishing; one minute we were having coffee, surrounded by an entire combat group. The next, we were totally on our own; seven *Alouettes* in the middle of Angola, without a soul in sight.

Fortunately, we were just out of range of the Fapla guns.

Our new HAG was situated a few kilometres to the east, on the edge of the Cuvalai River. The *Pumas* had returned from Ondangua with the 'Bats' and the envelopment started in earnest.

Captain Harry Anderson and his wingman, Lt Mike Kohler were tasked to give top cover to the *Puma* drops around the enemy camp.

During the deployment, Anderson detected a Swapo *Gaz* truck hidden under the trees. As he veered closer, the driver decided to make a break for it. Anderson turned for the attack; his flight engineer, Sgt Jock van der Westhuizen, opened fire, killing both driver and passenger.

Once all the troops had been deployed on the ground by the *Pumas* and the sweepline started moving through the objective, it quickly became obvious that the entire Swapo contingent had pulled out, except for a handful of men who seemed to be confused as to which direction they should escape. They were quickly eliminated by the ground forces.

Lt Pete Welman, flying his gunship on the eastern flank spotted another *Gaz* truck trying to get away. Its driver was also killed.

One of the more confusing and frustrating aspects of the op was the amount of radio traffic. Only one VHF frequency had been allocated. All ground-to-ground, ground-to-air and air-to-air radio traffic for the operation had to pass through this one channel. And even though there was no real contact with the enemy, radio discipline was poor. I was in the command and control trooper with Colonel Pieterse trying to coordinate sweeplines and aircraft movements.

After ten minutes a message was patched through from 'Telstar'; Sector 10 HQ requested a SITREP. The reply was relayed back: nothing to report. This happened several times in the next hour, and always the same reply.

Then came a demand; find something to report! My immediate reaction, through 'Telstar' was to tell HQ that there was nothing to report and when there was I would let them know. Until then they should f*** off. A reply came back promptly; 'OC Sector 10 sends his compliments. Message understood'.

I had the feeling that it would not be the last I heard from the Sector 10 OC, Brigadier 'Witkop' Badenhorst."

What should have been a great setback to Swapo's forces – the Peoples Liberation Army of Namibia (Plan) – turned out to be a missed opportunity for the South Africans. The destruction of the Swapo Military Command Post would have successfully put an end to any joint Swapo and Fapla plans to retake the towns of Ongiva and Xangongo in south Angola. Both were then in the hands of the South Africans.

For the loss of one 32 Battalion soldier, from Lt van Staden's Company, Swapo lost two valuable vehicles and five men. Apart from the vehicles, they had managed to completely evacuate their main camp in what appeared to be a well-organised exercise.

Once again planning had not allowed for vast distances. It took four-and-a-half hours to deploy all the troops by helicopter. The use of a para-drop some time before an attack on a temporary Swapo base was also questionable. Ellis and his associates knew that any use of airborne needed to be coordinated with the deployment of ground troops. P-Hour should always be at the same time – or as close as possible – to H-Hour, he had always stated.

The more activity in the sky and on the ground during an attack always confused the enemy and allowed for more kills.

The inexperience of the senior planners of the operation was evident; they seemed to believe that Swapo temporary base camps were permanent structures, with elaborate systems of defence coupled with underground bunkers. Clearly, Pieterse and his staff were not familiar with the terrain, the enemy or the strategies employed by them. The result was that the attack was planned along

conventional lines, *against an unconventional target*.

A Swapo temporary base (TB) was invariably built with shallow shellscrapes for the protection of personnel from attacks. There were no trenches and, as Ellis stated, "we could have told them so".

"We also knew that the elaborate trench system was only in use at more permanent Swapo bases that were in remote areas to the north, well beyond our own tactical capability. It was also true during the war that many inexperienced SADF officers were unable to adapt their planning to unconventional conditions and, as a result, we all suffered," he said.

1 AUGUST

The day was spent preparing for an assault on 'A' Battalion. Air reconnaissance carried out a few days previously had confirmed the siting of the camp. The decision was made to go ahead with the attack without deploying any reconnaissance teams.

The new base was situated on the edge of a *chana* – an open grassland or swamp feature in Angola's southern bush-covered terrain – marking the Jamba River. It appeared to be a perfect target for a heliborne assault operation.

The estimated strength of enemy forces was approximately 200; there was one clearly visible AAA position situated on the northern side of the camp, overlooking the open *chana*. According to intelligence, the anti-aircraft guns were ZSU-23s, the much-vaunted twin-barrelled Soviet optically-guided weapon.

From the analysis of air photographs of the camp, Ellis felt that they were 14,5mm single-barrelled guns; smaller than ZSUs, but immensely potent in this kind of bush war. If they were not taken out early, they would definitely prove to be a problem for any ground forces advancing over the open *chana* areas to the north and east of the camp.

The most obvious enemy escape routes were to the west and south of the camp.

The initial plan drawn up by Pieterse and his staff was to initiate the strike with a *Mirage* bombing attack. The air plan was for four *Mirage* F1s to hit the AAA site with bombs and napalm and eight more of these jets to bomb the camp area. There would also be two F1s on standby for CAS if necessary.

Immediately after the run-in, the main assault group – which comprised Eric Rabie's Company – was to be choppered into a position on the other side of the open *chana* to the east of the camp. *Pumas* would be used for this purpose. Also, stopper groups were to be deployed to the west and south of the camp.

The *Alouette* gunships, in turn, would also play a role as stopper groups until the anti-aircraft guns had been

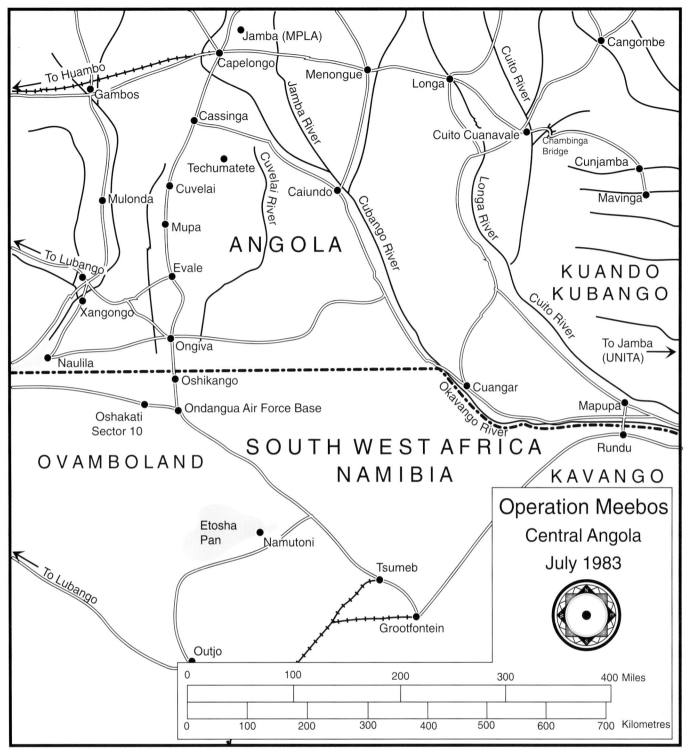

Operation Meebos
Central Angola
July 1983

neutralised; they would then would move over the camp to give close-air support to the troops in the sweeplines and stopper groups.

Ellis and one or two other pilots disagreed with the initial plan. Rabie would have a problem with the AAA if the *Mirages* failed in their task, he said. Ellis would have preferred to have placed the assault group to the west of the camp; bush cover was thicker and the advancing troops would not be threatened by large calibre fire while advancing. Everyone was aware that 23mm or 14,5mm AAA employed as ground fire were formidable weapons. Stopper groups to the east and south would have channelled the enemy into the open *chana* to the north which pro-

vided an ideal killing ground for the gunships.

2 AUGUST

Dawn revealed a perfect day; there were no clouds in the sky and no wind.

This was a good omen as the strike aircraft should have no difficulty in finding the target. Without wind, the *Alouettes* could maintain a perfect orbit. The veldfire hazard to the sweeplines and stopper groups would also be reduced. Ellis goes on:

"I had a thing about going to battle unshaven. After a quick shave, I joined the

181

other crews for a breakfast of 'dog-biscuits' and tea sweetened with condensed milk; 'plastic' tea as we called it. While we watched the sun rise, we went over our plans and looked for gaps.

Once again the problem of the assault group was discussed and I decided to make a minor adjustment. Eric Rabie's Company would be dropped on the southern side of the open *chana*. This would mean that at least his left flank would have the protection of thick bush. After our preparations were completed, we waited for the *Pumas* to arrive and the final briefing.

During the briefing we were told that there was a change of plan. Two *Impala* jets with napalm were to drop their ordinance approximately four kilometres to the west of the camp at the same time as the main bombing strike.

The rationale behind this decision was that those in the target camp would be awed by the blast and the ensuing fire and would run in the opposite direction. Again I couldn't help feeling that this was a decision which indicated a distinct lack of experience on the part of our commanders. No one on the ground – and in thick bush – can see for more than 20 or, at most, 50 metres; here was an expectation that they would spot the strikes from four kilometres. The change of plan caused a few guffaws and hardly helped to relax the men.

Brigadier Badenhorst told me that he would be in the command and control helicopter with me. He needed first-hand information on the battle as he was not prepared to be told to f*** off again!

Pieterse was not too happy with this decision, especially when I told him that fuel allowed for only one extra person. Both Pieterse and Badenhorst were large, heavy men; to take both of them would have meant that I probably would have less fuel than the gunships. I was not also prepared to ferry what I considered to be a superfluous commander into a combat situation.

At 10h30, we walked out to the aircraft for pre-flight inspections. All six gunships as well as my trooper/command and control chopper fired up satisfactorily for a 10h51 lift-off. The flying time was 16 minutes and we were coordinated to arrive five minutes after the bombing strike had taken place.

Just before 11h00B, I made contact with the *Mirages*; the strike time would be delayed by three minutes. This suited me fine. It meant that we would arrive over target while, hopefully, there was still confusion in the camp.

The lead *Mirage*, flown by Colonel Dick Lord, a graduate of the US Top Gun Academy, called while rolling in on his strike. Soon afterwards the first bombs exploded, thudding home in a series of huge explosions below us. It all looked impressive.

While listening to 'jet jockey' commentary on the lack of anti-aircraft fire, I heard another voice over the radio shouting, 'Going underneath!' For a moment I caught movement; the next, an *Impala* had shot past below me, followed by the distinctive blast of a jet engine. I was placed at about 50 metres above the trees and the gap between my *Alouette*, the trees and the *Impala* must have been minimal. They were pulling out after their napalm 'strike'.

I have always been sceptical when I am told that anti-aircraft fire is inactive when evidence such as aerial photography clearly confirms the presence of these weapons.

When a *Mirage* jet rolls in from above 20 000 ft and releases its bombs at about 15 000 feet and the pilot tells me that there is no effective AAA, I must believe that the man knows what he is talking about. But still, experience has taught me to approach a target very cautiously.

A report of no anti-aircraft retaliation can only mean one of two things; either the camp is deserted or the enemy is waiting for easier targets such as the slower, lumbering troop-carrying *Pumas*.

My apprehension proved to be a fairly realistic appreciation of the situation. I had decided to come in from the south-west. As we came abeam of the target the familiar 'rattle' of Soviet weapons fire began with the accompanying tracer flashing past the nose of my chopper.

As Team Leader of the formation and with the Brigadier in the aircraft, I fought against the temptation to swing down and pull away; instead I carried on climbing to determine what type of fire we were experiencing. And when we saw it, it was a shock!

I glanced towards the position where the AAA site was supposed to be. Straight away I picked out one of the guns; out of a small cloud of dust there protruded a regular pattern of red flame about two metres long. These were definitely AAAs; 14,5mm.

By this time the formation had split up to fly to the pre-planned orbits, Lt Pete Welman and his wingman were hovering to the west of the target; Lt Mike Hill's team were to the east. Anderson had been designated to cover the south, but I told him to stay with me as attacking a

14,5mm position with a .303 machine-gun was not exactly appealing. Also, I felt that with the volume of fire being directed at me that it would be preferable to spread the odds a little...

I immediately called to Mission 262, the *Mirage* CAS pair to do a restrike on the gun position. These F1s were being flown by Captains Jan Henning and Nic Oosthuizen and once more they came in and rocketed the target below us.

With Anderson and his wingman, we tightened our orbit to put us in a more favourable firing position. What we could observe from where we hovered was astonishing; as we started towards the gun emplacements, the Swapo gunners would swarm, like termites, out of their underground bunkers and man their guns once more.

Once the *Mirages* swung into their dive modes the men on the ground would scatter underground for cover. As soon as the rockets had exploded, they would emerge again and reman their 14,5s.

Once they started firing, it seemed as if everyone in the enemy camp had decided to get in on the act; the volume of small arms fire became intense. I had my normal day-glo panel stuck to the *Alouette's* tailboom and because of the amount of tracers passing ahead, to port and starboard, coupled with RPG-7 explosions around us, I thought I was the only one being shot at. Anderson assured me afterwards that he was also picking up a lot of flak.

The battle soon developed into a duel between chopper gunships and the AAA, with the two *Mirages* putting in strike after strike until all their ammunition had been expended.

The two jets ended up breaking every rule in trying to silence the guns. At one stage they were coming in so low to improve the accuracy of their strike that I expressed concern about a mid-air collision with our choppers in orbit. Fortunately, they did manage to destroy one of the guns.

Once they had departed, I knew that it would take another hour to get more ground-air support from the *Mirages*. It was now up to us to knock out the remaining anti-aircraft guns and it had to be done before Rabie and his men could be successfully deployed and the operation have any hope of success.

Anderson and his wingman were magnificent. They were hanging in – above the gun position – letting go with everything they had at the targets below us. I couldn't help but marvel – and, in retrospect, I was attracted to the phenomenon almost like a moth to an open light – at the long tongues of flame spitting ahead as they fired at us. There were also more RPG-7 missiles exploding in the air around all the choppers and for a while I was concerned that we might lose one of our machines. But at that moment the enemy broke and ran.

So are heroes born! Anderson was awarded the *Honoris Crux* decoration for bravery after the action.

As soon as all the AAA were silenced, I called in the *Pumas* with Rabie's company and deployed them. If Anderson and his wingman had not knocked out the larger weapons, they would most certainly not have been able to sweep through the camp; the *chana* was completely exposed and Rabie's contingent would have offered an ideal target.

As it was, his right and centre flanks ended up in some heavy scraps with enemy elements who had taken shelter in their bunkers. Rabie and his men managed to cross the open ground with only one casualty.

The *Pumas* returned with the 'Bats'; they were deployed in their pre-planned position to the west where many of the enemy had started to head after their breakout. Once Swart and his men had deployed and formed up in a sweepline, they immediately exchanged fire with escaping enemy troops and some heavy battles developed. By then the *Pumas* were out of the area.

When the Swapo commanders became aware that there was a stopper group to the west, they reversed course and struck out across an open *chana*. Welman and his wingman moved across and mowed down the moving targets.

Conditions on the ground for the troops in the sweepline were appalling. An easterly wind had sprung up and fanned the fires caused by the bombs. The result was that Rabie and his troops were threatened from behind by a raging veldfire with flames of up to 10 metres high, sweeping towards him and the Swapo forces ahead of his position.

I could see everything clearly from where I hovered; it was perfect from a control point of view. There was no necessity to urge our troops to advance more quickly; the fire was doing it for them. Swapo forces had, by now, realised that the west was bottled up and they started to put up fierce resistance.

This placed Rabie in a precarious position as some of his troops were picking up burns from the flames. In fact, when the fire had passed through our and Swapo lines and reached the 'Bats', a few troops virtually had their clothing burnt off their bodies. One section had to turn tail and dash for safety.

By now we were being affected by the bush burning below us. The smoke was so dense that the gunships were flying in IF conditions; there were a few near misses. It had now become difficult to spot enemy troops on the ground, with the result that the prospect of close-air support was abandoned. The control of sweeplines was almost impossible. Swapo made good use of the situation and gave our orbiting choppers quite a few 'snotties'.

Once the fire had passed, the battle started again in earnest. By now the sweeplines were approaching each other with some Swapo cadres inbetween.

This was a tricky situation as both sweeplines were totally hyped by the battle. In the poor visibility they were liable to shoot at each other without querying the source of fire. At one stage the sweeplines were about 30 metres apart and because of the thick bush – even after the blaze had burnt most of the undergrowth away – were still not able to see each other. Some deft manipulating of radio frequencies brought both sweeplines to a halt.

Once the battle was over, all that remained was to move through the camp collecting weapons, ammunition, destroy food and collect any documents to further confuse the Int boffins. During the troop uplift, the seven *Pumas* led by Captain Cor Greef landed on the open *chana* to the south-east of the camp.

Anderson was overhead in his *Alouette* giving the aircraft on the ground top cover and supervising the uplift. As the *Pumas* took off for the TAC HQ, Anderson happened to spot three Swapo troops lying underneath a tree, their AKs trained on the lead *Puma* only 50 metres away.

'They never fired their guns and there is no reason for their reticence except, perhaps, that they did not wish to draw more fire,' said Anderson later. 'If they had, they could have caused considerable damage to the aircraft and possibly killed quite a few of the 'Bats'.'

As it was, a short burst from Anderson's gunner took care of the three insurgents.

Overall, the day was quite successful. Own Forces casualties were one dead and two wounded, all of them 32 Battalion personnel. The official body count was 104 Swapo dead. The figure was actually much higher as it did not take into account the number of Swapo killed in the bunkers. Quite a few weapons were recovered as well as large amounts of ammunition.

Once again the *Alouettes* had performed brilliantly. That day, above all others, it had been proved that the French-built *Alouette* is a versatile and rugged little fighting machine that is also able to take a punch. We had conclusively shown that with the correct tactics and adequate pilot tenacity it is possible for an *Alouette* to neutralise an anti-aircraft gun emplacement. Quite a few of our machines needed 'patching'.

There were a few other developments shortly afterwards. 61 Mech, acting on intelligence received about a convoy transporting supplies from Mulondo to Cuvalai managed to deploy in time to lay a successful ambush. The lead Fapla truck detonated one of our mines in the road and with the convoy brought to a halt, the *Ratel* Infantry Fighting Vehicles managed to knock out five vehicles. A reaction force consisting of two *Alouette* gunships and the command and control chopper were deployed to the area.

Once the troops had swept through the area, the vehi-

cles that could be recovered were taken in tow by the *Ratels* and the rest blown up, complete with food and ammunition that was not needed by Own Forces. One of the trucks was carrying a full load of macaroni. We went into wide orbit to watch the blasts; these were followed by an impressive 'shower' of macaroni over a wide area.

The following day we were told that the politicians in Pretoria were unhappy with the fact that the convoy had been knocked out. That Fapla openly sided with our enemy, Swapo, seemed to make no difference to these distant observers and we were aware that reports like this did tend to lower morale.

We could never understand that if we were required to wage war against Swapo, then everything and anyone opposed to us should be wiped out, particularly if they got in our way.

Another aspect which disturbed those of us in the Operational Area was the lack of sufficient resources to effectively do the task required of us. We knew that if we were to embark on an operation the size of *Operation Meebos* and penetrate up to 200 kilometres into enemy territory – in this case Angola – then more aircraft should have been made available. With more *Pumas*, we should have had a better capability to put Own Forces on the ground and therefore we would have obtained better kill ratios. We could not help but get the impression that we seemed to approach each operation half-heartedly and half-cocked and not with everything that we needed at our immediate disposal."

FRIDAY, 6 AUGUST

"Apart from knocking out the convoy, very little happened after the attack on 'A' Battalion.

The TAC HQ had now been in the same area for some time and to pre-empt a possible attack, it was decided to move the camp to a new site on the Cuvelai River.

This was a most pleasant change, with high trees for shade and deep pools to swim in; at least we were able to wash. We had to watch for hippos and crocodiles, though. There were also fish in the river which allowed for a change of diet. Surviving on a 'ratpack' becomes monotonous after a while. Then hostilities started again.

Intelligence had reported the presence of a Swapo logistics base at Techumatete. Major Bulla Nieman from 32 Battalion and myself had been trying to convince Colonel Pieterse that we should attack the base before Swapo decided to head north and seek succour at the main Swapo base near Cassinga.

We knew that there were about 50 Swapo soldiers in the camp at the time and suggested that a heliborne assault with six *Pumas* and four *Alouette* gunships would easily be able to overcome any resistance. But Pieterse was not prepared to authorise an onslaught; he was wor-

CLOCKWISE FROM ABOVE: SAAF *Mirages* lined up on the runway at Ondangua in preparation for ground-air support operations during a cross-border raid. Note drop tanks in the foreground; South Africans uncover a large cache of Soviet weaponry; A Swapo suspect is unceremoniously hauled towards a waiting *Puma* for interrogation at Sector 10; Final swing into Ondangua with *Impalas* and *Mirages* lined up on the apron; *Dakota* DC-3s were used to ferry men and equipment in and out of tiny forward airstrips often deep inside Angola.

ried about interference from the Angolans. He also felt that the troops needed a rest after the 'A' Battalion battle. This was frustrating, but there was nothing we could do."

MONDAY, 9 AUGUST

"The preceding week produced little evidence of the presence of Swapo and the 32 Recce group commanded by Captain Willem Rutter had been deployed in the area to the north-west of Cuvelai to try and locate what, according to intelligence, were Swapo's B Battalion, the Socialist unit as well as the Central and Eastern Area Headquarter units. We were told that they had grouped together. It was accepted by all of us that if this were the case, we would be up against a really formidable force.

Each of the units would consist of up to 150 men providing a force with a total of approximately 600 well-armed troops. And each element would have its own AAA battery; it would give them a minimum of twelve or more 14,5mm AAA weapons.

Rutter was due for uplift at midday, but the previous evening he had reported that he was quite certain that he had spotted the location of an enemy concentration. He had picked up fresh vehicle tracks and wanted to follow them through to where he believed the base would be. Having requested a 24 hour extension to 'recce' the area, this was refused. It was felt – although there was evidence to the contrary – that the enemy had either left the area or split up into smaller units. In their wisdom, our leaders decided to deploy troops to carry out area operations.

The operation was scheduled for early afternoon. All pilots attended the briefing and Rutter suggested that the *Pumas* avoid the area where he suspected the enemy were encamped. Two *Alouettes* were tasked to give the *Pumas* top cover during the drop.

The gunships, flown by Captain Mike Hill and Lt Chris Louw would route straight to the area in the hope of picking up evidence of enemy on the ground. There were eight *Pumas* for the assignment which would be split into two elements of four each with a time gap between each formation.

At approximately 14h25B, while routing into the area, the *Pumas* – fully laden with troops – unwittingly flew over the *chana* where the Swapo concentration had deployed their AAA. These guns were grouped close together and were therefore able to send up a powerful volume of fire.

The leader of the formation was Captain A.J. Botha; Number Three of the formation, Captain Ian Solomon described what happened:"

'We were following the *Alouettes* to the LZ. I was in the Number Three position, just behind Captain John Twaddle in a loose Vic formation. As we moved along a chana, I was flying over the bush on the southern edge of the clearing with Twaddle lower down the chana *itself*. We were low, on the trees almost. I suddenly saw a long flame and a curtain of tracer emanating from the bush on our left. I realised that we were under heavy AAA and small arms fire.

All of a sudden I saw John's aircraft pitch up with a high nose attitude. The tailboom separated and somersaulted through the air. The aircraft rolled onto its back, dived into the ground with a steep nose-down attitude and exploded.

I was not able to distinguish what type of weapons were fired at us. It all happened too quickly.'

This was a tragic loss to the South African forces. All the aircrew, Captain John Twaddle, Lt Andre Pietersen, the Flight Engineer Sgt Grobbies Grobbelaar and twelve Parabat national servicemen were killed. Hill and Louw immediately turned back and flew to the area in the hope of spotting survivors. Lt Louw describes what happened:

'While on the way to the LZ, we heard Cor Greef shout over the radio that Number Five had gone down. Hill immediately gave the order to turn around and fly to the crash area. It was easy to determine the crash site from a column of thick black smoke that rose from where the Puma had gone down.

At this stage we were not sure if the aircraft had actually been shot down; while routing through the area we had not seen any indications of Swapo's presence. Then when we were approximately a kilometre from the wreck Sgt-Major Thomas, my gunner/flight engineer shouted over the intercom that he had enemy visual.

I immediately put the aircraft into a hard bank to the left so as to position for firing. Below us was a group of about thirty Swapo running towards the crash site. Thomas began shooting at the group.

During the manoeuvre, we were hit by a number of rounds. I immediately looked at my instruments and saw that the rotor RPM was winding down. I was afraid that we had an engine cut and immediately attempted to initiate a forced landing in the chana ahead of me.

Thomas called that the engine was working perfectly and that we should clear the area; there were too many enemy about. I was already in the flare, but pulled up and drew away approximately two metres above the ground. I continued at this height passed the wreck and could see immediately that no person could have survived the crash. There was a large group of about 100 Swapo dancing around the wreck in jubilation. They were jumping up and down with their rifles held high above their heads. Those nearest to me started shooting at us but, in their excitement, they were not accurate and we were not hit again.

We cleared the area and Hill escorted us to the mini-HAG which was about ten kilometres away where we landed to inspect damage.

I think there were two aspects which saved our lives that day. First was the fact that Thomas urged me to carry on flying when I thought we should land. Second was my inexperience, in that I flew so low past the wreck, that the AAA – which was situated on a slight hill to my right – was not able to depress enough to hit us.

Another more experienced pilot would probably have climbed and provided the AAA guns with a more adequate target.'

The MAOT commander, Major Kiewiet Maree, scrambled the remaining gunships at the HAG. These were despatched to support Hill who, after escorting Louw back to base, had returned to the scene of the disaster to search for survivors. Hill was later awarded the *Honoris Crux* for bravery during this action. Louw achieved the Southern Cross medal for flying his aircraft to safety. Major Kiewiet continues:

'When we arrived in the area, we could see the wreck, but could not get too close. The 14,5s were active; it was difficult to pinpoint their positions as the smoke from the massive veldfire caused by the fuel explosion made visual identification very difficult. Swapo had dispersed and we were receiving small arms fire up to four kilometres away from the crash site. The enemy also seemed to have an unlimited supply of SAM-7s. Three F1 Mirage aircraft from Ondangua were tasked to give us CAS, but they were armed with rockets and because of the difficulty in pin-pointing the AAA sites, accurate FAC was not possible.

There was a lot of confusion and when it became apparent that we would probably lose another aircraft because of the intensity of the enemy ground fire, I decided then that all aircraft should return to base where we could go into a planning session for the 'rescue' attempt.

But time was running out and an appreciation of the situation indicated that it would not be possible to deploy troops in a position where they could reach the wreck before last light.

It was decided to leave Rutter and his recce teams on observation positions along the Colonga River in the hope of detecting any evidence of a Swapo withdrawal; we know that it was their tactic to leave the area as soon as they had been compromised. The chances were likely that they would head north.

A number of pilots had reported seeing a large herd of cattle near the contact area. Swapo often kept cattle in tow as a source of 'mobile food' largely because, unlike us, they did not have the luxuries of refrigerated trucks! We knew that if the cattle could be detected, the main body of troops would be nearby. The OPs were tasked to keep a lookout for any evidence of beef on the hoof.'

10 AUGUST

"We arose early this morning in order to come on standby in the event of the Swapo force being detected. There was an underlying feeling of anger at the loss of the men and the *Puma*. Everyone needed to settle a score.

Normally, on operations, the camp took some time to get its act together at the start of a day, but not this time. Reaction Force troops were ready and waiting at the LZ at sunrise, even though the *Pumas* were not due to arrive for another couple of hours.

I was tasked with two gunships as escorts, for a 08h00B take-off to ferry Colonel Pieterse to coordinate his ground forces and 61 Mech Bde vehicles advancing on the crash site. As we were flying to the area, one of Willem Rutter's OPs – callsign *Charlie Lima* – reported that he had a large herd of cattle visual moving in a northerly direction towards the Calonga River.

I decided to investigate and flew down the river in a westerly direction. As we were passing a bend on the river – some 30 kilometres due north of Cuvelai – I saw a movement out the corner of my eye. The distinctive smoke trail of a SAM-7 missile passed through the centre of our loose Vic formation.

We were at about 800 feet above ground level and I immediately turned the formation around and headed back towards the position from where the SAM had been launched. It was about a thousand metres away and in the cool, early morning air the trail led right back to the launch pod. On approaching the source of our problems, the clatter of small arms fire accompanied by a wall of tracers reached out at us. And there they were; the long spitting flames of 14,5mm AAA with the blasts of RPGs intermingled in the smokey, deafening confusion. Another four SAM-7s were launched at us, but they missed.

We immediately went into an orbit around the position and were able to clearly see the enemy anti-aircraft positions. The sun was still quite low on the horizon, with the result that the dark shadows under the trees accentuated their muzzle flashes.

I counted twelve sites which meant that at least four detachments were moving together. I realised then that we had found the main body of the Swapo force trying to escape to the safety of the north. I immediately reported the situation on the radio.

The enemy had grouped together and spread out over an area of approximately two square kilometres. If the first SAM-7 had not been launched, we would probably have flown over the detachment and been none the wiser.

During the furious initial stages of this action, the only battle damage was received by Lt Mike Kohler who took a hit from a 14,5mm round at the attachment point of his tail-guard on the boom. Fortunately the dislodged guard did not strike his boom. The problem was later sorted out with 'Boere technology'; a piece of fencing wire.

The South Africans back at Oshakati's Sector 10 HQ had been waiting for this news. Immediately the remaining gunships were scrambled. I requested additional air support from strike aircraft on standby at Ondangua.

Unfortunately the Pumas had still not arrived at the HAG from Ondangua and I knew that we would not be able to contain the main Swapo breakout once the contact had been closed; these choppers only arrived at our position with troops at 10h30B; two hours after the contact had begun.

For once the Mirages did a good job. Between them and the gunships, the big AAAs were quickly silenced.

It was quite impressive watching the F1s launch their rockets and being followed out of their dives by one or two SAM-7s hanging on to their tails. On pulling out of a dive the jets dispersed flares to confuse the missiles' IR homing devices.

At one stage I felt uncomfortable; there seemed to be more RPG bursts in our vicinity than before. To make matters worse, all the explosions were at the same height as our orbit. It did not take me long to realise that the air bursts were not from RPG-7s, but from self-destruct 30mm shells fired by the Mirages in their dive approach. We were sitting at about 1 200 feet in a bid to make it more difficult for the gunners on the ground, and here were our boys pumping 30mm shells into our perimeter.

Once the AAAs had been silenced, we moved over the main body of the enemy and started picking them off. There was still a lot of small arms fire and RPG rockets being directed at us, but after a while the continuous fire began to feel like an every day occurrence. It was interesting to see how soon the pilots became impervious to danger, but much of that had to do with bad aiming from the ground. Swapo never really shaped under fire during the course of the war, although there was the occasional exception.

The enemy commanders must have been aware that we were intent on avenging the loss of John Twaddle's Puma the day before; they were clearly fighting to survive. Swapo forces were aggressive in their defence and the fact that there were none of our troops on the ground yet, might have stimulated their resolve. We knew that they were convinced that if they directed enough heavy fire at our choppers, we would eventually withdraw. It was the shortage of fuel that caused us to pull out in the end, but it was not long before we were back after having topped up our tanks at the nearby TAC HQ.

At approximately 10h30B, the first Pumas arrived with the ground backup that we had asked for. On radio we were able to tell them that the main breakout appeared to be along the river towards the west and the north-west. Lt Harry Ferreira, another 32 Battalion veteran, was dropped along this waterway to cover the western end while Lt Tinus van Staden created a barrier a little farther towards the north. Major Jab Swart and his 'Bats' went in north-east of where we flew.

Once again veldfires in the powder dry grass created a problem.

Not long afterwards we heard that some of Ferreira's men had been trapped by the inferno sweeping ahead of the wind towards the west along the river; several had to be evacuated with serious burns. According to the troops on the ground, the flames were up to 10 metres high; there was no escaping them.

As with the attack on 'A' Battalion, smoke from the veldfires caused visibility above the contact area to deteriorate sharply, and when an overzealous pilot attempted to poach in another gunship's killing field, there were several near-misses.

With the blaze burning itself out, we were eventually able to come down to a lower level where it was easier to pick out the enemy, some of whom had taken refuge in thick bush.

At the end of the day, we uplifted the troops and returned to base satisfied with our efforts. Twaddle's death still hung heavily on our minds. But the final body count for the day was 116 Swapo dead and two prisoners.

Of particular satisfaction, was the fact that we were able to take, intact, many of Swapo's 14,5mm guns.

Own Forces suffered no more deaths. Still, the results might have been better had the Pumas not had to return to Ondangua every night. This always resulted in troop deployment coming much too late in the day for us to

CLOCKWISE FROM ABOVE: Eenhana army base near the Angolan border landing strip, foreground; A wounded officer is airlifted back to base in a *Puma*; Unloading a mine-protected vehicle from one of the SAAF transporters; Loading captured munitions into a *Puma* from a base in Angola; Preparing *Alouette* gunship's 20mm cannon for action.

OVERLEAF: Unita troops with a captured Russian T-54/55 tank knocked out during one of the engagements.

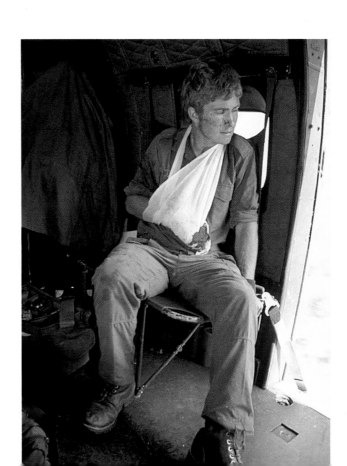

obtain any significant results, even though, on this occasion, Swapo detachments – on the hop, with us close behind – were completely caught off balance. They were never able to organise themselves in any effective form of defence.

On this occasion the river offered us a natural barrier to prevent escape and we were able to make the best of their bad luck.

If we had had troops on the ground earlier that day, it is quite possible that we could have wiped out as many as 400 of the enemy force."

THE NEXT DAY

Roland de Vries and his armoured force had managed to reach Twaddle's wreck the previous day. According to those who surveyed the disaster, there was no hope of anyone surviving the crash. They spent much of the time sifting through the charred remains and placing what was left of the occupants in body bags for airlifting back home for burial.

An examination of the wreckage indicated that the tail rotor gear box could have seized when it had been penetrated by a 14,5mm round. This probably caused the tailboom to separate from the fuselage.

Operation Meebos produced little of value after 10 August. Troops were deployed to carry out area operations, but all ensuing contacts were isolated and hardly significant.

An attack was carried out against a Swapo log base at Techumatete a week later, but the event yielded nothing; the occupants had fled northwards to the main Swapo base at Jamba (not to be confused with the Jamba base of Dr Jonas Savimbi about 600 kilometres farther east). Willem Rutter who had 'recced' the camp earlier said the last of the stragglers had left early on the morning of the attack. It was almost as if they had had a warning of our impending arrival.

It was a disappointment, of course. Had we attacked the previous week, we could have delivered a powerful blow.

The camp was a large one and appeared to have stored vast amounts of ammunition and food supplies. Once again, lack of initiative and experience on the part of HQ planners had lost us an opportunity.

A few days later, General Jannie Geldenhuys – then Chief of the Army – was flown from Oshakati to the TAC HQ for a staff visit. After being briefed on the situation and the results, he was silent for a long time. Then he addressed us. He said that it seemed to him that the operation had lost much of its initial momentum, and that we were wasting our time by staying in Angola any longer. If he was in the shoes of the commander, he stated blandly, he would pack up camp and return home.

And that was it. The same night the new TAC HQ commander, Colonel Bert Roos, gave orders for camp to be broken and moved back to Ongiva the next day.

CHAPTER 22

NIGHT OPERATIONS IN THE OPERATIONAL AREA

The early eighties saw a fairly dramatic development in Swapo operations within northern South West Africa because of a more aggressive Security Force role in the conflict zone. Most insurgent groups trying to infiltrate southwards out of Angola were obliged to move at night to avoid being detected. They tended to employ any means that could move; pick-up trucks, bicycles and donkeys. Many groups came into the operational area on foot.

Although a curfew was enforced, the security forces found it impossible to cover the whole area. A decision was made by Sector 10 Operational Headquarters at Oshakati towards the end of 1982 to establish whether the flow could be stemmed by using *Alouette III* gunships on night surveillance patrols. Apart from infiltrating bands, other targets were enemy concentrations in the area of operations (AO).

LIMITATIONS

A number of problems had to be overcome. The first of these was the lack of instrumentation fitted to *Alouette III* helicopters for night flying. There was also the question of identifying curfew breakers; it would not do to intercept and indiscriminately shoot at innocent people moving between their villages after dark. It had always been the custom among tribespeople all over Africa to visit each other at night and it was difficult to put a stop to, war or no war. Such are the vagaries of life in the bush. Also, this kind of action could have an adverse effect on the 'hearts and minds' programme launched by the army in Ovamboland.

A third problem was to position troops on the ground to arrest curfew breakers and, if necessary, to offer medical aid to any person who was perhaps wounded during operations.

The first issue was overcome by restricting operations to nights where there was sufficient moonlight for the pilots to have a visible horizon. Flying an aircraft low level, at night, does place a disproportionate work-load on the pilot; without an horizon, disorientation can easily occur. Moreover, pilots were not given any night vision equipment and had to fly with the naked eye.

In a bid to upgrade the safety factor, only pilots with a minimum of 400 hours on *Alouette III* helicopters – plus 40 hours night flying experience (of which 15 hours had to be on type) with experience in bush operations – were considered for this role. Flight engineers – the gunners – had to achieve a weapons delivery assessment of exceptional high average and were not permitted to wear corrective lenses.

Initial tests showed that it was no problem to visually acquire vehicles travelling at night. But as soon as the occupants heard the sound of rotors, they would switch off their lights and stop. *Alouettes* could be heard some distance away and a darkened vehicle was difficult to spot in the bush when stationary. Consequently, it was decided to equip the gunner with locally-manufactured night vision equipment. This had the advantage of visually acquiring and identifying the target. In addition, to improve accuracy, a laser designator was mounted onto the 20mm cannon.

The gunner was able to see the beam through his night vision goggles and the new equipment also helped target the objective for the second aircraft in the formation.

To provide mutual support during a contact and to give assistance in the event of a helicopter being downed, the Air Force always deployed two gunships at a time. It was the same with the *Pumas*.

There was also the threat of SAM-7 anti-aircraft missiles being launched. For this reason, no navigation lights were displayed. This shortcoming, in turn, caused the additional problem of the two pilots not 'bumping' into each other in the dark. The problem was settled by allowing only rear tail lights to show; all other aircraft lights were masked off.

Initially, *Pumas* were considered for deploying troops on the ground. However, landing a large helicopter in the dark and on a dusty LZ without lights was not considered viable. It was accepted that a helicopter approaching an LZ with landing lights on was an ideal target for anyone lurking nearby. The problem was solved by positioning a vehicle reaction force on the ground in constant radio communication with the pilots at various points in the AO.

LUNAR OPS

The term 'Lunar Ops' soon became current in the area adjacent to Angola; it signified helicopter night operations using *Alouette IIIs*. To make the point that the curfew was to be more strictly enforced than in the past, a campaign was launched by the Army COMOPS (Psyops) department using pamphlet drops from aircraft and local commercial radio broadcasts.

Local inhabitants were warned that if a helicopter circled their position, they were to stop and await the arrival of ground forces for questioning. If the transgressor still attempted to move away it would indicate that he was enemy and would be attacked.

MODUS OPERANDI

During the 'Lunar Ops' period, the AO was divided into sectors; vehicles were deployed after last light at predetermined points. There were no Security Force ground operations in that specific sector.

Before a mission, all participants were given a detailed briefing on operational aspects; the exact location of ground forces, any other aircraft carrying out night operations in the vicinity, what targets could be fired upon as well as any restrictions that should be observed.

The *Alouettes* would take off after last light. When movement was detected they would orbit above the suspected target and, if necessary, fire warning shots. The *Alouettes* flew at different heights, with only the lower aircraft permitted to fire.

If the suspect did not stop after warning shots had been fired, the gunner would disable the vehicle by firing at its tyres. Some *Alouette* gunners were able to deliver most accurate fire; with one round many of them could deflate a tyre on a vehicle on the ground a hundred metres away. If any person still tried to escape they were instructed to shoot to kill.

Once the suspect vehicle or group had halted, their position would be determined and a grid reference radioed to the nearest reaction vehicle. One of the helicopters would then head off in the direction of the reaction force and guide them to where the suspects were waiting.

PARATROOP REACTION FORCE

The use of the vehicle reaction force ultimately proved to be time-consuming and not really as effective as had been hoped. The reaction time was too long, sometimes up to 20 minutes. Often, by the time the troops reached the area, suspects on the ground were able to sneak away from the scene and troops would arrive to find an abandoned vehicle. The other problem was that the helicopters could not orbit the area indefinitely. They needed to refuel, sometimes leaving the suspects unguarded.

The next step in the evolution of 'Lunar Ops' was to drop paratroops from a DC-3 *Dakota*. The *Dakota* customarily transported two sticks of ten paratroopers ('Bats') each and, after take-off, would orbit in a pre-arranged holding pattern waiting for Mission Leader to call for a drop.

The lead helicopter carried the troop commander to monitor his men on the ground after they had landed. Like the gunner, the Army Commander wore night vision goggles.

'GREEN LIGHT'

If the gunships engaged an insurgent party or had a reason to call for airborne troops, the procedure was as follows:

The lead helicopter marked the target by dropping three lumi-sticks (luminous chemical light sticks) approximately 200 metres apart. The Number Two helicopter then climbed to a predetermined height and made radio contact with the fixed-wing, passing on the heading and distance to the target.

As the conflict adjacent to – and often inside Angola – developed, a requirement was identified in the early eighties to carry out night trooping with *Puma* helicopters. The arms embargo against South Africa made procurement of night vision equipment virtually impossible and the Air Force was obliged, at great cost, to develop their own sights, which they did very successfully, considering the limitations of this kind of high-tech expertise.

Thus, using locally manufactured night vision goggles and modifying *Puma* cockpit instrumentation, night flight tests were initiated in the mid-eighties.

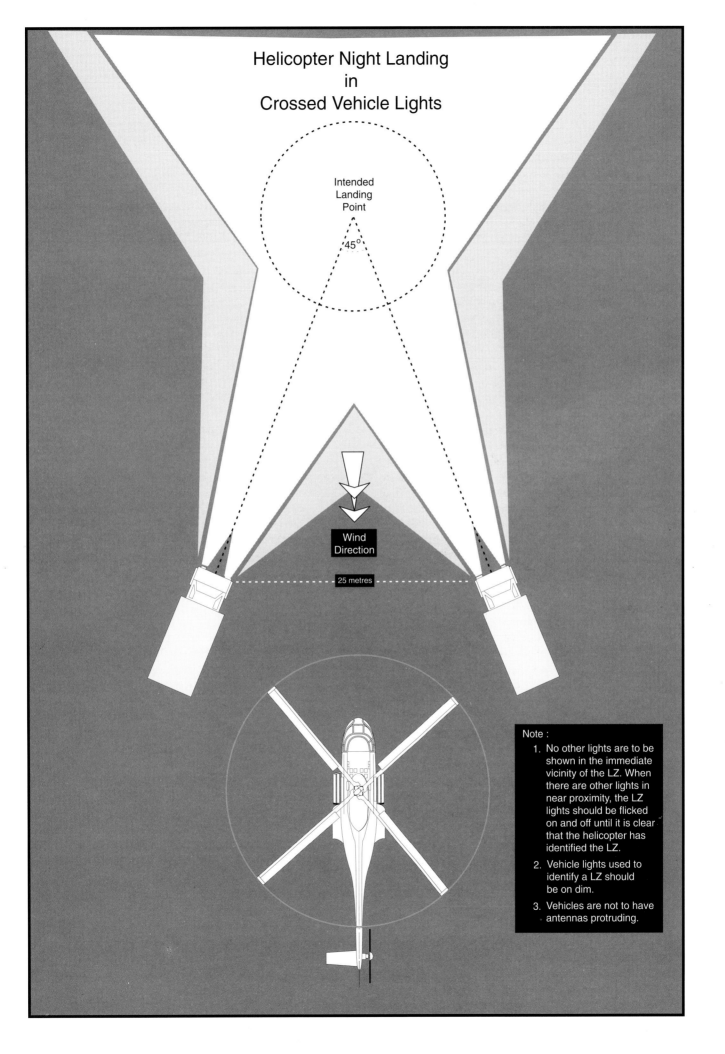

PLANNING FOR NIGHT OPERATIONS

It was quickly found that night operations extended the scope of border operations; there was suddenly the additional advantage of surprise.

In order to capitalise, thorough planning was needed. Only very experienced crews were deployed; a minimum of 500 hours command on type and 50 hours command night flying hours were prerequisites. In addition, the aircraft commander had to have a valid instrument rating.

OPERATIONAL EXPERIENCE

As a result of Angolan war experience, South African Air Force helicopter pilots are regarded today as among the most experienced night operation veterans anywhere.

Night flights had become a reality earlier in the Border War, largely for the purpose of evacuating the wounded. Pilots would fly their helicopters with limited navigational aids and radio communications in atrocious weather conditions – day or night – often to a point up to 200 nms from base and usually to a remote point on the map. All this to uplift an injured soldier, but that was how this war was fought by the South Africans.

Whatever else one might think about them they have always been brave and resourceful. It is not generally known that during World War 2, South Africans were rated first and third among Allied and Commonwealth fighter aces in the number of enemy planes destroyed. 'Pat' Pattle had the highest tally – in excess of 41 German and Italian planes shot down and 'Sailor' Malan with 35 confirmed kills.

The Angolan missions were sometimes characterised by aircraft coming under heavy enemy fire – small arms and anything up to 23mm – particularly when airlifting wounded troops.

During *Operations Modular, Hooper* and *Packer* in 1987-1988, *Pumas* were the only aircraft that were able to fly night after night in southern Angola in all weather conditions, largely because they had to.

The task given to *Puma* aircrews was to bring in essential supplies, personnel and on occasion, ammunition to forward elements and to return the same night with casualties. The pilots would take off from Rundu airfield in Caprivi in northern South West Africa at last light and return again at dawn. They would often fly up to eight hours under extremely demanding and sometimes hazardous conditions.

To avoid acquisition by enemy radar, the maximum height allowed above ground level was between 70 and 100 metres. If the trees were 30 metres high and the night was dark, that allowed very little margin for error if a distance of several hundred kilometres had to be flown. They embarked on these missions mostly without night vision or sophisticated navigation equipment, usually on the look-out for a tiny clearing in the bush, often marked by no more than 'Coke' tins that had been filled with a mixture of sand and aviation fuel. The mixture would burn with a small flame and mark the designated LZ.

At times – particularly during the summer months – the area would be exposed to heavy thunderstorm activity. Rain would restrict forward visibility through the cockpit perspex; this made the task of searching for a small LZ in the pitch black darkness of a remote corner of tropical Africa almost impossible. Few missions were aborted, though.

The only plus associated with tropical storms was that it kept enemy MiG fighters on the ground and Own Forces were able to send up flares to act as visual beacons without fear of a bombing raid.

The trees in much of south Angola are, on average, 30 metres high; as the pilots approached forward elements positioned near Cuito Cuanavale, the terrain became slightly undulating. And while the pilots could not – on a dark or cloudy night – see the ground below them, they would monitor the radio altimeter needle oscillating wildly up and down, indicating that at times trees were less than 15 metres below.

On one occasion, two *Pumas* were tasked to drop off a reconnaissance team at a point behind enemy lines in the early hours of the morning. It was a particularly dark night. The pilots were briefed to use their landing lights only in an emergency during the approach and the landing itself.

Having landed successfully without lights, the formation leader felt uncertain about his position and risked flashing his landing light at the area immediately ahead. He discovered that both helicopters had settled in a river bed; its banks towered roughly 12 metres above them.

If they had taken off, both choppers would almost certainly have flown into the bank no more than 15 metres from the LZ.

On another occasion, during a heavy rainstorm – while approaching a LZ to land – a pilot flew his aircraft through the upper-most branches of a tree. Fortunately damage was minimal; nothing more than a smashed perspex panel and a bruised ego.

There are countless stories of missions flown at night in the operational area, many of them remarkable; much of it is the stuff of adventure novels. None of it is fiction, though. Listening to some of the pilots relate their escapades, it is astonishing that there were not more SAAF helicopters lost in a war that eventually lasted 21 years.

CHAPTER 23

OPERATION SUPER: MARCH 1982

SAM Missiles vs Helicopters

"Your mission – to provide top cover to the Pumas during the 'recce' drop at last light on the 9th and then to be on standby for close-air support for the duration of the operation".

Neall Ellis, flying an Alouette III was the Gunship Commander during Operation Super. This is his report:

A pair of SAAF *Pumas* en route to the arid bush country of the Kaokoveld, just south of the Swapo infiltration area of Angola where *Op Super* took place.

The Intelligence officer told crews attending the briefing that a 'source' had reported an unconfirmed Swapo presence in the Cambino area, approximately ten kilometres to the north of Iona in a remote desert-like region in south-west Angola, not very far from the border with South West Africa/Namibia. Iona is situated in a valley 30 kilometres north-east of the Marienfluss valley – or 'Fluss as we called it – a magnificent isolated region with great herds of game and few local people living there, in the north-western Kaokoveld.

The plan was for a reconnaissance commando patrol to be dropped by helicopters in the area to determine if there was an insurgent presence or not.

We all knew that the sea was less than 20 minutes flying time to the west, and since most of us had never fished off the Skeleton Coast before, it could be interesting.

Also, the mouth of the great Kunene River which empties a large Angolan catchment area into the icy south Atlantic Ocean was one of the better fishing spots in the region. Certainly the crocodiles were the biggest and most aggressive in Africa.

After sorting out a few domestic arrangements, Captain Angelo Maranta and myself left the briefing room at Ondangua to prepare for a late morning take-off for the 'Fluss on 8 March.

I had been in the Marienfluss a few years before and found it to be one of the most beautiful places imaginable. When I saw it in 1975, it was a vast valley, approximately 120 kilometres in length and 15 kilometres wide. The memory that stayed with me was of an expanse of waist-high yellow grass and hundreds of grazing animals, from gemsbok to elephant, rhino to zebra, all of them seemingly unaffected by our worldly affairs. At that stage the war had not touched the region.

This time, however, I was in for a shock. The 'Fluss had become a barren stretch of desert. There was neither grass nor grazing animals; years of drought had laid the 'Fluss to waste.

Our Tactical Headquarters (TAC HQ) was situated alongside the runway, which was really little more than two rows of rusty 44-gallon drums half-buried in the sand. Next to a lifeless windsock surrounded by a ring of white-washed stones, three 12x12 army issue tents had been erected, our home for the next couple of days. There was not a tree in sight; it could have been the Sahara Desert. The heat was the worst; it was just bearable and from the expletive Maranta muttered, I was aware that this was not an easy posting.

The TAC HQ commander was an Army Captain Vissie Verster. Sgt Jose Dennison was the reconnaissance patrol leader and was formerly Angolan: he had ten men in his team. All troops in support of the operation were from 32 Battalion, under command of Captain Jan Hougaard.

Our Air Force complement consisted of two *Alouettes* and two *Puma* transport helicopters. There was also a *Bosbok* light aircraft to act as 'Telstar' for communications relay back to base while we were operating in 'Indian country', once over the border in Angola.

The morning of the 9th was spent with the patrol, planning aspects such as regular frequencies, alternative frequencies in the event of jamming by the enemy and battle frequencies. Final briefings were held on escape and evasion for aircrew in the event of being shot down. There were also rendezvous points if crew became separated from each other, and what recognition aids were being carried by troops and aircrew.

The drop was timed for just before last light, at a point north-west of the suspected infiltration area. Here a road roughly followed the course of a river through the mountains. Once Dennison and his men had been dropped,

they were to mine the road at the entrance to the pass. The idea was that should the 'recce' presence have been detected by the enemy, any force entering the pass would detonate a mine and these men would be forewarned.

Everything went according to plan with the drop. All aircraft returned safely to base to await their first report. That night, having settled down around the fire for the evening's session of war stories, at approximately 21h00B under the most brilliant African night sky imaginable, a muffled explosion to the north was heard.

Contact! Something had happened and it was not too far away, even though the mountains could have carried the sound a great distance. There was a mad rush to the ops tent to find out if Dennison was okay and if he knew what had caused the blast. He was on the radio before we were and reported that a large Mercedes truck had passed him coming from the direction in which they were walking. It must have detonated one of the landmines.

Clearly, there was enemy activity close to the border. Our original intelligence source had been correct. Now it was Dennison's task to establish what that presence was doing there.

10 – 11 MARCH 1982

The 10th was spent on standby, speculating if the 'recces' would encounter any enemy patrols sent out to investigate the mine incident. The land was sparse; few trees or defiles where ten men could secrete themselves in daylight hours. We were aware that if the enemy was onto them they could be hunted down by good trackers.

There was nothing to report from the 'recce' team that evening which, in a way, was a disappointment. We had hoped for action. That night the heavens parted and a huge rainstorm drenched us all to the bone. It does not often rain in these desert climes, but when it does it is usually a cloudburst. It was quite an experience listening to the Kunene River rushing down in flood. Although the river was a good half-hour walk from where we were camped, the noise of the water roaring over the rapids was awesome.

We rose early in Kaokoveld. It was best to make the best of the cool morning air before the heat became overpowering. Then any physical movement would become an ordeal. Major Paula Kruger, the *Puma* chief, suggested a 'recce' along the Kunene River to look for potential insurgent crossing points. It was also felt that the camp food supply lacked protein, of the kind usually associated with ocean waters. Consequently, our 'recce' would have to go all the way to the Kunene Mouth and we would take fishing gear. We tasked a *Puma*, largely to show some of the non-combatants – cooks and bottle washers – what this great desert area looked like from the air.

CLOCKWISE FROM TOP: Arid, desolate and isolated, the Tactical Headquarters of the strike force involved in *Op Super*; All supplies had to be flown in – some were dropped by parachute; Captain Neall Ellis in his distinctive garb at the time of the chopper strike and; 32 Battalion members with some of the captured Swapo hardware which included landmines and SAM-7s.

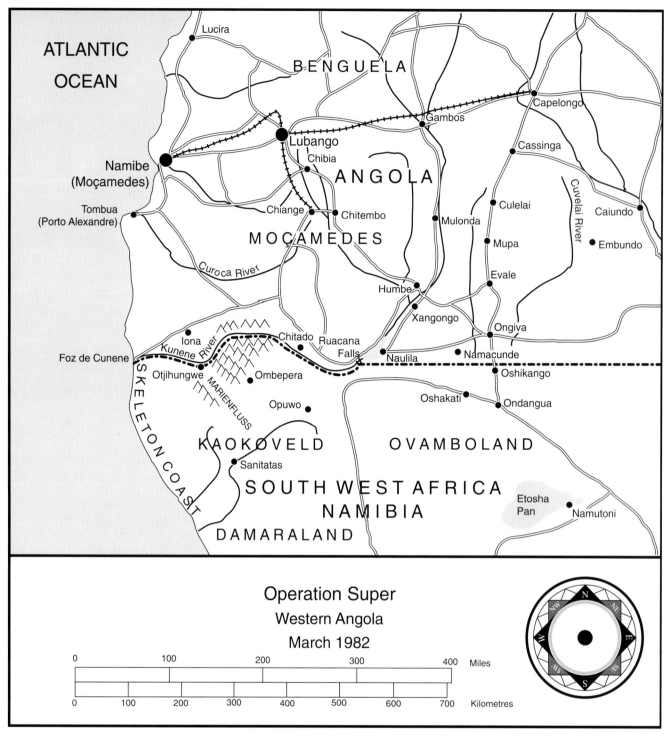

Operation Super
Western Angola
March 1982

0	100	200	300	400	Miles

0	100	200	300	400	500	600	700	Kilometres

I was particularly keen to get to the beach, as the last time that I covered the south bank of the Kunene was just before *Op Savannah* while carrying out a fuel dump check. In those days – before the war became intense – drums of aviation fuel were stashed along the river unguarded, and these had to be checked at regular intervals for evidence of fuel contamination. We touched down on the beach, caught nothing and headed back to base.

About 10 minutes out from the 'Fluss, Kruger passed a headset back to me and indicated that he wanted to talk. Dennison, he said, had a Swapo patrol of platoon strength in sight. Contact was imminent. The war was on again and we weren't ready for it. We had been fishing...

Our problem was to get to Dennison and his men before the shooting started. I was worried that we might arrive too late to be of any assistance and for some minutes, all of us had visions of having to evacuate the entire 'recce' team in body bags. Had we been back at base – where we should have been – this would not have happened.

On arrival at the TAC HQ, we found Verster in a state of apoplexy. He had been trying to contact us all the time that we were on the beach. He told us that the team had just come over the radio. They had been compromised and contact could not be avoided.

After a quick briefing on the position and possible

deployment of troops, we took off in our *Alouette* gunships. The *Pumas* followed behind with the reaction force, all 16 of them; their airspeed was better than ours.

I spoke to a very unhappy Dennison just after take-off. The Swapo strength was approximately 18 men; they had began to fire on his position with light mortars. Twenty minutes later, we arrived overhead and there was much evidence of battle on the ground below; the bush had started to burn. The smoke had served as a homing beacon.

Dennison and his team had taken cover on a small *kopjie*, about 100 metres high, adjacent to a large rocky ridgeline. There were steep cliffs overhanging the contact area. The top of the *kopjie* was flat and Dennison and his team were in defensive positions facing the enemy.

It was hardly necessary for him to indicate the enemy position. Bush cover was sparse and the opposing players could easily be spotted, prone, weapons pointed in the direction of the *kopjie*. They were halfway up the hill, the nearest approximately 40 metres from where Dennison crouched.

I could see that the enemy had spread out alongside each other and were advancing steadily using well-disciplined fire and movement tactics. The *Pumas* arrived moments later.

Because there was only one section of heliborne-troops, deployment would be restricted to a single sweep-line and no stopper groups. However, I was aware that if Swapo could be duped, the sweepline could initially act as a stopper group and once the main punch-up was over, these men could then sweep through the contact area, mopping up remaining resistance. I instructed Sgt Steve Coetzee, my flight engineer, to start firing towards the rear of the attacking group. I was hoping that this would cause confusion in the cross-fire between Dennison and myself and force them to withdraw. We would then know in which direction to deploy our stopper group. Moments later, the first of the Swapo cadres broke and ran towards open ground.

Before the break became panic, all 32 Battalion troops were deployed. Those insurgents that had not been killed by our initial gunship fire ran headlong into 32 Battalion on the ground. All that remained was for the stopper group to sweep through the area, count the dead and take prisoners.

At this stage both Maranta and myself were low on fuel. As one of the *Pumas* had not returned to supply us, we had to land and monitor our forces from the top of one of the cliffs overlooking the battle field. Throughout, the insurgents offered very little opposition, directing minimal fire either at us or the newly deployed ground forces. The sudden appearance of the helicopters had taken them completely by surprise.

We suffered no casualties; the final Swapo tally was 14

dead, seven captured.

Immediately after we had landed back at base in the 'Fluss', the intelligence officer began his work. It was ascertained from the prisoners that they were, in fact, Swapo and not, as we had feared, Angolan regular army. They said that their task was to build a transit camp and cache arms for a new infiltration route through the Kaokoveld into central South West Africa.

According to the prisoners, there were about about 250 to 300 insurgents in their main camp. They confirmed the presence of shoulder-launched, anti-aircraft SAM-7 missiles, but were not certain of anti-aircraft fire-power.

They were well armed with the normal squad weapons such as RPGs, AKs, RPDs, PKMs and RPKs. In addition, there were vast quantities of anti-vehicle mines and rifle grenades.

Once it had been established how big and how vital the target was to the Swapo war effort, Sector 10 at Oshakati put in motion efforts to fly in extra helicopters, troops, fuel and ammunition. The concern was that if the camp was not attacked within the next 24 hours, the remainder of the group would disappear into the bush. It had happened before.

12 MARCH 1982

Most of the previous night was spent listening to the interrogation of the prisoners and going over details of logistical planning for the extra aircraft and troops. There was a critical shortage of fuel and ammunition; to truck in supplies from Windhoek – 800 kilometres to the south over bad roads – could have taken days. A fuel drop by air was requested.

This was subsequently carried out by *C-130/C-160* transport aircraft and completed by lunchtime the following day, which was not bad since it had to be decanted into 44-gallon drums and then flown in from Pretoria, half-way across the sub-continent. The ammunition and the rest of Hougaard's company were brought across from Ovamboland by *Dakota* and *Puma*.

Two *Alouette* gunships from Ruacana on the Angolan border to our immediate north-east were attached to the TAC HQ. The pilots were Major Charlie Bent and Lt Andre Schoeman. By midday, everything was in place, and we were ready for the attack.

Headquarters had decided that the onslaught would be launched late in the day; at 16h00 that afternoon; not a clever choice as far as the pilots were concerned because a base attack needs a whole day to clear up the mess afterwards. One of them made the point that if the action was rushed, casualty figures would escalate.

Says Neall Ellis: "We were tasked to take off at 15h40

for a 16h00 strike. After the briefing we left, only to have to abort because of a rainstorm over the target area. I was looking for any excuse to cancel the attack, so I was pleased. Planning was not to my satisfaction and I was sure that the intelligence boys had not determined the exact location of the camp.

"A senior intelligence officer who had arrived at the 'Fluss managed to obtain a clearer picture of where the Swapo camp was situated. He built a sand model of the area and, at last, was able to pin-point our destination. This was fortunate as the position initially indicated by the prisoners on the sand model was 35 kilometres away from the one we were given earlier."

The ability of enemy prisoners to 'rat' on their former comrades never ceased to amaze the South Africans. In most instances, interrogation boffins did not need to use coercion to make these captives talk. There were times when security forces would be able to follow up on this kind of information by launching an attack within an hour of determining where the base was situated. All that was required was some food and a soft drink and, as far as these survivors were concerned, the war was over. There were, of course, exceptions, but not often.

13 MARCH 1982

Ellis continues:

"I awoke at first light. There was definitely a sense of imminence about the camp. It was all going to happen that day, I felt. But it would not be easy.

"The camp was the biggest enemy base that I had attacked; we were not strong on the ground or in the air. Total forces were 45 men from 32 Battalion led by Captain Jan Hougaard – good soldiers, granted, but too few of them – an 81mm mortar group, four *Alouette IIIs* and five *Puma* medium transporters for troop deployment. Because we were thin in terms of firepower, the plan had to be simple but thorough.

"Any delay in troop deployment or lack of fuel at the mini-HAG (Helicopter Administrative Group) could cause us to lose the initiative.

"The basic plan was to initiate the strike at 08h00. We knew from our own intelligence sources that Swapo paraded each morning at that time, when orders for the day were issued. This suited us. The sun would be high enough to lighten the shadows and enable those of us over the target to spot any enemy hiding in the sparse bush cover.

"Maranta and I were to search for the camp and, once identified, deploy the sweepline and stopper groups. Four *Pumas* were tasked to transport these forces into position. The fifth *Puma* would bring in the mortar group.

"Once the men had been deployed, the two remaining

Alouettes would give top cover to two small groups that had taken up position to the far north of the camp; it would monitor the road, basically waiting for Swapo reinforcements and prevent any of the enemy from escaping in the direction from where they had originally come.

"The mini-HAG was to be established about 12 kilometres away from the target. The gunships would refuel and rearm there, and if a *Puma* could not get into an LZ in the contact area for a casevac, the wounded man would be transported by *Alouette* back to the mini-HAG. The *Puma* would then airlift him to the TAC HQ where a temporary base hospital had been established.

"After a quick breakfast of dog biscuits and 'plastic' coffee, we went over the plan once again to make sure that the intelligence picture had not changed overnight, and that everyone understood communications. The 'devil-dodger' finished off with a prayer and we were at our aircraft at about 07:20 hours.

"Take-off was uneventful. No snags were reported and we proceeded to the target area. Visibility was good; no rain clouds were present or expected.

"Once over the river, I busied myself with navigation. We needed to stay as low as possible so that the enemy would have no warning of our approach. This was difficult as the *Alouettes* had no navigational aids and I had to keep tracking our course on the charts.

"At the two minute mark I called for the climb and confirmed that the *Pumas* were in the holding area. As I lifted my machine over the ridge which dominated the Swapo camp I could only pray that we had achieved surprise.

"The target area was in a large natural geological 'bowl', completely surrounded by mountains. We came in close to the mountainside, hoping to confuse the enemy as to our direction of approach and also to use our camouflage to prevent or delay visual detection. By now I was apprehensive as the AAA capability that the enemy might have in the camp had still not been determined.

"For some moments I had expected to see the camp stretched out below me. Surely, I thought, a camp of that size would be easily identified. But I saw nothing. There was only flat scrub.

"I entered another orbit. Even if the camp was deserted, I argued to myself, we should still be able to pick up the path pattern. And where was the parade ground? Obviously, they were there somewhere, but all I could see was a large number of dew soaked rocks, very dark brown in colour. I sent Angelo to the north of the area to 'recce' for any signs of the camp."

Just then, Coetzee called over the intercom that he had spotted tents below. Ellis looked about him but could still see nothing. Coetzee remained adamant that he had tents visual and described them as squarish and dark brown in colour.

To Ellis the scene unfolded; dark brown rocks became

bivouacs and the path pattern emerged like a spider web on the ground. In places clothing had been hung out to dry and the camp debris, carefully concealed, came into focus. Then, jackpot!

Under every bush lay inert 'toy' soldiers, sometimes five or six to a bush. One small shrub looked like a starfish; they had covered their torsos but not their legs. Ellis again:

"I had never seen so many enemy on the ground before. They were all over the place. The camp was built around an old derelict *kraal* and covered an area of roughly 1 000 by 1 500 metres square.

"By now, the adrenalin was pumping. I had the feeling of having been punched in the gut. The first task was to get our troops on the ground as soon as possible. Once Swapo started to run it would become a flood. I knew that we had to keep them guessing as to whether they had been spotted or not and I instructed Maranta to widen his orbit, to climb higher and to try and act as nonchalant as possible.

"I decided to drop the sweepline to the west of the camp and the stopper groups along the river lines to the south and south-west. There was a conical hill quite close by on which the mortar team could be deployed; it overlooked the camp and they would easily be able to observe the fall of their bombs and make their own corrections. I radioed instructions to the *Pumas*.

"The enemy had still not made any effort to reveal their positions. But some of them had started to crawl slowly towards the edge of the camp. Then I saw the *Pumas* approaching below me and the insurgents must have been alerted at the same time. Clearly, we were onto them. At this point I opened fire.

"Experience had shown in the past that once one person moves in a direction, the rest would follow and it would be difficult to contain the panic.

"The first rounds from our choppers stopped the run and the insurgents dived for cover. Then all hell broke loose. I heard a large bang towards the rear of the aircraft as an RPG rocket exploded behind me, while Maranta shouted over the radio, 'SAM launch: six o'clock!' I could see the distinctive thick whitish-grey smoke trail of a SAM-7 twirling up into the sky towards us. I immediately put on more bank to find the firing position.

"As I turned through 180 degrees a second SAM-7 was launched towards us. This time it was directed at Maranta. I called hastily 'SAM launch: nine o'clock!'

"We were so low, that by the time I had used my radio the missile was already travelling at Mach 1.5. It passed by harmlessly just in front of his nose. SAM-7s were not fitted with proximity fuses.

"By now we were coming under heavy automatic fire. The sound of rounds, RPG blasts accompanied by a curtain of tracer was deafening, even with headsets on; a

chattering clattering cacophony.

"The SAM firing position was easy to trace because of the smoke from the launch area rising lazily into the air. I approached the position and spotted the missile operators trying to take cover beneath the bushes. Coetzee, my gunner, quickly killed them.

"By now both Maranta and I had become principal targets. More RPGs were being launched and they self-destructed above our heads at 900 metres.

"Although fairly ineffective against aircraft, RPG-7s do explode with an extremely loud blast accompanied by a large puff of black smoke almost like flak out of a World War 2 movie. And this can cause distractions while trying to direct a battle.

"Another SAM-7 shot past the nose of my aircraft. Once the firing position had been identified, Coetzee again killed the missile team. By now, the *Pumas* were quite close to the LZ I had identified. I shifted my position to mark the spot with a smoke grenade and to provide top cover.

"The LZ was just under two kilometres from the camp and with the breakout, I had observed some of the enemy running in that direction.

"The troops from the four *Pumas* formed up quickly and started moving towards the objective. The next task was to drop off the mortar group. This too was accomplished without problems. After they had been placed, the larger choppers returned to the 'Fluss to uplift the stopper groups, fuel and ammunition needed to form the mini-HAG."

It was at about this point that the enemy realised that they had been contained. They again started directing heavy fire at the two gunships as well as mortars onto the troops in the sweepline. Although neither was effective, it was, according to Ellis, disconcerting, as apart from all the other fire coming their way, there were also mortar bombs passing through their orbit. Maranta neutralised the emplacement soon afterwards.

Once the South Africans on the ground started moving through the outskirts of the enemy camp they came under heavy fire and their progress slowed. This was not a serious problem as the gunships had limited the breakout. But ground fighting had become intense.

At one stage Coetzee was killing isolated pockets of enemy approximately five metres from our forces. And since the lethal radius of a 20mm cannon shell is five metres, the South Africans had to keep their heads down during gunship support fire. After the battle, some of the troops had to be treated for light 20mm shrapnel wounds.

On another occasion, two of the enemy had climbed a tree to get a better line of sight on the advancing troops. Coetzee picked them off as well.

About 20 minutes after the sweepline had been dropped, the *Pumas* returned with the rest of the force which had been taken in as stopper groups. Maranta was detailed to give top cover to the *Puma* which was dropping callsign *Blackie*.

While this helicopter was in the process of flaring prior to setting down, a group of about 30 of the enemy had managed to identify the LZ. Maranta engaged them and became involved in a fairly stiff fire-fight, neutralising the position in a few minutes, but not before his gunship had taken light battle damage from small arms fire.

Ellis meanwhile was giving top cover to the *Puma* dropping off callsign *Nella*. This *Puma* had just begun short finals for the LZ, when he picked up some of the enemy running along the same gully into which the *Puma* was going to land.

The defile was rocky with steep sides and the rebel group could not climb out of it. They were trying to escape, to no avail. It was like a duck shoot. All that Coetzee had to do was fire above their heads and the ricocheting shrapnel did the rest. Ellis continues:

"However, by the time the *Puma* had taken off again, a few more of the enemy had progressed to within 50 metres of the LZ and Nella was himself immediately involved in a contact only seconds after touching down. His position was exposed and we had a few anxious moments before we were able to knock out the survivors.

"By this time Maranta and myself were short on fuel; both of us were out of ammunition. Bent and Schoeman positioned their gunships overhead to carry on with the task of controlling the sweepline and giving close air support. Hougaard had his first casualty as we were pulling out. A sergeant was badly wounded and Maranta put down to pull him out. He carried out the evacuation under heavy fire, landing only metres behind the sweepline."

After refuelling and rearming, the two gunships returned to the scene of the contact and relieved Bent and Schoeman. Both gunships had positioned themselves to the north and east of the camp to act as airborne stopper groups.

Throughout the battle, the South Africans had *Impala* ground strike aircraft orbiting the area for close-air support, if that need arose. Towards the end of the battle, their ground forces encountered a particularly aggressive group of insurgents that had managed to keep them at bay. It was Ellis that decided to call in a strike.

PREVIOUS PAGE – FROM TOP: The lower reaches of the Kunene, the biggest river in the region had to be forded by Swapo infiltrators heading south; *Pumas* in a semi-brown-out situation starting engines in the desert prior to *Op Super*; SAM-7 taken by South African troops; Converted *Buffel* modified by SAAF electronic boffins for communications work in cross-border raids.

After passing on target information and marking it with smoke, he eased away to give the jets a clear run in.

Some minutes passed but there was still no sign of the *Impalas*. Ellis called on the radio to find out what was up. The answer came back, "We have been orbiting the position you gave us, but can find no signs of the battle or see your smoke. Are you sure that you are in the right valley?" So much for back-up in the African bush.

Although most of the opposition had been neutralised, there were still pockets of die-hards which had to be sorted out before a final body count could be made. During this period, Hougaard lost two more men, a black soldier and one of his platoon commanders, Lt Nel (Nella), who was posthumously awarded the *Honoris Crux* Silver Decoration for bravery. Nella had accounted for many kills during the action. Some of his contacts were at point-blank range.

The clearing-up operations took the South Africans into late afternoon.

The final body count was 187 Swapo dead with one capture; the camp cook, who soon made it clear that he was not too interested in making war.

Total kills for the operation, including the results of the contact on the 11 March were 201 dead and eight captures. With clearing-up operations completed, the next day's events revealed huge arms caches concealed in the rocky slopes of the surrounding mountains. One cache alone had 1 000 anti-tank and personnel rifle grenades, more than three hundred 82mm mortar bombs, 150 landmines, ten SAM-7 anti aircraft missiles and fifty AK-47 rifles.

The end result was that Swapo, intent on opening an infiltration route to the farmlands to the south through the Kaokoveld, had taken a heavy knock. And, while military activity in the Kaokoveld did intensify over the next few years – they laid thousands of landmines, making many roads impassable – their leaders never again tried to launch any large-scale operation in the barren and beautiful arid land on the edge of the Western Front.

32 Battalion troops move towards a *Puma* during ongoing operations in south-central Angola. These helicopters are regarded as among the most reliable anywhere.

CHAPTER 24

OPERATION SHARP EDGE

US Marine Rescue in Liberia

Protecting civilians abroad is a job Navy and Marine amphibious forces do frequently – but never routinely. This operation showed the team at its best – but the Middle East dominated the news and few have heard of it. Lieutenant Colonel T.W. Parker tells us how it was.

From 5 August 1990 until 21 August 1990, the 22nd Marine Expeditionary Unit (Special Operations Capable) executed classic MEU (SOC) missions:

Protection and evacuation of noncombatants
Security operations
Show of force

Men of the 22nd Marine Expeditionary Unit (22 MEU) board a Marine Medium Helicopter Squadron 261 (HMM-261) CH-46E *Sea Knight* onboard the amphibious assault ship USS *Saipan* (LHA-2) in preparation for *Operation Sharp Edge* off the coast of the West African state of Liberia.

On 27 May 1990, the 22nd MEU (SOC) – then serving as Landing Force Sixth Fleet – left the Mediterranean for coastal waters off Monrovia, Liberia, in response to continued unrest and threats to US citizens and property. Little has been written about the operation, which was overshadowed by Iraq's seizure of Kuwait and the subsequent US and coalition buildup.

Nevertheless, *Operation Sharp Edge* highlighted the unique capabilities of the Navy-Marine Corps teams to deploy rapidly a sea-based force capable of remaining on station indefinitely, prepared to conduct special operations with particular emphasis on the evacuation and protection of noncombatants.

Stern view of the USS *Saipan*, the American amphibious assault ship that took part in *Operation Sharp Edge* off Liberia.
INSET: US Marines preparing to board in preparation for the rescue mission.

BACKGROUND

Liberia has had a long-standing relationship with the United States and is the location of a number of important US telecommunications sites. The major cities are Monrovia, the capital; Buchanan, an important port; and Harbel, just south of the Firestone rubber plantation – the largest in the world.

On 12 April 1980, a coup led by Army Master Sergeant Samuel K. Doe overthrew the government, suspended the constitution and imposed martial law. A new constitution was drafted and on 15 October 1985 elections were held. Elected president, Doe was inaugurated on 16 January 1986.

In December 1989, Charles Taylor, a Gio tribesman, launched an insurgency against the Doe government. Taylor, a former director of the Liberian General Services Administration, had been accused of corruption and had fled the country. His insurgent organisation became the National Patriotic Front of Liberia (NPFL), and was initially composed of 100-200 hard-core members. The organisation grew as dissatisfaction with Doe increased; as the NPFL gained strength, elements began a slow advance toward Monrovia.

During pre-deployment training, the 22nd MEU staff had focused on Liberia as a potential trouble spot, gathering intelligence continuously; indications were that the NPFL might bog down during the approaching rainy season.

Representatives from the staff of the Commander-in-Chief, US Naval Forces Europe, briefed the 22nd MEU (SOC) Staff on the situation when the unit arrived in the Mediterranean, and provided maps, photography, and other valuable background information. Preliminary "What if..." sessions focused on possible sources of action, should the unit be deployed.

DEPLOYMENT

In late May, the Marines were conducting routine training ashore in France while Amphibious Squadron Four (PhibRon Four) ships – the *Saipan* (LHA-2), *Ponce* (LPD-15), and *Sumter* (LST-1181) – were undergoing an upkeep period in Toulon, France.

The Battalion Landing Team (BLT) 2/4, Marine Medium Helicopter Squadron (HMM)-261 (Reinforced), and MEU Service Support Group (MSSG)-22 were training at Camp De Canjuers, France. The squadron's AV-8B detachment was shore-based at Hyeres Naval Air Station, east of Toulon.

On 25 May 1990 the Chairman of the Joint Chiefs of Staff directed PhibRon Four to embark the Marines and proceed to the vicinity of Monrovia, prepare to evacuate noncombatants and conduct security operations at key US installations. The order came as no surprise, and the ships departed Toulon on 27 May.

An initial plan was presented to the Commander, Sixth Fleet on 28 May. This quick response was a direct result of the emphasis placed on rapid-reaction planning during all MEU (SOC) training. Although use of other forces was considered, it became apparent at this point that the 'maritime option' was the preferred course of action.

COMMAND RELATIONSHIPS

Under normal command relationships in the Mediterranean, the Landing Force, Sixth Fleet – in this case the 22nd MEU (SOC) – is designated Task Force 61 and the amphibious squadron – in this case, PhibRon Four – is Task Force 62. Traditional blue-green amphibious relationships exist for planning and execution, i.e. parallel planning prior to embarkation as Commander, Amphibious Task Force (CATF), and the Commander, Landing Force (CLF), for execution.

Because *Sharp Edge* was a maritime operation, the US Commander-in-Chief, Europe (USCinCEur), designated Commander, Sixth Fleet, as Commander, Joint Task Force (COMJTF), to facilitate adding additional forces, if required. The MEU and the PhibRon reported directly to COMJTF.

Command relationships were clear. All elements of the Sixth Fleet and CinCEur staffs worked closely with the MEU and PhibRon.

The Commander, Sixth Fleet, attached the USS *Peterson* (DD-969) to the task force to provide an improved signals intelligence and naval gunfire capability. As the situation unfolded, this decision proved fortuitous.

As the MEU transited the Straits of Gibraltar, the latest maps were flown to the ships and a forward command element (FCE), led by the MEU's executive officer, was flown to Rota, Spain. The FCE's mission was to fly to Monrovia, establish contact with the US Embassy, and provide detailed information to the forces afloat.

Communication with the Sixth Fleet headquarters was maintained on two satellite nets, and the European command net was monitored on the bridge of the *Saipan*. The *Sharp Edge* net was also the primary means of communicating with the FCE at the embassy. High frequency (HF) radio was used as a backup. Ultra-high-frequency (UHF) radio nets were used when the ships arrived off Monrovia.

The forward combat element included the battalion executive officer, the officers-in-charge (OICs) of the SEAL and Air-Naval Gunfire Liaison Company (ANGLICO) detachments, and a radio operator. The SEAL OIC provided valuable beach and hydrographic information while the ANGLICO OIC, an aviator, gave timely and accurate analysis of proposed landing zones. The BLT

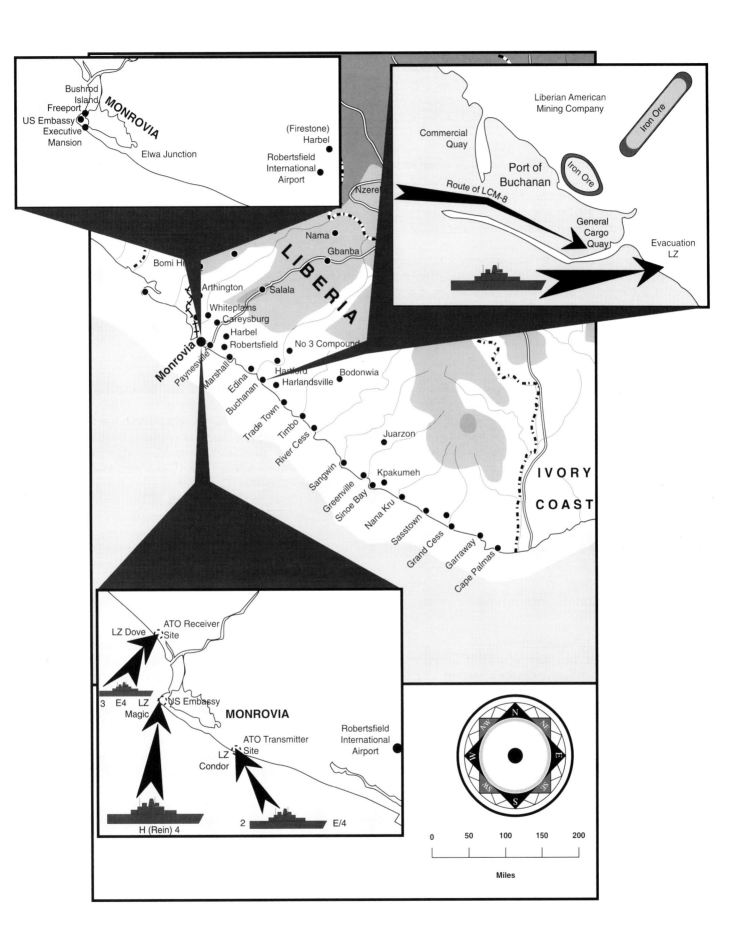

Inset (top left) — MONROVIA

Bushrod Island
Freeport
US Embassy
Executive Mansion
Elwa Junction
MONROVIA
(Firestone) Harbel
Robertsfield International Airport

Inset (top right) — Port of Buchanan

Liberian American Mining Company
Commercial Quay
Port of Buchanan
Iron Ore
Iron Ore
Route of LCM-8
General Cargo Quay
Evacuation LZ

Main map

Nzere
Nama
Gbanba
Bomi Hi
Arthington
Salala
Whiteplains
Careysburg
Harbel
Robertsfield
No 3 Compound
Monrovia
Paynesville
Marshall
Edina
Buchanan
Hartford
Harlandsville
Bodonwia
LIBERIA
Trade Town
Timbo
River Cess
Juarzon
Sangwin
Greenville
Kpakumeh
Sinoe Bay
Nana Kru
Sasstown
Grand Cess
Garraway
Cape Palmas
IVORY COAST

Inset (bottom left) — MONROVIA

LZ Dove
ATO Receiver Site
3 E4 LZ Magic
US Embassy
MONROVIA
Robertsfield International Airport
ATO Transmitter Site
LZ Condor
H (Rein) 4
2 E/4

Scale

0   50   100   150   200
Miles

executive officer provided tactical assessments from the ground combat element perspective and the MEU executive officer dealt with embassy officials (to include the ambassador) as the direct representative of COMJTF, the 22nd MEU, and PhibRon Four. The team landed at Monrovia's Roberts International Airport on 31 May, after a flight from Rota in a Navy C-130.

As the situation deteriorated, particularly in Monrovia, the requirement to reinforce the embassy assumed higher priority. This made it imperative to get a helicopter-borne force within range of Monrovia as quickly as possible. Even steaming at more than 20 knots, the *Saipan* could not close this distance until 3 June. Accordingly, a CH-46 and a 75-man security force composed of a reinforced rifle platoon and a SEAL detachment were embarked on the *Peterson* to sprint ahead of the *Saipan* at 30 knots.

The *Peterson* arrived off Monrovia on 2 June, 24 hours ahead of the *Saipan*. The situation had changed, however, and the *Peterson's* force was not immediately required. On 3 June, the security force returned to the *Saipan*.

During the transit to Monrovia the forward command element relied on satellite communications to maintain contact with the forces afloat. This link provided indispensable updates on the situation ashore and enabled all elements of the Marine Expeditionary Unit to conduct realistic rehearsals for possible action ashore.

EXECUTION

During June and July and into the first days of August, the NPFL and a splinter group, the Independent National Patriotic Front of Liberia (INPFL) under Prince Johnson tightened the noose around Monrovia. US forces continued to rehearse possible actions – day and night – at least once a week. The MEU issued ammunition, used role-players to simulate evacuees, and conducted mass-casualty drills. No-notice rehearsals were also held, and all evolutions received immediate critiques.

All hands became familiar with planned landing zones, debarkation, ammunition issue, treatment of casualties, handling of evacuees, and the rules of engagement.

At the end of July, fighting around the US Embassy intensified and the MEU was placed on a one-hour alert, as possible reinforcements. The killing of approximately 200 civilians at the Lutheran Church of Monrovia added a new sense of urgency to the situation.

On 4 August, Prince Johnson threatened to take US hostages. That evening, the US Ambassador advised the forces afloat that he was requesting assistance from the National Command Authority. Shortly thereafter, the forces afloat were directed to:

Secure the US Embassy with a reinforced rifle company

Evacuate embassy personnel, US citizens, and designated foreign nationals from the US Embassy and area telecommunications receiver and transmitter sites

Provide logistics support to the US Embassy

At sea, the Navy and Marine Corps staffs met at 21:00 (local time), 4 August onboard the *Saipan* to refine the plan. A final brief was conducted at 05:00 on 5 August.

Few changes were required; L-hour (touchdown in the LZ) was set for 09:00 the same day – 5 August.

All ships closed to within six nautical miles of Monrovia that morning. HMM-261 helicopters launched with visibility restricted by rain. Predeployment and shipboard training, which emphasised flight operations in reduced visibility, paid dividends; the helicopter crews found their landing zones without incident.

Five CH-46s landed a rifle platoon from Echo Company in LZ Dove at the area telecommunications office (ATO) receiver site; by 09:13, eighteen US citizens were on their way out. Within minutes, the platoon followed them.

Two CH-46s and one CH-53D another of Echo Company's platoons in LZ Condor landed at the ATO transmitter site; by 09:29, three US citizens and all the Marines were on their way to the *Saipan*.

Simultaneously, a mix of CH-46s and CH-53Ds landed Hotel Company (Reinforced) – 234 Marines and six fast attack vehicles – in LZ Magic at the US Embassy. The company set up security and deployed heavy weapons and 60mm mortars to cover likely avenues of approach and planned targets. Defensive positions were established at each gate and Marines patrolled the embassy perimeter; forty US citizens and foreign nationals were processed at the embassy and flown to safety on the *Saipan*.

AH-IT attack helicopters and UH-IN command and control helos orbited all three LZs ready to provide close-in fire support; two AV-8Bs maintained a five-minute alert on the *Saipan's* flight deck. The *Peterson* was positioned in a predetermined fire support area three miles west of Bushrod Island to provide naval gunfire support.

Daily, from 6 August through 21 August 1990, 22nd MEU (SOC) helicopters continued to evacuate US citizens and foreign nationals from the embassy. On 16 and 18 August respectively, 359 and 754 people were flown to Navy ships from LZ Magic, a one-helicopter landing zone.

Screening of evacuees was conducted at the embassy by Marines and State Department personnel. Detailed processing was done onboard ship by ship's company and Marines. The intent was to move evacuees quickly to the ships, where detailed processing would be conducted. The evacuees were then flown by helicopter to Freetown, Sierra Leone, where they were met by their embassies.

On 11 August 1990, NPFL leader Charles Taylor communicated his willingness to provide safe passage from Monrovia for Spanish, Swiss, German, and other diplomats (e.g. from the Vatican) and their families who wanted to leave. Fighting was intense and assembling these people at the US Embassy was not a realistic option. The plan called for NPFL soldiers to escort an overland convoy to Buchanan, Liberia, beginning at approximately 16:00 on 12 August. Helicopters would then evacuate the diplomats to the ships.

The *Saipan* and the *Peterson* were designated to support the evacuation at Buchanan and arrived on station five miles from the port at 05:30 on 13 August. At this point, the OIC of the Naval Special Warfare detachment and a SEAL security force departed the *Saipan* in an LCM-8 to link up with NPFL officials in the port. They docked at the general cargo quay at 08:25, and the OIC met with NPFL representatives to identify a suitable LZ.

After the LZ had been designated, MEU and US State Department representatives landed at 09:48. A quick-reaction heliborne force supported by AH-ITs remained on deck alert onboard the *Saipan*.

Negotiations continued in the LZ about the particulars of the evacuation. Flights began at 11:18, using four CH-46 aircraft cycling into the LZ one at a time and flying evacuees to the ship for detailed processing. A total of 96 evacuees were flown out and three were moved by LCM-8 from the port. The mission was completed at 13:38.

ABOVE: US Marines of the 22nd MEU ashore near Monrovia in preparation for the evacuation of refugees. BELOW: Marine at a forward 'hot' position in Monrovia during the evacuation process.

LOGISTICS

More than 35 000 gallons of JP-5 in fuel bladders were staged at the US Embassy. Pumps from the squadron's helicopter expeditionary refuelling system transferred fuel from the bladders to tanks that supplied the embassy's generators. HMM-261 flew 28 pallets of food, two pallets of medical supplies and 4 800 gallons of water to the diplomatic compound. Helicopter support teams handled the supplies at the LZ.

LESSONS LEARNED (OR RE-LEARNED)

Three broad categories stand out:
> The basic MEU (SOC) concepts and principles are valid
>
> Simple plans, thoroughly rehearsed (to include critiques) provide enough flexibility to respond to rapidly changing situations
>
> The MEU (SOC) requirement to respond quickly (within six hours) is valid

The 22nd MEU/PhibRon Four Special Operations Capable Exercise during training highlighted many of the challenges later faced in Liberia.

The commander's intent was always clear: to use the smallest tactically feasible force and move evacuees by the quickest means to amphibious shipping for detailed processing. All plans were rehearsed in detail, in both daylight and darkness.

Having trained under the six-hour, rapid-planning guidance during workups and the deployment, the MEU and PhibRon responded quickly to orders. The process also ensured a capability to plan for new missions while revising current plans. Demonstrating this capability should continue to be a hard-and-fast requirement for deploying units.

More than 1 600 US citizens and foreign nationals were removed from a threatening situation while US installations were protected. The restraint, professionalism, and *esprit* of the individual Marine, when called upon to carry out a sensitive mission, was proved again under demanding conditions. Realistic training and effective small-unit leadership were keys to success.

The value of the MEU (SOC) as a forward-deployed Marine Air-Ground Task Force (MAGTF) in stability operations and limited-objective operations was reinforced by *Operation Sharp Edge*. MAGTFs operating from amphibious ships capable of remaining on station for extended periods are uniquely suited for employment in low-intensity conflict.

On 22 August 1990, the 22nd MEU (SOC) was relieved by the 26th MEU (SOC).

CHAPTER 25

THE NAVAL FACTOR IN THE SOUTH ATLANTIC

The Cold War waged in the South Atlantic was, in its own way, every bit as intense as elsewhere, largely because of the strategic importance of the sea route around the southern tip of Africa – the Cape Sea Route as it was referred to in strategic briefings in Whitehall, the Pentagon and elsewhere.

A great deal of the Western World's oil has always been routed around the Cape. The Suez Canal had proved during two fairly recent Arab wars with the Israelis to be vulnerable to blockage or to sabotage. And, in the event of an all-out war with the Soviet Union and its Allies, southern Africa's coast would have become a pivotal factor to the survival of the West if the larger proportion of its oil from the Middle East were to be routed around Africa. Clearly, the Soviets were well aware of this, which is why they paid so much attention to southern African liberation groups. But all that is now history.

In the face of United Nations arms sanctions, an embattled and isolated South Africa was hard-pressed to keep pace with the demands made on their 2 000-kilometre coastline and the Cape Sea Route. Its fleet of ageing frigates, destroyers and submarines were, clearly, no match for what any modern adversary could field. Yet, manoeuvres involving the South African Navy and the SAAF were held annually and effort was expended to keep abreast of maritime developments elsewhere in the world.

South Africa's *Wager* Class helicopter-carrying destroyers were extensively upgraded and converted between 1961 and 1966 to operate Westland *Wasp* HAS Mk1 manned anti-submarine, torpedo-carrying helicopters (MATCH) for stand-off weapons delivery.

OPPOSITE: The destroyer USS *Peterson* DD-969, which played a major role in *Operation Sharp Edge* off the West Coast of Africa. ABOVE: South African Air Force Westland *Wasp* in air-sea rescue exercises off the southern African coast.

DURING THE COLD WAR THE SOUTH ATLANTIC WAS AN ACTIVE THEATRE OF MILITARY ACTIVITY

CLOCKWISE FROM ABOVE: *Wasp* landing on the quarterdeck of one of the SA Navy's *President* Class frigates; Maritime *Puma* stowed, rotors folded, in the hangar onboard SAS *Drakensberg*; French-built *Super Frelons* were widely deployed at South African coastal bases, but were not successful in African conditions; *Wasp* approaches afterdeck landing; Pilot's eye-view of quarterdeck landing; SAS *President Steyn* was involved in several clandestine landings on the Angolan coast during the early phase of the war; *Puma* at the hover at sea.

CHAPTER 26

DISASTER AT SEA

The Sinking of the *Oceanos*

The MV Oceanos, a beautiful but rather anti-quated ocean passenger liner, sailed from East London on Saturday, 3 August 1991, bound for Durban. She had 571 people onboard; passengers and crew. At 22h30B that evening, the East London port captain received a distress call from the Oceanos stating that her position was approximately 100 nautical miles north of that port city which lies on the east coast of South Africa. The ship was taking on water and had developed a list to starboard. Clearly, the situation was critical.

Within minutes the distress call was relayed by the East London port captain's office to the South African Air Force Maritime Rescue Co-Ordination Centre (MRCC) at Silvermine near Cape Town, about 1 200 kilometres to the west. The officer on duty immediately activated his command post and informed SAAF Headquarters in Pretoria of the impending disaster.

From that moment on, a coordinated joint operation between the four components of the South African Defence Force; the Air Force, Army, Navy and the SA Medical Services was put into action; its planning and exe-

cution resulted in the recovery of everyone onboard the ship. There was no loss of life.

It was the first time in modern history that such a large rescue mission had been implemented and total success achieved in what was probably the worst storm to hit this south Indian Ocean coast for several years. Gales had gusted up to 120 nautical miles earlier that evening and swells were often in excess of 20 metres. Damage to shore installations and reefs hundreds of kilometres farther up the coast was severe. Aliwal Shoal, just south of Durban – and more than 500 kilometres away – was badly mauled by wave action.

The rescue attempt was no easy task. Where the *Oceanos* eventually sank was in a remote region far from the major centres and with few basic facilities. Essentially, there was little of the kind infrastructure as we know it in the West. One of the pilots phrased it this way:

"If a theoretical exercise were carried out to select the most remote corner on the entire South African coast between Cape Town and Durban, the answer would, in all probability, be between The Haven and Coffee Bay, two sleepy little hamlets on the coast of the Transkei, a nominally independent black state in the Eastern Cape. In both villages there is little more than a single road, a post office and a small hotel, usually closed during the winter. August in the Southern Hemisphere is mid-winter, a time when these waters are to be avoided. The Transkei coast, especially, is notoriously treacherous; it always has been. Ships have been driven ashore along the coast since the Portuguese first navigated these seas five centuries ago."

It was a tiny position on the charts, three or four kilometres off the coast – between these two hamlets – that the *Oceanos* sank. But she stayed afloat long enough to allow the South Africans to launch their rescue operation.

The comparative distances to the ship from the points where the aircraft were deployed are as follows:

Durban to Coffee Bay = 300 kilometres; a distance equivalent to that between London and Paris. Or New York and Washington

Pretoria to Coffee Bay = 1 040 kilometres; London to Berlin. Or Chicago to Washington

Cape Town to Coffee Bay = 1 070 kilometres; London to Nice. Or Quebec to Washington

Officially, the town of Umtata in the adjacent Transkei is the 'capital'. Even by African standards, facilities are very basic, but Umtata does have an airport with an Air Traffic Control service, and it is capable of handling larger aircraft. There are also limited supplies of jet fuel.

From Umtata, flying time by *Puma* helicopter to the scene of the disaster is approximately 15 minutes; but to drive by vehicle on a secondary dirt road takes about an hour-and-a-half between the capital and Coffee Bay.

Officers attached to the Maritime Rescue Co-ordination Centre were aware, of course, that the Transkei, being an 'independent' country, required the authority of that government to overfly its territory. Fortunately, unlike several other rescue operations in Africa that have bogged down in delays and bureaucratic red tape, which has sometimes resulted in loss of life, authority was granted immediately.

For the planners that momentous night, there were several physical obstacles to overcome; each had a bearing on the outcome.

The warm Agulhas Current which flows down the east coast of Africa in a southerly direction comes very close inshore along the Transkei coast. Its width at that point is fairly narrow and this results in an increase of the flow speed. Currents of up to three metres a second (six knots) are not unusual off Coffee Bay. Even when there is calm weather this kind of movement poses a severe hazard to ships that come too close inshore.

Earlier on the day of the disaster, a massive cold front had passed to the north-east of the disaster area. A big storm with gale-force winds had approached the region; the seas had become wild and it is astonishing that the captain of the *Oceanos* even considered leaving port.

The weather system was complicated still further by a strong current moving in the opposite direction to the wind, causing frequent ten or fifteen or even twenty metre swells. Some of these huge waves broke at the crest. By the time the rescue started on the Sunday morning, the sea had abated somewhat.

Meanwhile, there was much activity among SAAF personnel in the Air Force Command Post (AFCP) at Air Force Headquarters in Pretoria. This system which they implemented is geared for emergencies such as this and facilitates cooperation between all the service arms of the South African Defence Force. It works like this:

Air support in South Africa generally is maintained by the location of Forward Air Force Command Posts (FACPs) with corresponding Army regional headquarters, both of which are on permanent, round-the-clock standby. There are therefore FACPs in all the main cities of South Africa; Cape Town, Port Elizabeth, Bloemfontein and Durban, and each is responsible for the region in which it is based in the event of an emergency.

In recent years, though, South Africa – like many other countries – has not escaped rationalisation. The 'Cold War' is over and the threat of imminent conflict is gone, so cuts are made at all levels. The Air Force has been particularly hard hit; a number of air force bases, squadrons and units have been disbanded. The main effect of all this on the *Oceanos* disaster, was that the aircraft originally based in Port Elizabeth had been withdrawn.

But there was a contingency measure; aircraft and crews at all air force bases in the country were put on standby at night and over weekends. In the case of *Puma* helicopter squadrons, two aircraft – and their respective crews – were on a two hour notification basis in Pretoria, Cape Town and Durban. That is how the system operates at present.

Additionally, each Air Force Command Post is tasked to ensure cooperation with the emergency organisations within its region of operations. At a moment's notice, for instance, the Air Force can co-opt the assistance of experts in many different disciplines of emergency or rescue activities.

To allow standby personnel some free movement after normal working hours, a recall pager is issued to each member of the crew. This system certainly proved itself that night.

A positive factor that contributed to the success of this operation, was that the headquarters of all four services are situated in one central city, Pretoria. The Operations Staffs of the Air Force, Navy, Army and Medical Services had formed joint teams, both professionally and informally, and this arrangement had allowed joint operations to function without any of the inter-service rivalry that one sees in many other countries.

There were two major problems facing the planners on the night of the disaster: the first communications, the second was fuel.

Force 12 winds had blown down all existing telephone lines in the Coffee Bay area, which was a disaster since this village was to become the Air Force rescue base for the next 12 or 15 hours. These hamlets were effectively cut off from the outside world.

The obvious solution was to provide an alternative communications system as soon as possible and this was done without delay.

At 04h14B a C-160 French-built *Transall* aircraft took off from Waterkloof Air Force Base in Pretoria for the Transkei; it was to be used as the first 'on scene commander' to provide initial intelligence. Flares and marine markers were also to be dropped to assist merchant shipping nearby to locate the many lifeboats that had already been lowered.

By 08h25B on Sunday morning, a Mobile Air Operations Team (MAOT) under the command of Air Force Major Louter van Wyk had arrived by air from Cape Town. His Tactical Air Force Command Post was quickly set up at the Haven Hotel; each team was equipped with operator and VHF/HF radio equipment. Communications were now taken care of.

The fuel problem remained a major issue. All *Puma* helicopters had been fitted with long range tanks before their departure from the various centres to get them to the Coffee Bay area without refuelling. But what about afterwards?

When these choppers landed at the MAOT site at Coffee Bay, the additional tanks were removed to reduce weight and to allow greater internal space while hoisting *Oceanos* survivors into the aircraft.

Pumas from 15 Squadron in Durban, only 300 kilometres from Coffee Bay, were each able to haul extra 200 litre drums of fuel; this enabled them to refuel at the scene and commence rescue operations almost immediately.

All subsequent refuelling of helicopters was done at Umtata, an extra 15 minutes flying time away.

At each SA Air Force base, there are two *Puma* helicopters and crews on round-the-clock standby. However, when the callout for support was given, the word quickly went round among other crews and the various squadrons were able to supply more units than originally requested. *Pumas* were dispatched from Durban, Pretoria and Cape Town. The final score was as follows:

    5 *Pumas* from 30 Squadron (AFB Ysterplaat, Cape Town)

    4 *Pumas* from 15 Squadron (AFB Durban)

    2 *Pumas* from 19 Squadron (AFB Swartkop, Pretoria)

    2 *Alouettes* from 15 Squadron (AFB Durban)

    1 *C-160* from 28 Squadron (AFB Waterkloof, Pretoria)

    1 *C-130* from 28 Squadron (AFB Waterkloof, Pretoria)

    3 *Dakota* DC-3s from 35 Squadron (AFB D.F. Malan, Cape Town)

The two *Alouettes* were dispatched from Durban at first light. Their task was to search the rugged and by now foam-lashed coast in the vicinity of the sinking ship for evidence of survivors or, at worst, the bodies of those who had drowned, but they were not utilised during the operation. By now many lifeboats had been despatched from the *Oceanos* and these were being picked up in mountainous seas by merchant shipping that had been alerted to the area by emergency radio calls.

Additionally, the *C-130* sent from Pretoria brought 48 doctors and nurses and all their equipment to Umtata. This was a major effort to bolster the medical support already at the scene.

Ultimately nine *Pumas* were used to hoist survivors off the stricken ship. Two more were deployed to transfer personnel, equipment and fuel between the coastal villages.

The first four *Pumas* arrived off Coffee Bay at first light with medical personnel and naval divers. They immediately dumped their excess loads and, not long afterwards, the first two helicopters were over the badly listing *Oceanos*.

The pilots were immediately faced with serious problems: the gale force wind had dropped, but it was still

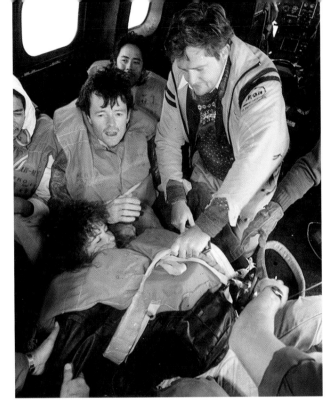

CLOCKWISE FROM ABOVE: Within a short while, the *Oceanos* disappeared below the waves; Survivors helped ashore by a *Puma* crew; Observer's view of the stern, as the ship lists harder to starboard; A survivor group after they had been brought onboard a *Puma* by winch from the ship.

about 60 knots which made the use of a hoist extremely difficult. In addition, a ten-metre swell required the hovering pilots to do some pretty deft juggling in getting the hoist strop onto survivors; as big as she was, the *Oceanos* was bucking like a mustang snared. Of necessity, the flight engineer had to allow a lot of slack to avoid the passengers being snatched into the air one moment and dropped onto the deck again on the rise of the swell the next. This necessitated an extra-long hoist line with the additional danger of snagging the ship's superstructure on lift-off.

The third problem was caused by the illuminating stringer cable which held a line of festival lights aloft; it was rigged from the bow, over the top of the masts all the way to the stern. This cable and its attendant wires had to be cut away before any attempt could be made at hoisting and this was the first job of the Navy divers.

The first passengers were lifted off the *Oceanos* soon after these cables had been removed. But then another setback presented itself soon thereafter; long hoist cables meant long periods between hoists; this was unacceptable as the ship was unstable and could go under at any time.

Pilots improvised quickly and developed a pattern of their own, whereby a helicopter was positioned over the bow and another at the stern: they used double-collared hoisting strops which allowed two persons to be lifted at a time. As soon as a couple were lifted off, the chopper would move away from the crippled vessel to complete the hoist.

Puma pilots alternated their positions until the sheer weight of survivors hoisted onboard each helicopter necessitated their return to the shore. By using all nine helicopters, an efficient shuttle service was soon established.

There was a stage when a moment of panic spread like a ripple among the passengers still onboard. When they spotted the first four *Pumas* heading inland to Umtata for more fuel, they thought they had been abandoned. The orbiting C-160 relayed a message to the *Oceanos*' radio room, which was then passed down the deck explaining the situation and calm returned among those still onboard.

The last person hoisted off the ship was lifted free at 11h20B, less than six hours after the start of the operation. By then, a total of 225 survivors had been taken off the *Oceanos* by the *Pumas*. One of these, on its own, was able to hoist a total of 64 survivors to safety; the crew started at 06h30B and returned to the ship four times, lifting off, in turn, 16, 20, 22 and, finally, the last six people to leave the sinking liner. Forty minutes later the *Oceanos* sank.

The enormity of the task involved in this rescue mission can be illustrated by the hours flown: the crews of the first two *Pumas* left AFB Durban at 03h30B and were finally able to relax after a total of seven hours and fifty minutes of flying. Five of those hours were associated with hoist operations in the storm.

In a bid to assist with hoisting, Navy divers were initially lowered onto the ship. These youngsters ensured the orderly and uninterrupted flow of survivors for'ward and aft, to where the *Pumas* were hovering. This was obviously a dangerous operation as the ship was listing more to starboard with each hour, making movement over the decks precarious. Two of these divers (both young men doing their two years' national service), Paul Whiley and Gary Scoular were eventually decorated for bravery with the highest South African military honour, the *Honoris Crux*. Whiley got his in gold.

Looking back on the disaster, there were other factors that contributed to the success of the evacuation. Throughout, none of the passengers panicked. Women and children went first and the men onboard waited their turns. No one jumped the queue. As one survivor recalled later, there was a quiet dignity about it all; *everyone accepted their lot. . .*

After the passenger list from lifeboats rescued by merchant ships in the area had been compared with those survivors lifted off the *Oceanos* by helicopters and had been consolidated, it was found that everyone onboard was safely off the ship. Not a lifeboat had been lost, though there were some lucky escapes. One man, with only a lifevest for safety, was swept out to sea more than 12 kilometres; he was spotted by a lookout on one of the merchant ships and brought to safety. Another was almost drowned when he jumped into the sea, his pockets bulging with coins that he had looted from the ship's slot machines. He dumped his 'treasure' in order to stay afloat.

The rescue was an involved, complicated and difficult operation. What has not yet been acknowledged is that it was highlighted by excellent planning, improvisation where necessary, and the professional flying ability of the South African pilots. There was also an underlying will to succeed, which is not a feature of events in so much of Africa these days. We salute them all.

CHAPTER 27

MOCAMBIQUE – THE POST-INDEPENDENCE PHASE

Mocambique, it seems, has always been at war. First, there was the 20-year guerrilla struggle against Portuguese colonial rule. This started when the first Makonde insurgents infiltrated into the country across the Ruvuma River from Tanzania. Then, after independence in the mid-seventies, a conflict of another dimension developed; a civil war involving Government and Frelimo forces and Renamo, a brutal Western-orientated movement that was totally opposed to Mocambique's Marxist policies which, for a time, was backed by Rhodesia and then South Africa.

Now, peace, of sorts, has come to this vast country along the East African seaboard. Problems persist; problems more of nature's making than of man's. Mocambique is dogged into the nineties by some of the worst droughts in its recorded history. And when the rains do come – usually cyclones or hurricanes – they are torrential and devastating, washing away towns, villages, crops, bridges and people.

Some of these floods have resulted in the collapse – as rudimentary as it is in this country regarded by the United Nations as the third poorest in the world – of the social system.

The only help that is available is from the various international aid bodies that are active in the country. With more than a million deaths from war and starvation in Mocambique since 1975, there is only so much that these organisations can do. There is only so much money available …

Even to the most detached observer visiting Mocambique today, this is a country that needs a great deal of assistance from the world at large. Either that or the country is likely to fade into total obscurity as developed nations are preoccupied with more pressing problems nearer home.

Crewman prepares to drop bread rolls to flood victims in the Zambezi Valley. This region suffered some of the worst flood disasters this century during the eighties.

CLOCKWISE FROM ABOVE: Mocambique civilian chopper hovers over flooded kraal in the Zambezi Valley; For most of the 20 years since independence, Mocambique has been wracked by conflict, bloodshed and civil war and; civilians bring food parcels ashore for flood victims.

CHAPTER 28

UNTAG: THE UN IN NAMIBIA

As the 20th Century heads towards its close, more United Nations operations will be seen in an Africa that refuses to be 'pacified'. Already we have had major deployments of multi-national forces in countries such as Namibia, Liberia, Somalia, Mocambique and elsewhere. Some of these peacekeeping efforts have been successful; others have not. But their role in Africa has been instructive.

emerged from a two-decade guerrilla conflict that had taken tens of thousands of lives. Most of the insurgency had come from Angola, itself caught in the vortex of a bloody civil war.

There, Cubans, East Germans, Russians and a dozen other states had been giving support to the South West African Peoples Organisation (Swapo) – a liberation group that is today ensconced in power in the nation's capital, Windhoek.

The deployment of blue-helmeted forces in the United Nations Transition Assistance Group (UNTAG) did not go without incident. The country that had formerly been known as South West Africa had, by the end of the eighties, just

CLOCKWISE FROM BELOW: Italy provided the helicopter contingent for the 11-nation military component of Untag. Their main base was at Windhoek; Operations with the peacekeeping force in Ovamboland and; preparing one of the Italian Air Force choppers for flight.

Johan Liebenberg took this shot of one of the Italian helicopters in the Untag force in Namibia; Remains of a Swapo improvised anti-aircraft position in the bush after the 'invasion' – it was a disaster for everyone.

The transition was not easy. Peace was only brokered after years of effort on the part, principally, of a United States team led by Dr Chester Crocker and, to a lesser degree, by the Angolans, South Africans, Russians, Cubans as well as several European nations.

Change did not come easily. Early April 1989, a Swapo force of 1 500 crossed into Namibia from Angola and attacked dozens of military posts, the majority only lightly manned because of the ceasefire. In the entire region there were only five *Alouette* IIIs, by then stripped of their cannon and used largely for monitoring purposes. Nine days of bitter fighting followed until the South Africans once again took control of the border region. Several hundred of the insurgents had been killed. It was *Koevoet* that did the damage (see Chapter 16).

The first stage of the peace process that was eventually to be implemented was to take place on 1 April 1989 with the drastic reduction of South African forces and confinement to their bases in Namibia of those who

remained behind. There was also to be the release of all Swapo prisoners and detainees. The final phase came in July 1991 with the withdrawal of Cuban forces from Angola.

Altogether 21 countries supplied military personnel to supervise the transition to independence: Australia (96), Bangladesh (25), Canada (60), Czechoslovakia (20), Denmark (132), Finland (43), India (20), Ireland (20), Peru (19), Poland (32), Spain (49), Sudan (20), Switzerland (46), Togo (25) United Kingdom (79), Yugoslavia (25).

Clearly, many of these contributions were of a token nature. Some of the countries involved could have found more useful work for their nationals in their own countries rather than in a remote and desolate corner of Africa.

Subsequent UN operations in Africa have been launched on a much grander scale. The UN contingent in Somalia, for instance, at one point approached 35 000 . In Mocambique, early 1994, it is in the region of 6 000 men and women.

CHAPTER 29

AMERICA'S SECRET SOMALIAN RESCUE

Operation Eastern Exit

American Forces, busily engaged in the military build up prior to *Operation Desert Storm*, were suddenly faced with an emergency in a country that, at the time, few people had even heard of: Somalia. In spite of the imminence of conflict in the Gulf, a carrier force was detached to deal with a critical problem. It was a huge gamble, but the Americans pulled it off.

The amphibious assault ship *Guam* (LPH-9) during her period of service in the Persian Gulf and off Somalia on the East Coast of Africa.

As a trouble spot Somalia is as familiar a name to Americans as Iran or Nicaragua were a couple of years ago. American service personnel – men and women – are active there. Some of these young people have died in the line of duty in the Horn of Africa.

Yet, long before names like General Farrah Aideed or Mogadishu had become news, a drama of horrific proportions was busy unfolding in this troubled East African land where violence seems to have ruled for centuries. That happened at roughly the same time that American and Coalition Forces were gathering their strength to invade Saddam Hussein's Iraq.

Captain Robert Doss, a United States Marine Mission Planner and CH-46E Sea Knight helicopter pilot with HMM-263 during Operation Eastern Exit *– for that is what the rescue mission was called – takes up the story:*

The arrival of 1991 found Amphibious Group Two and the 4th Marine Expeditionary Brigade wrapping up their fourth month in the Middle East. The USS *Guam* (LPH-9), with Marine Medium Helicopter Squadrons (HMM)-263 and 365, and elements of 1st Battalion, 2d Marine Regiment, left the Persian Gulf to conduct night-vision goggle (NVG) training and support Maritime Interdiction Force operations in the North Arabian Sea.

A detachment of HMM-263 helicopters onboard the USS *Trenton* (LPD-14) had shortly before intercepted two defiant Iraqi vessels, the *Ibn Khaldoon* and the *Ain Zalah*, for the UN-sanctioned boarding and inspection by an embarked naval raid force.

President George Bush's 15 January deadline for the Iraqi withdrawal from Kuwait loomed ominously. We remained uncertain that the Gulf War would begin in two weeks, even as we continued to prepare intensely for it. Our force, literally, had issued arctic gear for a NATO deployment on one August day, replaced it with desert camouflage the next, then departed for the Middle East a few days later. For the Marines in the Brigade responding to these rapidly changing events, the words "every clime and place" from the Marines Hymn rang true.

Rumours always find a home onboard ship, and, as day turned into night on 2 January, a new bit of 'scuttlebutt' started about trouble in Somalia. The country was being torn apart by a brutal civil war that ravaged the capital city of Mogadishu.

The US Embassy there was under a furious challenge, as rebels and government forces roamed the streets outside, leaving a wake of terror and indiscriminate death and violence.

When our aircraft were recalled to the ship that evening, we learned we were headed to Somalia to conduct a 'noncombatant evacuation operation' to rescue Americans and foreign nationals from the US Embassy compound which lies to the immediate north of Mogadishu Airport.

We were told that other navies, air forces, and commercial carriers had attempted evacuations, but the fighting drove them away.

As the aircraft carrier *Guam* and the amphibious transport dock *Trenton* (LPD-14) started south, information about the threat, evacuees, and landing zones had not yet begun to arrive; no one knew the exact location of the embassy compound and, of course, there were no adequate maps.

The first word we received from the US Ambassador in Somalia, James Bishop, detailed the desperate situation there. Each message provided a small piece of the planning puzzle, but kept us wondering if we were doing enough. More important, were we doing it in time?

Mission-planning cells worked feverishly to construct a plan for the evacuation. Fortunately, problems with communication and coordination never materialised; aviation, ground, and Navy units on the *Guam* had developed a rapport in the preceding months that supported close cooperation.

Incoming communication from the US Embassy gave some of us the distinct impression that they were being written from cover, beneath a desk as a fire-fight raged nearby; one message reported that a rocket-propelled grenade had slammed into the compound; others described automatic-weapons fire and armed aggressors being repulsed as they scaled the walls of the compound.

The ships were making best speed southwards out of the Persian Gulf, but despite the intensity with which we planned, we could not forestall those who threatened our embassy and diplomats.

Our course paralleled the coast of Somalia, a lengthy stretch of shoreline just north of Kenya that leads to Mogadishu.

In the very early hours of 5 January, following another frantic call from Ambassador Bishop, we moved to within the range of our CH-53E *Sea Stallion* helicopters, with their aerial refuelling capability. The most recent messages from the embassy indicated that the compound was in imminent danger of being overrun – with the logical implication to all of us that the evacuation effort would be lost as well.

Two giant *Sea Stallions* from Marine Heavy Helicopter Squadron 461 on board the *Trenton* were loaded with troops and sent on a 466-mile overwater night flight to reinforce the compound and assist with the evacuation: *Operation Eastern Exit* was begun.

This flight was not without event. During the first refuelling a pressure seal on the second CH-53E failed. Fuel

apparently sprayed into the cabin but the leak was quickly fixed by the crew chief and refuelling continued. Also, because the choppers' Omega Navigation Systems were not functioning properly, the pilots had to rely on the re-fuelling C-130s as well as directional control from the ships.

After two en route aerial refuellings by Marine KC-130s from VMGR-252 and 352, the helicopters arrived in

ABOVE: Squadron of 5 Marine CH-46E *Sea Knights* from HMM-263 leaving the flight deck of the USS *Guam*.
BELOW: General view of the US Embassy compound in Mogadishu and adjacent areas which contained the main US contingent during the subsequent UN phase, early 1993.

EASTERN EXIT CHRONOLOGY

DATE	EVENT
5 December 1990	Ambassador Bishop recommends the voluntary departure of non-essential US personnel
19 December	Number of official US personnel reduced from 147 to 37
30 December	Full-scale fighting between Somali government and rebel forces breaks out in Mogadishu
1 January 1991	US Ambassador requests authority to evacuate Embassy
2 January	Ambassador Bishop requests military assistance for evacuation; the *Guam* and *Trenton* get under way at 23h30 local time
4 January	Gun battle between US Embassy personnel and looters; Italian and Soviet attempts to evacuate via fixed-wing aircraft fail
5 January	CH-53Es launched from *Guam* 466nm from Mogadishu, insert a 60-man evacuation force, and return to *Guam* with 61 evacuees aboard
6 January	Four waves of CH-46s evacuate the remaining 220 evacuees and the 60-man evacuation force in the early morning. Mission declared complete
10 January	Baby born on board the *Guam* in early morning
11 January	Evacuees offloaded in Muscat, Oman

the compound as dawn broke.

Altogether a 60-man Marine evacuation force, including a nine-man SEAL team were landed in the embassy compound, supplementing the five Marine security guards who had been 'holding the fort' until then. They were a most welcome addition to the team.

Their 'run-in' was not without event. Because of the lack of adequate maps, the CH-53Es spent 20 minutes to-ing and fro-ing over Mogadishu looking for the embassy compound. They found it eventually, but it was a close thing.

The first of the evacuees were gathered and carried to the safety of the *Guam*, still more than 300 miles and another aerial refuelling away. Italian C-130s started another evacuation effort at the airport, but increasingly

bitter fighting kept them from returning to Mogadishu that day.

Mission planning onboard the *Guam* continued. The timing of the main evacuation was a key concern: as the team considered a daylight mission, it also developed a night alternative.

Daylight would afford us the opportunity for an evenly paced hands-above-the-table evacuation. If we could be recognised as a neutral third party attempting an *overt* evacuation of innocents, we might proceed unmolested. The likelihood of locating the US Embassy in the daylight was also considerably better than trying to spot it in the dark; particularly since pilots had only recently obtained a few black-and-white photographs and 1:50,000 scale maps of area for navigation purposes.

If we flew into Mogadishu at night we could do so under the cover of darkness; but, there was a risk that a night mission – if compromised – might be construed as a sneak attack on behalf of one or other of the civil war adversaries.

Night-vision goggles would permit us to see in the dark, and we could turn off all of our aircraft lights and become 'invisible' to those on the ground, depriving hostile forces of much of their precision. Nevertheless, any advantage gained by flying in the dark would be lost by meandering flights searching for a darkened landing zone over extremely hostile positions with unlimited supplies of ammunition.

To make matters worse, the LZ was described as extremely sandy and filled with unspecified obstacles …even in the daylight, landing five helicopters in such a confined area would be a challenge.

More messages continued to arrive describing further mayhem and conflict around the perimeter of the embassy compound. The erratic nature of these attacks convinced us that our helicopters would almost certainly be targeted if spotted. With the report that the fighting appeared to decrease at night, the decision was made: we would go in under cover of darkness.

It is axiomatic that a night operation poses more dangers than any daytime mission. But these were problems over which pilots could exercise control. That was another factor: at this point, our night option made better tactical sense, simply because we were a force that presumed a capability to strike at night against Iraq. Consequently, there was no reason to balk at a night strike into Somalia.

At 23h30 on 5 January, the first of our two waves of five armed CH-46s, led by aviation mission commander Lieutenant-Colonel R.J. Wallace, prepared to launch from 30 miles at sea. We were now close to the capital.

Once in the air, Mogadishu was easy to see through our night-vision goggles. The sky at sea was clear, though the city, itself, was overcast. A pall of smoke drifted to seaward.

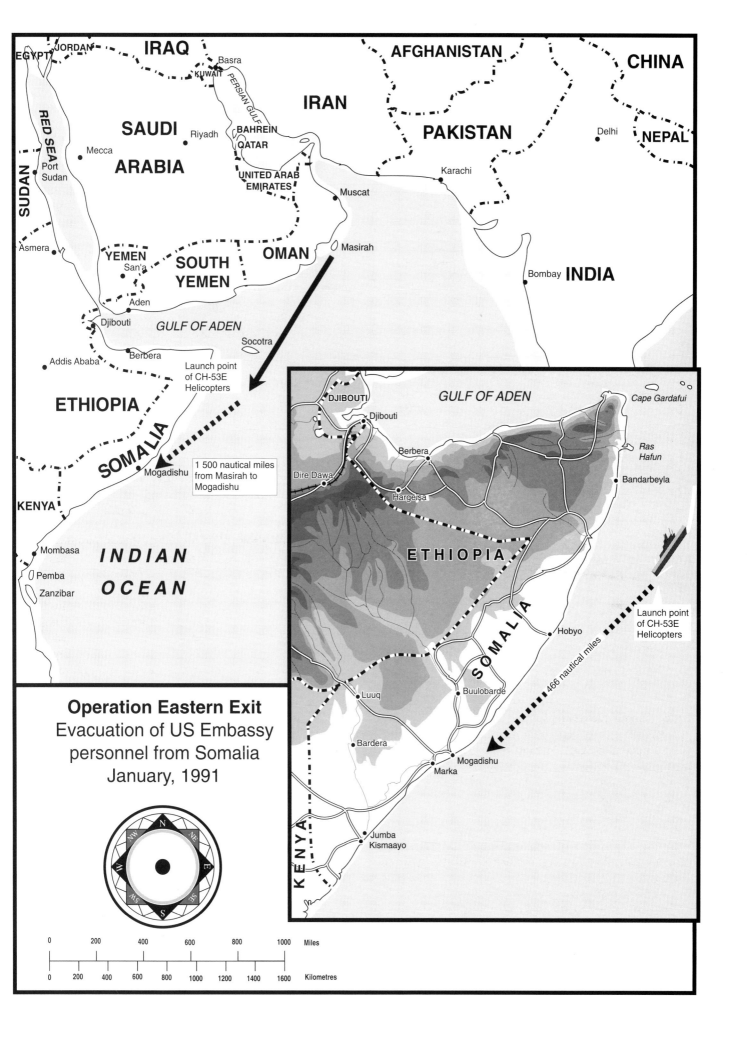

Operation Eastern Exit
Evacuation of US Embassy
personnel from Somalia
January, 1991

ABOVE: Captain Robert Doss, alongside his CH-46E *Sea Knight* **shortly after returning to the Persian Gulf from East Africa.**

LEFT: Marines board a *Sea Knight* **helicopter, similar to the ones used in the Somali** *Operation Eastern Exit.*

RIGHT: Official map of Mogadishu handed out to flight crews. The US Embassy compound is top, left.

It surprised us that Mogadishu still had electrical power. Occasionally we could see flashes of battle and the occasional line of tracers, but not much more. The Initial Point (IP) – the point at which the flight intended to cross the coast – would not be easy to find, but the importance of flying over it on the first crossing had been stressed during planning and briefing.

An error of a thousand metres to the right would take the flight directly over known surface-to-air missile (SAM) and anti-aircraft artillery (AAA) sites (and presumably troop concentrations). A thousand metres to the left would head us off the edge of our maps. They were the only ones we had, so the intial effort was crucial to the success of the whole operation.

The flight crossed the IP as planned and descended to 100 feet. We slowed down to about 80 knots. Lieutenant-Colonel Wallace spotted the embassy compound's infra-red strobe light that marked the LZ and transitioned to land.

The decision to put a little distance between aircraft during this final transition proved critical; the LZ was more confined than anticipated and each helicopter 'browned-out' in the whirling sand and debris swept up by the rotors just prior to touch-down.

When the dust settled, we were presented with a view of what it was all about; through our NVGs, we could see groups of civilians huddled near an embassy building. The

CONTINGENCY MAGTF ORGANISATION AND FORCES AVAILABLE

CE   Command element (CE) comprised of 4th MEB Bravo CE staff and detachments from 2d SRIG, 8th Comm Bn, 2d Intel Co, and 2d Recon Co. Commander was Col J.J. Doyle, CO, BSSG-4

GCE   Consisted of Headquarters Company, a rifle company, and 81mm mortar platoon from BLT 1/2. Potential augmentation of seven to nine provisional rifle platoons from the CE, CSSE, and ACE. Commander was Lt-Col R.P. McAleer, CO, BLT 1/2

ACE   Consisted of HMM-263 (12 CH-46s), HMM-365 (12 CH-46s), MWSS-274, det HMLA-269 (2 UH-1s armed with 2.75 inch rocket pods), and det HMH-461 (2 CH-53Es) Commander was Lt-Col R.J. Wallace, CO, HMM-263

CSSE Consisted of a headquarters detachment, MP platoon, a landing support det, and a medical/dental section that would be responsible for ECC. Commander was Maj. W.N. Saunders, XO, BSSG-4

Additional Marine Corps forces involved (not in Contingency MAGTF): Three KC-130s from VMGR-252 and VMGR-352 in Bahrain for Desert Shield.

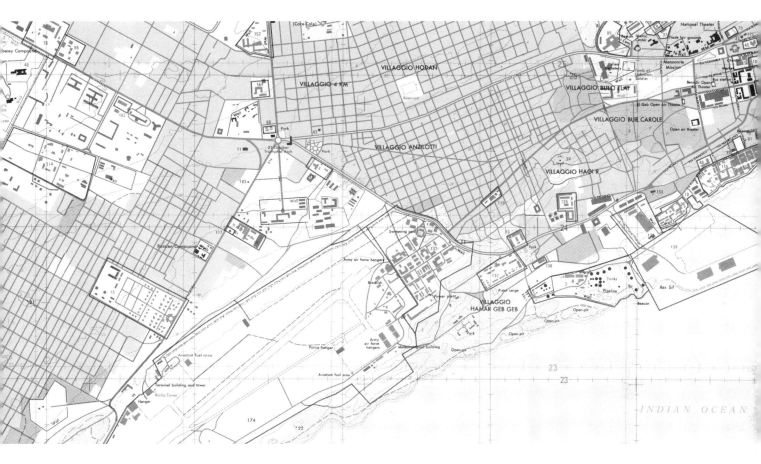

evacuees moved quickly in organised groups of 15 to board the helicopters.

Once they were seated, the aircraft launched and signalled the second wave of five aircraft to begin its ingress.

Like ships, almost, our aircraft passed each other in the night – five *Thunder* aircraft from HMM-263 returning to the ship and five *Rugby* aircraft from HMM-365 inbound to Mogadishu. Continuing the process, *Rugby* departed the embassy with evacuees and *Thunder* prepared to launch from the ship and return to the city.

Suddenly, the silence of the radios was broken by a call from the ambassador's office saying we'd been ordered to cease the evacuation immediately. We were told to leave Somalia or be shot down. Some of us were surprised it had taken the Somalis so long to react.

Since we had begun our operation – with the understanding that the environment was hostile – the threat had no effect on our mission. Crews did however double-check their body armour, and there were some hasty discussions reiterating procedures for the transfer of flight controls between pilots if one of them was hit. There were also rules of engagement passed on to the gunners.

Moments after *Thunder's* departure from the ship, the overhead Air Force AC-130 reported that his radar warning receiver had detected an active SAM system to the west. Message noted by all of us.

We continued to the embassy and were aware that the situation could only get worse if we delayed the outcome any longer. Approaching the LZ, this time, we received SAM radar-search indications from the east, but by flying low and keeping our airspeeds high, we prevented acquisition and lock-on possibility.

The evacuations continued. One more load for *Thunder* and another for *Rugby*.

As the number of evacuees dwindled, the security force began to pull inward into a tighter security perimeter in the embassy compound. At this point, as reported by Adam Siegel in *Proceedings: US Naval Institute*, there were some curious developments. "As the second wave arrived, a more serious threat emerged. A Somali major approached the gate with two truckloads of troops and threatened to shoot down the helicopters if the 'illegal operation' did not cease immediately.

"With the concurrence of the US Ambassador, the operation continued unimpeded as Ambassador Bishop negotiated with the major. Because the ambassador, his immediate staff, and the Marine security guards had been scheduled to go on the third wave, it took off for the *Guam* with only a portion of the planned evacuees (and only four helicopters instead of five).

"Before the arrival of the final wave, the Somali major withdrew his opposition in exchange for several thousand

229

dollars in cash and the keys to the ambassador's car. The last wave, therefore, had six helicopters."

Final head counts were taken and the last helicopter prepared to leave the LZ. Armed guards massed at the embassy gate and our gunners were prepared to repel and attack, but none materialised. When we were certain no evacuees remained, the last aircraft left Mogadishu, but not before the two-man Marine communications team was almost left behind because of a misunderstanding. They were not aware that this was the final wave.

The State Department later reported that the embassy was sacked, its doors blasted down with grenades soon after the evacuation was completed. Two days later, Italian C-130s and a French warship evacuated more foreign citizens from the city.

Heavy fighting kept the Italian C-130s from returning until 12 January, when they completed their evacuation. That was barely a year before the United States sent its troops into Somalia as part of the United Nations *Operation Restore Hope*.

Each aircraft passenger manifest told a story. One listed the names of Kuwaiti and Soviet diplomats; there were 39 Soviet nationals in the group. Another roster contained the name of a woman who had been shot. One more named the Sudanese ambassador's wife, who was about to give birth – which she did shortly afterwards – and still another included a woman who boarded a helicopter with a parachute draped around her – the only 'personal belonging' that she had managed to salvage from her home.

Altogether 281 men, women and children from 30 other nations moved to the aircraft elevator onboard the *Guam*. The ship looked like an international bazaar, with a curious assortment of apparel from various cultures and countries.

At 03h00, after a final accounting of evacuees and troops, the last two helicopters landed and *Operation Eastern Exit* was over.

The ships turned north and headed out of Somali waters, back to the Persian Gulf, towards that other "clime and place" where, eleven days later, another mission was about to begin: *Operation Desert Storm*.

CHAPTER 30

WOMEN IN UNIFORM IN SOMALIA

Women in the United States forces have been active in several theatres of military activity, but not on quite such a scale as in Somalia. The trouble is that that country on the Horn of Africa is a dreadful reflection on the rest of a very volatile, unstable continent.

There are many women in uniform in Somalia, most of them in a potentially hostile zone carrying modern infantry weapons or sidearms.

There were, among others, Australian women military police, Royal Air Force pilots, flight engineers and loadmasters, Scandinavian drivers and security personnel, as well as American women in their light-patterned *Desert Storm* fatigues in every unit imaginable.

BELOW: A flight of five UH-60 *Blackhawk* assault helicopters take off from Baledogle on a strike on Afghoi late January 1993. BOTTOM: A casualty is lifted aboard one of the 159th Medical Company *Blackhawks* at Baledogle, Somalia.

CLOCKWISE FROM LEFT: Women in the US Marine Corps have been well represented in the Somali operation. Somalia's biggest river makes a turn just north of Mogadishu creating a beautiful oasis; Army PFC Robert Bunting and Spec Ginger Pence being airlifted to Bardera; Checking water supplies for contamination at Mombasa US base; Soldiers of the 2nd Batt, 87th Infantry, 10th Mountain Division, prepare to board; Australian woman driver at Mogadishu Airport; Tented camp conditions in the dust and heat of Somalia were hard on the women who served there.

233

Many were pilots: UH-60 *Blackhawk* Medevac choppers and huge twin-rotor CH-47 *Chinooks* of the kind that were used for air-supply in the war against Iraq. There were also women flying C-130 transporters and the humble OH-58 *Scout*, a Vietnam-vintage helicopter in Somalia, as elsewhere, usually deployed ahead of the gunships to pinpoint enemy fire. Or used for scouting work, for which, as the name implies, they were originally designed.

Most of these *Kiowa* choppers remain unarmed to increase their speed payload and manoeuvrability. The female pilots accepted that shortcoming as 'part of the package'.

There were women in uniform everywhere; in Mogadishu, the capital; up-country at the huge abandoned Soviet air base at Baledogle; in the port of Kismaiyu where there have been numerous exchanges of fire with dissidents and at refugee centres such as Bardera and Baidoba where Somalis are still battered by the vagaries of a civil war that simply refuses to end.

They are a diverse lot, these girls. Like the men, they do not regard their posting to the Horn of Africa as either gratifying or enjoyable. To most of them it is simply a job to be done; the sooner it is over and they can get back Stateside, the better.

Of course the Americans, in particular, curse the heat and the filth. They abhor the desert wind and the primitive washing and toilet facilities as well as the general discomfort.

They had to make do while in Somalia with a camp bed and sleeping bag that was often covered with sand by morning. And after a week on an unrelieved diet of MREs (Meals, Ready-to-eat) the diet begins to pall, even though American forces in Somalia did get one cooked meal a day when I was there.

Like the rest of the 22-nation Allied force, few of these American soldiers have any affection for the Somalis; who are regarded by those who have had dealings with the people there as a crass and brutal nation, heedless of the suffering and death of its children and now oppressed by over a dozen warlords intent on acquiring weapons and drugs and war with no thought for the starving millions, many of them children.

To the American in uniform Somalia is not the sort of place any of them would visit twice. That sentiment is shared by most of the men and women there.

Pauline Knapp – Major Knapp to the several hundred US soldiers at the makeshift base at Baledogle, north of Mogadishu, was one of these – though she was too discreet to record her sentiments on tape.

She flew a *Blackhawk* helicopter in *Desert Storm* in Saudi Arabia, and tells stories about the dourness of the Somalis while their children were dying everywhere.

"The last time we despatched a flight to Mogadishu it

was diverted to take a two-year-old child to hospital; it had had its leg staked to the ground in a squalid hut infested with ants and mice while its parents spent the day chewing *khat* in town. *Khat*, she explained, is a leaf brought from Kenya and the Ethiopian Highlands every day and chewed by practically every Somali; it is a mild narcotic and has been classified as a drug by the World Health Organisation. The authorities tried to ban the leaf in Ethiopia, Djibouti and the Yemen, but without success.

While in Somalia Major Knapp was in command of the US Army Aero Medical Evacuation Company with the motto: "Anywhere, Any Place, Anytime; You Call – We Haul!" There were 16 UH-60 *Blackhawk* helicopter gunships adapted for medical evacuation and 129 personnel – many of them women – under her command in dirty, dusty and distant Baledogle, about 40 minutes' flying time north of Baledogle.

She is a tough and very professional lady, a graduate of Rutgers University who originally hails from "the wrong side of the Hudson in New Jersey". Of combined Spanish and East European Jewish descent, this diverse gene-pool seems to be the basis of much of her charm.

Major Knapp had her work cut out for her while posted to Somalia. She and her crews needed to cover almost the

A Marine Corps chopper CH-53D *Sea Stallion* airlifts a cargo truck 'Gamma Goat' to a forward position. OPPOSITE: Three *Sea Knight* CH-46Es lift off an amphibious assault ship in another African operation, off Liberia (See chapter 24).

entire country, roughly speaking several hundred thousand square kilometres. Their task was to bring casualties (and the dead) through to forward field hospitals as quickly as possible, no matter what the hour. She, herself, has been in the air, with crew, within minutes of receiving an urgent Medevac call-out.

Her command included servicing all 22 Allied nations, besides the occasional dying Somali.

A trim figure in uniform, she is married to an Executive Officer in an Armoured Cavalry Unit in Germany. Obviously, their careers tend to take them in opposite directions all over the globe and she regrets that they missed an Austrian skiing holiday when she was posted to Somalia at 24-hours' notice.

"We're lucky if we can manage a weekend a month together. But when we do make contact, it's quality time," she says with a smile.

"But I run a lot. It keeps me sane."

For the future, Major Knapp aspires to another degree at one of the US Army military colleges. "We don't even think of children. It's just not on. Not with this kind of career."

After 13 years in uniform she has her sights on the half-eagle on her lapel.

Significantly, the women in the US Army and Air Force serving in north-east Africa regard themselves as soldiers first and only secondly as females. Other nationals are surprised to learn that men and women in the US forces wear the same uniform and receive the same pay. But then they are allocated to the same daily drudgery, and often dreary details. In Africa all this is compounded by dust, the heat and the filth. And also the fact that water is rationed in this semi-desert environment.

They point out that although there were women involved in Saudi Arabia in *Operation Desert Storm* against the Iraqi forces of Saddam Hussein, this is the first time that women in uniform have come into direct and forceful contact with an African nation at war.

There are women commanders who have had to make snap decisions about implications relating to the use of force and, sometimes, whether to retaliate to armed aggression or not, usually when out in the towns.

Living in close confines with men, it is no secret that romance does feature in the lives of these men and women so far from home. The US Army is non-committal.

Dalliance between the sexes in the forces is discouraged; but, as another *Blackhawk* pilot, Chief Warrant 4 Officer Dave Coates – one of the few members who fought in Vietnam – says: "It happens, but God help the man who gets into bed with one of the girls under him." The pun was not intended, but it is appropriate. The events are rather appropriately termed 'career terminators'.

For all that, life on the Baledogle base is remarkably well integrated. Male and female latrines are usually placed side by side with the men's urinals visible to all; the 'lilies' are screened off only by a waist-high sheet of board.

Hygiene is rigorous. It is the unglamorous job of one at the women at the base to remove night-soil from the latrines every morning, douse it with kerosene and burn it.

"Helps to keep the flies down," said Colonel Mike Dallas, Commanding Officer of the 900 men and women attached to the 10th Mountain Division 2nd Brigade Headquarters at Baledogle. It certainly worked.

There are moments, though, when sex is irrelevant, as when a three-metre spitting cobra, darted into the women's showers.

159 MEDICAL COMPA

BELOW: US Army base at Baledogle, Somalia – it had for
region; CLOCKWISE FROM TOP LEFT: Insignia of the 159
UH-60 *Blackhawk*; Colonel James Kelley and his wife, C
weekly *pour deux* of canned cheese and pate; Some of the
these canisters at Mogadishu Airport; A flight of *Blackhau*
New York, is also in Somalia with her husband – the graffit
posted to Somalia; Private Denise McCracken, a heavy wh
hawks; 'Brown-out' at Baledogle; An everyday sight to thos

ON OPS IN SOMALIA

...en a Russian Air Force headquarters in the Horn of Africa
... Company (AA); Major Pauline Knapp at the controls of her
...tte Kelley, who served together at Baledogle enjoying the
... brought back by the 159th Med. Co. were ferried home in
...00 feet over Afghoi; Medic SSgt Elaine Clarke of Carthage,
...can; The smiling face of one of the female flying instructors
...e mechanic using the drill on one of Major Knapp's *Black-*
...ns who served in Somalia's interior.

Naked ladies dispersed in all directions. Some of the men tried dragging a dead snake on a string through the women's shower a few days later, but it was a non-event.

Baledogle is infested with snakes. In the first five weeks two soldiers, one of them a woman, had been bitten, both by vipers. In both cases Major Knapp's unit had to fly the victims to Mogadishu at night.

The fact that there are several married couples at Baledogle and other American bases in Somalia is unique. One such couple is a husband-and-wife flying team under the command of the Flight Operations Officer, Lt-Colonel James Kelley. His wife, Captain Yvette Kelley, is adjutant of the Aviation Brigade, and spends most of the day in front of a computer terminal.

They met a few years ago at a military base in California and served together in *Operation Just Cause* in Panama, where Yvette, a graduate of UCLA and West Point, flew combat helicopters.

While I was there they slotted their week into two really big occasions, or evenings, rather. Once a week they take in a movie, usually on a Thursday night at one of the open-air video screenings on base. Monday or Tuesday is a 'dinner occasion' *pour deux*, when cans of tinned food from home are carefully laid out on the operations room table, *sans* cloth, together with a bottle or two of water. A can of pate or shrimps is usually the start of the event.

In compliance with General Order Number One of *Operation Restore Hope* in Somalia, no alcohol is available to US forces; only fruit juice and water. Unlike the French and the Australians, the American forces are 'dry'.

The only iced drinks among the thousand personnel at Baledogle were in the medical tent and, curiously, in the warrant officers' caravan. By the time I had arrived, several weeks of heavy pressure in that stifling climate had disabled the warrant officers' fridge. The Coke that I was offered was lukewarm. In that heat it tasted like glue.

Generally, the United States forces in Somalia appear to be on a tight budget. There are few excesses; the troops have only that gear that they brought with them in their kitbags. Some of the women needed to replace their uniform, but this was not possible, until more supplies arrived. Hats, for instance, were constantly being blown away by the desert winds.

The PX Store was open for only a few hours a week in Baledogle, usually on a Saturday morning. Women's necessities were in short supply. Even cigarettes were not always in stock in the outlying PXs. It was interesting that the US military establishment in Somalia had come down firmly against the tobacco habit. "You can chew Skoal but you can't light it!"

I saw perhaps a couple of dozen of the men (and not one of the women, although I am sure there must be some) who smoked. Naturally, the unit at Baledogle was physically all the better for it. The day began with a volun-

tary five- or ten-kilometre run for all. It usually ended, before sunset, with more PT and games. This was a very fit unit indeed.

The women told some interesting stories when they were asked why they had joined the forces.

One, a radio operator, confided that she had left her husband one morning and signed up. Just like that!

"I had had enough of his bull," she declared with vehemence.

Another saw it as a way of seeing the world and getting paid for it. She had become a flight engineer and had been in several military theatres, including one involving an airlift of civilians from Liberia in dangerous turmoil. She had also spent a few months in Saudi Arabia.

"Now I'm in Somalia. It's the pits," she said. She hated it, and, being partly Afro-American herself, she felt that her African heritage had been 'betrayed' by the Somalis who so maltreated their own starving people. But then I pointed out that the Somalis were not true African. History had made them half Arab, accepted neither by Arab nor pure African people.

Captain Patricia Stout from Portland, Oregon, learnt to fly huge CH-47 *Chinook* transport helicopters at Fort Rucker, Alabama, in 1989, and then spent a year in Korea; yet she is still only 26. She joined the US Army as a career option. She was the Battalion Staff Officer or S-1 at Baledogle, running the flying operations room when I was there and it was she who coordinated my chopper flights into the interior every day.

An attractive, unmarried, no-nonsense operator she will return to her unit in Germany when the Americans eventually leave Somalia. Captain Stout is undecided about the future, except that she is proud of her uniform.

Another pilot in Somalia was 25-year-old Kristen Townsend, whom I met on my last day in the north of the country. She had just returned from Kismaiyu on the coast, where her unit had seen action against the forces of one of the more notorious Somali warlords, Colonel Morgan of the Darod-Majertain clan, which, for a while, was linked to the deposed dictator, the former President Said Barre.

This movement had been giving the Coalition Forces a rough time at this once-beautiful palm-fringed seaport; at least that was so until the Americans made a ground and air assault on their positions in Kismaiyu.

First-Lt Townsend's wing destroyed one of the armed vehicles known locally as 'technicals'.

Lt Townsend, from Michigan, is a graduate of West Point. She flies a UH-60 *Blackhawk* gunship and the US Army is her long-service career. She hopes to get sent on an Officer's Advanced Course and become a captain; at least that's what she aspires to.

What does she think of Somalia? "If I never see Africa again, it will be too soon," she replied. This is sad, since

CLOCKWISE FROM ABOVE: Mechanic Sgt Terese Vaughan came to Somalia from Germany; *Kiowa* pilot's view of one of the many Somali villages in the interior – armed bands often operated from such settlements; and, Captain Patricia Stout from Portland, Oregon usually flies CH-47 *Chinooks*. At Baledogle, she was in charge of the flying operations room.

Somalia, strictly speaking, is not 'Black Africa'. The Somalis are an Hamitic people.

Her impressions had been largely conditioned by the brutality of the people whom she had encountered and by the never-ending horror of starving children and adults, a spectacle she had seen almost everywhere in-country.

Sadly, the Somalis are perhaps their own worst enemies. It is impossible to walk about the streets of Mogadishu without a military escort. Even then, when you are driving through the market quarters between the airport and the US Military Headquarters – which is in the old compound of the US Embassy – you clutch your possessions to keep them from being snatched.

I wound the stout strap of my Nikon camera and motor drive round my arm while travelling in a *Humvee*. Even so a man grabbed at it and tried to run; he ended up under the wheels of the vehicle that I was in. We had stopped a moment before. God knows what the thousands of Somalis in the street around us would have done if he been been killed or hurt, even though he had initiated a hostile

action. It is clear that the Somali people need little provocation to send volleys of stones at passing vehicles. And there are a lot of stones in East Africa!

Two women workers of an European international aid organisation, were robbed of everything that they had on them except their clothes. They had stopped briefly at the market to enquire about a group of people who had asked for assistance. An Irish Concern aid worker was murdered in Kismaiyu shortly before I entered the country.

Many soldiers have had their glasses snatched off their faces as their vehicles moved slowly through the throng. Others had their wristwatches torn from their arms. I lost the pen in my top pocket; a hand appeared from nowhere through a *Humvee* side-window and snatched it.

Most American troops moving through the area usually have their carbines or pistols at the ready, cocked and locked. Others carry big sticks called 'Somali dissuaders' to deter thieves, and they use them with grim determination on Somali skulls when the people try to board the vehicles to steal.

239

The difficulties facing an effective peace-keeping operation in Somalia are almost insuperable. Not one of the women in uniform that I spoke to, whether British, Australian, Scandinavian or American, was prepared to go anywhere in Somalia without an armed escort. They were concerned, not so much with the possibility of getting into an exchange of fire: they had all been trained for that.

What they feared most was the possibility of being stabbed in the back while walking about or getting their throat cut while asleep; or of being seized and held hostage by people who set more store by the Nikes on their feet than their lives.

As they say, welcome to Mogadishu!

CLOCKWISE FROM BELOW: The airport at Mogadishu is a huge establishment, miles long, but occasionally under attack from dissident Somali warlords (note derelict Somali Air Force MiG jets and transporters, abandoned; bottom left); Major Pauline Knapp was in command of the US Army Aero Medical Evacuation Company while she served in Somalia; Squadron of US Army *Blackhawks* attached to the 159th Med. Co. Many of the pilots serving in Somalia were women.